A GENERAL HISTORY OF EUROPE

GENERAL EDITOR: DENYS HAY

A GENERAL HISTORY OF EUROPE

General Editor: Denys Hay

For many years the volumes of Denys Hay's distinguished *General History of Europe* have been standard recommendations for university students, sixth formers and general readers. They offer broad surveys of European history, in which the detailed discussion (on a regional or continent-wide basis) of social, economic, administrative and intellectual themes is woven into a clear framework of political events. They set out to combine scholarship with accessibility in texts which are both attractively written and intellectually vigorous. Now the entire sequence is under revision by its original authors – most of the volumes for the first time since they were published – and the books are being redesigned and reset. The revised *General History of Europe*, when complete, will contain twelve volumes, three of them wholly new.

* *Available in the original edition*

◇ *New edition published in the revised format*

□ *New title in preparation*

EUROPE

1780–1830

SECOND EDITION

FRANKLIN L. FORD

LONGMAN
LONDON AND NEW YORK

Longman Group UK Limited,
Longman House, Burnt Mill, Harlow,
Essex CM20 2JE, England
and Associated Companies throughout the world.

Published in the United States of America
by Longman Inc., New York

First published 1970
Second edition 1989

British Library Cataloguing in Publication Data
Ford, Franklin L. (Franklin Lewis), *1920–*
 Europe 1780–1830. — 2nd ed —
 (A General history of Europe, 1770–1870)
 I. Title II. Series
 940.2

 ISBN 0-582-03378-0 CSD
 ISBN 0-582-49392-7 PPR

Library of Congress Cataloging-in-Publication Data
Ford, Franklin L. (Franklin Lewis), 1920–
 Europe, 1780–1830/Franklin L. Ford. — 2nd ed.
  p. cm. — (A General history of Europe)
 Bibliography: p.
 Includes index.
 ISBN 0-582-03378-0
 ISBN 0-582-49392-7 (pbk.)
 1. Europe — History — 1789–1815. 2. Europe — History —
 1815–1848.
I. Title. II. Series.
D308.F65 1989   88-744
940.2′7 — dc19   CIP

Set in Linotron 202 10/12pt Bembo

Produced by Longman Singapore Publishers (Pte) Ltd.
Printed in Singapore

CONTENTS

11 THE EUROPEAN STATE SYSTEM AFTER 1815   271

LIST OF MAPS

PREFACE TO THE SECOND EDITION

In the seventeen years since this volume first appeared, there have been significant additions to the store of available sources for the history of Europe between 1780 and 1830. Equally important, debates over interpretation have continued to modify our very conception of some of the problems, while sharpening the questions to be put concerning others. We know rather more now than in 1970, I think, about what was going on in a number of countries during the period involved – especially in those lying outside the once dominant British–French–German centre of attention – with the result that a general work can refer to Russia or the Balkans, not to mention Spain, Scandinavia or the Netherlands, simply by having recourse to a growing shelf of valuable studies.

At the same time, reflective essays such as François Furet's *Penser la Révolution française* (1978, English translation 1981) have thrown new light on even so venerable an issue as how the great upheaval was rooted in the conditions and aspirations of Frenchmen, rulers and subjects alike, prior to 1789. Having mentioned Furet's work, I should perhaps add that it has not, despite its excellence, confronted me with any unwelcome necessity to make major changes in the initial version of *Europe 1780–1830*. The latter already included an attempt, less elegant and for obvious reasons less fully elaborated than his, to balance what was incontrovertibly new in the French Revolution against what it owed to the centralizing and, in a sense, homogenizing policies of the old monarchy, combined with the popular cry for equality. On this score, the debt to Tocqueville we both share with countless others is self-evident.

Certain broader historiographical trends of the past two decades have influenced the chapters which follow, albeit to varying degrees. The same, of course, can be said of their impact, lasting or ephemeral, on contemporary historical thought as a whole. To cite one example, the demand for a fuller study of *mentalités*, while doubtless worthy in itself, did not launch a new age of historiography, largely, I assume, because interest in popular attitudes, the role of folklore, the power of symbolic pageantry and related subjects had not been wholly lacking even before a new word was introduced to encompass them. The uneven record of that verbal crusade has nevertheless proven to be more impressive than the meteoric transit of 'deconstructionism' as a means of wresting the truth from our purportedly uncomprehending ancestors and their heretofore misleading documents. At the other extreme, the development of women's studies as a serious enterprise has had an undeniable effect on how one perceives, and thus how one describes, human experience, an effect whose real strength is demonstrated by the fact that as it becomes more pervasive and less self-conscious, it also shows fewer traces of either angry reproach or nervous apology, offering instead to enrich our understanding of the past as a whole.

Any reader of this book who has occasion to compare the revised with the original version will at once perceive that, save for the use of a concluding bibliographical essay in place of the previous chapter bibliographies, the volume's organization has not been altered. However, although the earlier framework remains, scarcely a page has emerged unchanged from the endeavour to incorporate new knowledge or find clearer ways of saying things, or both.

In this work of revision I have benefited from access to the libraries of Harvard University, Bennington College (during summers in Vermont) and both Duke University and the University of North Carolina in 1983–84, while a fellow of the National Humanities Center. To all of those institutions, and to colleagues who have supplied valuable suggestions along the way, my sincere thanks. In particular, let me acknowledge with gratitude the help of my research assistant, Nancy Koehn, a young historian whose diligence and ability have made the resulting manuscript at once more readable and more accurate than it could possibly have been in their absence.

CAMBRIDGE, MASSACHUSETTS   F. L. FORD
May 1988

For
Stephen, Becky and John

1

INTRODUCTION

For an age much given to discussing 'the history of mankind' an
opening word is perhaps in order concerning the scope and intent
of the present volume. It is, like its companions in the present
series, devoted to European history. Admittedly, the period
with which it deals saw Europe's influence still spreading across
the world, continuing a process begun three centuries before with
the first modern age of discovery. At the same time, non-
European forces were beginning to work back with increased effect
upon the old continent and its principal islands. Nevertheless,
such a book can scarcely aspire to global coverage when so many
European developments must themselves be passed over, or at
best treated only briefly. Particularly for an American, who
despite inherited attitudes and attachments is bound to look at
Europe itself somewhat from the outside, it would be folly to
attempt *world* history as seen primarily from a European angle of
vision.

Within these unavoidable limits, we shall be concentrating on
a central problem of interpretation, namely, the relationship
between Europe before and Europe in the aftermath of the
Revolutionary-Napoleonic crisis. Was the quarter-century that
began in 1789 the great historical watershed it has often been
called? Or were deep currents, running from the eighteenth
century on into the nineteenth, strong enough to discredit any
notion of a deep cleavage between two different ages as merely
an illusion born of too much emphasis on exciting events?

The best way of attacking the question of continuity versus
change, in any period, is to give thoughtful attention to the

1

'before', the 'after' and the 'in-between'. Hence, this book involves narration, but narration interspersed with reflections and preceded, as well as followed, by descriptions of European society around 1780, and then again around 1830. The chronicle of public actions – of treaties and battles, legislative enactments and executive decisions – is not ignored. Neither is the record of European thought and artistic accomplishment. For it is an underlying premise of the ensuing chapters that events, abstract ideas and popular attitudes, as well as attempts to capture beauty in colour or form or sound or language have all contributed to, even as they have reflected, the patterns and movements of society in general. If, however, any one theme is accorded special emphasis, it is that of *relationships among groups of people*, variously defined in legal, economic, honorific and political terms. That, I think, is how the central issue can be most clearly framed. Was European society at the end of our period only superficially different from what it had been five decades earlier? Or had there occurred a transformation so fundamental as to mark the dawning of a new age?

One of the most difficult balances to maintain in a book about Europe, 1780–1830, lies between according due emphasis to France and providing adequate coverage of other regions or states. There are dangers on both sides. It would be a serious mistake to view this period as nothing more than a dramatic segment of French history, in which the other peoples of Europe were compelled or privileged, depending on the historian's point of view, to play their parts. At the other extreme, another kind of distortion, less apparent perhaps, but no less harmful to full understanding, would result if we were to underestimate the power, by turns destructive and creative, of the French engine throughout this segment of the European past. Close attention will therefore be paid to the France of Louis XVI, of Robespierre, of Napoleon and of the restored monarchy after 1815. We must also, however, try to keep clearly in view affairs and conditions in the British Isles, the Germanies, the Low Countries, the Iberian peninsula, Italy, the Austrian Habsburg lands, Russia, Poland, Scandinavia and southeastern Europe.

Because the period to be examined was so full of violence, innovation and abrupt reversals, there is a natural temptation to visualize its eighteenth-century background in excessively pale colours. In a similar vein, although to a lesser degree, we are sometimes inclined to speak of 'the nineteenth century' as though things *settled down* after 1815.

Actually, of course, the Old Régime had been far from static. It had witnessed, amid intense argumentation and questioning, the rise and fall of kingdoms, churches and social groups. Every state in Europe was in important respects far different in the 1780s from what it had been in 1715, to say nothing of 1648. By the same token, one need only think for a moment of Germany and Italy, France and Britain, Russia and Austria-Hungary, as they came to exist by the 1890s, let us say, to realize how much was to change in the three-quarters of a century *after* the fall of the Napoleonic Empire. The Revolutionary-Napleonic era was, as we shall see, turbulent enough to exercise the most dramatic imagination; but it cannot be fairly described as sandwiched between two other epochs marked by relative calm. By any comparative standard, Europe has never been quiescent.

Our present task requires a different approach, one that involves examining the end of the pre-revolutionary era, then the great crisis itself and finally the emerging outlines of the post-Napoleonic European world. It must be remembered that what we are analysing represents a single slice from the annals of a civilization as self-critical and changing as it has been proud and traditionalistic. When we have finished, it will be time to consider whether the years between the beginning of the 1780s and the end of the 1820s saw a break between an old world and a new one too striking for any historian to ignore. Or did they witness nothing more than the passing disruption of a European system which resumed its earlier characteristics with remarkable speed and completeness once the storm had passed?

2

THE SOURCES

No historian concerned with Europe in the age of the Revolution, Napoleon and the Restoration should complain of special difficulties or claim unique advantages in the matter of sources. He may sometimes envy the medievalist's concentration on a relatively small number of documents. On occasion he may wish that, like the analyst of very recent history, he could look at motion pictures and hear recordings of his human subjects – or even interview them in person. On the other hand, he may take comfort from the greater range of published sources bequeathed by the period 1780–1830, as compared with earlier times, owing to an undeniable increase in both the quantity and the statistical exactitude of official records dating from this period. By and large, however, the source problems he confronts are shared in one form or another by all students of history.

His chief problems are best characterized by two terms which are only superficially paradoxical: incompleteness and profusion. No matter how many pieces of information the scholar may have available, he is bound from time to time to feel that the few indispensable ones are precisely those he lacks. There will always be gaps in the fullest documentation. On the other hand the researcher cannot escape some degree of consternation when he considers the materials he might, given limitless time and invincible eyesight, bring to bear on any question of interpretation. Total comprehension of the past, like total recall, eludes us.

A volume such as this cannot be based throughout on primary sources. Instead, it must rely upon countless studies which do rest on documentary inquiry. Some of these monographs, as well as certain interpretive works of a more discursive nature, are cited with appreciation in the selective bibliographical essay to be found at the conclusion of the present work. Even a general history, however, profits from some direct reference to primary materials, both for the concrete details they provide and for the sense of the period which they, and only they, can impart. In any event, the reader deserves to be reminded of the various bases on which our knowledge rests. From each major category of evidence a few examples have therefore been chosen for inclusion here at the start.

First in order of generality are wide-ranging collections of texts, such as H. T. Colenbrander's *Gedenkstukken der algemeene geschiedenis van Nederland van 1795 tot 1840* (The Hague, 1905–22). These 22 volumes bring together precious data on almost half a century of Dutch history from archives and private holdings not only in the Netherlands, but also in England, France and other countries. Another vast assemblage of different kinds of papers, in this case bearing on one aspect of a national history, is the *Collection de documents inédits sur l'histoire économique de la Révolution française* (Paris and other cities (1906–), edited by numerous experts under the auspices of a special commission of the Ministry of Public Instruction. This series, which already runs to over 100 volumes, is still being extended. Marc Bouloiseau, for instance, has edited the *Cahiers de doléances du Tiers état du bailliage de Rouen pour les Etats généraux de 1789*, in four volumes, with Philippe Boudin (Paris-Rouen, 1957–1974).

Few students, of course, have much need for these detailed accumulations of material. Many shorter publications, however, offer the chance to get acquainted with history through original documents, under careful editorial guidance. The Historical Seminar of the University of Bern, for example, has been issuing a series of paperbound books, *Quellen zur neueren Geschichte* (Bern, 1944–), averaging fewer than 100 pages apiece and valuable for the well-selected texts they include. To illustrate, the first item in the series, entitled *Vom Ancien Régime zur Französischen Revolution*, contains the electoral regulations for the Estates General of 1789 and sample lists of grievances (*cahiers*) addressed to that body, as well as the full text of the Constitution of 1791. Other numbers are *Europa Politik zu Beginn des 19. Jahrhunderts* (Heft 2); *Napoleonische Friedensverträge* (Heft 5); and *Des Ende des Alten Reiches* (Heft 10). A useful volume assembled by an American scholar,

J. H. Stewart, is the 800-page *Documentary Survey of the French Revolution* (New York, 1951). For Great Britain, the best and newest selection for the period we are interested in is *English Historical Documents*, vol. XI, under the general editorship of D. Douglas. That particular volume, prepared by A. Aspinall and E. A. Smith (London, 1959), comprises 587 items from the years 1783–1832. (Volume III in the revised edition of this collection will deal with the same period but is not yet available at the present writing.)

An era of revolution, war and repression was inevitably a time of expanding governmental action in almost every European nation. State papers thus represent a major class of sources, subdivided by nationality, by originating agency and by type of activity involved. Legislative records are a rich but unavoidably uneven source of information, being limited to countries which enjoyed some degree of parliamentary rule. In the case of Great Britain, there is no need to elaborate on the importance of William Cobbett's 36-volume *Parliamentary History of England*, containing actual speeches in the House of Commons down to 1803, to which has now been added Sheila Lambert's edition of *House of Commons Sessional Papers of the Eighteenth Century* (London, 1975). The First Series of Thomas Hansard's *Parliamentary Debates* – 'Hansard' as we still know it – runs from 1803 to 1820 in 41 volumes and was kept up to date on an annual basis after 1812, when Hansard took over Cobbett's interest in the enterprise. The so-called New (or Second) Series covers the ten years of George IV's reign, to 1830, in 25 volumes. Much less familiar, since they deal with the legislature of a short-lived Italian satellite of revolutionary France, are the 11 volumes on the *Assemblee della repubblica cisalpina* (Bologna, 1917–48), edited by C. Montalcini, A. Albert, *et al.* More significant as a national body, but far more difficult for the reader of western European languages to get at, was the Diet of Hungary, summaries of whose debates were translated into German for the benefit of Habsburg officials in Vienna.

As might be expected, legislative documentation for France in this era is particularly voluminous. Beginning with P. B. Buchez and P. C. Roux, who edited the still useful though haphazard *Histoire parlementaire* in 40 volumes (Paris, 1834–38), and continuing with the *Archives parlementaires*, Série I: 1787–99, edited by J. Mavidal, E. Laurent, *et al.* (Paris, 1875–), the publication of such records has proceeded to a point of almost incredible specificity. For example, the Institute for the History of the French Revolution has launched a *Recueil des documents relatifs aux séances des Etats généraux, mai-juin 1789*, the first volume of which, edited by G. Lefebvre and A. Terroine (Paris, 1953), deals entirely with preparations for the Estates General and with one day's session, that of the opening on May 5!

In the matter of administrative and legislative documents, an inevitable preoccupation with France – not limited, by the way, to French historians – deserves credit for the publication of countless volumes of Revolutionary and Napoleonic archives. British ministerial papers, of course, have also appeared in print, often as appendices to various special studies, while the notes and memoranda exchanged by public figures, whether German or Russian, Austrian or Spanish, help us to gain partial entry into the once secret council chambers of other governments. Yet despite the need to retain some degree of European perspective, again and again one is forced to return to the massive French documentation mentioned above. It constitutes a phenomenon already visible before F. A. Aulard began publication of the huge *Recueil des actes du Comité de salut public* (Paris, 1889–1951). Leaving aside later editors concerned with the files of individual prefectures and local governments, the briefest catalogue for France as a whole must acknowledge the efforts of E. S. Lacroix and R. Farge on the Commune of Paris, 16 vols. (Paris, 1894–1914); A. Debidour on the Executive Directory, 4 vols. (Paris, 1910–17); and C. Durand on the Napoleonic Council of State (Gap, 1954).

Public records, broadly defined, comprise many items in addition to minutes, protocols and correspondence. Census reports began to be published in some European countries during the late eighteenth and early nineteenth centuries, lifting the veil of official secrecy that from time immemorial had concealed virtually all demographic data. Governmental appointments, promotions and reorganizations were regularly announced in such publications as the royal Bavarian *Regierungsblatt* (1805 ff.). Papers of both official and private origin can frequently be combined to good advantage. We should note as well the rapidly growing body of business archives, often published in connection with the histories of famous old commercial or industrial concerns. In their collection, *Les patrons, les ouvriers et l'état: Le régime de l'industrie en France de 1814 à 1830* (Paris, 1912), G. and H. Bourgin showed the use that could be made of the texts of prefectorial and police reports concerning labour conditions, together with the proceedings of the *Conseil des Manufactures.*

At the mere mention of the phrase 'documentary sources', the category most likely to spring to mind is undoubtedly that of diplomatic papers. It was such documents or 'diplomas' (whence the name) that the learned archivists of the seventeenth and eighteenth centuries preferred to turn when compiling their pioneer editions. Many dominant figures of nineteenth-century historical writing, from Leopold von Ranke onward, tended to view ambassadorial reports, cabinet instructions to envoys, drafts and final texts of treaties as at once the richest and the most reliable sources for any student of the past. The faith of these historians in the 'primacy of foreign policy' was daily reconfirmed by the very nature of their favourite materials. Modern scholarship has tended to be more reserved in its enthusiasm for this admittedly clear, but often thin and lifeless, stream of observations and opinions. Perhaps the decline of secret, round-table diplomacy in our own century has influenced our attitude towards its functions and worth in other times. More likely, the recognition of influences acting upon all governmental policy decisions in ways seldom clear to the diplomatic reporter have diminished the reverence once accorded those neatly tied bundles of foreign office dispatches.

Whatever its cause, however, no such reaction can, or should, rob diplomatic papers of their undeniable value for the study of an age filled, like our own, with international conflict – an age which produced such famous diplomats as Talleyrand and Castlereagh, Capo d'Istria and Czartoryski, Metternich and Canning. The numberless minutes, drafts, instructions and dispatches published in the last 150 years, whether in separate volumes or as documentary appendices to monographic studies, remain indispensable aids to research. The same is true even of such hoary collections of treaty texts as F. de Martens and F. de Cussy, *Recueil manuel et pratique des traités* (Leipzig, 1846–57) in seven volumes, or single-nation compilations including L. Neumann, *Recueil des traités et conventions conclus par Autriche . . . depuis 1763*, vols. I–IV (Leipzig, 1855–58). An illustration of the value of ambassadorial reports for reconstructing more than just diplomatic manoeuvres will be found in *Gesandtschaftsberichte aus*

München, 1814–1848, edited by A. Chroust (Munich, 1935–51). In these dozen volumes we have, from the separate points of view of the French, Austrian and Prussian envoys to Bavaria, a running analysis of general conditions within that south German kingdom during the first half of the nineteenth century.

It is not always easy to draw a clear line between official sources and other, overlapping categories. Individual correspondence is a case in point. The letters of important public figures generally range all the way from the level of significant state papers to that of trivial, albeit revealing, personal notes to friends and relatives. An example of this variety is found in the six volumes of *Correspondence of King George the Third*, edited by Sir John Fortescue (London, 1927–28). Though the collection ends in 1783, early in the period here discussed, it was later carried forward by A. Aspinall's massive edition of *The Later Correspondence of George III*, which appeared in five volumes (Cambridge, 1962–70). The correspondence of Napoleon began to receive serious editorial attention with the 32 volumes published in Paris, 1858–70. Today the number of the Emperor's letters in print exceeds 40,000. A useful selection of some 750 of these items, translated, is J. E. Howard's edition of *Letters and Documents of Napoleon.* vol. I, *The Rise to Power* (London, 1961). Much of the official, as well as personal, correspondence of Austria's (indeed Europe's) leading statesman between 1809 and 1848 appears in the eight-volume collection, *Aus Metternichs nachgelassenen Papieren*, edited by his son, Prince Richard von Metternich-Winneburg (Vienna, 1880–4). More recently, an excellent new edition of letters and other state papers of Freiherr vom Stein, *Briefe und amtliche Schriften*, has been appearing under the editorship of W. Hubatsch, assisted by the preparations of the late E. Botzenhart. Ten volumes have been published so far (Stuttgart, 1957–74), carrying the Prussian leader's career through his reform ministry, that is to 1808.

Not all worthwhile correspondence comes from the files of rulers and leading ministers, of course. The Swiss burgher, Peter Ochs, left an invaluable portrait of his native Basel during the revolutionary period in his *Korrespondenz*, ed. G. Steiner, 3 vols. (Basel, 1927–37). A different type of commentary, by an important English economic theorist but not a major politician, emerges from the letters that fill ten volumes of *The Works and Correspondence of David Ricardo*, edited by P. Straffa and M. H.

Dobb (Cambridge, 1951–55). Often we profit from the observations of a relatively obscure individual who was nevertheless well placed to comment upon a scene or a movement of great significance. Thus an entertaining view of the Italian liberal refugees in London, forerunners of subsequent revolution and unification, can be found in Giovanni Berchet's *Lettere alla marchesa Costanze Arconati.* vol. I: *Febbraio 1822–Luglio 1833* (Rome, 1956). Another important example is Liddell Hart, ed., *The Letters of Private Wheeler, 1809–1828* (London, 1951) for which we are indebted to one of Wellington's infantrymen.

As the examples of Metternich, Stein and Ricardo show, correspondence is frequently published as only one element in a collection comprising other personal papers: essays, notes, speeches. Or again, letters may be printed in company with their writer's memoirs. As a means of checking and verifying this class of literature, correspondence has obvious value; but one should be wary of editorial techniques designed to make the letters, supposedly 'primary' sources, appear to corroborate the assertions of the memoirs. The danger of misinterpretation resulting from purposeful omissions is a real one. All the same, it is quite common to find the correspondence published with memoirs the most valuable portion of the edition, sometimes revealing more, one suspects, than either author or editor intended. This is true of one of the chief sources for Russian imperial policy and Polish affairs in the early nineteenth century, the two volumes of *Memoirs of Prince Adam Czartoryski and His Correspondence with Alexander I*, edited by A. Gielgud (London, 1888). It is even truer of Paul Léon Talleyrand's *Mémoires du Prince de Talleyrand* (Paris, 1953–55), since the letters contained in these seven volumes are seemingly authentic, wheras the original manuscript of the memoirs was hidden by the Prince's heirs and has in fact never been recovered.

With respect to the recollections of most statesmen, the insertion of special pleading is too obvious to constitute much of a threat. That is to say, the student knows the circumstances under which the writer may have fallen from power, or the actions and policies he or she is seeking to justify. Armed with that knowledge, a careful reader can recognize the apologetics for what they are, while making good use of the assertions either corroborated by other accounts or inherently plausible in the absence of any apparent motive to distort or falsify. Thus the six volumes of

Memorias de Don Manuel Godoy (Paris, 1839–41) are a transparent defence of his own record by Charles IV's chief minister from 1794 until 1807; but they also provide a wealth of reflections by a Spanish courtier and administrator who was as shrewd about most matters as he was unscrupulous in some. Another minister, a Prussian responsible for both reform and repression during the dozen years prior to his dismissal in 1819, was K. A. von Hardenberg, whose five-volume set of *Denkwürdigkeiten* (Leipzig, 1877) was edited by Ranke. We remain as heavily indebted to the *Mémoires du Général de Caulaincourt*, edited by J. Hanoteau (Paris, 1933), for their portrait of Napoleon and his policies from Tilsit in 1807 to the collapse in 1814, as we are to the 56-volume *Collection des mémoires relatifs à la Révolution française*, edited S. A. Berville *et al.* (Paris, 1821–27), for a long series of personal accounts. Or, turning to still another quarter of Europe, the memoirs of General Makrygiannēs, *Strategou Makrugianne Apomnemoneumata* (2nd edn, Athens, 1947), have proven indispensable to students of the Greek struggle for independence in the 1820s; but readers of English may also turn to R. Clogg, ed., *The Movement for Greek Independence, 1770–1821: A Collection of Documents* (New York, 1976).

The direct, undoctored jottings of genuine diarists are more difficult to find in print, and hence more precious, than are reworked memoirs, at least where prominent and controversial figures are concerned. It is a curiosity of the revolutionary era that so few diaries seem to have survived and that among those that do still exist, fewer still have been deemed worthy of publication. Perhaps the eighteenth century's dedication to letter-writing, with all its volubility and frankness, remained an acceptable alternative to the keeping of day-to-day journals. In any event, we can be grateful that at least one form of diary, travel notes, had never gone entirely out of style. Among the liveliest and most informative were those of the English agronomist, Arthur Young, *Travels in France during the Years 1787, 1788 and 1789* (Cambridge, 1929), edited by C. Maxwell.

Still more characteristic of the period was a tremendous upsurge of interest in, and production of, periodical literature of all kinds. Newspapers in particular assumed an importance scarcely imagined earlier in the eighteenth century. The decades after about 1760, it is true, had witnessed a very considerable increase in the number, scope and influence of journalistic ventures. Nevertheless, it took the public excitement of the revolutionary crisis to make the reporter and the editor what we now generally concede them to be: members of a 'Fourth Estate'. Accentuating this development were improvements in printing technique, typified by the London *The Times*'s adoption of the rotary principle on a flatbed press, which came in 1814.

At one extreme stood the solemn official bulletins, featuring legislative enactments, foreign news and descriptions of public events. The French *Moniteur universel*, though born in the super-charged atmosphere of November 1789, retained nevertheless a serious tone throughout the stormy years that followed. It can still be read in the 32-volume *Réimpression de l'ancien Moniteur* (Paris, 1840–45). Another French publication, the *Journal des débats*, founded in 1789 to report proceedings of the National Assembly, became increasingly formal until in 1805, renamed the *Journal de l'Empire*, it became as obviously a governmental organ as was the *Gaceta de Madrid*, that decorous reflector of views at the Spanish court regarding European affairs in general. Other papers, though heavily engaged in the issuance of official announcements, managed to be something more than governmental puppets. The sedate old *Wiener Zeitung* and London's *Daily Universal Register*, founded as such in 1785 but renamed *The Times* in 1788, expressed in cautious tones some of the tensions in Austria and England respectively during the tempestuous years of struggle abroad and economic strain at home. More openly dedicated to the strong expression of opinion was *Der Rheinische Merkur*, which Joseph Görres of Coblenz made into a powerful mirror, and by the end of Napoleon's reign a magnifier, of anti-French feeling in western Germany. Finally, at the opposite extreme from the *Moniteur* or the *Gaceta de Madrid* were the combative, abusive, often obscene tabloids produced by writer–editors in every trouble spot where such polemics dared appear. In Paris alone, the early Revolution was punctuated by the verbal salvos of Camille Desmoulins's pastiche of humour and libel, the *Révolutions de France et de Brabant*, Marat's scurrilous *Ami du Peuple* and Hébert's foul-mouthed but effective *Père Duchesne*, to mention only three leading exemplars of the art.

Pamphlet literature retained its already long-established place in popular affections and hence its significance as a source for historians. Even at their worst, the countless folds and broadsides hawked on European street corners remind us of the era's passionate interest in topics that in retrospect often appear ephemeral. At their best, of course, pamphlets were powerful tools for shaping attitudes towards key issues. Publications such as the Abbé Sieyès's *Qu'est-ce que le Tiers état?* of 1789 or the first instalment of Tom Paine's *Rights of Man*, which appeared separately as a booklet two years later, merit treatment not only as sources but as major events in their own right.

The monthly or quarterly magazine of the period, more substantial than a newspaper and published more regularly than a pamphlet, was in most of Europe less likely to be a political organ than a literary review, a scholarly journal or a collection of fashion notes and other women's features. While it may retain great interest for the cultural and social historian, the student of public affairs and institutions will generally have to seek his or her information elsewhere. England, however, represents an important exception in this regard. There the journal of opinion had enjoyed an assured place since the first triumphs of *The Spectator* in the early eighteenth century; and beginning in 1758 parliamentary debates had been summarized in the *Annual Register*, edited until 1788 by no less a figure than Edmund Burke. The years after 1800 saw the founding of the *Edinburgh Review* (1802) and the *Quarterly Review* (1809). The first of these mixed literary criticism with political commentary – successfully, to judge from a rapidly acquired circulation of 10,000, an awesome figure for the day – while its rival, the *Quarterly Review*, was founded to respond with more conservative arguments. An idiosyncratic but nonetheless significant publication was William Cobbett's lively and aggressive *Political Register*, which appeared for certain periods under such titles as the *Weekly Political Register* and *Weekly Political Pamphlet* from 1802 to 1835. To have fathered what might, under varying definitions, have been considered a magazine or a particular kind of newspaper or even an uncommonly long pamphlet series is nothing if not characteristic of its irrepressible editor. An excellent guide to periodical literature in general is G. A. Cranfield, *The Press and Society: From Caxton to Northcliffe* (London, 1978).

Before leaving popular media, we should remark two other categories, less familiar perhaps than printed news and comment, but scarcely less illuminating. One is the political caricature, especially prized in the era before photography had assumed its place as the handmaiden of journalism. Cartoons ranging from the light and clever to the gross and brutal were sold in profusion, either separately or with accompanying squibs treating questions of current interest. The pictures were tacked up in private homes, handed about in cafés and pubs and, occasionally at least, filed or pasted into scrapbooks. M. D. George alone succeeded in cataloguing over 17,000 such prints belonging to the British Museum (as it then was) and published two volumes of selected volumes of selected reproductions, *English Political Caricature: A Study of Opinion and Propaganda* (Oxford, 1959), with illustrations extending down to 1832. Comparable collections have appeared in France, exploiting the holding of the Bibliotheque Nationale's Cabinet des Estampes. Germany, the Low Countries, Austria, Italy, Spain all have contributed smaller but still welcome shares to this fund of graphic evidence.

A second category to be noted here is that of popular jingles set to music. Some of these were printed, either with notation or with references to traditional tunes for accompaniment. Many more have been saved for us by collectors with a penchant for jotting down lyrics, if that is not too dignified a term for some of the verses. A useful compilation of 90 items has been published by C. B. Rogers, *The Spirit of Revolution in 1789: A Study of Public Opinion as Revealed in Political Songs* (Princeton, 1949). The variety and vehemence of opinions reproduced in Rogers' book help us to get at the reality behind more formal documents such as the *cahiers* and edited texts of parliamentary speeches.

At the other extreme from the doggerel recited or sung in the streets of European cities stands the body of written work produced by leading thinkers of the period. It is never easy to use such material for purposes of historical reconstruction; for a philosophical treatise is by its very nature partly normative, that is, concerned with things as its author believes they ought to be. To that extent it offers a potentially deceptive picture of things as they are, or were. One such theorist may emphasize the dark side of the contemporary scene, hoping to shock his countrymen into supporting major changes. Another, revealing a more positive cast of mind, may emphasize signs of an emerging Utopia, if only to minimize the difficulty of going the rest of the way. Still a third may attempt frankly to achieve results by satire, exaggeration, overstatement. Allowance made for these possible refractions, however, we can scarcely afford to ignore the insights afforded by the writings of thoughtful individuals.

It might appear at first glance that metaphysicians such as Immanuel Kant and George Wilhelm Hegel could tell us little about their Germany or about Europe as a whole in the late eighteenth and early nineteenth centuries. Yet in his *Critique of Judgment* (*Kritik der Urtheilskraft*, 1790) or his *Conflict of Faculties* (*Der Streit der Facultäten*, 1798), to cite only two examples, Kant expressed in quite concrete terms his fascination with the revolutionary drama spreading outward from France. Similarly, dispersed through Hegel's writings on law, power, freedom and history are references to the lessons he felt could be drawn from the Napoleonic experience and applied directly to the Prussia of his day. It is equally possible to read the British fathers of modern political economy, from Thomas Malthus through the more engaged, and engaging, David Ricardo to that tireless crusader for reform, Jeremy Bentham, not only as prescribers but as describers as well.

Some fairly ponderous works composed between 1780 and 1830 were intended as tracts for their times, not efforts at preaching to the ages. Johann Gottlieb Fichte's *Addresses to the German Nation*, delivered in Berlin during the winter of 1807–8, while they range over great expanses of history and religion, gave voice to a most specific set of reactions to conditions in Prussia under French occupation. To take another instance, the historian Karamzin's *Memoir on Ancient and Modern Russia*, translated and analysed by Richard Pipes (Cambridge, Mass., 1959), spoke for unyielding conservatism in the face of foreign and domestic pressures for change under Tsar Alexander I. Whatever their importance as a gospel for modern conservatives, Edmund Burke's *Reflections on the Revolution in France* (London, 1790) illuminates, by both approval and condemnation, the divided opinions of the British ruling class concerning events transpiring across the Channel. A number of the prolific Count Joseph de Maistre's treatises, perhaps most notably his *Considérations sur la France* (Basel, 1797), reveal the mixture of political and religious advocacy in the life of an anti-revolutionary Savoyard nobleman.

From the theoretical disquisition, used as an 'intellectual' source, it is only a step to any of several other categories of literature. One such consists of travel books. Arthur Young's journals have already been mentioned; we have available to us an army of other, often more stylish, works of description based on their authors' journeys through places of general interest. An invaluable item in the immense library of travel records left by several centuries of Englishmen is William Coxe's three-volume *Travels in Poland, Russia, Sweden and Denmark* (Dublin, 1784). Another work, this one by a knowledgeable Frenchman who was shortly to become ambassador in Madrid, is Jean François Bourgoing, *Nouveau voyage en Espagne, ou tableau de l'état actuel de cette monarchie* (Paris, 1789); and in a more bellelettristic vein there is Goethe's account of his introduction to Mediterranean culture, the *Italienische Reise* (1786–88). No student of Russian society at the end of Catherine II's reign should overlook the *Journey from St. Petersburg to Moscow* by A. N. Radishchev, who paid for the frankness of his agrarian portrayal with a long exile in Siberia. This famous exposé, first published in 1790, has been translated by L. Wiener and edited by R. P. Thaler (Cambridge, Mass., 1958).

Travel literature is at least ostensibly based on observations of the existing world. When the historian turns to works of fiction as descriptive sources, he or she undertakes to sift factual information from what are primarily creations of imagination. It is generally conceded that some, perhaps most, of the greatest works of dramatic literature and prose fiction are among the least valuable sources of history, precisely because part of their greatness lies in their universal, timeless quality and in a perception of the human condition common to many different locales and ages. It is also true that a novel's historical significance may or may not correspond to the author's degree of personal proximity to the people and events embodied in the plot. The success of Jane Austen's novels obviously did rest on their creator's intimate knowledge of the restricted English scene with which they deal, as well as on her ability to detect and recreate every psychological nuance of the situations she conjured up in her imagination. On the other hand, two of Heinrich von Kleist's greatest dramas, *Die Hermannschlacht* (1809) and *Prinz Friedrich von Homburg* (1810) – though the first treats the struggle of Teutons against Romans in antiquity, while the second is laid in the court and camp of Brandenburg's seventeenth-century Great Elector – manage to express in passionate terms the patriotism and the call to martial valour aroused in Germany by Napoleon's autocratic rule. These plays are fascinating not only for the literary historian but also for the analyst of political propaganda at the highest level of art.

Certain later works of fiction, some of them based in part on their writers' own recollections but all of them heavily reliant on the accounts of other people who had lived through the situations and events described, nonetheless contain a great deal of solid history. The depiction of contemporary Italy, with reflections on Napoleonic warfare, in *The Charterhouse of Parma* by Stendhal (1839) reflects the vision of a great literary artist who had witnessed some of the Emperor's battles and known veterans of many more. His characterization of the petty despotisms of Restoration Italy in the same novel is if anything still more significant. Tolstoy's *War and Peace*, viewed simply as the Russian epic of 1812 (though written in the 1860s), contains brilliant and informed characterizations of such central figures as Speransky and Kutuzov. With Anatole France's novel of the French Revolution, *The Gods Are Athirst* [*Les dieux ont soif*] (Paris, 1912), as with Theodor Fontane's *Before the Storm*, set in the Prussia of 1812–13 but published in 1878, we are too far from the events described to speak any longer of primary sources. However, Anatole France was born in 1844 and Fontane a generation earlier, in 1819 (he had also served as a war correspondent from 1864 to 1871). Both had talked at length with survivors of the great crisis at the turn of the century, and these youthful conversations contributed an at least semi-documentary quality to their eventual novels.

Poetry as a source of history poses difficult problems, not least of which is the historian's uneasiness, even sheepishness, at seeking to extract literal data from verbal evocations of mood, emotion and often fantasy. Nevertheless, naturalism and anti-intellectualism in Wordsworth, glorification of the German middle ages in Wackenroder, revolutionary enthusiasm in Shelley and Byron, impatience with formal aesthetics in Chateuabriand, national and cultural pride in the Hungarian Alexander Kisfaludy, are without doubt significant characteristics of the era dealt with here.

Still more elusive than poetry, but at least comparable in its power to recall the tone of a vanished epoch, is music. Who can listen to a Gregorian chant and not gain added appreciation of the medieval scene, or a composition of Lully without a sense of having walked in the courtly surroundings of Louis XIV? Political songs have already been mentioned; but these we seldom prize for their musical qualities, exception made for France's *Marseillaise*. Firmly installed in both music and history, however, are Haydn's stately 'Lord Nelson Mass' of 1798, Beethoven's martial

Fifth Symphony and the lavishly romantic *Symphonie fantastique* of Berlioz, written in 1830, to mention only three illustrations.

The pictorial and plastic arts speak to us in more explicit terms than do the voices of poetry and music. Through the genius of Thomas Gainsborough we actually see at close range the English upper-class subjects he painted in the latter half of the eighteenth century. Jacques-Louis David, he of 'The Tennis Court Oath', 'The Death of Marat' and 'The Coronation of Napoleon', was an active participant in some and a graphic recorder of many more great scenes of the Revolution and the Empire. Francisco Goya conducts us from the eighteenth-century courtiers of Charles III's Spain and the cartoons (designs) he executed for huge rococo tapestries, through the changing aspect of the revolutionary era, to the horror of the Napoleonic invasion and the French occupation of Madrid. Géricault's 'Raft of the Medusa' or Delacroix's 'Massacre of Chios' (the former inspired by a shipwreck in 1819, the latter by a tragic incident in the Greek war of independence) take us directly to the centre of romantic sensibility and melodrama.

As for architecture, the most imposing of the historian's material sources, the age we are examining produced its full share of contributions to Europe's store of monuments and buildings. The Brandenburg Gate, completed in 1791, was a proud tribute by Berlin to the Prussian military tradition of Frederick the Great and the *Junker* aristocracy (though the first victorious troops to march under it were the French regiments of Napoleon in 1806). Paris, of course, bristles with the emperor's own memorials in stone, dominated by the Arc de Triomphe. In the pleasure palaces of the park surrounding the Escorial near Madrid, we can observe the luxury and the imitation of France that marked the Bourbon monarchy in Spain. No one could claim to have grasped the full extent of classical revival and Philhellene (pro-Greek) enthusiasm during and after the 1820s without having considered the buildings designed by the Prussian Schinkel and the Bavarian Klenze at the behest of their royal patrons.

Even this brief tour of sources has of necessity omitted the mass of still unpublished documentation which in countless libraries, archives and family collections awaits the researcher who has the requisite time, interest, patience and resources for travel. The study of original manuscripts has no place in a general history. Their existence, however, is signalled by the printed selections referred to here, as by much of the monographic research on which our generalizations rest. A reader wishing to form some impression of the nature and range of government documents might examine the printed inventories of the Archives Nationales in Paris, the Haus-, Hof- und Staatsarchiv in Vienna, the Archivo Histórico Nacional in Madrid, the Public Record Office in London, and so on. He or she might also become acquainted with less official sources by looking through the catalogues of the Cabinet des Manuscrits of the French Bibliothèque Nationale and the corresponding listings for a number of provincial cities, or by consulting the various reports of the Historical Manuscripts Commission and the *Catalogues of Additions to the Manuscripts* in the British Library.

When all available materials have been brought together, however, their sum total is not yet history. The analyst may pore over contemporary accounts, dissect statistical reports, listen to music, gaze at paintings, tramp through historic neighbourhoods – and the final indispensable steps will still remain to be taken. He or she will have to select, interpret, in short give meaning to the evidence. In so doing, an historian assumes a degree of personal responsibility which no one need bear so long as the data remain unevaluated and unorganized; but it is a responsibility he or she cannot at last evade. The relationship between sources and history is one of reciprocal dependence. Documentary evidence, both verbal and non-verbal, awaits the application of individual judgement in matters of accuracy, adequacy and relevance. On the other hand, no history can be better than its sources. What does it matter, after all, how brilliantly the causes of an event are explained, its implications weighed and correlated, if upon closer examination the event itself proves never to have occurred?

3

THE OLD RÉGIME: SOCIETY AND CULTURE

Throughout this and succeeding chapters references to 'the Old Régime' (or its French original, *l'ancien régime*) will appear repeatedly, in a number of differing contexts. For most students of our period the term itself carries strong associations, some favourable, others deeply hostile; but for present purposes any expression either of nostalgia or of animosity toward an age long past would seem out of place. There will be time enough at the end to weigh conflicting value judgements. Let us instead begin simply by identifying a number of social and cultural features discernible, with the usual amount of local variation, in most European countries prior to 1789.

An initial warning is in order concerning the temptation to visualize the Old Régime as something that extended back to the Middle Ages more evenly, and ended more abruptly and completely with the coming of the Revolution, than was the case. There was in fact mounting evidence, even during the eighteenth century, of dislocation and fundamental change. Quite apart from the climactic earthquake in France, the 1780s in particular were marked by a series of premonitory shocks in a number of separate places.

One important indicator of further changes to come was especially portentous, although its significance was not immediately apparent to contemporaries. Europe's population, after several centuries of relatively slow and periodically interrupted increase, began to increase from an estimated 140 million in 1750 to 187 million by about 1800. This phenomenon carried with it a host of implications for the narrative of the period, and we shall have occasion to refer to it in various connections.[1]

There was another sign of transition, less quantifiable than demographic data, but not less significant. This was a growing confusion in the *terms used to describe society*. The analysis of social structure, to be sure, is always beset by difficulties. In the Europe of 1780, however, these difficulties were particularly acute; for while old terms showed signs of growing inadequacy, no new vocabulary had as yet been invented to replace them.

SOCIAL STRATIFICATION

Let us begin by distinguishing three separate categories: (1) *orders*, (2) *status groups* and (3) *classes*. All three can be found in the structure of late eighteenth-century European society, though only the first would have been recognized by a man or woman living at the time. In most countries of continental Europe, an *order* was a category defined by law. Nobility, bourgeoisie, clergy and peasantry constituted the four largest and most frequently encountered of the traditional orders; but it should be noted that each of them was subdivided into a multitude of *corps* or *corporations*. A particular corps might comprise all the noblemen of a province or the bourgeoisie of a single town or the chapter of a particular cathedral. Although much of the relevant law was archaic and even more of the phraseology inadequate to express the social realities of the day, contemporary arguments went on employing 'orders' as units of social organization.

The nobility offers a case in point. Europe's noblemen comprised several million individuals whose material circumstances ranged all the way from great affluence to genuine poverty, whose individual social prestige might be as high as that of a duke or as low as that of a rustic bumpkin. With respect to its collective identity, the nobility existed solely as a legally defined order. In theory at least, every genuine member could produce proof that his title had been rightfully acquired, by inheritance, by purchase, by free conferral at the hands of a ruler or by occupancy of an ennobling public office. If a man had such proof, he and his family members both male and female were endowed with noble rank and the privileges, usually including tax exemptions, that went with it. If not, whatever his wealth and power, a commoner he remained in the eyes of the law.

A non-noble might or might not belong to another order, the bourgeoisie. The modern confusion over the proper use of 'bourgeois' and 'middle-class' has tended to obscure the fact that in the eighteenth century, bourgeoisie meant something very specific. A bourgeois (burgess, burgher) was not just any townsman. He belonged to the corporation that monopolized political rights in his municipality, and indeed *was* the municipality under the terms of its charter. Hence, he was one of a privileged minority among Europe's town dwellers. Like the nobleman, he was assumed to have documentary evidence – in his case, the official roll of burgesses – to prove it. His neighbours who had not won places on that roll, through time in residence, formal admission to the corporation and payment of set fees, were not bourgeois. They were listed under some such category as 'inhabitants' or 'residents'.

The two other great orders descended from the middle ages could not boast even the theoretical solidarity of the nobility and the bourgeoisie. The clergy, splintered since the Reformation, now encompassed Scottish Calvinist ministers as well as Italian cardinals of the Roman Catholic Church, Orthodox priests in Russia no less than Lutheran pastors in Germany, Scandinavia and elsewhere, Methodist preachers in addition to Anglican bishops. As for the peasantry, it had no institutional form at all, save in certain western European farm communities, where the villagers had some share in local government, or in Sweden, where they actually elected deputies (themselves not peasants but bourgeois) to a fourth estate in the national legislature. Yet the clergyman and the peasant, like the noble and the bourgeois, still seemed to contemporaries to be identifiable by order before all else.

The reader will have perceived the chief reason why orders cannot provide our only units for social analysis, namely, that they did not take in all of society. It is important to know whether a particular European of 1780 was a nobleman, a bourgeois, a clergyman or a peasant – but there is an excellent chance that he may prove to have been none of the four. Hence, we must introduce terms and subdivisions which are more modern in origin. One such concept is that of the *status group*, as defined by the famous German sociologist, Max Weber. While orders must be thought of as defined by law, status groups are categories representing degrees of social honour. There was, of course, some overlapping. Any nobleman was apt to be treated with more respect than *most* bourgeois, and certainly more than any peasant. Similarly, any enrolled burgess enjoyed a kind of prestige not shared by even the wealthiest non-bourgeois of the same town or city. In general, however, orders were at once too formal and too sprawling to be usefully thought of in terms of shared status.

The nobility, to return to this familiar example, was criss-crossed by innumerable status distinctions within its own membership. The contrast between the restricted British peerage and the horde of Polish gentry illustrates one such distinction, that of size. Even between clergymen of the same denomination, a Catholic archbishop and a village priest, for example, the social distance was practically immeasurable. The bourgeoisie or legal *citizenry* of a given town, be it Geneva or Frankfurt or Toulouse, extended from the proud heads of senatorial families to obscure shopkeepers and artisans who clung to an often empty franchise as their only claim to acknowledged standing of any kind. As for the peasantry, how could one compare the self-esteem of a French *laboureur*, virtually a free-holding farmer, with that of his own hired hands? It would be still harder to relate him to an Austrian serf, struggling under the system of *Leibeigenschaft* (literally 'bodily possession'), or to one of the millions of Russia's 'bonded people'.

In some of their aspects, status groups took account of distinctions which had no place in the original conception of an order of men. One of these sprang from religious variations. In an officially Catholic country, such as France or Spain or the Habsburg dominions, non-Catholics of all ranks suffered not only from legal disabilities but also from varying degrees of social inferiority. The same was true of both Roman Catholics and dissenting Protestants under the Dutch Calvinist theocracy or under the Established Church in England. To all this must be added the age-old discrimination against non-Christians, primarily the Jews.

Still other ingredients went into that elusive but powerful concept, status. Education, or the lack of it, was such an element. From the humble qualification of being able to read and write, which guaranteed the scribe, the schoolteacher, the parson some degree of local respect, up to the levels of erudition or literary skill which gave an entrée into aristocratic society, learning had a distinct value of its own. Partly for that reason, leisure, or the time to acquire education, was as prized by those who enjoyed it as it was envied by the less fortunate. But leisure was important for other reasons as well. Not to have to work to feed and clothe oneself had for centuries been the hallmark of 'the noble living nobly', in the language of the Old Régime. Hence the wealthy merchant gazed down proudly on his fragile slippers and his uncalloused hands as badges of honour even more impressive than his bank account.

The mention of a bank account nevertheless suggests one other distinction calling for attention in its own right, namely, degrees of wealth. It is obvious that wealth or poverty, both directly and through their bearing on leisure and education, helped to determine social status. Such is the independent power of economic variation, however, that we need to introduce still a third type of category, *class*, defined as a collection of individuals who share comparable *material* circumstances. Stated thus baldly, the notion assumes nothing about religion, legal titles, education or any other factor except the economic one. It was not a conception familiar to the eighteenth century; and had it been explained to the people of 1780, it would have outraged their assumptions about social structure.

Yet nothing in the social evolution of their own epoch had been more apparent, and for conservative onlookers more infuriating, than the emergence of 'the rich' as a stratum which cut abruptly across older lines of legal order and social status. Traditionalists, despite grumbling, could not easily object to the familiar sight of wealthy nobles or churchmen, or even merchant princes descended from the later Middle Ages and the Renaissance. But what was one to make of an English *nabob*, back from India with bulging pockets, an Austrian profiteer in arms or grain, a French speculator in luxury imports or royal tax revenues? Some of the oldest feudal coats of arms, it is true, had themselves been 'regilded' by fortunate investments or marriages into newly wealthy families. But other great fortunes were entirely in the hands of men too recently successful to claim any aristocratic connection. Such a man might buy a title for himself and his descendants, but for the present his power lay simply in riches. Wealth thus became another independent variable. By this I mean only that it is not enough to know of an individual that he was, let us say, a nobleman, a communicant of his ruler's faith and a member of an old family of the neighbourhood. The historian may also wish to know whether he was rich and, if so, *how* rich.

The usefulness of class analysis extends to all economic strata. The eighteenth-century 'middle class', as we have seen, was not the same as the 'bourgeoisie'. The latter was both older and narrower, in legal and political terms, but covered a much wider economic range. The former, while restricted to people neither wealthy nor depressed, was sufficiently elastic to include substantial farmers as well as townsmen. Finally, the notion of a 'lower class' reminds us that the poor under the Old Régime, whatever their religion and regardless of whether they suffered want in cities or in villages, constituted a reservoir of bitterness and potential violence. What could people in their situation care about the other, finer distinctions so dear to lawyers and social climbers?

PRIVILEGED GROUPS

With the three concepts of order, status and class in mind, we can appreciate the differences which separated the Europeans of 1780. That in turn allows us to consider actual groupings, before turning to national or regional variations within them.

At the top of the social pyramid, in country after country, were to be found the large landholders, led by royalty itself. The special prestige of landed wealth stemmed partly, no doubt, from its association with noble functions and with noble pastimes. Still more important, however, was the idea of the land as a source of income theoretically unsullied by commercial bargaining, a dignified form of property which permitted even a commoner to 'live nobly' on the labour of others. Living nobly did not as a rule mean living exclusively on one's lands as a manorial lord. Such holdings could also support their proprietor at court or in an urban residence. Mere possession of large parcels of land, however, remained in itself the highest mark of social success.

In the cities, of course, the plutocracy existed in the midst of leisure, comforts and opportunities for amusement unmatched by any but the very greatest country seats. As already remarked, few owners of town houses were without rural interests as well, and intermarriage combined with the comings and goings of wealthy town- and country-dwellers to produce a substantial mingling between them. Yet the magnate who clung to the city and its concerns remained different in his style of life from the true country gentleman.

Certain other elements helped to make up Europe's ruling group. Higher state officials – judges, fiscal administrators, career military officers – were with few exceptions recruited from both the urban and the rural upper classes. Yet the officialdom, in its training, its professional interests and its direct voice in public affairs, was clearly distinguishable from the men who devoted their full energies to the life of the manor or the private counting house. The same was true of the higher clergy. It was heavily dependent on the landed nobility for its leading personnel in Catholic countries and in England, rather more on the urban patriciate in Protestant lands on the Continent and on a mixture of both in eastern Orthodox regions. Everywhere, however, it was set apart by its special powers and responsibilities. Lastly, the ruling aristocracy included the most influential members of the professions: lawyers consulted by public authorities, medical doctors residing at court, professors in certain universities.

These, then, were the directors of Europe under the Old Régime: holders of wealth in land and money, wielders of judicial and military power, formulators (or at least executors) of religious policies and the custodians of specialized knowledge. Together they formed an elite which clearly overlapped the order of nobility but which had long since been expanded to include certain rich or talented commoners as well. In terms of status, the very concept of an aristocracy sprinkled with titles and blessed with leisure meant that this was the top stratum of social honour. It coincided in large measure with the highest economic class, though certain of the ecclesiastics and scholars – and even a few of the government officials – were men of only moderate means, while some rich Jews and other religious dissenters remained outside the charmed circle of the socially elite. The question soon to be posed by events was brutally direct: could this aristocracy rooted in the medieval past, however modified it may have been by centuries of adaptation, adjust to the newer demands and discontents of European life?

RURAL PRODUCERS, URBAN CONSUMERS

Turning from the ruling to the subordinate groups in late eighteenth-century Europe, one at once encounters the producers and purveyors of food. Most of the continent's long coastline bristled with ports offering shelter and manpower not only to warships and merchant vessels but also to the far more numerous fleets of fishing craft. Like fishing, hunting remained a full-time occupation in the wooded areas of Scotland and Scandinavia, Poland and the Balkans, Bohemia and Germany, Switzerland and France. Human survival, however, depended primarily on products extracted from the soil, either directly in the form of crops or indirectly, in that of domesticated meat animals. Farmers remained by far the largest occupational group, and the first effects of the eighteenth-century population rise had only accentuated their immense preponderance. In Spain, for example, where the population is estimated to have grown from 7.4 million in 1747 to 10.4 million in 1787, there were at the latter date still only four cities with more than 100,000 inhabitants (Madrid, Barcelona, Valencia and Cadiz), while just four others exceeded 50,000. The Spanish case may have been extreme, but it was not uncharacteristic. In one country after another, it was the growing number of farm folk, not the vanguard of a future army of industrial workers, that impressed observers in the 1780s.

About no other element in pre-revolutionary European society is it quite so difficult to generalize as about farmers, particularly because during the preceding 50 to 100 years age-old differences had been sharpened and in some instances new ones introduced. Prosperous and independent freeholds were to be found scattered across most of north-western Europe, though their numbers, except in France and western Germany, had been declining as a result of avid consolidation of property by the wealthier classes. On the other hand, even those among western farmers who had lost the independence of peasant proprietorship had never appeared more fortunate in relation to the sinking multitude of eastern European bondsmen. The latter had paid, in both personal freedom and economic wellbeing, for the policies adopted by their rulers out of deference to privileged aristocrats.

Despite this bewildering variety of conditions Europe was in 1780, as it still is, one of the world's most fertile and productive regions. Threatened by periodic blights and freezes, hampered by

27

tolls, tariff duties and local or national export restrictions, the stream of food nevertheless poured towards the cities. Marketers of food thus formed one of society's largest occupational groups. It was a group not only populous but also elaborately subdivided according to specialities. Even today, the advent of supermarkets notwithstanding, many European householders still rely heavily on smaller stores, picking up their bread from the bakery, milk, butter and cheese from the dairy, vegetables from the green-grocer, meats from the butcher, seafood from the fishmonger or a freshly killed hare from the game store. In so doing they re-enact, no doubt without realizing it, scenes from the lives of their eighteenth-century, and even older, forebears. The author once perused a list, dated 1785, which gave the occupation of 132 heads of families in a southwestern German village. Of this number, 68 were primarily engaged in selling foodstuffs to the remaining 64 and, of course, to one another!

Other townspeople included petty officials – constables, collectors, sextons, clerks – as well as school teachers and members of the lower clergy. Service personnel formed a major category: household servants, coachmen and wagoners, innkeepers, restaurateurs, pedlars. Craftsmen and shopkeepers, under guild control, sold clothing and utensils to those of their neighbours who could afford to buy from experts instead of having to rely on household industry. Finally, the larger cities contained a growing number of day labourers who worked for wages, using materials and occupying premises supplied by their employers – in other words, early factory workers. It would, however, be a mistake to exaggerate their number. Industrial labour, as distinct from the traditional journeymen who worked in small guild enterprises, was to be found concentrated only around the larger mining establishments, the as yet very limited scattering of private plants and the workplaces for state manufactures. It must be emphasized that in this period the 'putting-out' system, under which weavers, for instance, took home yarn or thread issued to them by an industrial entrepreneur and were paid when they brought back the finished pieces of cloth, was far more prevalent than was the central organization of a London brewery, a French cannon shop or one of the new Russian iron works. Nevertheless, an early proletariat, composed of both insecure journeymen and industrial labourers of the newer type, was becoming an increasingly important feature of the urban scene.

The social structure of Europe included of course some groups which were essentially unproductive. Soldiers, for example, were a regular component of the population of any garrison town and an irregular one of other places through which troops passed from time to time. Their demands for billets and supplies, not to mention their characteristic amusements, might disrupt the life of an otherwise stable community; but in general the professional military was accepted as essential to stability itself. Other groups, such as entertainers and prostitutes, attracted a similar mixture of distaste and tolerance on the part of society's consciously respectable elements. The same could not be said of the beggars, the vagabonds, the mentally ill, who were hounded into jails or driven from one locality to the next as fast as the constables could overtake them. In such circumstances, despite the savage penalties provided by law, the criminal population was large, counting among its numbers not only the petty thieves and cutpurses of the town but also the murderous gangs that preyed on all but the best-policed highways. For despite the crowded humanity of its cities, Europe still had great regions of loneliness, regions where an unexpected sound or flash of light might be either a source of comfort or a cause for terror, but never a matter of indifference.

BRITAIN

Needless to say, even the swiftest tour through late eighteenth-century Europe showed a traveller countless departures from the general pattern just sketched. If he started in England, he encountered at once a major exception to the prevalent definition of nobility: the division between the peerage (dukes, marquesses, earls, viscounts and barons), on the one hand, and on the other, the gentry. In Britain, only the former were styled 'noblemen' or defined as such by law, though baronets and knights were clearly equivalent to the lower ranks of the continental *noblesse*. Also, while England had its bourgeoisie, technically defined, the old town corporations were rapidly being swamped by the large, vigorous army of newer merchants and manufacturers, an army containing many representatives of the gentry and not a few younger sons of the peers themselves. Nowhere else was the aristocratic prejudice against money-making weaker, nor the alliance of land and trade quite so strong.

Since Parliament stubbornly refused to authorize a national census until 1801, detailed population figures for Great Britain are difficult to come by; but it is clear that the island kingdom shared in the demographic revolution. By 1750 England, Wales and Scotland combined had perhaps 9 million inhabitants, and this number swelled to about 11 million before the end of the century. Even in 1780 many English cities were growing faster than urban centres on the Continent. This was especially true of the northern factory towns, such as Manchester; and had it not been for London's phenomenal climb towards the 1 million mark, the south would have been completely left behind in the population boom.

This precocious development of cities was not solely the result of an early swing towards factory production. Also involved was a crisis affecting the agrarian poor of England and Wales, the peasants who had once eked out a farm labourer's meagre wages by growing subsistence crops and grazing a few animals on village common lands. As more and more of these commons were enclosed by parliamentary enactment (the eighteenth-century peak was reached in the decade 1770–80 with 642 such Acts 'dividing, allotting and enclosing'), the gentry and other substantial freeholders acquired tracts large enough to permit efficient exploitation through the application of improved agricultural techniques. For peasants and other marginal farmers, however, enclosures meant expulsion or restriction to tiny plots which could not feed them and their families. Their only choice lay between full-time employment as hired hands or migration to urban centres. Ugly as most of the cities unquestionably were, they offered escape to thousands, soon millions, of country dwellers who apparently felt that escape was necessary. Recent studies of the problem have therefore revised the older view that the false lure of factory wages seduced misguided rustics away from an idyllic, or at least wholesome, rural existence into one of sooty degradation. The actual alternatives seem to have been at once grimmer and less flattering to rural life.

North of England, the Scottish scene – both in the agricultural regions of the Lowlands and in the Highlanders' remote strongholds – offered a set of bewildering contrasts. A nobility which reached its summit in the Scottish peers, sixteen of whom were selected by the others to sit as representatives in the British House of Lords, also included a wide variety of lairds and clan chieftains. At its worst, the tightly knit Presbyterian church structure enforced the petty tyranny practised by a stern regiment of clergy and lay elders. At its best, it supported an uncommonly strong and effective system of education. Thus, a vigorous and relatively well-taught population provided skilled labour for an expanding industry while, at the other extreme, many indentured miners were bound to their pits jobs under conditions approaching those of slavery. Despite economic progress, Scotland's high percentage of unproductive terrain made it particularly difficult for this partner in the United Kingdom to absorb the population increase of the eighteenth century. In growing numbers, Scots were therefore setting forth to make their mark on the outside world – including England.

On 'John Bull's other island', as some contemporaries saw fit to call Ireland, the social pattern differed from the European norm primarily because it was viewed by its English rulers as conquered territory, and treated accordingly. Ulster Protestants enjoyed relatively high status, when contrasted with their 'papist' neighbours in the the north and the far more numerous Catholics in the south. Under the English bureaucracy and army, however, no Irish subject, regardless of his or her religion, could look forward to much social, let alone political, advancement. Much of the country's income was enjoyed by great lords, mostly resident in England, and by the Anglican hierarchy of the Church of Ireland. Catholic priests, with the surviving Irish gentry and burgesses, for the time being retained their status only at the price of docility. The introduction of the potato had recently added a cheap and comparatively dependable food to the diet of the poor, while linen weaving was beginning to show promise as a putting-out industry; but the bulk of the population, estimated to have grown from about 2.7 million to 4.2 million between 1771 and 1791, lived a rude agrarian existence, and a precarious one at best.

IBERIA AND ITALY

The traveller who sailed southward from the British Isles to the Iberian Peninsula found in Spain's 10 million people and

Portugal's nearly 3 million an entirely different set of variations on European themes. Traditional elements of the Spanish way of life strongly resisted the efforts to change them initiated by Charles III's reform ministers, as Portuguese habits had earlier done when challenged by the Marquis de Pombal's still more autocratic projects. In Spain, the aristocracy comprised the great *señores* (110 *grandes* and 535 *titulos de Castilla* in the census of 1787). It also included the *caballeros*, each appointed by the crown to life membership in one of the four great crusading orders that enjoyed the income from almost 800 localities earlier reconquered from the Moors. In addition there were an estimated 500,000 individuals, many of them only poor *hidalgos* (sons of someone), who nevertheless claimed the legal status of nobility. When to this figure is added that representing 200,000 ecclesiastics, over half of them monks and nuns, the overloading of the social distribution in favour of privileged groups becomes apparent.

Of the peasant proprietors, who constituted something over 20 per cent of the Iberian farm population at the century's close, many held plots too small to distinguish their possessors very sharply from the depressed mass of *péons*. An urban middle class existed, to be sure, and was actually increasing in size and influence. The Mediterranean cities of Barcelona and Valencia in the east, the north coast centres of Bilbao, Santander and La Coruña, together with Lisbon in Portugal, all witnessed the emergence of a new, expansionist breed of businessmen. However, while these capitalists were sufficiently numerous and articulate to frighten the older elite, the mass of illiterate peasants and shepherds could generally be counted on to join with their traditional 'betters' in opposing any radical change.[2]

From Iberia our attention moves naturally to Italy, where Spanish influence had been paramount in the sixteenth and seventeenth centuries. Italian society in the 1780s was as variegated as the Italian political map was confusing. The three surviving city republics of Venice, Genoa and Lucca, despite their decaying commerce, were still ruled by the haughtiest of patricians. Savoy and Piedmont, on the other hand, had relatively few towns but numerous proud families of mountain nobility. Or to take another example, fully one-third of the Papal States' adult population consisted of members of the clergy, while in Rome itself an indolent aristocracy enjoyed the support, in pensions and appointments, of the Holy See.

In the Papal States, in the kingdom of Naples and on the island of Sardinia, the Italian peasantry doubtless fared as badly as did the Spanish. In parts of the north, on the other hand, the rural economy compared favourably with that of any other area in Europe. Increased hardship resulting from population growth – from an estimated 11 million at the beginning to 18 million at the end of the century – did not bear down on all parts of Italy to the same degree. Tuscany in particular, ruled since 1765 by Grand Duke Peter Leopold von Habsburg, had profited from an impressive series of reforms: fairer distribution of tax burdens, abolition of legal restrictions on agricultural modernization, the ending of legal serfdom, efforts to reduce the excessive number of clergy. Not all of these reforms could be pushed as far as the ruler had intended, and some were destined to be reversed in the reaction after 1790, when Leopold left Florence for Vienna to succeed his brother Joseph II as Holy Roman emperor. Tuscany's lower classes, however, would never again be remotely comparable in poverty to those of the south – the *Mezzogiórno* – nor its nobility so vulnerable as that of Rome to the bitter description, 'vain swans on a lake of misery'. Albeit somewhat less strikingly than the Tuscan state, the Austrian province of Lombardy also occupied a favourable place in the Italian complex. Under the relatively mild supervision of distant Vienna, native Lombard officials compelled the upper classes in Milan and the rich Po Valley to accept many of the urban and agrarian improvements already decreed in Florence. In this instance, Italian commoners reaped undeniable, if not widely recognized, benefits from foreign rule.

FRANCE

Pushing northward into France, the oberver on tour entered what he had reason to consider the heartland of western Europe, a nation of 25 to 26 million, two-and-a-half times the population of either Spain or the United Kingdom. Blessed with uncommonly plentiful and varied natural resources, supporting fewer nobles than did Spain, boasting a higher percentage of landowning peasant proprietors than did Great Britain, France could not fail to impress visitors fresh from poorer lands. It too, of course, had its famines, its less fortunate peasants, its beggars and criminals; but to a contemporary traveller the French monarchy must have seemed a veritable giant of mobilizable power.

Yet not all of France's special characteristics could be described in such positive terms. Given the obvious wealth of the kingdom, the public bankruptcy which seemed always just around the corner was more humiliating, more suggestive of duplicity and fraud in high places than equally inept financial administration might have appeared in a less richly endowed country. The nobility, albeit less inflated than in several other areas of Europe, was quite large enough (perhaps 400,000 individuals) to enrage vigorous commoners who could not secure access to it as quickly or completely as they would have liked. More serious, this same *noblesse*, as one of its most brilliant descendants, Tocqueville, was sadly to reflect, still enjoyed social pre-eminence over a non-noble population which seldom looked to it for administration at the local level, no longer respected its fighting ability and had long since ceased to feel markedly inferior to it in economic terms. The French nobleman's privileges fanned the resentment of neighbours who felt no need for his protection.[3]

In these circumstances, perhaps the most ominous feature of the French situation was the aristocratic resurgence which the nation witnessed in the decades preceding 1789. The ministerial reform efforts of the early 1770s had been repudiated when Louis XVI came to the throne in 1774. In the 1780s the law courts (the preserve of the so-called *noblesse de robe*), the army and navy, the civil administration and the church hierarchy were once more in the grip of the higher nobility to an extent unmatched throughout the preceding 100 years. A royal ordinance of 1781, for example, required that each candidate for an officer's commission in the army have a coat of arms showing four family ties with the nobility. From 1783 to the Revolution, every French bishop was a nobleman. Clashing with the increasing freedom of religion and the progressive collapse of obstacles to commercial and industrial enterprise, the couner-offensive of the privileged orders at the social and political levels represented an ominous departure.

THE LOW COUNTRIES

Across France's northern border lay the Flemish and Walloon

(French-speaking) provinces of the Austrian Netherlands, the future Belgium. Here the ruling group included a fairly small cadre of officials sent from Vienna to Brussels, a larger number of Belgian administrators, a stratum of strongly Frenchified native nobility, the prelates of the Catholic hierarchy and the burghers who controlled such cities as Ghent, Bruges and Antwerp. Because cities contained an uncommonly high proportion of the 3 million people in this compact region, the urban oligarchs were especially proud and influential. Their influence, however, was no more progressive than that of titled noblemen in many other lands. It was the town guilds, in fact, that led Belgian resistance to the Habsburg Emperor Joseph II's attempts to limit special privilege, as we shall see in Chapter 5.

Proceeding up the Atlantic seaboard, our traveller would have entered the Dutch portion of the Netherlands, resembling the Belgian in its heavy urban development but different in being officially Protestant (Calvinist) and politically independent of foreign control. The United Provinces, led by the richest of them, Holland, had suffered political confusion and relative economic decline since their seventeenth-century apogee of commercial success, naval power, colonial expansion and diplomatic influence. By the 1780s, the very question of aristocratic leadership was at issue. Patricians belonging to the regent families, who monopolized seats in the various town councils as well as in the provincial estates and the national States General, found themselves faced by increasing opposition from other commercial elements, scarcely inferior in terms of economic class but discriminated against under the existing social and political arrangements.

Roughly a third of the Dutch population, nearly 700,000 out of 2 million, were Roman Catholics and, as such, excluded from government positions, army and navy commissions and high commercial posts, such as those in the Dutch East India Company. Another 10 per cent were Jews or dissenting Protestants (Mennonites, Quakers, etc.), who shared the Catholics' disabilities. Finally, although the little country's trading and banking structure still represented an imposing national asset, business had unquestionably suffered from foreign, especially British, competition. The number of poor journeymen and able-bodied unemployed both angered and depressed the Calvinist oligarchs, with their firm conviction that poverty, like illness, was a sign of defective character.

SCANDINAVIA

Still farther north, in Lutheran Scandinavia, the two kingdoms of
Sweden and Denmark-Norway recalled the Dutch experience in
that since the seventeenth century both had fallen from positions
of considerable power. Sweden's warlike past had left the nation
with a turbulent nobility; but under the imperious rule of Gustav
III, king since 1771, the nobles found themselves treated with
suspicion at court and forbidden to initiate public proposals
through the *Riksdag*, or diet. Weak in industry (since 1730 even
its famed iron works had been cautiously limiting their own
production), Sweden had seen once flourishing market cities, such
as Wisby, shrivel in size and decline in wealth. Peasant farmers,
who made up the vast majority of the Swedish ruler's 2 to 2.5
million subjects, were working hard to improve production by
clearing and enclosing large plots, introducing new crops such as
potatoes and turnips and adapting for their own use the new
agronomic theories originating in England. A major problem for
both agriculture and industry, however, was that a large share of
the capital needed for improvements had to come from foreign
investors. The result was that the Swedish economy was
especially sensitive to international disturbances over which the
country had little or no control.[4]

If the approximately 800,000 Norwegians, stretched thinly
along their hundreds of miles of Atlantic coastline, appeared less
advanced economically and less diversified socially than the
Swedes, the compact realm of Denmark, also with a population
under 1 million, seemed by contrast much closer to the main-
stream of European life. With its handsome capital, Copenhagen,
its busy shippers and merchants, its numerous small craftsmen,
seamen and fisherfolk, its relatively prosperous farmers and still
outwardly secure nobility, the Danish kingdom proper (as distinct
from its crown's possession, Norway) showed a close family
relationship both to the Low Countries and to certain German
principalities.

THE GERMAN LANDS

The Germanies themselves – the loose structure of the Holy

Roman Empire scarcely constituted a single 'Germany' – presented a social range which came close to mirroring that of Europe in its entirety. The nobility included princes who were vassals of the emperor at Vienna, but were themselves suzerains (overlords) of their own territorial nobles and virtually sovereign rulers of their subjects. In addition, especially along the Rhine and in south-western states such as Württemberg, there were about 1,000 imperial barons and knights, holding fiefs of only moderate size but intensely conscious of their own 'immediacy', that is, their direct fealty to the emperor without owing allegiance to a local prince.

Eastern Germany – Saxony, Mecklenburg and, above all, Brandenburg-Prussia – had its own special type of nobility, the Junkers, who profited from large estates employing staffs of overseers and exploiting the labour of serfs, near-serfs and tech-nically free tenants to grow rye and other grains. East of the Elbe, though personal *servitude* was declining, peasant proprietors of independent farms were exceedingly rare. In Prussia, the eight-eenth century had seen the Junkers acquire not only increased economic power over the peasantry, but also an ever tighter grip on high military appointments. At the same time, they had succeeded in invading the upper levels of the civil service, partly through appointment to bureaucratic posts, partly through inter-marriage with non-Junker families of the administrative elite. Frederick II 'the Great', forty years on the throne in 1780, had worked to harness the Junkers for military and civil service in this way, while he condoned their growing exploitation of the lower classes. He assumed that social stability and a loyal aristocracy could be bought for this price; but by the time he died in 1786, it was clear that the Prussian monarchy faced a peculiarly tough and arrogant alliance of privileged elements within its realm.[5]

Far different from the Prussian scene was that to be found in Hamburg, Frankfurt-on-Main, Nuremberg or any of the approxi-mately fifty other imperial free cities, each with its ruling caste of senatorial dynasties. Still different was the pattern in the large southern duchy of Bavaria, south-western states including Baden, Württemberg and Hesse-Darmstadt, or the north German possession of the British royal family, Hanover. Each of these and some 250 smaller principalities had its landed nobility, its official bureaucracy, its merchants and shopkeepers. In each, however, the small farmer – often a landowner in the Rhineland and the south-west, but just as often a poor tenant or serf – was the predominant social type.

Comparable in importance to its several varieties of class structure was Germany's diverse religious geography. In officially Catholic Bavaria, the aristocrat who was also a communicant of the Church of Rome quite naturally stood at the top of the status hierarchy. The same distinction was assured the Lutheran patrician in Frankfurt and his Calvinist equivalent in Bremen. In the sprawling Prussian kingdom, on the other hand, the situation was complicated by the fact that a royal family which professed to be Calvinist ruled over some 6 million subjects, the majority of whom were Lutherans but who also included many Catholics in Prussia's Rhenish outposts as well as in its recently won southeastern province of Silesia. Small wonder that Prussians viewed religion as a less significant status factor than did Frenchmen or Dutchmen or, for that matter, Bavarians.

SWITZERLAND

In the thirteen cantons of the Swiss Confederation, religious differences between the Catholic and Reformed churches were compounded by the mixture of German, French and Italian ethnic groups within this small country. A landed nobility and numerous clergy survived in Switzerland, most notably in the Catholic forest cantons of Schwyz, Uri, Zug and Unterwalden. Among the three most populous urban cantons that of Bern contained the most exclusive patriciate, absolutely closed to newcomers since 1651 and by 1780 limited to just sixty-eight families. Basel, half of whose inhabitants qualified as citizens or burghers, was ostensibly more democratic; but even here the top positions in the social hierarchy and in the government as well were in the grip of the leading members of a single guild, that of merchants.

Geneva was still an independent republic outside the Confederation. Its French-speaking population of 25,000 made it larger than any of the technically Swiss cities, and it contained a much more complex society. Scaling down from citizens who could hold office, through burghers who could only vote, to *habitants* and *natifs* who could do neither, the Genevan social structure appeared almost a caricature of local distinctions in eighteenth-century Europe. More important, it served as a microcosm from which much could be learned about the stresses of the period we are examining.

AUSTRIA AND HABSBURG CENTRAL EUROPE

Still north of the Alps, its German Austrian provinces forming part of the Holy Roman Empire, lay the bulk of the Habsburg domain, with a total population of about 27 million. Austria proper, in many of its social traits, resembled Bavaria and other south German regions. Its landed nobility and its Catholic clergy were numerous, its farmers divided between small proprietors and many more dependent peasants on large estates, its urban development unimpressive by western European standards. The great exception to this last was, of course, Vienna, which contained not only a substantial bourgeoisie and a mass of poor inhabitants, but also the aristocracy of court and administration. Unlike the German gentry of the rural areas, this ruling elite in the capital was an international amalgam of titled lords and high officials: Germans, Bohemians and Hungarians, with smaller delegations of Italians, Belgians, Croats and Slovenes.

The Habsburgs' Slavic states – Bohemia and Moravia, Slovenia, Croatia, Polish Galicia – supported some of Europe's wealthiest landlords on the backs of some of its most miserable peasants. Queen Maria Theresa (often incorrectly referred to as 'Empress') agreed with her enemy, Frederick the Great of Prussia, on at least one point, namely that a loyal nobility was essential; and despite honest efforts at reform on her own estates she had allowed a multitude of farm labourers under seigneurial control to be reduced to what was, under various technical names, a state of serfdom. Her son, Emperor Joseph II, was committed to improving the lot of the agrarian masses, but the resistance of the privileged orders was as stubborn as it was oppressive. The notorious Bohemian *robot*, for example, a system providing for several days of compulsory service by the bondsman for his lord each week, has become in a number of languages a byword for abject subjugation to another's commands.

Hungary was famous for its numerous, self-willed and warlike aristocracy, the Magyar nobles who filled the Hungarian Diet and controlled local government through the *comitats* or county councils. Natural growth and territorial conquest, combined with immigration by Slavs and Germans, had swelled the Hungarian population from 1.5 million in 1700 to over 6 million by 1780. Yet this figure still amounted to less than a fourth of the French total. Consider then the fact that the Hungarian nobility was roughly equal in size to that of France! Only a few of these Magyar lords moved at the cosmopolitan level of great magnates with palaces in Vienna, the Esterhàzy family for example. The rest stayed at home, sharing in the profits from their country's grain production and horse breeding. A small bourgeoisie, largely confined to a few towns, notably the twin Danubian cities of Buda and Pest, had no great role to play in Hungarian society. As for the peasants, the relatively high fertility of the area helped many, probably a majority, of them to live somewhat better than did Poles and Czechs; but in general they shared the weary life of their counterparts elsewhere in eastern Europe.

THE BALKANS UNDER OTTOMAN RULE

The social conditions of the Balkan Slavic peoples and their Albanian and Greek neighbours to the south are by no means easy to reconstruct. Few natives of the region could write, and those who could, primarily Orthodox Christian clergymen, appear to have felt little inclined to compose descriptive chronicles. Foreign visitors generally recorded only superficial impressions, limited for the most part to a handful of cities. Such documents as do exist, furthermore, have all too frequently been interpreted by Balkan historians in the light of their nationalistic resentment against the former Turkish rulers and used to paint a picture of unrelieved misery. Actually, the surviving data, when treated dispassionately, suggest that the lot of Europeans under Ottoman rule, while certainly not enviable, compared favourably with that of the corresponding classes in other continental countries.

The Turks exercised their rights in a far from uniform manner. In Albania and Montenegro, for example, the native mountaineers paid only nominal tribute to Istanbul (Constantinople) and saw little of their Ottoman masters. The port city of Dubrovnik on the Dalmatian coast, a genuine trading centre, sent financial payments to the Sublime Porte, as the Turkish imperial government was called, but in other respects enjoyed almost complete freedom to pursue its commercial rivalry with Venice. The Rumanian principalities of Moldavia and Wallachia had their own nobility, the *boyars*. These no longer chose the princes or *hospodars* of the two states, now selected by the sultan exclusively from a few Greek families called *Phanariotes*; but the boyars did represent an indigenous Balkan aristocracy. In Greece, on the other hand, while an elite of clergymen and scholars certainly existed, it would have been difficult to see them as native Greek aristocrats. (The only Greek-speaking nobility, apart from the Phanariotes in faraway Rumania, was that of the Ionian Islands, which were under Venetian rather than Turkish control.)

Seen in the broadest terms, the society of the Ottoman-governed Balkans revealed two or three characteristics of particular interest. One was the even more than ordinarily sharp distinction between urban and rural populations – not only in their ways of life but also in their ethnic composition. The million or more Turks whose ancestors had settled in Europe since the fourteenth century were concentrated in cities such as Athens, Salonika, Belgrade, and in a number of smaller centres, supporting themselves as civil servants, garrison troops, craftsmen and merchants. In this last profession, they were joined by Greeks in some areas, by Jews in others. The countryside, on the other hand, was left almost completely to the indigenous Bulgars, Serbs, Rumanians and so on. Hence there usually existed between any Balkan city and its own hinterland not only the difference in life styles to be found everywhere in Europe, but also ethnic and even linguistic differences of still greater moment.

Another Balkan peculiarity lay in the set of almost exclusively financial obligations imposed upon the peasantry under the Ottoman form of feudalism and its manorial substructure. On a fief, whether it was a large *ziamet* or a smaller *timar*, the *spahi* or landlord received a regular tithe (theoretically just 10 per cent of each tenant's produce), while the sultan's government claimed a head tax or capitation. Forced labour, on the Bohemian or even the Prussian model, was remarkably rare in the Balkan version of the lord–tenant relationship. For this reason, among others, modern researchers have tended to revise the once black picture of lower-class existence in European Turkey.

One more circumstance casting doubt on that picture was the protection which the Sublime Porte accorded the Orthodox Christian clergy. Since the conquest of Slovenia and Transylvania by the Austrians at the end of the seventeenth century the Turkish empire had ceased to contain many Catholics. Nevertheless, the Orthodox establishment, presided over by the Patriarch of Constantinople, was still given privileged treatment as a purveyor of anti-western sentiments and a defence against the missionary zeal of the Roman Church. The result, ironically enough, was that the Orthodox clergy within this Muslim empire enjoyed more security and higher social status than did any but the most elevated churchmen in Christian lands.

It would obviously be ridiculous to over-react against old stories by suggesting that the Balkan peoples lived under a benign foreign master whose rule they should have cherished. Capricious ferocity and periodic extortion had in fact become increasingly characteristic of the Porte as its international position deteriorated and as Ottoman administration decayed. Yet the traveller moving northward into Poland might have been forgiven the thought that there were definite advantages for the mass of a population in having some government other than an unrestrained aristocracy.

POLAND

In one sense, such a judgement would have been unfair. A segment of the Polish nobility, reacting to the humiliating loss of territory in the first partition eight years before, had by 1780 managed to initiate a serious campaign in support of both constitutional and social reforms. There even seemed to be some hope of bringing at least a modest amount of order to the mass of *szlachta* or gentry (numbering perhaps as many as 750,000 in a population estimated at 9 million). In the event, Poland's aggressive neighbours prevented these reformers from showing what might be done, but it must be said that the purely internal obstacles confronting them were enormous from the start. Nowhere else in Europe did one perceive such a ludicrous exaggeration of noble privilege. It was apparent in the defencelessness of a peasantry denied the admittedly sporadic relief offered the lower classes by the central governments in many other nations. It was apparent too in the virtual collapse of the once considerable but now increasingly isolated Polish bourgeoisie. With its Catholic clergy demoralized by political conflicts and disciplinary lapses, its public order constantly threatened by rebellious confederations of nobles, and many of its cultured aristocrats more at home in St Petersburg or even Paris than in Warsaw, Polish society presented a baffling challenge to its would-be rejuvenators.

RUSSIA

In distant Russia, the traveller doubtless expected, and assuredly found, some particularly sharp departures from western and central European conditions. This expansive empire, its population already nearing 25 million, incorporated a huge peasantry, a relatively small industrial labour force concentrated in a handful of cities, as well as in the Ural iron region, and a still smaller, deeply conservative merchant class. The Russian nobility was itself divided, according to occupation and domicile, into the great families of courtiers and magnates, the 'service nobility' of the imperial administration, the provincial gentry and, of course, the military officers' corps, many of whose members were by this time also serving as local administrators (especially after retiring from active duty). The sprawling mass of Orthodox clergy included types as diverse as the easygoing, often ignorant village priests, on the one hand, and on the other, the better educated, celibate 'black monks' who monopolized the higher ecclesiastical posts. All these social distinctions were further complicated by regional differences: between the still partially nomadic Ural branch of the Cossacks, for example, and the farmers of the Ukraine and White Russia, or between both these elements and the coastal Balts and woodland Finns of the northern frontier. No other realm we have considered, not even the Habsburg possessions, displayed quite the ethnic and economic heterogeneity of 'all the Russias'.

Some of the most striking characteristics of the Russian scene had to do with the position of the bonded peasantry. Because of the prevalence of legal servitude, a tsar or reigning tsarina disposed of millions of 'souls', as they were termed with unconscious irony. Hence, instead of describing his or her gift to a favourite courtier or successful general as such-and-such a tract of land, the successor of the Tatar khans would say: 'Let him be given so-and-so many thousands of my souls.' The bonded peasantry on the Romanovs' own estates remained the largest single block of subjects, but by the end of the eighteenth century the number of *pomyetscheke* peasants, those bound to other noble lands, had probably risen to at least 10 million. Directly tied to the status of agrarian labour was one final peculiarity of Russian society: the effort to build industry by simply assigning serfs owned by the crown or certain great nobles to designated mines and factories. Unlike western businessmen, early Russian entrepreneurs did not try to attract workers from the countryside, nor did they sweep up the unemployed of the cities. Rather, they contracted to have adequate numbers 'ascribed' (as the practice was called) on a regimented basis; and the 1782 census listed 75,000 such possessional serfs working for private manufacturers, to say nothing of mine operators who controlled thousands of others. All in all, an observer who strayed very far from the cosmopolitan, French-speaking court of St Petersburg knew that he was on the very fringe of 'Europe'.

THE CULTURAL SCENE

Thus far we have centred our attention on distinctions defined by legal order, by status honour, by varying degrees of economic security and comfort. Before ending our survey of social structure we should do well to ask how these distinctions were reflected in other facets of European culture. The latter term should be understood here in its broadest sense. That is, it includes not just the highest flights of human intellect and artistic taste, but also the humbler forms of expression and communication and enjoyment which together characterize a particular civilization. This extension is necessary precisely because the life of Europe in 1780 was so strongly marked by the division between a high culture, the shared possession of the wellborn, the wealthy, the educated of all countries, and a host of 'lower' cultures embodying the ethnic variety and local traditions which were no less European than the cosmopolitanism of privileged groups.

For the upper classes there were really two international languages. Latin had by no means lost its place in scholarship and education, where it permitted learned treatises to be discussed and academic lectures to be understood by people speaking a score of different native tongues. Amid the linguistic confusion of central Europe in particular, it served as an important administrative tool. For example, German and Czech officials in Vienna agreed with many Magyar-speakers in Budapest that Latin ought to remain the official language of Hungary. Another of its major uses lay in the rituals and the communications of the Roman Catholic Church. Lastly, though no longer the sole medium of diplomacy, it was still used for certain international agreements.

Latin's successful rival as a diplomatic language was French, more flexible than any ancient prose could be, but at the same time, after a century-and-a-half of rigorous purification, more precise and orderly than any of its modern rivals. English, Spanish, Italian and, increasingly, German were recognized for their literary contributions; but French alone could qualify one as a cultured individual. This fact will help to explain the extraordinarily swift and general impact of French events, beginning in 1789, on the literate of Europe.

The vernacular tongues, on the other hand, were in many cases all but ignored by the upper classes of the very nations in which they were spoken. A well-known personification of this tendency was Frederick II of Prussia, who spoke and wrote almost exclusively in French, maintaining until the end of his life a scornful indifference towards German writers of the calibre of Goethe and Schiller. Local dialect, with its mysterious slang and elusive peculiarities of pronunciation, was apt to be even less attractive to the man of education than was the literary form of his national language. There were exceptions. Herder and Goethe, having become masters of High German (albeit in Goethe's case only after a youthful infatuation with French), found a special charm in the archaic Swabian and Alemannic expressions of Alsace. Neither the Cockney speech of London, however, nor the *argot* of the Parisian streets had comparable admirers. Was the Florentine gentleman, with his beautiful Italian, the *lingua toscana*, really using the same language as the Calabrian peasant's mixture of vulgarized Latin, Spanish, Arabic, Levantine and other Mediterranean words? In Greece, scholars employed the debased but still recognizably classical *katharevousa*, while the masses spoke a 'demotic' blend of uninflected Greek, Turkish and Slavic roots. In the Balkans generally, the church Slavonic of the Orthodox clergy was as great a mystery to a Dalmatian fisherman as to the wife of a Macedonian farmer. Beneath the contempt of educated people, the future national languages of eastern Europe survived only by word of mouth. The first book printed in Bulgarian, for instance, did not appear until 1806.

As in language, so in formal education, the lines of cleavage followed boundaries of class and, as earlier remarked, helped to determine lines of status. Certain Catholic and Orthodox seminaries, as well as a number of Protestant universities, admitted and supported prospective clergymen recruited from the humbler levels of society. Otherwise, however, education above the elementary level was almost exclusively reserved for the aristocratic and the well-to-do. Universities were only beginning to free themselves from the desiccated and inert state in which most of them (outside Germany) had existed during the eighteenth century; yet they alone could certify individuals for admission to the professional corps of scholars. Furthermore, their importance in training civil servants would soon rival their old function as finishing schools for young gentlemen.

Education below the university was somewhat more accessible to the needy, through parish and charity schools. The demand for working hands on family farms and for apprentices in family shops nevertheless prevented most of the sons and virtually all the daughters of farmers or artisans from learning even the rudiments of numbers and spelling. Any numerical analysis of the European population in 1780 would almost certainly show a vast majority to have been illiterate. The more prosperous segments of the urban middle class provided some secondary education for their children (again with heavy preference shown to boys); but for more sophisticated instruction in languages, the classics, history or mathematics, it was necessary to rely on private tutors whom only a relatively small minority of the population – nobles, patricians and some rural gentry – could afford.

In view of this very narrow base of systematic training, the scholarly and scientific achievements of Europe's high culture in the late eighteenth century seem truly impressive. It is important to bear in mind that the Scottish economist Adam Smith, the French chemist Antoine Lavoisier, the Italian physicist Count Volta, the Prussian philosopher Immanuel Kant, and the other great intellectual figures of the time were members of a tiny elite. It was by no means an elite wholly confined to the richly or nobly born (Smith was the son of a minor customs official, while Kant's father was a saddlemaker in Königsberg); but by virtue of its training and interests, a select fragment of the population it remained.

Belles lettres offered a career which was easier than scholarship for poor men to enter, if only because it demanded less formal preparation. Germany's Friedrich Schiller and Scotland's Robert Burns were both of humble farm stock, while Caron Beaumarchais, author of the *The Marriage of Figaro* and *The Barber of Seville*, was the son of a Parisian watchmaker. Equally representative of the literary calling in their day, however, were Goethe, the wealthy patrician from Frankfurt, and Harrow-educated Richard Brinsley Sheridan, witty playwright, member of Parliament, friend of some of Britain's most influential aristocrats and politicians. Two great compatriots, respectively the fathers of modern Italian comic and tragic drama, illustrate the contrasts that were possible. Carlo Goldoni began his career as a strolling player from Modena. Count Vittorio Alfieri came of one of the Piedmontese nobility's richest families. But perhaps more significant in this connection is the fact that even the low-born among the writers referred to above, save for the tragically shortlived Burns, eventually acquired fortunes and social recognition. Schiller was honoured, and paid, as a history professor *and* literary artist in residence by the enlightened Duke of Saxe-Weimar from 1789 until the poet's death in 1805. Beaumarchais, now styling himself Pierre Augustin Caron *de* Beaumarchais, became a brilliant figure at the French royal court. Goldoni too was invited to Paris and there given a pension by Louis XVI. The ruling aristocracy of the Old Régime knew how to flatter writers, though in some cases, including that of Beaumarchais, it did not even attempt to make them stop ridiculing the existing social order.

In the other arts, with one major exception, the high culture of the waning eighteenth century was more notable for elegance than for power or originality. Architecture seemed locked in the stiff neoclassical formalism exemplified by the Pantheon in Paris (completed in 1781) and by Berlin's Brandenburg Gate (begun seven years later). The suffused colours and fantastic lights of rococo decoration sought to make the most of the hard, regular spaces provided by formal domes and rectilinear building shells;

but the resultant effect was generally one of display, as distinct from genuine sensitivity.

Formalism and insipidity characterized painting as well, at least on the Continent, blanketed as it was by representation of idealized Greeks and Romans or inhumanly pretty aristocrats at play. The English painters, Gainsborough, Reynolds, Romney, at least retained contemporary costumes and recognizable types in their portraits, together with superb mastery of detail. England, for once in her history, was pre-eminent in a field of graphic art – while potters like Wedgwood and furniture designers like Chippendale, Hepplewhite and Sheraton made her a leader in the useful arts as well.

One of the most striking features of pre-revolutionary European painting in general is not the absence of talent, for that remained plentiful throughout the period, but rather the extent to which prevailing canons of style suppressed the talent of men who would soon display it in full measure. The Jacques-Louis David of 1780, while already thirty-two-years old, suggested little of the vigorous and opinionated interpreter of dramatic events to come (though as early as 1785, his 'Oath of the Horatii' announced a vivid new school). And who could have detected the depth of tragic feeling, the versatility, in short the genius, of the mature Francisco de Goya in his first sedate designs for tapestries and his portraits of the Spanish court?

The great exception to this impression of relative aridity was music. Much that was inconsequential was being composed, of course, with the full approval of a large part of Europe's aristocracy, the custodians of 'high culture'. In musical composition, however, to a degree unmatched by any other art form, creativity seemed to gain discipline and precision from a set of formal requirements, yet soar above them to new heights. The sonatas and symphonies of Haydn, exquisitely tooled for the music room or concert hall, nevertheless wove together Croatian peasant tunes from the master's boyhood. With Mozart, European music reached a level of combined craftsmanship and feeling scarcely approached before and seldom equalled since. A modern Protestant philosopher writes of this Austrian Catholic genius: 'He has heard the harmony of creation as providence in coherent form of which darkness is also a part, but in which darkness is not eclipsed.'[6] The child prodigy who grew into such a composer of light and darkness had outflown the boundaries of the rococo.

Opera deserves special mention because the late eighteenth century saw it well on its way to becoming in northern Europe, as it had long been in Italy, a polished form which was nonetheless meaningful to large sections of the general public. Gluck's most influential works, such as *Orpheus* and *Alceste*, belong to the 1760s; but their author was still alive in 1780, and the fame of his dignified, intricate technique was at its peak. In the Low Countries and France, all across the Germanies to Vienna and even St Petersburg, the opera was settling in as a feature of city life. With Grétry of Liege, whose *Richard-Coeur-de-Lion* flattered royalty and aristocracy alike, Belgium found its most widely admired composer of the early modern era. With less pomposity, the Italians Cimarosa and Paisiello (the latter a precursor of Rossini in setting *The Barber of Seville* to music) sustained their country's mastery of the form.

It is worth repeating that despite the use of folk tunes by Haydn and others, despite the fascination which popular stories and vernacular idiom held for many writers, what we have been looking at was essentially an upper-class culture. As such, it was the possession of a thin, cosmopolitan stratum running across the top of European society. In its literacy, its opportunities for travel, its dress, its food and drink, its shared enjoyment of wit in the salon and high stakes at the gaming table, the 'upper crust' gave a deceptive impression of stability and uniformity. Beneath it were strong forces of localism – and discontent. Popular poetry, for example, with its slanderous rhymes about easily identifiable lords and ladies, politicians and clergymen, found a graphic counterpart in the crude cartoon literature of the streets. Strenuous dances, coarse foods, heavy beer and thin wine cheered the life of Europe's poor, in so far as it was cheerful at all. In the distance between such pleasures and those of the ruling elite lay a warning scarcely perceived by men and women content to reassure one another that: 'It has always been this way.'

One final observation takes us back to the realm of folk literature. Dependent though they were on transmission by the spoken word, Europe's vernacular languages nevertheless cherished classics of their own, poems and songs and tales which the next century would rejoice in committing to print. If such humble favourites had any common characteristic that could be assigned a degree of social significance, it was their glorification of the rebel, the hunted victim but also the resister of the *status quo*.

From the pirates and highwaymen of Scottish ballads and England's rediscovered Robin Hood to the defiant heroes of the Serbian epics, from the south German legends which inspired Schiller's *William Tell* and *The Robbers*, to the Greek *klephtika* or 'outlaw songs', this theme runs through the popular culture of Europe. It is not to be ignored by a student of the coming upheaval.

NOTES AND REFERENCES

1   C. Cipolla, *The Economic History of World Population* (7th edn, Baltimore, 1978); also M. W. Flinn, *The European Demographic System, 1506–1820* (Baltimore, 1981).

2   W. J. Callahan, *Church, Politics and Society in Spain, 1750–1874* (Cambridge, Mass., 1984).

3   A. de Tocqueville, *L'Ancien Régime*, trans. M. W. Patterson (Oxford, 1949), Chap. 2, pp. 27–36.

4   G. Utterström, *Jordbrukets Arbetare* (Stockholm, 1957). English summary.

5   H. Rosenberg, *Bureaucracy, Aristocracy and Autocracy: The Prussian Experience, 1660–1815* (Cambridge, Mass., 1958).

6   K. Barth, quoted in G. Clive, *The Romantic Enlightenment* (New York, 1960), p. 39.

4

THE EUROPEAN STATE SYSTEM

The phrase 'state system', as applied to Europe before the French Revolution, has several advantages over 'international relations'. Many of the pieces on the chessboard of eighteenth-century power politics were either too tiny or too sprawling to be considered 'national' as that term is used today. While some were already recognizable as nations, others were supranational empires and still others much smaller entities surviving from the past. As for the reference to a *system*, it might prove misleading if taken to indicate a rational, self-adjusting relationship between and among individual governments. Such a relationship certainly did not exist. But if we mean simply that there existed an acknowledged list of monarchies, principalities and republics, each of them occupying a specified territory or series of territories and each expected to observe certain formalities while asserting its own interests, then we may safely have recourse to the notion of a state system without exaggerating its coherence or completeness.

One other feature is covered by the term, namely, a rough hierarchy of states, grouped by degrees of size, mobilizable power and hence ability to affect the course of European events. By visualizing several such orders of magnitude, we can better understand the characteristic duels among sovereigns, as well as the disruptive impact of the quarter-century that began in 1789.

THE MAJOR POWERS

The late eighteenth century knew five 'great powers': Britain,

France, Austria, Prussia and Russia. Against demands made by any of these a smaller neighbour was virtually helpless unless supported by another of the Big Five. By the same token, it required several of the latter, acting in concert, to extort any significant concession from one of their peers (*see* Map 1).

Great Britain's claim to inclusion in this select circle rested neither on geographical concentration nor on numerical superiority. Its standing army was limited in size and scattered from Dublin to the West Indies, from Quebec on the St Lawrence to Calcutta in the Ganges delta. Yet because of its commercial resources, sustained by a redoubtable maritime tradition, the United Kingdom was assured an influential voice in any European dispute it chose to enter. The very dispersion of its colonial empire, like the intangible quality of its financial strength, gave British power a resiliency which could frustrate more massive opponents. Whether or not George III's inherited German title as Elector of Hanover should be viewed as an asset was more problematical. To the extent that it facilitated diplomatic access to central Europe, Hanover seemed a useful possession; but whenever the Electorate's vulnerability to attack by continental enemies threatened to embroil the island kingdom, London rang with indignant outcries.

Across the Channel, the French monarchy could no longer challenge the rest of Europe as it had done a century earlier under Louis XIV's imperious motto: *Nec pluribus impar* (Not unequal to many). However, with its large army, its natural wealth and its strategic location, which permitted direct assaults upon a variety of possible opponents, France remained the Old Régime's most feared land power. Its not inconsiderable navy denied even England's Admiralty the pleasures of complacency. Despite colonial losses during the first two-thirds of the century, the French still commanded important bases overseas: Pondichéry in India, Gorée in Equatorial Africa and such valuable island possessions as Martinique in the Caribbean. Even after the humiliating peace with England at the end of the Seven Years' War, the French crown had managed at last (a) to secure, by inheritance in 1764, the Duchy of Lorraine (thereby closing the gap that had previously separated its older dominions from Alsace on the Rhine), and (b) to acquire Corsica, by purchase from the Genoese republic in 1768.

On a simplified political map, the great continental rival of France might appear to have been the Holy Roman Empire of Germany. A closer look, however, reveals the true nature of this venerable monument to medieval statecraft. With its elective emperor in Vienna (the crown had been in the Habsburg family almost continuously for three-and-a-half centuries), the ponderous Imperial Diet at Regensburg, its supreme court in Wetzlar and its periodic levies for common defence against external foes, the *Reich* still maintained a pretence of unity. But it was only a pretence. From the eight electoral principalities[1] down to the tiniest county or free city, the more than 300 states in the Empire acknowledged only formal allegiance to the Kaiser – and often behaved as though they owed no allegiance at all.

For the real *loci* of power in central Europe, therefore, we must turn to two monarchies, each a member of the Holy Roman Empire by virtue of territorial possessions within the latter's boundaries, but at the same time endowed with important territories outside those limits. One was the Habsburg complex, which for convenience we call Austria, as contemporaries generally did. Its ruler, Joseph II, was Holy Roman emperor by election. By inheritance he was archduke of Austria, duke of Styria and Carinthia, count of Tyrol, king of Hungary and, quite separately, of Bohemia, margrave of Moravia and overlord of Slavic possessions which stretched from Polish Galicia in the north to Slovenia and Croatia in the south. In addition, Lombardy in Italy and the Austrian Netherlands acknowledged his rule. This immense array of people comprised a population larger than that of France, with a corresponding potential in terms of military manpower. The main obstacles to the full realization of that potential were obvious: a profusion of scattered commitments (pp. 434–5, Map I, 'Europe in 1780') and the difficulty of welding Hungarian cavalry, Croatian infantry and other diverse elements into a single army under commanders of diverse backgrounds.

Smaller, but scarcely more compact, were the lands of the Hohenzollern dynasty, Austria's principal rival in central Europe. At his death in 1786, Frederick II was an elector of the Holy Roman Empire, in his role as margrave of Brandenburg. He was also grand duke of Silesia, annexed by conquest forty years earlier. Outside the Empire, he was king of (technically 'in') Prussia, including the western Polish lands snatched in 1772. His realm further included west German territories: the small but rich duchies of Cleves and Mark in the Rhineland, the principalities of Minden-Ravensberg on the Weser and East Frisia on the North Sea coast. Far to the south, he was sovereign prince of Neuchâtel, a member of the Swiss Confederation. Finally, through family connections, he controlled the collateral fiefs of Ansbach and Bayreuth in central Germany. All that held the Prussian kingdom together was the crown itself, seconded by a large bureaucracy and an army that had earned great prestige from its victories over Austria in the 1740s and still more from its success against the French–Austrian–Russian coalition of 1756–63. By the end of Frederick the Great's reign both the bureaucracy and the army had become calcified to an extent which threatened their high reputation, but Prussia's right to consider itself a great power was beyond dispute.

Under the German-born Catherine II, the fourth reigning tsarina in half a century, Russia too was a major factor in European affairs. Since Peter the Great's death in 1725, the vast empire of the Romanovs had been extended northward into Finland at Sweden's expense, westward by virtue of the Polish partition of 1772, and southward through concurrent victories over the Turks. Its right to sail ships in Turkish waters, to intervene in the Rumanian principalities and, within vague limits, speak on behalf of Christians living under Ottoman rule, had been acknowledged at Kuchuk Kainarji in 1774. In the 1780s Catherine was entitled to congratulate herself on results achieved by her own ruthless will, by the stamina of Russian troops and by the high ability of General Suvorov, the 'Scourge of Islam'. The voice of St Petersburg had never been stronger.

LESSER POWERS

A number of states which had been significant components of an earlier Europe had declined markedly by the end of the eighteenth century. The most catastrophic plunge had been that of Poland. Once the centre of a great Slavic realm, the Polish kingdom now appeared helpless in the grip of social paralysis, crippled by the losses of 1772 and bereft of natural boundaries for defence against further Prussian, Austrian and Russian depredations.

Still more rapid, though destined to have a less abrupt and dramatic conclusion, had been the decline of Ottoman power. Only a century before, in 1683, the Turks had swept all the way to the walls of Vienna. With the raising of that siege, however, had begun the long Austrian counter-offensive down the Danube, a reconquest from the Christians' point of view, but from the Sublime Porte's a torment matched only by more recent defeats at Russian hands. Weakened by internal corruption, this great empire was threatened on all sides, Persian and North African no less than Balkan and Caucasian. Its only hope so far as Europe was concerned lay in the restraints imposed on assailants there by other great powers pursuing interests of their own.

Not all the beleaguered mighty of the past shared the extremity of Poland's and Turkey's peril. Many others had simply fallen, with varying degrees of awareness of the change, to the second rank. Spain, with its poorly equipped armies and sluggish fleets, could no longer be seriously compared with the prestigious force it once had been. More and more clearly, the Spanish crown's ability to act in the diplomatic–military arena had come to depend on its old enemy (but since 1700 its Bourbon dynastic ally) France. Such respect as the kingdom still commanded rested on its colonial possessions in Latin America, the Caribbean and the Pacific. When the 1780s opened it, like France, was seeking to capitalize on Britain's colonial troubles both for revenge and for territorial profit.

The neighbouring Portuguese had never recovered the status of a great power since their subjugation by Spain in the late sixteenth and early seventeenth centuries. Though restored to independence in 1640, they had suffered heavy naval and colonial losses at Dutch hands, only to become dependent on England in the eighteenth century. Yet Portugal retained considerable importance, not only because of the British alliance but also because of its own overseas holdings in the East Indies and the Indian subcontinent (notably Goa), on both coasts of Africa south of the equator and, above all, in South America, where Brazil already promised to dwarf the mother country.

The United Provinces constituted the third of these former colonial giants, sunk to intermediate rank by the 1780s. Like the Spanish and Portuguese, the Dutch controlled far-flung holdings: the lion's share of the East Indies, Ceylon off the tip of India, the Cape Settlement in South Africa, even a slice of Guiana on the

South American coast. Unlike their old Iberian rivals, however, they had shown the commercial and financial astuteness needed to translate these distant resources into economic strength in Europe. That this demonstrated capacity for survival had not brought the United Provinces genuine security was due above all to the continuing threat posed by Great Britain, whether as an enemy in war or as an implacable trade rival even in times of peace. This external frustration was the most important source of Dutch social tensions, already referred to in Chapter 3. The loss of genuine independence might be hidden by ostensible sovereignty, but it was a felt loss none the less.

Less prominent in the world of commerce and colonies, but in earlier days, under Gustav Adolf and Charles XII, even more potent than the Dutch as a military factor, Sweden now retained only scraps of its former Baltic empire. On the German coast, despite Prussian resentment, the Swedes still held the island of Rügen and a sliver of Pomerania. A large part of Finland was also ruled from Stockholm, but Russian ambitions posed a constant danger on this flank. King Gustav III scarcely bothered to deny that he hoped to take back from the tsarina the southern Finnish districts lost in 1721 and 1743. What restrained him, apart from uncertainty about Russia's strength, was the probability that in any Baltic struggle Sweden would be attacked by its old Scandinavian adversary, Denmark. The latter kingdom, even taking account of its control over Norway, would be no match for the Swedes in a land campaign. With either Russia or Prussia as an ally, however, the Danes held the key to the 'northern enigma'. Furthermore, given their position at the mouth of the Baltic Sea and a navy capable of harassing any fleet in those waters, they loomed large in strategic calculations of ministers as far away as Paris and London.

Another order of geographical considerations made little Switzerland more important to the European power balance than it could possibly have been on the basis of population and wealth alone. Its internal religious divisions, combined with a prudent distrust of involvement beyond its frontiers, generally prevented the Swiss Confederation from taking a decisive stand in any major international dispute. On the other hand its Alpine passes, invaluable to allies but difficult for an enemy to seize from the stubborn militia of the cantons, retained their military significance. It would be difficult to imagine a more startling act of aggression than a direct blow at Switzerland.

In Italy several states qualified as intermediate powers. One was the kingdom of Naples, comprising the foot of the Italian boot and the island of Sicily. Like Denmark in the north, this realm looked seaward to a maritime bottleneck of critical importance. Unlike the Danes, however, Naples lacked naval forces capable of disputing the passage of the central Mediterranean against a first-class fleet. Under the influence of Queen Maria Carolina, daughter of Maria Theresa, it relied increasingly on Habsburg Austria for support and rather less on King Ferdinand's Bourbon father, Charles III of Spain. Some such bulwark appeared vital in any case, and the importance of naval defence made even distant England a possible alternative.

The other Italian monarchy, albeit named Sardinia, was less important for its possession of that western island than for its ruler's patrimony on the mainland: Piedmont, Nice and the mountainous duchy of Savoy. King Victor Amadeus III, though his dominions had a sizeable military nobility and a record of past adventures abroad, was generally as conservative in foreign as in domestic affairs. The only danger of Sardinia-Savoy's disrupting the status quo in Italy lay in its long-standing ambition to annex the maritime republic of Genoa.

Not all the rulers of Europe's middle-sized monarchies were kings. The peaceful but strategically located grand duchy of Tuscany in north central Italy was a case in point. Germany contained two others, each ruled by a duke who also qualified as an elector of the Holy Roman Empire. One was Bavaria, stretching northward from the Alps, across the Danube valley to that of the Main. The other was Saxony, with its beautiful capital, Dresden on the Elbe, its burgeoning industrial area and its crucial, if vulnerable, location between Prussia and the Habsburgs' Bohemia.

While monarchy was eighteenth-century Europe's prevailing form of government, references to the United Provinces and Switzerland remind us that it was by no means the only one. We have no reason for surprise, therefore, at finding yet another oligarchy, Venice, among the secondary powers. The Most Serene Republic had been able to maintain its hold on the upper Dalmatian coast of the Adriatic and on the Ionian Islands between

57

Greece and Italy largely because of Turkish distractions elsewhere. In the late eighteenth century, it re-enacted each year the pageantry of former power, marrying its Doge (the ruling magistrate) to a sea which had ceased to be an avenue to riches and become instead a perilous arena for Venetian war galleys and merchantmen. Nevertheless, while no longer the imperious city of the past, Venice exploited its ancient prestige and its proverbial diplomatic cunning to sustain an impression of influence in Italian and Mediterranean affairs.

THE 'SWARM OF GNATS'

In addition to the five great powers, we have identified a dozen kingdoms, duchies and republics of lesser, but by no means negligible importance. Still to be considered is yet another category, a host of individually insignificant polities, some of them situated as enclaves within the territory of larger states, others grouped into what amounted to buffer zones between strong neighbours. Together, these relics of Europe's morselized past continued to account for a substantial fraction of the continent's total area and contained several million of its inhabitants.

This 'swarm of gnats', as an exasperated younger Pitt once called it, could be subdivided into several basic types. First, there were the ecclesiastical principalities, ranging from the Papal States of central Italy (comparable in size, though not in power, to several units discussed earlier), through Avignon in southern France, also a possession of the Pope, to the prince-bishoprics and archbishoprics in the Holy Roman Empire. Second, we should note the smaller secular principalities. The Germanies alone contained about 200 such microcosms, not to mention the 1,000 or more fiefs of all but independent imperial knights (*see above*, p. 37). Some were as considerable as the duchies of Württemberg and Mecklenburg-Schwerin or the margraviate (*Markgrafschaft*) of Baden and the landgraviate (*Landgrafschaft*) of Hesse-Cassel, while others were as minute as Reuss and Saxe-Weimar. The closest equivalents elsewhere were the Italian duchies of Parma and Modena-Reggio. Third and last, an important category was that of free cities. Most of these acknowledged a flimsy allegiance to some distant ruler – Dubrovnik on the Adriatic to the Turkish

sultan, for example, of Bremen, Hamburg, Frankfurt, Nuremberg and their lesser German counterparts to the Holy Roman
emperor. Genoa, in northern Italy, on the other hand, claimed an
independence no less complete than that enjoyed by Venice, as did
Geneva, yet to become a member of the Swiss Confederation.
The distinction, however, was academic – all maintained garrisons, conducted diplomatic correspondence and acted as free
agents in foreign affairs.

DIPLOMATIC THEORY AND PRACTICE

This array of jealous states, from great powers through intermediate ones to the often tiny organisms just discussed, shared
a set of institutions providing for the exchange of views, the
collection of information about one another, the application of
pressure by threat or bribery, the conclusion of alliances and the
settlement of conflicts. The diplomatic machinery of eighteenth-
century Europe was one of the most highly developed bureaucratic features of the age. Every government had some kind of
specialized foreign office and reserved a major share of the time
of its ruling councils for the discussion of external affairs. Every
government also had representatives and correspondents stationed
abroad, though their number and rank, like their pay, varied
enormously among states of differing sizes. Thus, while the king
of France or the empress of Russia each maintained a score of
ambassadors from Lisbon to Constantinople, plus a number of
envoys to lesser courts, a petty German prince was likely to have
formal representation only in the larger states directly adjoining
his own, and possibly at Vienna and Berlin.

The origins of late eighteenth-century diplomatic practices can
be traced back to Greco-Roman, and even earlier Middle Eastern,
antiquity. The direct line of development, however, begins in the
Christian middle ages, specifically with heralds as official messen-
gers and with the papal nuncios of the Catholic Church. Two
subsequent periods had seen lasting extensions of diplomacy's
scope, together with increases in its technical complexity. One
was the fifteenth century, when the Renaissance Italian states, led
by Venice, had carried ambassadorial reporting to an unprece-

dented level of both volume and expertise. The other was the late seventeenth century, when the France of Louis XIV had awed Europe not only by its armies but also by its elaborate machinery for espionage, persuasion and intimidation. The use of codes and ciphers for secret communications had acquired new precision and intricacy at Versailles. Diplomatic protocol had been subjected to explicit rules of the type so dear to Louis's etiquette-conscious court. And it was the Sun King's government that had perfected the 'circular', a uniform set of instructions dispatched to every representative accredited to a foreign government involved in a given issue, so that the French point of view could be presented simultaneously and in identical terms (allowance made for local interests) to a whole array of capitals abroad.

As a result of the demonstrated virtuosity of Louis's government in this field, eighteenth-century diplomacy was marked by what one authority calls simply 'the French system'.[2] It did not necessarily follow, of course, that France retained unchallenged its earlier leadership in the art. Prussian diplomacy under Frederick the Great had earned a great reputation for both diligence and cynical astuteness, though like military and civil administration, this branch of Hohenzollern government had declined in efficiency by the 1780s. The British, while less dependent than the French on specialized professionals, displayed at least equal ability in the complex peace negotiations of 1782–83 and a clear superiority in responding to the critical developments in the United Provinces during the period 1784–87. Nevertheless, titles, documents, terms such as *chargé d'affaires* and *détente*, the organization of foreign offices and even the arrangement of their archives tended almost everywhere to follow the French model.

Regardless of nationality, Europe's foreign service personnel shared certain characteristics more significant than the momentary success or failure of any particular government. We are speaking now not of the numerous spies, informers and part-time commercial agents, but rather the ambassadors and ministers, the councillors and secretaries who enjoyed diplomatic rank, observed diplomatic protocol and claimed diplomatic immunity from local regulations. Despite the occasional appearance of a gifted commoner, there was no more solidly aristocratic calling. Foreign ministers and ambassadors were generally noblemen of high rank. Charles James Fox, Britain's secretary of state for foreign affairs in 1782 and again in 1783, was an exception but scarcely an extreme one, for despite his lack of a title of nobility he had been brought up as a member of England's ruling class.[3] It might be added that his three successors in the foreign secretaryship during the remainder of the century were Earl Temple, the marquess of Carmarthen – later duke of Leeds – and Lord Grenville. Subordinate posts were normally filled by gentlemen and often by scions of great houses. Even republics, the United Provinces or the free city of Frankfurt-on-Main, for example, customarily reserved diplomatic appointments to members of their oldest patrician families – in part, no doubt, because ambassadors were expected to pay their own way, using private means.

A professional group thus constituted had definite advantages in the conduct of negotiations. Formed by comparable educations, speaking the same language in both the literal and the figurative sense, aware of class and status interests shared across boundaries and across the conference table, the diplomats of the Old Régime communicated with an ease and an understanding which the twentieth century has learned to envy. Their common desire to uphold the structure of privilege imposed not so much generous restraint toward opponents (consider the fate of Poland!) as a prudent reluctance, in most cases, to push issues to violent conclusions. Wars of annihilation were known to be risky, and drastic peace settlements generally regarded as counter-productive. In their caution and their sceptical understanding of one another, these practitions sought to avoid a holocaust.

As is so often the case in history, the potential weaknesses of the system were inherent in its strengths. Men who spoke each other's language would have found it hard to understand the common people of their respective homelands, had they cared to make the effort. They were soon to experience the difficulty of comprehending, to say nothing of controlling, mass emotions of a diffusion and intensity unknown to the cool world of dynastic calculation. Viewing war as a subordinate arm of policy, they were unprepared for an age in which militarism and militarists would make a handmaiden of diplomacy itself. Finally, because they believed in the underlying stability of the state system, such men could scarcely imagine a nation or a ruler prepared to wipe out the network of old frontiers and inherited claims they knew so well.

ARMIES AND NAVIES

Not that the eighteenth century had been either peaceful or static in terms of military development. Many of the strategic and tactical issues soon to be tested in violent action had already been agitated by several generations of theorists.[4] With relatively few exceptions, however, the soldiers of Europe's Old Régime, like its diplomats, remained deeply conservative, satisfied with the narrow range of operational choice imposed by the methods of early modern warfare.

It was assumed, for example, that the best armies were limited in size, recruited on the basis of long-term enlistments and composed of professionals whose lack of emotional identification with the governments they served was viewed as irrelevant. Britain's King George III found it objectionable that regiments of troops contracted for with German princes should fight in North America against rebellious colonists who claimed the 'rights of free Englishmen', but his own ministers overcame the royal scruples. Ireland and Switzerland continued to supply mercenary soldiers to states all over Europe. During the 1780s, more than 40,000 Swiss citizens were regularly in service with a half-dozen foreign armies. France maintained the largest Swiss contingent, some 15,000 strong; but Spain and the United Provinces each had several thousand of these businesslike specialists from the cantons. Even countries with elaborate laws demanding enrolment of their citizens for militia duty in fact relied very little on citizens in arms. Russia required its peasantry to provide one conscript from each specified group of households; but since the men thus called to duty had to serve at least twenty-five years, they were fully as professional and as divorced from their civilian countrymen as any mercenaries could have been.

For half a century or more, a technical debate had been in progress over the relative advantages of two methods of disposing troops for combat. One of these orders of battle was the reigning system of thin lines, dependent on the fire power of their disciplined ranks. The theoretical alternative was to rely on more massive columns or phalanxes whose effectiveness would depend on the shock effect of a bayonet charge. The line formation, its champions argued, had proved itself in countless battles, notably those of the 1740s, 1750s and 1760s in which Frederick the Great's Prussian infantry had cut larger enemy units to pieces and broken cavalry charges by steady musket fire. On the other side were the still more recent successes of Suvorov's Russian columns against the Turks in pitched battles decided at close quarters after furious mass assaults.

In France, where the debate over the *ordre mince* (line) and the *ordre profond* (phalanx) reached its highest verbal intensity, the 1780s ended with no decision yet agreed upon.[5] The brilliant Count de Guibert refused to believe that the alternatives were mutually exclusive, arguing instead that movements in both line and column could be combined with dashing cavalry actions and supported by the improved, mobile field artillery developed by General de Gribeauval. In practice, however, this synthesis was to be without effect until the next decade, when a new France at last began to heed the prophets of the old army. In the meantime, on drill fields from Potsdam to Dublin, regiments practised the sinister minuet of manoeuvres in line and volley firing by long ranks of standing or kneeling soldiers. Only a few experiments with irregular advanced lines of skirmishers revealed any awareness in Europe that across the Atlantic red men fired prone from shrubbery and white men who had learned from the Indians crept to battle along creek beds or behind stone walls.

Old assumptions about naval warfare had been subject to only a few challenges during the eighteenth century. In the 1780s the short-barrelled naval cannon, or carronade, had just begun to swell the fire power of British ships at close quarters with the enemy. War galleys dependent on oarsmen had gradually disappeared from all except a few stretches of Mediterranean coastal waters, while the launching in 1782 of a huge French man-of-war, the 118-gun *Etats de Bourgogne*, announced a new scale of magnitude in shipbuilding. Despite such changes in equipment, however, the criteria of sea power and the tactical rules for its use remained essentially what they had been for 200 years past.

By the time peace was concluded in 1783, Great Britain, with her 174 ships of the line and her much larger number of supporting vessels, towered over all potential rivals. It is true that France's eighty ships of the line could mount a considerable challenge, especially if joined by Spain's sixty to seventy; but the battle of The Saints in 1782, when Rodney and Hood defeated De Grasse off Martinique in the West Indies, served to underline the danger of facing the British at sea. To be truly vulnerable, the Royal Navy would have had to be crippled by an especially heavy desertion rate or by a more protracted interruption of its supply of timber for hulls and masts than any opponent had yet managed to inflict upon it.[6] As for other fleets, the Dutch and Portuguese had long since abandoned any pretence of independent naval power; while Catherine II's Russia, though its thirty to forty ships of the line in the Baltic and another twenty or more in the Black Sea made it a newcomer of considerable importance, could not seriously affect the balance of forces outside those restricted waters.

TRADITIONAL RIVALRIES: BRITAIN AND FRANCE

There is no need here to recount every minor diplomatic exchange and military clash of the 1780s. We should, however, pay attention to a few episodes grouped around the two most important rivalries involving European states before the Revolution: the English–French and the Austrian–Prussian–Russian. Sometimes these zonal conflicts overlapped, but in each case the principal axis remained distinct. The issues at stake, the alignments formed and the characteristic modes of action will provide a basis for comparisons and contrasts with later episodes. The nature of these confrontations may also help to explain the conditioned reflexes of conservative governments during the ensuing era of upheaval. In most countries, after all, it was statesmen molded by the old diplomacy who would have to face the changes wrought by its apparent breakdown.

When the decade opened, the chief issue exercising the chancelleries of western Europe, and momentarily those of the German-Slavic East as well, was the lonely position of Great Britain. To the long revolt in the North American colonies, begun five years before, had been added a no more portentous but, from London's viewpoint, a far more dangerous renewal of the far-ranging struggle between the United Kingdom and the Bourbon monarchies of France and Spain. In 1778, encouraged by American victories in the Hudson Valley, the Count de Vergennes as French foreign minister had committed his government to a fresh assault on its old British enemy. The following year, Spain had accepted a French promise of territorial prizes, including Florida and Gibraltar, and had joined the alliance against George III.

So far as European observers were concerned, battles in remote places with names like Cowpens and Savannah appeared less significant than Vergennes's determined effort to organize continental opposition to England. The French minister found his opportunity in the angry disagreements between London and most other capitals over definitions of contraband, blockade and freedom of the seas. His Majesty's government insisted that ship-building materials and in some circumstances even foodstuffs, especially cereals, were liable to seizure by the Royal Navy if found aboard any vessel bound for a French or Spanish port. Those neutrals who faced a threat to their trade in timber and grain from northern Europe entered particularly sharp protests; but the British continued to take prizes on the Admiralty's own terms. Paris and Madrid, meanwhile, were loud in their protestations of respect for the rights of neutrals everywhere at sea.

Still, most trading nations were reluctant to be drawn into open hostilities against England; and France, as a belligerent, could scarcely assume the leadership of a band of neutrals. In this situation, the initiative of the empress of all the Russias proved decisive. Catherine II had begun in 1779 by expressing as much indignation over Spanish attacks on some of her grain ships as over British searches and seizures. The latter, however, proved far more numerous than the depredations by the Bourbon navies; and as the months passed, Vergennes played skilfully on the tsarina's gratitude for his friendly role in recent Russo-Turkish negotiations. Gradually, St Petersburg swung towards the provisions urged by France: (1) free passage for neutral vessels except through an effective blockade; (2) rejection of 'paper blockades' announced by belligerents but not actively maintained by naval units covering a definite zone; (3) limitation of contraband to mean only weapons and munitions. On 28 February 1780 Catherine sent a formal declaration to London, Paris and Madrid, containing the above stipulations and adding: 'Her Imperial Majesty, in making these points public, does not hesitate to declare, that to maintain them, and to protect the honour of her flag [and] the security of the trade and navigation of her subjects, she is preparing a considerable part of her maritime forces.'[7]

Within barely six months of this manifesto, Russia, Sweden and Denmark-Norway were linked by an agreement to arm their merchantmen and to coordinate convoy arrangements for the purpose of enforcing their definition of neutral rights. In January 1781 'Their High Mightinesses', the States General of the United Provinces, joined the growing League of Armed Neutrality, only to find themselves singled out by England for a full-scale naval war. Later the same year first Prussia, then the Holy Roman emperor joined the alliance; and in July 1782 a nervous Portuguese government followed suit. Finally, in February 1783, when preliminary peace treaties had already been signed by the former belligerents, the kingdom of Naples swung grandly, if somewhat irrelevantly, into line.

How significant Catherine II's League of Armed Neutrality really was has long been a subject of debate. Except for involving the Dutch in active hostilities, it can scarcely be credited with much influence on the course of the fighting. Its direct value to Britain's adversaries should certainly not be exaggerated; for the Americans were little interested in noncontraband shipments from neutrals (in *this* instance at any rate), while neither timber nor grain seems to have reached France and Spain in sufficient quantities to make an appreciable difference in the war capabilities of either nation. The League did, however, express European resentment of British naval supremacy and its uses. This first effort to organize the whole Continent against England held an augury of future undertakings by rulers bent on conquest, not mere neutrality. For the time being, however, the League's greatest importance doubtless lay in reinforcing the feeling of the British themselves that they were perilously isolated in a world of enemies and unfriendly neutrals. It was that feeling, combined with the economic strain of almost seven years of war and the discouraging course of events in America, which in February 1782 led 193 members of the House of Commons, just one short of a majority, to vote for an immediate peace.

These parliamentary proceedings doomed the ministry of Lord North, who resigned the following month after twelve years in power. They also led to the launching of formal treaty negotiations in Paris. The news of Rodney's and Hood's naval victory in April (*see above*, p. 63) helped to offset British gloom over Cornwallis's surrender to the French and Americans at Yorktown the previous autumn. Nevertheless, the new ministry of Lord Rockingham faced a number of unpalatable choices in dealing with France, Spain, the United Provinces and the United States.

At the outset, England's councils were divided. Charles James Fox, who as secretary of state for foreign affairs was charged with the European settlement, favoured practically unlimited concessions to the Americans, in order to get them out of the war and thus to weaken France. The secretary of state for home and colonial affairs, the earl of Shelburne, on the other hand, still hoped to escape with only a qualified grant of domestic independence for the thirteen colonies, which he believed might yet accept English leadership in matters of trade and foreign policy. The fact that each of these strong-willed politicians had his personal agents in Paris during the period of early soundings only added to the confusion and apparent unreliability of British peace offers. Not until Rockingham died in July could Shelburne assume what amounted to the premiership, as first lord of the treasury, and by naming his own men to the two secretaryships take control of all aspects of the negotiations.

The hostile coalition, on its side, also revealed conflicting interests which British diplomacy now set out to exploit. The American spokesmen, led by Benjamin Franklin, John Adams and John Jay, were intent upon securing full recognition of the former colonies' independence, plus as much land and freedom of action as the new nation could obtain on its western frontier. Vergennes, while seeking maximum gains from England in the West Indies and perhaps elsewhere, felt no enthusiasm over the prospect of an independent power on the North American mainland. He especially hoped that the United States might be left insecure enough, and sufficiently bitter against the British, to make French protection and supervision a continued necessity. Spain had its own territorial demands, specifically Florida and Gibraltar, though a four-year siege of the latter stronghold had failed to dislodge the British garrison from the Mediterranean gateway. In Madrid's calculations, everything depended on French refusal to reach a separate agreement with England before the latter acceded to Spanish wishes. Yet how could Vergennes, with his government in desperate financial straits, be expected to prolong hostilities in deference to Iberian pride? As for the Dutch, the most they could hope was that their unfamiliar Bourbon allies would help them to escape from the grasp of British sea power.

The outcome was a classic example of cold diplomatic bargaining. It required some concessions by an England long unaccustomed to making any concessions at all. Considering the military odds, however, it was an achievement for which Shelburne deserved something better than the parliamentary revolt that swept him from office only weeks after the preliminary treaties were signed. The solution he had worked out involved several steps. First, with respect to the newborn United States, he belatedly adopted the thesis of Fox, deciding that it would indeed be necessary to pay the price required to deny France any further hope of using the rebellious colonies for its own purposes. Britain therefore granted the Americans a separate treaty (November 1782) which recognized their full independence, acknowledged their claim to the Northwest Territory all the way to the Mississippi and guaranteed them generous fishing rights off Newfoundland. Then Shelburne turned to the Bourbon monarchies. In the general preliminaries signed at Paris in January 1783 and confirmed by the treaty of Versailles the following September, he conceded to France Senegal in Africa, Tobago in the West Indies and certain fishing privileges in the North Atlantic. For the rest, Vergennes secured only a mutual return of territories occupied during the war. Spain received Florida and the Mediterranean island of Minorca, but not its dearest prize, Gibraltar. The United Provinces, thus abandoned, were unable to arrange a settlement until well into 1784, when they yielded to Britain both Negapattinam, near India's southern tip, and trading rights in the rich eastern island chain, the Moluccas.

In some respects, no doubt, Lord Shelburne was building better than he knew. By his much-criticized generosity to the Americans, he left the United States free to reject French tutelage and to grow by slow stages towards another kind of partnership with England. Though His Majesty's government yielded some non-essentials to the Bourbon kingdoms, thereby isolating the hapless Dutch, the general restoration of occupied territories left Great Britain in possession of all its key strategic bases abroad. They would soon be needed more desperately than the men of 1782 and 1783 could possibly have foreseen.

The sequel, so far as Anglo-French relations were concerned, had two separate themes. One was continued rivalry, now transferred to the Dutch internal struggle, whose domestic aspects we shall consider in the next chapter. Here it is enough to observe that the political crisis within the United Provinces following the peace of 1784 was also a major test of great-power diplomacy. The republican opponents of Stadtholder William V had the support of France, with whom the States General concluded a treaty of alliance in 1785. Both Prussia and England, knowing that Louis XVI's government was in no condition to face a general war, were eager to upset this arrangement by restoring the stadtholder to power on terms which would eliminate French influence from the Hague. The young British minister there, James Harris (later rewarded with the title of earl of Malmesbury), proceeded with great skill and persistence, among other things arranging financial aid for the Dutch Orangists from George III's civil list. It was not until the summer of 1787 that the pro-French Patriots themselves supplied a pretext for armed intervention by insulting the princess of Orange, wife of the stadtholder and sister of King Frederick William II of Prussia. London and Berlin promptly agreed that a Prussian army should launch what proved to be a bloodless invasion, and on October 10 Amsterdam capitulated. Within six months, the triumphant William V formally repudiated the French treaty in favour of an Anglo-Dutch compact, and before the end of the summer an agreement was signed in Berlin making Prussia the third party to this new Triple Alliance.[8]

The other trend in French and English relations produced a move towards economic understanding which showed how swiftly eighteenth-century diplomats could shed national animosity when they chose to do so. The trade agreement signed in Paris on 26 September 1786, and commonly called the 'Eden treaty' in honour of William Eden, its British originator, marked an unprecedented experiment in commercial cooperation between the two kingdoms. The final mover on the French side had been the once seemingly irreconcilable Vergennes, on the British, William Pitt the Younger, prime minister since December 1783. Both sought peace and commercial recovery for their nations after the dangerous struggle which had ended only three years before. Both of them, the ageing Frenchman with only a year to live and the twenty-seven-year-old Englishman near the beginning of his long ministry, were groping towards something beyond the jealous mercantilism that for so long had dominated their governments' trade policies.

The treaty provided for a reciprocal lowering of tariffs on manufactured goods and foodstuffs, including beverages. A significant exception was silk cloth, which the French had hoped to see included; but the grain, wine and brandy of France could now enter the United Kingdom under tariffs lower than those charged on similar imports from any other country. Conversely, Britain's hardware, cottons and industrial products in general could invade the French market on a scale never before permitted. It was unfortunate for Vergennes's posthumous reputation that France was already gripped by an economic crisis, shortly to be intensified by a series of bad harvests. Under such conditions, with no great surplus of food or drink to sell in Britain and with many sectors of French industry at least temporarily suffering from foreign competition, it was easy to leap to the conclusion that France was being ruined by the 'English mechanics'. Free trade enthusiasts might insist that reciprocity would eventually bring compensating benefits to the French economy, but history refused them the time prove it. Both the treaty and the argument it spawned were about to be swept away by a quarter-century of Franco-British hostility unparalled by any the Old Régime had known.

TRADITIONAL RIVALRIES: AUSTRIA, PRUSSIA AND RUSSIA

While Britain and France were moving from armed conflict to a mixture of diplomatic fencing and shortlived economic under-standing, the powers of eastern Europe pursued their several aims with unswerving devotion to the law of the jungle. The joint seizure of Polish lands in 1772 had suggested a degree of community among Austria, Prussia and Russia which was thor-oughly belied by their subsequent actions. Joseph II, Holy Roman emperor since 1765 and after the death of Maria Theresa in 1780 sole ruler of the vast Austrian patrimony as well, inherited his mother's determination to recover Silesia from Prussia. In addition he hoped for various other gains which the house of Hohenzollern was certain to resist. In Berlin the elderly Frederick II sought to protect his Silesian prize and to increase his more recent Polish acquisitions by ingratiating himself with Russia, while checking Austria wherever possible. As for Catherine II, though she would not yield the slightest advantage to the two German powers with respect to Poland, her attention was increas-ingly directed southward towards the Ottoman empire. On this

Balkan–Black Sea front, Austria might appear at any given moment as either a valuable ally or a serious competitor. Prussia's importance, as seen from St Petersburg, no longer loomed so large as in the days when Russian interest had been riveted on the Baltic region.

In 1780 a visit by Joseph II to Russia set the stage for the next year's signing of a defensive agreement between Austria and Catherine's empire. This treaty has been called the 'second diplomatic revolution', though it scarcely marked a reversal comparable to the Austrian–French alliance of 1756. From Frederick the Great's point of view, the second 'revolution' did have drastic implications precisely because of the earlier one, in the sense that France, where Joseph II's sister Marie Antoinette now sat as queen, was also still a formal ally of the Habsburgs and thus a potential foe of Prussia. The nightmare of isolation continued to haunt Berlin.

It was Empress Catherine who seized the first fruits of the new alliance. Promising Austria immense rewards in the Balkans, claiming for Russia itself the western Caucasus, the Crimean peninsula and the left bank of the Dniester, her 'Grand Plan' of 1782 was also called her 'Greek Plan' because it invoked the vision of a restored Byzantine empire under a Romanov *basileus* or emperor. If the project were carried out, the tsarina's three-year-old grandson, named Constantine not quite by accident, would rule Greece, Macedonia and Bulgaria from the city of his namesake, once the latter had been wrested from the Ottomans by the Christian armies.

In the event, Russia settled for much less. Joseph II was not eager to alienate France by an all-out attack on the Bourbons' old Turkish client. Furthermore – and this was a recurrent theme of the period – he was reluctant to weaken his position vis-à-vis Prussia by becoming heavily engaged in the south-east. In 1783, therefore, the Russians struck alone. Announcing that conditions in the Crimea demanded intervention on behalf of the Tatar khan, technically a vassal of the sultan but actually a protégé of the tsarina, a Russian army occupied the entire peninsula. At this point, to her great chagrin, Catherine was prevented by Turkish appeasement from pursuing the Grand Plan any further. Under the pressure from Vergennes's envoy in Constantinople, the Porte wrote off the Crimea with unexpected alacrity and early in 1784 signed a treaty ceding it to Russia. For the time being, the tsarina halted Black Sea operations, sardonically thanking her embarrassed ally, the emperor in Vienna, for his 'measured behaviour' and 'benign prudence'.

These phrases contain a special irony in view of Joseph's own conduct in several other areas. A ruler of considerable intelligence and humane impulses where domestic reforms were concerned, he proved in foreign affairs as ambitious as he was predictable. Though not the ruthless expansionist portrayed by later generations of Prussian historians, he was prepared to agitate conditions in western Europe and in the Germanies, at the same time he continued to listen to Russian blandishments in the East. Hence, an inordinate amount of diplomatic excitement was generated in widely scattered capitals by his various projects during the 1780s.

At the very beginning of his personal reign, for example, he launched a frontal assault on existing treaty arrangements concerning the Low Countries. Ever since 1715 Dutch troops had occupied seven fortified towns on the southern frontier of the Austrian Netherlands, facing France. This 'Barrier' was intended to help forestall any resumption of French aggression after the manner of Louis XIV, and the original agreement had been an integral part of the transfer of the Belgian provinces to Austrian control. In 1781, however, the emperor suddenly announced that the Barrier Fortresses were no longer needed and ordered their Dutch garrisons to leave his territory at once. Protests from the Hague were brushed aside; and the United Provinces, already at war with England, had no choice but to abandon the old fortified positions.

Shortly thereafter, in 1784, Joseph repeated the same tactics against the beleaguered Dutch, abruptly informing them that 'his' River Scheldt was no longer closed to trade, as it had been ever since the Peace of Westphalia in 1648. This time the States General did not yield. The French government, as unenthusiastic as the Dutch over the prospect of commercial competition on the part of Antwerp, advised Vienna that there must be no unilateral repudiation of existing agreements. Prussia automatically joined the opposition to Austrian demands. Furious over the reverse, Joseph II nevertheless accepted a modest indemnity for damages to certain of his Belgian subjects' ships which had been fired upon by Dutch shore batteries – and the Scheldt remained closed.

The Austrian Netherlands during these years occupied the

emperor's thoughts in still another regard, this one primarily German in its implications. Joseph had already tried once, in 1777–9, to annex part of the big duchy of Bavaria where the last 'direct' Wittelsbach had died without legitimate offspring. That attempt had been blocked by Prussia and Saxony. In 1784 it became generally known that Austria had formulated a new project: a simple exchange of Bavaria for Belgium (minus Luxembourg and Hainault, which would go to France if it endorsed the transaction). Joseph would be rid of the remote and troublesome Netherlands, while the annexation of Bavaria by Austria would create a massive south German state fully capable of acting as a counterweight to Prussia in the councils of the Holy Roman Empire. The elector of Bavaria showed himself quite willing to move to Brussels. He was, after all, not a native Bavarian but a Rhinelander (having already been ruler of the Palatinate before succeeding his late cousin in Munich) and was easily dazzled by the promise of a° combined Belgian–Rhenish principality to be renamed the 'kingdom of Burgundy'. The trouble was that like his predecessor, this lazy, voluptuous prince had no legitimate children; and the next Wittelsbach in line, the duke of Zweibrücken, was a grown man who made clear his preference for the Bavarian patrimony.

In this situation, the attitudes of other continental powers became decisive. Russia's empress sent Joseph II vague good wishes and a cool refusal to help. For France, the choice was anything but simple. A weak Belgium under Wittelsbach control might well be an easier neighbour on the north than the Netherlands had been during three centuries of Habsburg rule. Luxembourg and Hainault constituted a handsome bribe, as the Austrian party of courtiers around Queen Marie Antoinette pointed out. Vergennes wavered, but his fundamental caution, fortified by dislike for the notion of a great south German power, inclined him to oppose the scheme. That, in effect, is what he did, by suavely insisting that the other German states must give their approval.

Prussia's Frederick II saw the chance to win his last contest with the Habsburgs. In gambling on either Russian or French support to cancel Prussian influence, Joseph II had actually defeated his own purpose; for he had frightened and enraged a series of German rulers who would otherwise have been suspicious of any initiative from Berlin. Instead they rallied behind Frederick's call to resist what he called the threatened destruction of the Empire. The League of Princes was ostensibly instigated by the margrave of Baden, but its act of association was signed at the Hohenzollern court in January 1785. Prussia, Saxony and Hanover were joined by a dozen lesser principalities in a formal declaration of intention to uphold the duke of Zweibrücken's rights, that is, the *status quo* in Bavaria. Vergennes now had his excuse to withhold any French endorsement of the exchange, and a further embittered Joseph II had his answer. Hope for an Austrian–Bavarian merger was dead beyond hope of resuscitation. The family compact between Versailles and Vienna, in turn, had been exposed for what it was, extremely weak.

One might suppose that Joseph had been thwarted on enough occasions to make him eschew further adventures abroad. That such did not prove to be the case was in part a result of the emperor's restless temperament. It must also be said, however, that his next undertaking stemmed partly from events which he had not set in motion. This final act in the confused melodrama of pre-revolutionary diplomacy and warfare opened in 1786, when Catherine II put forward a new set of designs for a joint assault on the Ottoman Porte. She had an excellent opportunity to do so, for Joseph went along on the tsarina's famous tour of the Crimea and the Dnieper Valley. In the event, her imperial guest returned to Vienna unconvinced that Russian plans contained anything of value from his point of view; but the prospects, as seen from Constantinople, were unnerving.

Had the Turks been aware of the lukewarm Austrian attitude, they might have felt less anxious to seize the initiative in the summer of 1787. Instead, fearing the worst and hoping to catch its menacing opponents off guard, the Sublime Porte suddenly presented Catherine II's government with an ultimatum demanding immediate cessation of Russian interference in the khanate of Georgia. When this was rejected, Ottoman forces attacked Prince Potemkin's inadequately prepared army, and five years of savage warfare opened amid unaccustomed Turkish victories. By 1788 Catherine II faced another danger, a Swedish assault launched against Russian holdings in Finland, only about 150 miles from her capital city of St Petersburg itself. This attempt at collaboration between Gustav III and the sultan seems to have frightened the tsarina more than any other episode in her tumultuous career.

The Turkish–Swedish alliance, however, enjoyed only brief success. In the north, King Gustav was soon distracted by Denmark's entry into the war against him; and though the Danes accomplished little or nothing in a military way, Sweden felt compelled to accept a *status quo* peace with Catherine in 1790. Meanwhile, Austrian intervention and the strengthening of Russian armies had already turned the tide on the Ottoman front. Unenthusiastic as he had been at first, Joseph II realized that he had no choice but to honour the treaty of 1781 and join the fighting if he hoped to retain any voice in Balkan affairs. Consequently, in the spring of 1789 a large Habsburg army invaded Serbia, where it captured Belgrade that autumn, while the Russians, now led by the able Suvorov, began a relentless campaign to occupy the entire Rumanian coast of the Black Sea.

As the decade of the 1790s began, the final collapse of the Ottoman empire in Europe and its division between the Austro-Russian allies seemed imminent. One more time, however, the balance wheel of eighteenth-century diplomacy swung back to restrain the rush towards a 'total solution'. Denied French support, as so often before, the Austrian government kept looking nervously over its shoulder at the danger of a Prussian attack. A threatened revolt in Hungary and an actual one in the Netherlands further weakened the hand of the new Emperor Leopold II. Early in 1790, therefore, a Turkish–Austrian truce was concluded; and the following year Vienna signed the treaty of Sistova, abandoning Belgrade and all other conquests save for a small segment of Bosnia. Russia fought on until January 1792, then at Jassy accepted the Dniester as its new frontier, returning the Rumanian principalities to Turkish rule. All things considered, the sultan could count himself lucky.

By the time these agreements were reached, events in France already promised to make western Europe once more the focus of attention. The shift, be it noted, was neither instantaneous nor complete. The Polish situation in particular would continue to engage Prussian, Austrian and Russian avarice until the denouement of 1795. Nevertheless, Europe was about to experience a series of unprecedented shocks from a force whose like had never been seen before: a nation in arms.

THE EUROPEAN STATES IN 1789

The last years of the Old Régime, far from being wholly aimless or static, had witnessed a series of important shifts in the European state system. To understand the setting for the revolutionary crisis, it is essential to bear in mind those shifts, at least in so far as they helped to determine the posture of the great powers in 1789. Great Britain, dangerously isolated only a half-dozen years before, had survived that predicament and now had a working alliance with Prussia and the virtually monarchical United Provinces. Prussia benefited in turn from this Triple Alliance, especially as a makeweight in dealings with Vienna and St Petersburg. Russia, engaged in the latest of its successful wars of expansion, was able to command Austrian support when needed, yet was basically strong enough to play its own game from the Baltic to the Black Sea. Austria, oscillating between its German–Belgian involvements and its secular struggle against the Turks, seemed tempted to intervene everywhere yet able to succeed nowhere in the absence of a major ally.

It was France, however, that had suffered most in those years of the Bourbon twilight. Despite an outward appearance of recovered prestige and influence in 1783, a tribute to the sophisticated intelligence of Vergennes, the threat of financial disaster had combined with the conflict of factions at court – 'Austrians' versus 'Anglophiles', 'expansionists' versus 'immobilists' – to leave Louis XVI's government practically impotent in foreign affairs. Within only a few years after the treaty of Versailles, mighty France had abandoned its Turkish protégé twice (in 1784 and 1787), deferred to Frederick the Great in the matter of the Bavarian succession, allied itself with Sweden only to refuse Gustav III any help in Finland, evaded the claims of another ally, Austria, for protection against Prussia after 1788 and allowed London and Berlin to manoeuvre the Dutch into an unforeseen alliance.

Coupled with undoubted strength, this posture of aloofness might have had much to recommend it; but in the French case each new disengagement seemed less a haughty assertion of strength than a nervous admission of weakness. The diplomatic record, in fact, supports the view that the French Revolution erupted in a country whose government was already paralysed.

It also helps to explain the reluctance of France's enemies to believe that anything very serious was about to happen to them.

NOTES AND REFERENCES

1   In 1780 these included the kingdom of Bohemia (ruled by the Habsburgs), the secular electorates (Brandenburg, Saxony, Hanover, Bavaria) and the archbishoprics of Mainz, Trier and Cologne.

2   H. G. Nicolson, *The Evolution of Diplomatic Method* (London, 1954), third lecture.

3   G. O. Trevelyan, *The Early Years of Charles James Fox* (London 1880), contains a masterful treatment of this governing aristocracy.

4   See the excellent chapter on 'Armies and navies' in M. S. Anderson, *Europe in the Eighteenth Century* London, 1987, pp. 210–36.

5   Recent studies of this topic include R. S. Quimby, *The Background of Napoleonic Warfare: The Theory of Military Tactics in Eighteenth-Century France* (New York, 1957), and Martin Van Creveld, *Command in War* (Cambridge, Mass., 1985).

6   R. G. Albion, *Forests and Sea Power: The Timber Problem of the Royal Navy, 1652–1862* (Cambridge, Mass., 1926).

7   J. B. Scott, ed., *The Armed Neutralities of 1780 and 1800* (New York, 1918), p. 274.

8   A. Cobban, *Ambassadors and Secret Agents: The Diplomacy of the First Earl of Malmesbury at the Hague* (London, 1954). The same author cites the figure of £89,100 as an extraordinary charge on the civil list for aid to the Orangists in 1787, 'British secret service in France, 1784–1792', *English Historical Review*, vol. LXIX (1954), pp. 234–7.

5

POLITICAL ISSUES IN THE 1780s

In the previous chapter we discussed relations among European states as though each of them actually had been the kind of unit shown on a solid-colour map. Even in treating diplomatic history, such simple and concrete language can be deceptive if not carefully used. To say, for example, that Prussia was openly hostile to Austria is not really to say, though it may suggest, that every Prussian was simultaneously glowering across the frontier at every Habsburg subject in sight. Still, the convention of personifying countries is justified by the nature of diplomacy, the organization of military power and the centralized structure of public finance. Governments did, and for that matter still do, speak for whole peoples in dealing with other governments.

The situation is abruptly altered when we turn to questions of domestic politics. Here states can no longer be treated as individuals in a many-sided competition. The point at issue becomes precisely the extent to which a particular regime does or does not represent the population under its authority. The two arenas are not altogether separated. Foreign policy is obviously affected by internal affairs, while events perceived as successes or failures abroad may influence profoundly a struggle for power at home. Such overlapping, however, constitutes only a small part of an exceedingly complex picture. Many other elements in a political situation derive from the internal problems of the state in question and have little or nothing to do with its external relations.

UNREST AND REFORM: MATERIAL AND IDEOLOGICAL PRESSURES

What is the first, the strongest and the most enduring impression imparted by a general view of Europe in the 1780s? Clearly, it is one of agitation, of a turbulence scarcely suggestive of the 'good old days' later generations tend to see in any period that precedes a great upheaval. Just as clearly, this turbulence can be explained only by a combination of separate causes, some of them operative for years or even generations past, but now especially active in a noisy decade.

One such cause sprang from fundamental changes in the physical conditions of European life. As we have already seen, the eighteenth century had witnessed a marked rise in population, an ascent that quickened its pace as the century went on and had, at least through the 1780s, been heavily concentrated in rural areas. The economic and political implications of such a phenomenon can scarcely be exaggerated. In good years more farm hands and the simultaneously advancing agricultural techniques had the effect of driving down commodity prices in the urban markets. In bad years, on the other hand, the unconquered threat of famine might still return to the countryside. Either way, the peasantry in many areas had reason to see in the much-touted 'agricultural revolution' a process of deterioration and to feel correspondingly bitter towards groups ranging from noble landlords to townsmen in general and government officials in particular.

Though the widespread population growth had yet to make its full impact felt in most cities, such increases as had already occurred were adding to the political strains experienced by urban centres. The master craftsmen and old patricians who had for centuries managed town affairs found themselves being challenged by a combination of technological developments and new social configurations. They had to face the resentful demands of manufacturers not all of whose methods and ambitions could have been fully accommodated under existing guild restrictions, even if the latter had been made sufficiently elastic to offer all of the 'new men' personal membership in these organizations. In addition, as one local study after another has shown, the 1780s witnessed an unprecedented increase in the numbers of factory workers in cities all the way from Manchester and Paris to Brno in the Habsburgs' Moravia and the Prussian provincial capital, Breslau in Silesia. Many of these workers were beginning to seek political rights for which the old distinction between burghers and other residents made no provision. Finally, as remarked in Chapter 3, the guilds had their own dissatisfied lower class, the numerous journeymen who could not look forward to admission as masters unless long-standing numerical quotas were raised, or better yet in their eyes, abolished altogether.

In an atmosphere of agrarian and urban discontent, ideas of reform, once enunciated, could produce unexpected reverberations and thus in themselves become a second, distinct source of political unrest. Much has been written about the political 'activism' of the Enlightenment, the intellectual ferment which Europe had been experiencing since the late 1600s; but it is difficult to estimate the precise amount of influence such questioning had on the course of public events. Philosophical criticism of the existing order came from more points on the social spectrum than was generally acknowledged by many nineteenth-century historians. It was not in fact a monopoly of middle-class reformers, since many influential members of the titled nobility joined in the chorus. But who was listening or reading? And who in the long run can be shown to have acted in direct, or even indirect, response to theoretical tracts?

By the 1780s the diffusion of numerous theories had combined with the altered circumstances of daily existence to make political argument a major activity for thousands if not millions of Europeans. Newspapers and journals of opinion, many of them far more audacious than their readers' grandparents would have believed possible, kept springing into print under the noses of censors even in supposedly autocratic states. The penetration of reformist ideas below the 'literacy line' in society is by definition all but impossible to document. The known popularity of certain street-corner orators, however, and the slogans memoir-writers tell us were shouted by mobs in countless cities even before 1789 suggest that poor and uneducated people had seized upon catch phrases that echoed, however approximately, the thoughts of philosophers and journalists. At the other extreme, numerous gentlemen of wealth and leisure prided themselves on being conversant with such ideas, and many a caustic witticism uttered in an elegant salon, if it had been overheard in a neighbourhood café or tavern, would have been judged seditious.

Had the Enlightenment put forward a coherent programme of political change including possible revolution? Once again, a simple answer eludes us. The century-old contractual theories of John Locke, for example, could be used to justify the overthrow of a tyrant, but they were also available to men in England's Parliament or Hungary's Diet who feared the actions of the populace. Montesquieu's *Spirit of Laws*, published in 1748, was critical of any monarchy which suppressed the established orders, but its message was assuredly not one of encouragement to mass rebellion. Voltaire was generally anti-aristocratic and always anti-clerical, but his form of political realism demanded a heavy reliance on royal power. Rousseau was in the 1780s better known for his views on religion, education and morals than for his sometimes confusing espousal of popular sovereignty as the ultimate basis for legitimate authority. In the latter regard, the author of the *Social Contract* had yet to become a patron saint of democracy; and it has been well said that the Revolution made Rousseau, not the reverse.

Yet despite all qualifications and reservations, there is no denying that the Enlightenment had bequeathed to the late eighteenth century a number of specific arguments and, still more important, a penchant for radical, probing criticism. Locke *had* declared that a government might forfeit its right to rule. Montesquieu *had* examined the nature of tyranny and conceded the danger that aristocrats might become selfish oligarchs. Both Voltaire and Rousseau, together with dozens of their contemporaries, *had* pointed fingers of scorn at a whole series of hallowed institutions. Even the most unpolitical of the *philosophes*, Beccaria in Italy, Lessing in Germany, Hume in England, had cast doubt, respectively, on cruel treatment of accused wrongdoers, on religious oppression and on the irrational nature of many hallowed traditional beliefs. All these men were dead by the 1780s, but Jeremy Bentham and his fellow Utilitarians in England were currently demanding that all behaviour, presumably including that of rulers, be judged in terms of its usefulness to all mankind. At the same time, a race of publicists far more extreme than the departed giants of Enlightenment – Tom Paine, Brissot de Warville in France, Karl Friedrich Bahrdt in Germany and many others – produced a flood of impassioned and sarcastic rhetoric. At the very least, it must be said that for the period we are examining no belief, no custom, no human relationship could claim immunity from criticism on grounds of either immemorial age or divine sanction.

To the compound of physical changes and reformist ideas must be added a third source of agitation: the American Revolution. Whether or not the colonists' struggle for *independence* was also a *social* upheaval continues to be a matter of sharp controversy. In any event, for most sympathizers in Europe, including numerous Englishmen, the important aspect of the American drama lay in its specifically political implications. The actors were no band of noble savages, but recently transplanted Europeans who were able to put forward their own *philosophes* in Franklin, Jefferson, Hamilton, Adams, Madison and others of the Founding Fathers. They had succeeded, with the help of several European autocrats to be sure, in defying the mightiest naval and commercial power of the day. Still more important, they were demonstrating that free men could frame, modify and reframe a lasting structure of responsible authority through the action of a startlingly new device, constitutional conventions.

It is difficult to say just how many European troops survived the fighting in America, but the figure almost surely exceeded 60,000 and may have approached 100,000 before the long war ended. There were an estimated 30,000 Westphalians, Hessians and other Germans alone. After peace came, perhaps a third of these men elected to stay in the new country, but the rest went back to their homes across the ocean full of stories of their experiences. All over Europe, enthusiasts extolled the triumphant colonists, often in terms which represent more good will than accurate information. Frederick II of Prussia, it is true, wrote sourly to his minister at the Hague in May 1783: 'I am very much persuaded that this so-called independence of the American colonies will not amount to much.'[1] The old king's sceptical judgement, however, was far from typical. The Italian dramatist, Alfieri, in his *Free America* (1783), wrote of

The raging storm
Which is bringing salvation and liberty to us.

A year earlier, the Russian social critic, Radishchev, had composed an *Ode to Freedom*:

To you my inflamed soul aspires,
To you, renowned land . . .

And from Holland, though written in French, came an anony-
mous epic, *America Delivered*, whose author cried:

Venerable Congress, of a people free and good,
You have cemented the glory and union; . . .
Clear-headed scrutinizers of our vain prejudices![2]

Not all discussions of American achievements, of course, were
so flattering. John Adams and Thomas Jefferson, from their
respective diplomatic posts in London and Paris, felt compelled
to defend various provisions in the new constitution of 1787
against sharp attacks by European commentators. Many of these
expressed disapproval of the strong presidency, while others
branded the United States Senate an aristocratic upper house. Still
more denounced the Society of the Cincinnati, a hereditary fraternity of ex-officers in the Continental Army and their descendants,
as an American nobility in the making. The very intensity of such
debates nevertheless testified to the importance of the New World
for the politics of late eighteenth-century Europe. Furthermore,
the criticisms just noted suggest the democratic note struck with
increasing frequency as discussion continued.

From America's revolutionary war it is only a short step to a
fourth cause of discord on the Continent and in Great Britain as
well. This was the record of foreign affairs, which we have
already recognized as *one* of the factors to be kept in view when
considering domestic politics. With the possible exception of
Russia, no European government could preen itself on having
recently given its people much reason for patriotic pride. The
concessions made by England in 1783, in order to escape severe
military difficulties, had sharp repercussions both inside and
outside the two Houses of Parliament. The French monarch,
greatest of the apparent victims in that year, embarked almost at
once upon the series of humiliating abdications of influence
summarized at the end of Chapter 4. The loudly denounced
commercial treaty with England in 1786, however well-
intentioned, seemed only to intensify the French sense of diplomatic misfortune. Defeats at the hands of the British hurt the
Dutch leadership's domestic standing in the early 1780s, while
Gustav III's authority in Sweden suffered from his rash embroil-
ment with Russia and Denmark in 1788. As for the Habsburg
dominions, Joseph II's numerous ventures in Germany and the

Low Countries fed the suspicious resentment which many of his subjects felt towards him on other grounds.

A fifth definable source of unrest was similarly rooted in the official actions of public authorities. It is customary to speak of the quarter-century preceding 1789 as the 'age of enlightened despots' *par excellence*. In almost every European country a strong ruler or minister had made determined efforts to impose reforms, at the same time clamping his own grip more tightly on the reins of power. Joseph II in Austria, Hungary, Bohemia, the Milanese and the Netherlands, Frederick II in Prussia, Pombal in Portugal, Charles III in Spain, Struensee in Denmark, Gustav III in Sweden, Grand Duke Peter Leopold in Tuscany, Turgot and Maupeou in France, Shelburne and, for a time, the younger Pitt in England, can all be said to have satisfied the above description, however widely they may have differed in their conception of Enlightenment and in the consistency with which they sought to implement its principles.

The important point here is that by the 1780s almost everywhere, save perhaps in Spain and Tuscany, enlightened despotism was in trouble, its limitations exposed to a public criticism couched in terms which reforming autocrats themselves had taught their peoples, its promise dimmed even in the eyes of many former enthusiasts among Europe's intelligentsia. The resistance was complex and highly variable from one country to the next, as we shall discover shortly. A regime might be denounced as too despotic or too enlightened – that is, too little mindful of traditional interests – or both. One ruler might appear too vacillating to carry through his own projects; another, too hypocritical to act on the very principles he claimed to embrace; still another, too impetuous and unrealistic to operate the complicated engine of state. Above all, however, there was a spreading conviction, the more easily expressed because 'enlightened' authorities had in many places relaxed the rules of censorship, that the best-intentioned autocrat could not be trusted to dispense final wisdom from on high.

The nature and the range of opposition must not be oversimplified. The diversity of liberal and in some cases democratic demands in itself constitutes a sixth distinct cause of confusion and acrimony. The proponents of change were deeply divided by their backgrounds, immediate aims and opinions concerning the best way to proceed. At the base of all the agitation lay popular demands for relief, demands containing an unpredictable, volcanic quality which disturbed more than a few sincere exponents of reform. Among the educated, these exponents included middle-class agitators, who almost everywhere tended to emphasize constitutional reform. There is no doubt that they also took economic freedom and opportunity very seriously, but the campaign to secure legal safeguards against capricious tyranny was viewed by them as the necessary first step towards economic justice.

It would be a great mistake to envisage all such reformers as businessmen. Their number would have been smaller, and their influence considerably weaker, if among them there had not been many lawyers and civil servants. We shall have to return to the role of public administrators as agents of innovation in many countries during the revolutionary and Napoleonic eras. Here it should be enough to note the significance of what one historian describes as 'the encouragement by the the civil service (*das Beamtentum*) of politically progressive strivings in the period after 1789, but also in definite ways before'.[3] Furthermore, as already mentioned in connection with the diffusion of the Enlightenment, Europe's aristocracy itself produced a number of reformers. The Yorkshire landlords who demanded English parliamentary changes, the Marquis de Condorcet and the Count de Mirabeau in France, Count Ignace Potocki in Poland, Baron Radishchev in Russia, these and scores of other critics of the old order were men of anything but humble origins. The general agitation of the 1780s was characterized by that extremely wide social range which throughout the western world has often marked progressivism at its least sharply defined.

The half-dozen separate factors we have now identified might appear more than adequate to explain the conflicts to which we shall turn in a moment. But there remains a seventh element which must be included in our reckoning, if the nature of these struggles is to be fully understood. This is the hardening of conservative resistance to all the pressures for change, whether these came from governments or from liberal agitators. In the absence of such resistance, many reforms would still have been attempted in one country after another, doubtless with varying degrees of success; but there would scarcely have been the series of outbursts which culminated in France.

For several generations it has been fashionable to explain the birth of modern conservatism as a natural reaction to revol-

utionary violence and hence, since it supposedly *followed* such violence, to see in it a product of the 1790s and the early nineteenth
century. According to this view, the revolutionary crisis that
began in 1789 was a sudden attack on unsuspecting traditionalists
who, however tardily, sprang to the defence of old values. In direct
repudiation of the sequence envisaged thus, R. R. Palmer has
argued persuasively that the conservative reaction had in fact set
in well before the 1780s and reached a new level of intensity in
precisely that decade.[4] He insists that revolutionary violence,
when it came, was directed not against a static eighteenth-century
situation but against a widespread campaign to push the the Old
Régime back to a renewed acceptance of privileges, viewed by
their proponents as essential to orderly existence. Privileged
groups for their part do indeed appear to have created much of
the rhetoric of modern conservatism in reaction not against the
'Great Revolution', but against the efforts at reform that preceded
it. Only after the pre-revolutionary conservatives had perished or
been driven into exile would the Terror turn on moderates and
'deviationists' among the insurgents themselves.

As we move from country to country in the pages ahead, this
resistance to gradual, often officially sponsored change will
manifest itself in a variety of ways. Generally speaking, however,
its propagators all over Europe will be seen to have belonged to
the same few groups: (1) the nobility of birth, (2) the hierarchies
of established churches and (3) other constituted bodies of the old
corporate system – assemblies of estates, judicial bodies such as
the French *parlements*, town governments, guilds. Not *all*
members of such bodies, it bears repeating, agreed that change
ought to be resisted at every point where demands for it appeared,
much less that, once effected, it should wherever possible be
reversed. We have already seen that individual reformers of quite
the opposite persuasion were recruited from every order and
almost every level of society. Nevertheless, without the resistance
of organized conservativism, sometimes extended to include
outright reaction, a constellation of forces able to mobilize
considerable intellectual resources of its own, the ensuing narrative would have read far differently than it in fact does.

ENGLAND AND IRELAND

When the 1780s opened, disturbances in the British Isles seemed particularly menacing to the established order. Both the unsuccessful course of the war in America and the increased taxes it entailed gave rise to widespread charges of misgovernment. Demands for reform arose from sources as different one from the other as Yorkshire landowners and radical spokesmen in Parliament's home borough, Westminster. The aims of all groups concerned revealed two quite separate tendencies, one economic or, more precisely, financial, the other political, being directed towards efforts to make the House of Commons responsive to the views of a larger fraction of the population. For a number of Whig politicians, including Edmund Burke, what came to be known as 'economical reform', especially the elimination of wasteful public expenditures, seemed both desirable in itself and advisable as a means of diverting the pressure for parliamentary reform *per se*. Such agitators as Christopher Wyvill and Sir George Savile, on the other hand, insisted that better financial administration would be an illusory gain as long as Parliament itself remained unrepresentative and open to corruption.

The parliamentary reformers called for annual elections, the addition of as many as 100 county members to the Commons (thus increasing the influence of the shires relative to the boroughs) and, above all, a thorough revision of the list of boroughs sending members to Westminster. Since that list had not been brought up to date since 1678, some adjustment seemed necessary if only to give seats to the many cities which were springing into new importance in the late eighteenth century. On the other hand, these critics argued, there was need to eliminate numerous 'rotten boroughs', which had become so depopulated over the years that some were now scarcely more than manorial villages, but which still enjoyed the right to elect members of Parliament. An M.P. in effect named by a single landlord, whether directly, on the basis of the lord's owning most of the local property, or indirectly, through bribes and instructions given the handful of remaining voters, did not impress the reformers as much of a bulwark against royal, ministerial or private influence.

Certain leading Whigs, among them Shelburne and Fox, adopted the cause of parliamentary reform, to the indignation of

Burke and others among their party colleagues. Despite the distrust which the more advanced extreme reformers felt towards these political leaders, the latter's opposition to the king and Lord North seemed by 1780 to ensure political changes. It appeared all but inevitable that major concessions would be extorted from both George III and the House of Commons as then constituted. That same year, however, two developments combined to frighten moderates out of the alliance. The first was the summons to an extra-legal General Association, issued in February by a handful of town and shire spokesmen who had assembled in London under the aegis of the Westminster radicals. The very thought of such an association's dictating to Parliament led most regular Whigs to abandon the entire movement – Shelburne being the only prominent exception.

Then, a few months later, came a second shock: the Gordon riots. Though actually unrelated to the constitutional question, this fiasco seemed to prove that revolutionary violence was too near the surface of English life for political changes to be safely discussed. Lord George Gordon, the unbalanced son of a Scottish duke, considered himself the appointed oracle of opposition to both the Pope in Rome and the North ministry in England. Becoming incensed over a slight measure of relief extended to Catholics in 1778 (the elimination of religious provisions from the oath of allegiance administered to military recruits), he proceeded to make himself the centre of anti-popish agitation in the poorer neighbourhoods of London. On 2 June 1780 Lord Gordon appeared in Parliament with a plea against religious toleration; and the crowd surrounding the building – an audience he repeatedly ran outside to harangue – became a raging mob. For almost a week, London was terrorized by rampant looting and burning. Not only Catholic homes but also those of unpopular officials were attacked. The emptying of several prisons only added to the general panic. By the time volunteer citizens' companies finally restored order, portions of the city resembled a smoking battlefield.

While the Gordon riots completed the destruction of the broad coalition which had briefly supported some democratization of British politics, the drive against corruption continued on the two established fronts. In 1782 Burke's Economical Reform Bill became law, improving the accounts kept of public funds and working a small reduction in the annual budget by eliminating certain useless offices. Simultaneously, the twenty-two-year-old William Pitt, newly elected to the House of Commons, moved a bill to modify parliamentary representation. It failed to pass in 1782, as did similar bills in the ensuing two years; but in 1785, now as prime minister, Pitt made his strongest bid for electoral reform. His proposal sought to eliminate thirty-six rotten boroughs, give representation in the Commons to expanding cities such as Birmingham, Manchester and Leeds, and simultaneously broaden the county franchise to include not only forty-shilling freeholders but also copyholders, as well as certain lessees, of land worth that much per year. Even this modest project could not get by a hostile-to-indifferent House; and with its defeat, Pitt abandoned the cause of parliamentary reform. Henceforth, he tried to make public administration increasingly honest and efficient, but in general he was content to hold power as a king's man who used 'treasury influence' to the full in marshalling political support for his ministry. Though other reformers below the ministerial level kept up the fight throughout the 1780s and on into the 1790s, their fate became bound up with English reactions to the French Revolution and will therefore be taken up in a later chapter.

In the same stormy period when the British Parliament found itself confronted by rebels in North America and rioters in London, it had also to face hostile agitation in Ireland. For political purposes, it should be remembered, 'Ireland' at this time meant essentially the 450,000 Anglicans or Anglo-Irish – a mere 10 per cent of the total population – plus a small number of Catholic and Presbyterian landowners. The Anglo-Irish Protestants' sense of being suspended between the British government on one side and a mass of disenfranchised Catholic farmers and town-dwellers on the other conditioned every phase of the parliamentary struggle dividing the two islands in the 1780s.

During the course of the American war, marked as it was by rumours that an invading French army would receive a welcome from Catholics in Ireland, London agreed to the organization and arming of a local militia. This was composed of upper- and middle-class Protestants, who took the name of 'Irish Volunteers'. By 1780 the Volunteers had increased in numbers and in popularity to a point where leaders in the Irish Parliament, notably Henry Grattan and Henry Flood, could use the militia as a source of pressure upon His Majesty's government. London granted an initial concession, a substantial reduction in export restrictions bearing on Irish trade; but by now more than commerce was at stake. The Irish Parliament, though firmly in the grip of the Anglican minority – Catholics could not even vote for its members – had for almost 300 years been subject to an English viceroy, the lord lieutenant. Furthermore, the Dublin body was subject to the commercial, diplomatic and military decisions of the British Parliament in Westminister. To escape this inferior status and to achieve equality with the British Parliament under the crown, Grattan and his fellow agitators mobilized protest meetings attended by tens of thousands of armed Volunteers. The similarities between their political role and that of American militiamen, including George Washington, following the end of the French-and-Indian War (1756–63) are self-evident.

Distracted by other military commitments, Lord North yielded. In 1782, the Irish Parliament was declared equal to the British, though still subordinate to the lord lieutenant acting in the king's name. Their immediate aim achieved, the Anglo-Irish abruptly ceased to protest and resumed a conservative stance. 'Grattan's Parliament', as it was called, still included in its House of Commons a majority of members named by fewer than 100 Anglican aristocrats. Somewhat grudgingly, it did agree to grant the Irish Catholics a few small economic and legal concessions after 1782, but scraps such as these could only whet the appetite for more sweeping change. Meanwhile, the Volunteers had shifted their field of agitation and were demanding both a broadened electoral franchise and the elimination of Ireland's own rotten boroughs.

In Ireland, as in England, parliamentary reform met total defeat. A Grand National Convention of the Volunteers in Dublin agreed in 1783 to support Flood's proposal for an expanded *Protestant* franchise, but the Irish Parliament voted the bill down by a ratio of two-and-a-half to one. The National Convention itself disbanded in 1785, amid numerous arrests and mounting censorship of anti-government publications. Meanwhile, the Irish battle lines were shifting, and no amount of repression could permanently conceal the altered distribution of forces. Irish Catholics and disenfranchised Protestants who had failed to benefit from Grattan's victory in 1782 were destined to become a revolutionary force beside which the memory of the Volunteers would seem pale indeed.

THE UNITED PROVINCES

Across the Channel, a different sort of revolution was beaten down in the Dutch United Provinces. While the immediate background of the crisis was the lost war against England, ending in 1784, the basic issues were deeply embedded in two centuries of Dutch history. The first stages of resistance of the House of Orange saw the regent families of wealthy merchants and the more radical Patriots collaborating in an effort to curb the powers of the Stadtholder, William V of Orange. Both elements charged that foreign affairs had been mismanaged and suspected that the cause was official corruption resulting from William's having intervened in civil administration. Both objected, in particular, to the stadtholder's efforts to control the choice of public officials by town councils and provincial assemblies of estates. Nevertheless, the conservative members of the opposition soon showed themselves to be equally alarmed by the threat of popular agitation. Democratic orators such as J. D. van der Capellen, a nobleman from the rural province of Overyssel, proved almost as harsh towards the merchant dynasties of the big cities as towards the House of Orange. No sooner had a Free Corps of armed burghers been formed, to offset William V's control of the army, than the division within the Patriot movement became apparent. The mutual suspicion between conservatives and radicals threatened to drown all consideration of common purposes in the National Assembly of Free Corps, meeting at Utrecht late in 1784.

During the next two years, what amounted to a three-way deadlock prevailed among (1) most of the regents, who sought to withstand the stadtholder's claims while avoiding concessions to the populace, (2) the Patriots, who demanded election of officials by all burghers, and (3) William V, who stubbornly refused to appeal to the democratic forces against his patrician enemies, though there existed precedents for doing so. The final test of strength began in Utrecht, where in 1786 the Patriots simply deposed the town council and replaced its membership with popularly chosen councillors.

As explained in the preceding chapter, the outcome was decided by outside forces. The Patriots considered themselves pro-French, and France did in fact appear to support their cause. The stadtholder, on the other hand, could rely on the sympathy of his brother-in-law, who in 1786 became King Frederick William II of Prussia, while Britain's minister in the Hague, Sir James Harris, was sparing no effort to rebuild a strong Orangist party tied to England. In the summer of 1787, sporadic fighting was already in progress between the rebellious Free Corps and William V's troops. The stadtholder's consort made an effort to reach Nimwegen, in the hope of gaining Orangist support there; but her coach was stopped by Patriots and forced to return to the Hague. In Berlin, her royal brother denounced this 'outrage' and, after issuing a peremptory ultimatum, sent a Prussian army corps across the Dutch frontier. Within a matter of weeks, the entire revolt was over, the Free Corps melting away before Frederick William's regiments from Germany. Henceforth the stadtholder would exercise virtually royal prerogatives, guaranteed in 1788 by the treaty with England and Prussia. The regents might grumble over the prince's victory, but they could breathe more easily with the popular agitation suppressed. As for the Patriots, their turn was still to come, with intervention by a different France in 1795.

THE AUSTRIAN NETHERLANDS

Another major complex of insurrections occurred in the dominions of Emperor Joseph II. The sharpest test took place in the Austrian Netherlands and especially in the big province of Brabant, with its active assembly of estates at Brussels. (There having been no Estates General since early in the seventeenth century, the importance of provincial bodies was correspondingly increased.) Relatively prosperous and until the 1780s generally quiescent, the Austrian Netherlanders reacted first with consternation, then with anger, to Joseph's drive to modernize his empire. By espousing legal equality for Protestants, suppressing several monasteries he considered superfluous and extending to the Low Countries the rest of his campaign against church privileges, the 'revolutionary emperor' infuriated Belgium's Catholic hierarchy. By ruling that guild monopolies and employment restrictions should end, he alienated the town oligarchies. By seeking in 1787 to abolish manorial courts, he turned the landed nobility against him.

At first, Belgian opposition to the emperor was marked by less social cleavage than had appeared in the Dutch rising. It appeared essentially conservative yet broadly based, for the defence of native traditon against the foreign innovator had the support of abbots and bankers, barons and professional men, village priests and master craftsmen. Such disagreement as existed among the rebels was confined to questions of tactics. Thus, the wealthy H. Van der Noot, favouring reliance on foreign aid, moved to Holland in 1788 and there sought support from the Anglo–Dutch–Prussian allies. The Brussels attorney, J. F. Vonck, took a different course, organizing from his secret headquarters in Brussels a patriotic movement calling itself the Society for Hearth and Altar.

Early in 1789 the long impending storm broke at last. Against a background of popular demonstrations which Vonck's society had helped to launch, the estates of Brabant curtly announced that no further monetary tribute would be sent to Vienna. Joseph II took several months to decide on a course of action, then in June dissolved the estates and abrogated Brabant's ancient charter of provincial rights. Unfortunately for Habsburg security measures, August brought a concurrent revolution in Liège, a prince-bishopric of the Holy Roman Empire which literally bisected the Austrian Netherlands. Belgian rebels by the thousand were now able to organize companies and to drill on Liègeois soil, then cross back into their own homeland to confront the depleted Austrian garrisons. Before the end of 1789, in a bewildering display of military weakness, Austrian power simply evaporated in the Netherlands. One after another the Walloon and Flemish provinces proclaimed their independence.

Only now, with foreign control seemingly at an end, did the familiar conflict between local conservatives and democrats come to light in Belgium as it had elsewhere in Europe. Under Van der Noot, the nobles, prelates and town fathers who dominated provincial assemblies stiffened their defence of traditional privileges, which were what they had been upholding against Joseph II all along. Around Vonck, on the other hand, tended to cluster those reformers who insisted on the right of their countrymen to remodel Belgian society in accordance with the wishes of the majority. Quickly reconvening in December 1789, the estates of Brabant seized the initiative by proclaiming themselves the sovereign authority in that province and shortly thereafter secured

the accession of the other provincial assemblies to a loose federation of quasi-independent units concerting their policies through
the hastily revived Estates General. The opposing party of Vonckists denounced the reactionary direction of these steps; but
cautious as Vonck's programme of democratic reforms may seem
in retrospect – he was far from espousing a truly broad franchise
– it was too radical for the majority of Belgians, including the
deeply religious peasantry. Aided by a veritable 'white terror', the
Estates Party by March 1790 completely crushed the Vonckists,
imprisoning some of their leaders while others fled abroad.

From his exile in France, Vonck warily opened negotiations
with Habsburg representatives. The democratic spokesmen turned
to the new Emperor Leopold II as they had never turned to his
late brother, Joseph. Paradoxically, considerable unintended
support for Leopold's efforts to recover mastery over the Netherlands came from the quarrelsome and inept Estates Party
leaders, who swiftly demonstrated their inability to give Belgium
either peace or justice. In so doing they sapped the country's
resistance to Habsburg rule; and late in 1790, when the emperor
ordered his troops back in, the Austrian forces resumed control
as swiftly as they had abandoned it the previous year. Leopold
kept his word by permitting the banished Vonckists to return
home. Further than that he would not go, for he feared the
unfolding crisis in France too much to antagonize conservative
forces anywhere in his sprawling empire. Time was to prove that
he need not have shown such deference to the conservatives, who
were little inclined to view the French innovators as allies, whatever Austria chose to do. Instead it was the Belgian democrats
who, having returned full of gratitude towards the Habsburg
monarch, only to find that he contemplated no basic reforms
affecting their homeland, soon concluded that real help could
come only from the side of revolutionary France.

HABSBURG CENTRAL EUROPE

In other parts of the Habsburg empire, Joseph II's innovations
gave rise to variations on the Belgian theme of conservative resistance.[5] Seeking to convert the serfs under his rule into a free peasantry, attacking the fiscal and judicial privileges of the nobility,

brusquely curtailing the prerogatives of the Catholic clergy, suspending aristocratic assemblies all the way from Bohemia's Diet to Milan's Council of Sixty, he appeared bent on destroying the very foundations of social hierarchy. Finally, in February 1789, he took what to traditionalists seemed the climactic step in this direction, proclaiming a uniform land tax to be paid by nobles and non-nobles at the same rate throughout all his dominions save the Netherlands and Lombardy. When Joseph died a year later, at the age of only forty-eight, he bequeathed to his brother, Leopold II, a general crisis in Bohemia, Austria, the Tyrol, not to mention the more distant troubles in Transylvania, Belgium and the Milanese. What added a note of panic to conservative protests was the apparent danger that a popular revolt might be touched off by imperial policies. With Czech peasants and the oppressed Vlachs of Transylvania beginning to stir beneath the rule of local masters, the problem of different levels of discontent was manifesting itself in the Austrian empire as clearly as it had in Ireland and the United Provinces.

Nowhere was the Habsburg crisis more profound than in Hungary. There the spokesmen for the aristocracy had first sought to oppose the emperor's will in the national Hungarian Diet, only to have him respond by refusing to convoke that body. The Magyar nobles could still express themselves through the county assemblies or *comitats*. Joseph, however, treated their protests with angry contempt, transferring Hungary's sacred iron crown of St Stephen from Pressburg (now Bratislava) to Vienna in 1784, decreeing that German should replace Latin as the country's official language and appointing non-Magyar officials to execute his commands. He even proposed to sweep away the *comitats* in favour of a system of German-style administrative districts or *Kreise*.

To an outside observer, many of the Emperor's judicial and economic reforms appear to have had much to recommend them; but in practice they infuriated the upper classes while encouraging the lower to take further action on their own. The nobles organized secret societies, created armed bands in defiance of imperial prohibitions and in 1790 at last compelled Joseph, literally on his deathbed, to permit the Hungarian Diet to assemble at Pest. Unfortunately for his successor's repose, this action, while it averted an open revolt by the nobility, did nothing to allay the fears and grievances of the farm population. Like the Vlachs in

Transylvania, the Hungarian peasants began a series of risings in the spring of 1790, attacking numerous manors and in the name of the emperor denouncing their landlords for misusing the power of the Diet.

The outcome again revealed Leopold II's eagerness to restore domestic peace, even at the cost of concessions to his brother's old opponents. Equally important, it showed the effects of the peasant rebellion on the Hungarian Diet, inalterably opposed to anything approaching a social revolution but now resigned to some of Joseph II's less extreme reforms. An Austrian army corps arrived in August 1790 and with the aid of the Magyar nobles managed to reimpose order in the country districts. Simultaneously, the Diet accepted a new *Diploma*, or charter, by which Leopold acknowledged the sanctity of many old customs, though he still insisted on the permanent abolition of personal bondage, as decreed in 1781. Despite this and a few other reservations, the document must be considered a victory for the conservative opposition. The new emperor had in effect agreed to the survival of a system his predecessor had hoped to revolutionize from above.

POLAND

A very different case, with a different ending, was that of Poland. It would not be accurate to speak of a Polish revolution in this period, if by that term is meant a violent repudiation of the existing government. In another sense, however, the work of the famous 'Four Years' Diet' which opened at Warsaw in October 1788 entailed departures from the existing situation too fundamental to be called evolutionary reforms. Many of the issues raised elsewhere in the present chapter are discernible here as well, modified by the peculiar nature of the Polish constitution but given increased scope and urgency by the acuteness of the nation's external peril.

From the outset, despite a sense of crisis which had pervaded the country since the staggering losses of territory in the First Partition of 1772, many of the lower nobles were hostile to constitutional change. It was equally clear that among Poland's neighbours, Russia in particular was opposed to any strengthening of the kingdom and generally ready to aid all local opponents of a stronger and more broadly based political system. On the other hand, a remarkable circle of aristocrats, including Prince Adam Czartoryski and Ignace Potocki, joined King Stanislaw II Ponia-towski in his desire to offer Polish subjects a new basis for loyalty and confidence. Nowhere else in Europe, to cite one indication of democratic ferment, does the American Revolution appear to have had greater intellectual and emotional impact – not surprisingly, since one Polish hero, Pulaski, had given his life in that struggle while another, Kosciusko, had come home to tell about it. When Catherine the Great's war against Turkey in 1788 temporarily reduced the threat of Russian intervention, the Polish king and his fellow innovators seized the opportunity to convene the Diet in Warsaw on terms which made it, unlike its Hungarian counterpart, virtually a constitutional convention.

Almost as soon as it was called to order, the Diet revealed its division into something like parliamentary parties. The aristocratic Republicans were pro-Russian in foreign affairs because they opposed any reduction in Poland's 'Golden Liberty', which is to say, noble privileges. The Moderates, who represented the king most directly, hoped to make a number of specific changes without giving Russia a pretext for military action. The Patriots were more radical both in their demands for a sweeping social advance and in their defiance of outside powers. The enactments which the king finally incorporated into the Constitution of the Third of May (1791) represented most clearly the Moderates' position, but the Patriots too had reason to rejoice. The Diet voted, for example, that landless nobles should no longer attend provincial assemblies, where the 'barefoot gentry' had previously turned by the thousand to do the bidding of this or that great lord. Another statute, sponsored by the brilliant orator, Niemcewicz, defined and extended citizenship in cities chartered by the Crown. In addition, it gave twenty-one such royal towns places in the Diet, where burghers would at last take their places beside noblemen. Still a third decision abolished the paralysing rule of unanimity in votes of the Diet, thus ending the notorious *liberum veto* by which irresponsible squires had often blocked important pieces of legislation. As proof of his unselfish determination to strengthen the central government, King Stanislaw put aside his own family pride and supported the institution of a monarchy which, instead of being elective as in the past, would be hereditary in the German house of Saxony.

An air of inescapable pathos surrounds this final effort at regeneration on the part of the old Poland. Very late, though they hoped it was not too late, some of the eighteenth century's most generous and intelligent aristocrats tried to redefine Polish freedom and give it meaning for a larger part of the population. At the same time, they sought to balance this freedom with enough recognized authority to assure their country a chance of survival as an independent nation. That neighbouring monarchs, in concert with unreconstructed elements in Poland itself, moved quickly to destroy the kingdom in 1793–95 does not prove the worthlessness of the Four Years' Diet. On the contrary, their action was in part a tribute to the prospects for a Polish revival, had the new constitution been given enough time to prove itself. But that is a part of the story still to come.

REFORM AND REACTION IN OTHER COUNTRIES

We need not give equal attention to the political narratives of every European nation in a decade which was of course more eventful for some than for others. Although Catherine II's Charter of Nobility (1785) was a recognition of aristocratic status more nearly comparable to that of western Europe than any previously known in Russia,[6] that empire during the 1780s witnessed no major domestic struggles. Radishchev's *Journey from St Petersburg to Moscow*, a searing exposé of peasant suffering, was completed, it is true, in the same year as the Charter of Nobility; but it was not published until 1790. The subsequent excitement over the book really belongs, therefore, to the record of foreign reactions to the French Revolution. For the time being, the tsarina simply made her deal with the nobility, and the millions who paid the price were silent.

Among the German states, a wide range of local conditions prevailed. A few principalities, notably Württemberg, retained assemblies of estates which continued to bicker with their rulers, over finances in particular. Popular agitation for democratic reforms flared up periodically in ecclesiastical states such as Cologne and Mainz, as well as in Frankfurt, Nuremberg and several other imperial cities. Even Prussia, that disciplined 'Sparta of the North', showed signs of internal tension following the 'Great King's' death in 1786. A combination of economic troubles and the unpopular influence of Frederick William II's pious favourites, Woellner and Bischoffswerder, produced a mounting chorus of criticism, especially from bureaucratic and commercial groups. Yet it does not appear that Germany as a whole was threatened by revolution in the 1780s. The most that can be said is that liberals and a small number of radical democrats were beginning to object to the system of small autocracies (*Kleinstaat-erei*) in terms which suggested that a revolutionary crisis outside the Empire might find a welcome from some elements within it.

Sweden's situation seemed potentially much more explosive than any to be found in the Germanies. The aristocrats whose prerogatives of the Freedom Era had been swept away by Gustav III in 1772 still nursed their hatred of the king. In 1786, when the royal government proposed to create a paid standing army, the *Riksdag* followed the initiative of the nobles and refused to vote the requisite taxes. Two years later, Gustav having committed what forces he had to the assault on Russia, a number of Swedish barons actually opened negotiations with the tsarina behind his back. Early in 1789 the *Riksdag* convened once more. This time it became deadlocked through disagreement among the four chambers, and the king saw a chance to strike another blow at his titled adversaries. Expelling all nobles from the session, he issued, and the remainder of the Diet accepted, an Act of Union and Security. Though certain high offices and court positions were still reserved to the nobility, a remarkable degree of civil equality was henceforth guaranteed to all subjects of the Swedish crown. Commoners were assured the right to own land, to be tried in proper courts and to hold offices below the few reserved to noblemen. Three years later, Gustav III was to pay with his life for his treatment of the aristocracy, but for the time being he had given the Swedish throne a broad popular base.

In several other countries reforms imposed from above produced less furore than in Sweden, either because the reformers moved more cautiously or because they succeeded better in linking social changes to economic advance. In Denmark, after twelve years of reaction against Struensee's ministry, the energetic

Count Andreas Bernstorff came to power in 1784 and within four years succeeded in practically wiping out what was left of serfdom. In Portugal, where the ferocious Marquis Pombal had finally been ousted from power in 1777, the nobles were able to reduce the pace of innovation to a crawl; but at least there was no violent reaction in the 1780s. Spain under Charles III and his gifted set of ministers – Campomanes, Floridablanca, Jovellanos – was enjoying its first real agricultural and industrial expansion since the sixteenth century.[7] We have already seen how the Spanish monarchy and the Italian grand duchy of Tuscany became the two realms that for the time being appeared to show the clearest margin of gain on the balance sheet of enlightened despotism.

Before turning to the massive problem of France, we should fit one last, small piece into the surrounding mosaic of European politics. This involves the little republic of Geneva, the violence that flared there and the bitterness it left behind. Despite an earlier struggle in the late 1760s, the government of this independent city state remained in the hands of the office-holding citizens and the less exalted, but voting, burghers. The disenfranchised residents, or 'natives', at last revolted in 1781, demanding admission to the ranks of the bourgeois voters. At first, the campaign for electoral reform appeared successful. The General Council, or town meeting, actually decided to admit to the status of burghers some 460 natives who were third-generation residents. The more aristocratic Small Council of Twenty-five rejected this concession and appealed to Geneva's 'guarantor powers', France and the Swiss cantons of Bern and Zurich, to uphold the existing government. In response, a French-Swiss army besieged the city for three weeks in 1782 and ultimately occupied it, though with a minimum of bloodshed. Secure once more, the patricians of the Small Council asked the guarantor powers to draft a pacification, called by its opponents the 'Black Code'. Not only did two-thirds of the newly enfranchised lose their rights as registered bourgeois, but the burghers' own General Council was stripped of all real power. The Small Council and its creatures, the four syndics, now ruled as an unrestrained oligarchy. In Geneva, however, as in Ireland, the Low Countries and various petty German states, hatred of the existing order left an ominous legacy to the coming years, when revolution moved from small areas to an undeniably major one.

FRANCE

Since the French Revolution will receive special attention in Chapter 6, the only question to be addressed here concerns the place of France in European politics *before* that crisis erupted. The point at issue is whether or not there was anything in the French situation before 1789 that marked it as peculiarly tense. In short, was the upheaval in France unique from the earliest moment it could be seen developing, or was it simply another variant of the unrest we have been observing in many other lands?

The beginning of the pre-revolutionary crescendo is usually dated from the publication in 1781 of Jacques Necker's *Compte rendu*. The choice of that event has much to recommend it, for the printed report of the recently dismissed controller-general of finances did bring into view the royal deficit, at a time when the expenses of the American war had just been added to the endemic evils of fiscal confusion and sweeping tax exemptions. It is reasonable to see in the ensuing uproar sardonic proof that injustice and inefficiency may be tolerable for generations, until they begin to be discussed openly and, above all, statistically. At any rate, a mounting wave of suspicion that both economic and diplomatic affairs were being administered by incompetents loomed large in the acrimony enveloping French public life. After 1781, for example, overt criticism of Marie Antoinette became more and more strident. A queen who was both a spendthrift and an Austrian seemed to personify financial chicanery on the one hand and an unpopular foreign alliance on the other.

In certain respects, however, the crisis had begun to unfold as early as 1774, when Louis XVI had opened his reign by overriding Chancellor Maupeou and giving back to the parlements, the great regional law courts containing well over 1,000 aristocratic judges, all the powers taken from them in 1771. Just two years after Maupeou's fall, the king had also dismissed Baron de Turgot as first minister, seeming thereby to obliterate all hope that the worst inequities of the old society might be alleviated by energetic, royally sponsored reforms. In a very real sense, the predicament in which Louis found himself by the mid-1780s had been prepared by his own timidity and incomprehension a decade before.

Wherever in time the onset of the *general* crisis is placed, one can scarcely avoid dating the beginning of its climactic stage in

1786, with a series of decisions reached by the controller-general, Charles-Alexandre de Calonne. Calonne was intelligent enough to recognize that only by making the wealthy and the wellborn contribute a fairer share of the state's revenues could he attack an annual deficit which had climbed to 110 million French pounds (*livres*), tripling the figure of just ten years earlier. He was also vain enough to believe that merely by avoiding the curtness of Turgot he could induce noblemen and Catholic church leaders to consent to a new, equitable land tax and to the elimination of many regional differences in payments. The body from which he proposed to obtain this consent was to be not the Estates General, which had last met in 1614–15, but instead a smaller 'assembly of notables', handpicked by the government to discuss and approve the new measures.

Its members, most of them titled lords and high prelates with a few wealthy bourgeois added, came together in Paris early in 1787 – and flatly rejected Calonne's pleas. They asserted that the privilege of exemption from general taxes was sacrosanct and advised the royal administration to cut expenditures in place of trying to increase revenues. Calonne was beaten, despite a desperate appeal for public support, which only reinforced the sensation created by Necker's revelations in the *Compte rendu*.

The notables having gone home, the new controller-general, Loménie de Brienne, archbishop of Toulouse, was left to deal with the stiff-necked judicial magistrates of the parlements. The 'nobles of the robe' had to register (that is, verify and pass along to the lower courts) any royal edict, fiscal or otherwise, in order for it to become a part of the law of the land. Thus during the long coma of the Estates General, the *parlementaires*, who owned their offices outright as private property, had grown accustomed to a quasilegislative role, negative though it was. Brienne did secure the parlements' overdue assent to ending the *corvée*, the enforced peasant labour to maintain roads and bridges, which would henceforth be kept up by workers paid out of public funds. However, he could not induce the courts to register his watered-down version of Calonne's tax reform. The king and his finance minister wavered between sternness and appeasement, first banishing the Parlement of Paris to Troyes during the summer of 1787, only to recall it to the capital that autumn. Then, in May 1788, the government announced that the nation's thirteen parlements were no longer fit to exercise the power of registration, which would henceforth be entrusted to a single Plenary Court composed of judges newly appointed by the Crown.

For the next four months France was in turmoil. What was taking place has been justly called an aristocratic revolt, centring in the outraged parlements and in the few surviving provincial assemblies of estates. It should also be pointed out, however, that a wide range of public opinion was for the time being strongly favourable to the opposition. The parlementaires in particular managed to portray themselves as spokesmen for the rights of all subjects against a corrupt court and a pack of ministerial despots. Faced with a campaign of resistance which was mounting in intensity and spreading in geographical scope, the Crown again backed down. In July Louis XVI pledged himself to convene the Estates General the next year. In August Loménie resigned, and Necker was called back to serve as finance minister. A few weeks later the Plenary Court was for all practical purposes dissolved, and the parlements triumphantly resumed their old functions.

To modern eyes it may seem strange that the French aristocracy should have congratulated itself on having compelled the king to revive the Estates General. At the very time when the government was preparing the formal summons to the great assembly, there was mounting evidence of popular discontent which might become dangerous to all vested interests, including those of parlementaires and other noblemen, if it found an institutional outlet. By the autumn of 1788, an extremely bad harvest was evoking the spectre of famine, while raising bread prices in the towns to almost unheard-of levels. These in turn contributed to an industrial depression which had been developing for several years, partly as a result of increased English competition, but even more, it would appear, as a cyclical response to over-expansion in particular areas of manufacturing.

The food crisis on the farms thus merged with – and indeed increased – the urban difficulties to form an especially ominous combination. Demands for higher wages inevitably followed the rising cost of bread, and beleaguered employers, faced with mounting labour costs, sought to conserve their capital by laying off workers. Food scarcity and spreading unemployment added a desperate quality to the political and social grievances already felt by masses of Frenchmen. State taxes and manorial dues alike began to appear not just burdensome, but literally unbearable. The implications of all this, however, were scarcely visible to aristocrats who hailed the Crown's surrender in the summer of 1788 as an unqualified victory for the established orders of the realm, summoned at last to resume their just place as the principal shapers of public policy. The actual sequence which would start to unroll with the opening of the Estates General the following May lay hidden in the mists of the future.

Was the French case then recognizably different from the others we have examined? Looking back from our present vantage point, we can find good reasons for saying that it was. If we call to mind the list of general sources of unrest which were suggested at the start of this chapter – (1) economic strains resulting from demographic and technological change; (2) political ideas popularized by the debates of the Enlightenment; (3) the contagious influence of the American Revolution; (4) frustrating reverses in foreign affairs; (5) the policies of often well-intentioned but seldom energetic or consistent public administrators; (6) demands for social and economic change advanced by a wide variety of liberal or democratic critics; and (7) the stiffening of conservative resistance – we note that *all* were represented to a marked degree in the developing French crisis.[8] As so often in the past, every wind blowing across Europe seemed to converge on France.

In two other respects the French situation has impressed subsequent observers as peculiarly acute. First, this was, despite its size, the most centralized nation in all of eighteenth-century Europe, a nation quickly responsive to events taking place at its centre, Paris. By establishing such a concentrated structure, as Tocqueville pointed out long ago, the old monarchy had itself prepared the stage for a truly national revolution. The second difference between the French crisis and any of the others we have discussed lay in a unique combination of power, prestige and physical location. Any major development in France was bound to be felt almost immediately everywhere else in Europe. On the other hand, no foreign monarch who found such a development unsettling could reverse the tide of events merely by sending in a small military force, as Frederick William II of Prussia had done in Holland, Emperor Leopold II in Belgium and Hungary, or Louis XVI himself in Geneva. If outsiders proposed to intervene in France, they could do so only at the cost of a full-scale European war.

Thus *we* reason and reflect, looking back at 1789 across the tumultuous quarter-century which was then beginning. From all that has been said, however, we should be prepared to sympathize with the many contemporaries who thought they saw elsewhere, especially in Great Britain and in the Habsburg dominions, revolutionary portents at least as serious as any then visible in France. This appeared to be equally true whether the threat of revolution was visualized as chiefly concerned with legal, financial and social privileges or was supposed to relate to the distribution of political power within the state. If the former, then the Austrian empire of Joseph II was a likely testing ground. If the latter, there seemed to be little need to look beyond England, that home of constitutional strife in the preceding century.

We may come to understand the problem most clearly if we ask ourselves what a European living in the 1780s conceived a revolution, any revolution, to be. What model did he or she have, given the historical lessons available? Was revolution essentially a popular rising in vast broad reaches of the countryside, a *jacquerie* like the German Peasants' Revolt in the 1520s or Pugachev's rebellion in Russia during the 1770s? Or was it more likely to be an outburst of mob violence, fired by religious passions or aimless frenzy, as in the Paris of the St Bartholomew's Day massacre (1572) or the London of Lord Gordon's riots (1780)? Was it best represented as a struggle for regional independence, on the pattern of the Dutchmen resisting Spain in the sixteenth and seventeenth centuries or of Americans rebelling against Britain in the eighteenth? Or was it, first and foremost, an internal political contest – and if so, should it be expected to recall the aristocratic *Fronde* of Louis XIV's boyhood, the English parliamentary assault on Stuart absolutist claims or, conversely, a palace coup such as Sweden's King Gustav III had carried out against his own nobility in 1772?

Many intelligent men before 1789 realized that a revolution need not assume only one of these guises and that two or even three different types of revolution might be interwoven. It is unlikely, however, that anyone visualized a revolution that would incorporate elements of *all* the known precedents, bringing together the rural *jacquerie* and the violence of town mobs, mingling aristocratic, liberal and absolutist political claims, reawakening separatist impulses in outlying provinces to bedevil the revolutionaries themselves. It was precisely because Europe's turmoil in the 1780 involved so many levels and lines of conflict that the situation proved bewildering to onlookers. And because the French Revolution, when it came, proved to be a whole cluster of revolutions, it has remained, in the words of a twentieth-century American scholar, 'one of the few events of modern history towards which, even today, a man may entertain a feeling of awe'.[9]

NOTES AND REFERENCES

1   M. L. Brown, Jr., trans. and ed., *American Independence through Prussian Eyes* (Durham, N. C., 1959), p. 201. A newer, and somewhat broader, treatment is H. Dippelt, *Germany and the American Revolution*, trans. B. A. Uhlendorff (Chapel Hill, 1977).

2   Quoted in R. R. Palmer, *The Age of the Democratic Revolution*, vol. I: *The Challenge* (Princeton, 1959), p. 76. The translations are Mr Palmer's and are quoted with his kind permission.

3   F. Valjavec, *Die Entstehung der politischen Strömungen in Deutschland, 1770–1815* (Munich, 1951), p. 83.

4   R. R. Palmer, *The Age of the Democratic Revolution*, especially pp. 55–82 and 308–17.

5   E. Wangermann, *The Austrian Achievement, 1700–1800* (London, 1973), stresses positive aspects of the eighteenth-century Habsburg reigns.

6   M. Beloff in A. Goodwin, ed., *The European Nobility in the Eighteenth Century* (London, 1953), pp. 172–89; but see also the more recent work by I. de Madariaga, *Russia in the Age of Catherine the Great* (New Haven, 1981).

7   R. Herr, *The Eighteenth-century Revolution in Spain* (Princeton, 1958), p. 21.

8   In addition to Labroussse, *La crise de l'économie française*, monographs devoted to special aspects of causation in the French case include D. Mornet, *Les origines intellectuelles de la Révolution française. 1715–1787* (Paris, 1933); J. Egret, *The French Pre-revolution, 1787–1788* (Chicago, 1977); and D. Echeverria, *Mirage in the West: A History of the French Image of American Society to 1815* (Princeton, 1957).

9   C. Brinton, *A Decade of Revolution, 1789–99* (New York, 1934), p. 1.

UPHEAVAL IN FRANCE

By the autumn of 1788, the royal administration in France had bowed to the demands of privileged opposition groups. Louis XVI's promise to convene the Estates General was greeted by such groups as an admission that the traditional social structure of the kingdom must be reconsecrated in some other way than by adopting the Crown's own projects for reform. Events would shortly prove that to view this as simply a struggle between the government and its conservative critics was both superficial and profoundly misleading. Easy to discern, if we recall the set of social categories introduced in Chapter 3, were other sorts of conflict taking form as the time approached for the Estates to assemble at Versailles.

FROM ESTATES GENERAL TO NATIONAL ASSEMBLY

Whatever eighteenth-century theorists liked to believe, traditional 'orders of men' were far from being society's only meaningful divisions. But even if orders *had* occupied this unique position, the relations among them in late 1788 and early 1789 promised tension and acrimony enough. The leaders of the clergy (First Estate) were well aware of past occasions when the nobility (Second) and commons (Third) had joined forces to make the Church bear the brunt of financial contributions to the Crown. The lay nobles, on the other hand, looked enviously at the riches of the ecclesiastical establishment, while at the same time rejecting the pleas of non-nobles for measures aimed at achieving a greater degree of legal equality. Above all, spokesmen for the Third Estate, including a host of busy journalists, were stressing the fact that an overwhelming majority of French subjects were neither clergymen nor nobles. The Abbé Sieyès in his famous pamphlet, *What is the Third Estate?*, published early in 1789, answered his own question in a word: 'everything', and added: 'What does it ask? To be something'. Specifically, these voices urged that the number of deputies accorded the Third Estate should be equal in number to those of the other two estates combined.

The king and Necker conceded this point with deceptive ease, announcing that in the elections set for March and April 1789 the First and Second Estates would choose 300 delegates apiece, while practically all other adult males, voting through a complicated system of district and subdistrict electoral assemblies, would name some 600 representatives. The 'doubling of the Third', however, still did not settle the question whether voting in the assembly of Estates itself would be by head or by order. If the former, then the commons had indeed won a great victory; but if each of the three Estates was simply to agree, as in the past, on how its single, combined vote should be cast, then to have more delegates would constitute no advantage. Despite mounting pressure to clarify this point, the government refused to make a decision in advance. Meanwhile, since the parlements roundly denounced the claims of the Third Estate, the aristocratic judges saw their earlier popularity quickly fade away. Instead of seeming to be tribunes of resistance to despotism, they now impressed more and more Frenchmen as reactionary exponents of the nobility's interests.

These rifts in the original opposition to the royal tax programme were clearly perceived at the time, because they were taking place within an acknowledged system of legally constituted orders. How much more confusing, then, were the clashes along what we should consider primarily economic, honorific and political lines. Through the lists of grievances (*cahiers de doléances*) drawn up by the various electoral assemblies to guide their representatives, poor men protested against manorial dues, ground rents, low pay and high prices. Late April 1789 brought the Revolution's first outbreak of mob violence in Paris, the *affaire Reveillon*, which entailed two days of rioting in the Faubourg Saint-Antoine, with twenty-five deaths at the time and three subsequent executions. This outburst, it should be noted, was touched off not by antimonarchist or antinoble passions but by the public statements of Reveillon and another rich manufacturer in favour of lower wage scales. It was, in short, an expression of class hatred in the modern sense.

At the same time the status consciousness of various groups was being sharpened by such arguments as those over ceremonial arrangements in the approaching Estates General. The commons ended by agreeing to march first (the least exalted position) in all processions, to occupy the lowest seats at any joint session of the three chambers meeting together and to wear simple black suits and three-cornered hats, in contrast to the high clergy's brilliant robes and the nobility's plumes and satins. Yet at the very time when these provisions were being more or less grudgingly accepted, a curious and significant reversal of status was manifesting itself. Responding to this change, the Count de Mirabeau and the Abbe Siéyès, along with certain other nobles and clergymen, decided to stand for election to the Third Estate, as the most 'honourable' segment of society. Even within the Third, however, status rivalry embittered the spring elections. In most towns members of the enrolled bourgeoisie, which had long controlled local affairs, bitterly resented, and were in turn resented by, other inhabitants now entitled to vote under the national franchise.

Conflict of an explicitly political nature was also beginnning to emerge, though its outlines were naturally indistinct until a legislative forum came into being. Through the pamphlet wars and public speeches of the winter of 1788–89, there took shape a rough division not unlike the split within the Polish Diet then meeting in Warsaw (Chapter 5, above). Men who differed widely in birth, occupation and economic position found themselves allied either in defence of what they considered the ancient constitution of France, or in support of moderate reforms, or in agitation for fundamental changes in society and government. Thus the interplay of orders, classes and status groups was more pregnant with implications for the future than any single level of conflict would have been alone, not least because that interplay was producing still another set of elements: parties defined in recognizably political terms.

Despite confusion and recriminations, the spring elections did produce the requisite lists of deputies to assemble at Versailles, where deliberations opened on 5 May. The roughly 600 deputies of the Third Estate were clearly dominated by lawyers, who made up over half of the total. Other major groups of commoners included government officials (many of them counting, because of their training, among the lawyers as well), merchants, investors and representatives of the so-called liberal professions, especially that of medicine. Farmers and artisans were apparently to be represented only by their 'betters'. The nobles included some individuals, such as the 'Marquis de Lafayette, who were willing to consider reforms but were nonetheless expected by their constituents to oppose any basic social change. Deputies of the First Estate were divided between prelates on the one hand and, on the other, a large number of parish priests, many of them quite radical in outlook.

It was clear that until the voting issue was settled there would be no way of determining what kind of legislative body had been called into being. Charged by the Crown with responsibility for deciding this question, the three Estates fell into six weeks of apparent deadlock. The clergy and the nobility (though the vote in the First Estate was only 133 to 114) favoured separate deliberations and *final voting by order*. The Third insisted with growing vehemence on a merger of the three chambers into a single body and voting therein *deputy by deputy*. Finally, on 17 June, the commons adopted the title of 'National Assembly' and invited the other two orders to join their number.

In one of his characteristic oscillations between severity and surrender, the king yielded first to the court party led by his brother, the Count d'Artois, and tried to coerce the Third Estate. On 20 June he ordered that the commons be locked out of their meeting hall, only to learn that they had adjourned to a nearby tennis court (the game was then played exclusively indoors) and had solemnly sworn not to dissolve until they had written a new constitution. In reponse to the Tennis Court Oath, which had enlisted even the more cautious members of the Third on the side of defiance, Louis XVI directed the commons to stop all talk of a National Assembly and to proceed with their proper business as one of the three established orders. The deputies, while they avoided being openly disrespectful, ignored the royal command. On 27 June, by which time a clear majority of the clergy and about fifty of the nobility were sitting with the erstwhile Third Estate, the king suddenly capitulated, appealing to the remaining noble and ecclesiastical deputies to join what thus received his formal recognition as a single legislative body. The Estates General had become the National Assembly.

THE DECLARATION OF THE RIGHTS OF MAN

In his famous work on 1789,[1] Georges Lefebvre suggests that while an aristocratic revolution had been necessary to bring the Estates back to life, what was happening between May and late June amounted not just to a further stage, but to a second revolution, this one engineered by the lawyers, civil servants and businessmen of the Third Estate. Even these two revolutions, however, might yet have been undone if the upper and middle strata of society alone had confronted the power of the Crown. Lefebvre argues that although Louis XVI remained unclear about the best course of action and was probably most concerned with avoiding bloodshed, a royalist *coup d'état*, using the army to arrest some and disperse the rest of the deputies at Versailles, was a genuine possibility at the beginning of July. On 8 July Mirabeau rose before the Assembly to express his alarm at the number of troops, perhaps as high as 20,000, then pouring in to reinforce the regular garrisons of the Paris–Versailles region. On the 11th, while demands that these regiments be sent away still echoed in the wake of Mirabeau's speech, the king suddenly dismissed Necker as controller-general, replacing this most popular of his ministers with the Baron de Breteuil, a member of Queen Marie Antoinette's inner circle of courtiers. Necker was known to have opposed the royal attempt at coercion prior to the Tennis Court Oath, and his displacement was greeted by many as a signal that the National Assembly and its supporters in the capital were about to be crushed by armed force.

The result in hungry Paris was anxiety which quickly turned to violence. For two days, 12 and 13 July, impromptu parades and public meetings helped to whip up feelings of fear and anger. Just how this excitement was channelled into an assault on the Bastille nevertheless remains a mystery, for the impulse to storm the old prison fortress on the eastern edge of the city seemed to arise spontaneously in a number of places and amid various groups of people. At any rate, early on the morning of 14 July a crowd began to form outside the Bastille's main gate, and negotiations designed to preclude any army action against the populace were opened between self-appointed civic leaders and the commandant. The latter, with only about 100 men under his command, was inclined to make concessions, perhaps even to surrender the fort itself; but the crowd, growing in size and increasing its armaments with each passing hour, became impatient. When desultory attacks on the outer courtyard drew fire from the garrison, a full-scale battle developed. Before it was over, perhaps as many as 125 of the crowd were dead; but the Bastille was taken, soon to be demolished and its stones distributed far and wide as sacred relics of freedom. The commandant and several of his men were killed after surrendering. All the prisoners were released from the cells, which had been expected to yield up a number of political martyrs but proved instead to contain five convicted felons and two helpless lunatics.

Thus, to the aristocratic and middle-class elements in the spreading insurrection, a third, popular wave of revolution had lent its shock effect. The very next day, 15 July, the king spoke before the Assembly at Versailles, announcing the reappointment of Necker, promising the withdrawal of the extra troops around Paris and explaining, perhaps quite truthfully, that they had never been meant to serve any purpose but that of maintaining order. Even now, however, there was still the possibility of a reversal in the course of events, if all revolutionary activity remained confined to the capital and a few other cities; for the countryside might offer a base for counter-revolutionary action. Hence, a fourth uprising may have been required to sustain the momentum created by the other three. This wave, whether indispensable or not, consisted of widespread risings in rural areas.

There had been already been attacks on certain manor houses, aimed at destroying leases and other documentary records of peasant indebtedness. In addition, raids on grain convoys by desperate villagers had been reported in various parts of France for several months past. But in late July and August agrarian outbreaks assumed a new intensity, seemingly the result of fear that either an aristocratic reaction or an invasion by brigands, or both, would drench the land in blood unless local vigilantes took up arms and struck first. This was the 'Great Fear' of 1789, a contagious agrarian panic which markedly increased the incidence of château burnings – and thus worked back upon the deliberations at Versailles.

It was in such circumstances, with the royal government seemingly cowed and with both town and country people engaged in sporadic violence fed by predominantly unfounded rumours, that the National Assembly took its first steps towards the framing of constitutional principles. One of these comprised the resolutions adopted on the night of 4 August, together with the acts subsequently passed to give them legal force. The other was the Declaration of the Rights of Man and of the Citizen.

It is not quite accurate to say that the night of the Fourth of August 'abolished feudalism', since *feudal* relations in the strict, medieval sense of relations between knightly vassals and their superiors or suzerains – which is to say, between aristocrats – were scarcely at issue. What the Assembly did do was to abolish the legal basis for the *manorial* or *seigneurial* system, as well as countless noble, ecclesiastical, corporate and provincial privileges. As speaker after speaker came forward to renounce on behalf of his order or his locality some ancient right or exemption, the structure of the old society seemed to crumble before men's eyes. Consider only the most striking features of that society which were now declared at an end: peasant dues based on personal subjection to a lord; all differences between nobles and commoners in matters of taxation as well as in judicial penalties; regional variations in tax rates; seigneurial as opposed to public tribunals; the ownership of public offices as private property, including the immensely valuable seats in the parlements and other sovereign courts; all church tithes and the annates previously sent to the Vatican; even the guilds' old restrictions on freedom to pursue a trade or craft. Some of these measures were reworded more cautiously in the days that followed; and the Assembly showed its concern for property rights by voting that officeholders should be paid for their lost offices and landlords compensated for the sacrifice of any income not based on earlier serfdom. Nevertheless, it is difficult to escape the impression that after 4 August the *ancien régime* in France was dead at its roots.

To this assault on old arrangements, the Assembly added a positive catalogue of principles to be followed in the making of the new constitution. The Declaration of the Rights of Man was formally adopted on 26 August, after several weeks of debate.

When its text announces in Article 1 that 'men are born and remain free and equal in rights', in Article 2 that 'these rights are liberty, property, security and resistance to oppression', and in Article 3 that 'all sovereignty rests essentially in the nation', it seems an abstract manifesto of liberalism. However, critics who have dismissed it as only that have missed the hard, practical quality revealed by many of the other articles. For the framers also had in mind a list of specific problems with which eighteenth-century Frenchmen were all too familiar. The document stipulated, for example, that 'every citizen may . . . speak, write and print freely' (Article 11); that 'no man may be indicted, arrested or detained except in cases determined by law' (Article 7); that 'only strictly necessary punishments may be established' (Article 8); that every man must 'be presumed innocent until judged guilty' (Article 9); and that 'all citizens have the right . . . to have demonstrated to them the necessity of public taxes [and] to consent to them freely' (Article 14). These points struck directly at particular abuses.

The incident which completed the initial drama of 1789 was the march on Versailles of 5 October. That day a large crowd of women formed in Paris, shouting for bread but also demanding that the king give his approval to the decrees of 4 August and the Declaration of the Rights of Man. The women, accompanied and to some extent perhaps led by male agitators, made the five-hour walk to Versailles and there invaded the Assembly's meeting place. In due course a delegation of marchers was admitted to the royal palace itself; and after temporizing, Louis announced his acceptance of the August legislation, as well as his determination to rush food supplies to Paris. Still the crowd would not disperse, but instead spent the night before the palace gates. In the cold, wet dawn of 6 October rioters burst into the great courtyard, insisting that the royal family move to Paris, where the king could be protected by his people – presumably against his courtiers. Once more Louis XVI yielded, this time loading Marie Antoinette, the Dauphin or crown prince and himself into a coach which the now jubilant mob escorted back to the capital. Ahead of it ran the cry that 'the baker, the baker's wife and the baker's boy' were on their way. With the royal family ensconced at the Tuileries in Paris, the National Assembly decided that it too should move into the capital. Henceforth, the political centre of France would be not Versailles, with its elegant parks and stately halls, but a great city of teeming streets and immense explosive power.

THE MONARCHICAL EXPERIMENT

For the next three years, French politics centred around an effort to find both freedom and stability under constitutional monarchy. It was an effort which disintegrated progressively over the second half of this period and which, even at the beginning, was beset by a host of difficulties. Quite aside from the task of devising new foundations of government (the National Assembly was called the 'Constituent Assembly' with increasing regularity after its move to Paris), royal officials and elected deputies shared a common concern with a number of individual problems. These included feeding the kingdom, reordering its local administration, buttressing its financial position, regulating the status of the Roman Catholic Church in France, creating dependable armed forces and conducting relations with foreign states. On the degree of success achieved by the Crown and the Assembly in attacking such issues, as well as on the shape of the emerging constitution, would depend the fate of what has been called 'the monarchical experiment'.[2]

Louis XVI is best known to history as a good man because of his lack of cruelty and his freedom from personal vices, but a bad king because of the indecisiveness and inconsistency which on occasion produced effects difficult to distinguish from those of conscious deceit. In 1789, in 1790 and well into 1791 he still possessed some considerable political assets. The aura of consecrated royalty was not quickly dissipated. Popular hatred of many of his advisers and even of his queen seldom extended to him personally. 'If our father, the king, only knew' was a common expression in the mouths of even his angriest subjects. Not one of the hundreds of *cahiers* of grievances drawn up for the Estates General had been an antimonarchical document. Yet the facts of power and the tides of opinion were such that in all probability only a royal genius, and perhaps not even he or she, could have ridden out the stormy transition from theoretically absolute to expressly limited monarchy. Louis XVI would have had to assume the role of arbiter, above parties and special interest groups. In particular, he would have had to repudiate, or at least very sharply reduce, his special concern for the nobility and a privileged church. How could this poor, phlegmatic king, with his gift for showing stubbornness and docility at just the wrong times, comprehend so demanding an assignment?

The Assembly too faced dilemmas and difficult choices. In the debates of August and September 1789 a clear division along party lines emerged with respect to constitutional principles. J. J. Mounier, a lower court judge from Dauphiné in south-eastern France, chief framer of the Tennis Court Oath and leading member of the first committee on the constitution, was the spokesman for what might be called the moderate wing. That is, he and his supporters favoured a set of checks and balances which reflected their admiration for the British system so admired by Montesquieu, as well as for the new government of the United States. They urged that the Crown be recognized as an important factor, that an absolute royal veto over legislation be written into the constitution and that the future lawmaking body include, in addition to a democratic lower chamber, an upper house or senate, not hereditary but reserved to the wellborn and the rich.

Opposing these views stood a faction led by the Abbé Sieyès, one of the three members of the clergy chosen as deputies of the Third Estate the previous spring. As a speaker in the Assembly, Sieyès brushed aside arguments that the royal veto might actually protect popular interests against aristocratic machinations. He did not trust the king and asserted flatly that no good could come from diluting the sovereignty of the people by surrendering great executive authority to a monarch. In addition, he denounced Mounier for wishing to save a privileged nobility by instituting an upper legislative chamber. While many other speakers took the floor during months of debate, the conflict between Mounier and Sieyès brought the issues into their sharpest focus.

The formal outcome was embodied in the constitution which took effect in 1791. The basic decisions, however, had been reached before the end of 1789. On 10 September, for example, the Assembly overwhelmingly endorsed the one-house legislature favoured by Sieyès. The next day, embracing a compromise arranged by a group around Lafayette, the deputies voted to give the king no more than a suspensive veto, which would permit him to delay legislation for a maximum of four years but not to block it once that limit had been reached. When these decisions were announced, Mounier resigned from the constitutional committee in disgust and soon afterward went home to Dauphiné, the first step on his road to exile.

The prickly question of voting rights was finally settled by classifying as a citizen every male twenty-five or more years old who had lived in one locality for a year and was not a domestic servant, but then stipulating that only those who paid taxes equivalent to three days' wages were 'active' citizens, entitled to vote in the lower or primary electoral assemblies. This provision reduced to 'passive' citizenship about one-fourth of the 6 million or more men who would otherwise have qualified as voters. In addition, it was initially decided that payment of direct taxes worth *ten* days' wages was required of an active citizen aspiring to serve as an elector in the higher assemblies which would choose all important elective officials, including national legislators. Finally, national deputies would be recruited only from payers of taxes worth a silver mark (54 livres), or as much as ten times the amount set for electors in low-wage areas. Despite certain changes introduced by the Constituent Assembly in its last weeks, the above provisions essentially governed the election to the new Legislative Assembly, the only national body chosen under the Constitution of 1791.

Between the National Constituent Assembly, from June 1789 to its dissolution on 30 September 1791, and the Legislative Assembly, which convened the next day, the change of personnel was complete; for the Constituent had passed a self-denying ordinance making its own members ineligible to hold office in the Legislative. Even earlier, many familiar figures had left the political arena, whether by choice, as in the case of Mounier and that of Necker (who resigned his ministerial post in the late summer of 1790), or by death, as when Mirabeau succumbed to a long illness in 1791. For the moment, however, it seems best to consider this period of limited monarchy as a whole, noting the disposition of the urgent problems mentioned above, the growing opposition to measures adopted and the circumstances under which the monarchy finally collapsed.

There is not much to be said about the food crisis, though it impinged on the political situation at many points, including the October Days of 1789 when the women marched on Versailles. For months thereafter, all the government could do to stave off massive riots was periodically to release stored grain and to send emergency shipments into Paris and other large cities. Then, with the excellent harvest of 1790, the threat of famine receded, not to return in full force until after the monarchy's fall and the establishment of the Republic.

To administer the distribution of food and other matters affecting public order, a system of local administration was urgently needed in place of the welter of provincial and municipal regimes doomed on the night of August 4. The new structure, as elaborated in 1790, provided for eighty-three *départements*, each of them named for a geographical feature of its area – Seine-Inférieure, Basses-Pyrenées, Haut-Rhin – in conscious repudiation of the historic names of provinces such as Normandy, Béarn or Alsace (*see* Map 2). Each department comprised several districts, each district two or more cantons and each canton a number of local units called communes. At every level, from the municipal or rural council and mayor of a commune up to the council, the directory and the syndic or procurator-general of a department, popularly elected officials were charged with administration. It soon became apparent that merely establishing such institutions did not make skilful officials out of often illiterate farmers and previously inexperienced townsmen. The system created in 1790 nevertheless provided the units which Napoleon would use to fashion the departmental, district and local hierarchy of modern France (*see* Map 2).

More pressing in 1789–92 than administrative needs or even food shortages was the issue of national finances. 'Patriotic loans', emergency taxes, dramatic appeals for public contributions of jewellery and precious metals, all failed to halt the flight of capital abroad. The difficulty of collecting taxes from a population inclined to see in the Revolution an end to taxation itself is shown by the fact that only one-third of the revenues assessed through the end of 1791 had actually been paid a full year later. Desperately seeking an escape from this fiscal crisis, the Assembly had long before, in November 1789, voted that church property could be disposed of for the good of the nation. In due course, as more and more nobles fled the country, the confiscated belongings of emigrants were added to those of the clergy as *biens nationaux*. The latter, amounting to as much as 25 per cent of the land in some departments, in turn provided the backing for what became the new paper currency of France, the *assignats*. In theory the assignats were notes given to creditors of the government, who could use them to buy confiscated land. In August 1790, however, when it authorized the issuance of additional assignats worth 800 million livres, the Assembly not only tripled the amount in circulation but also made the notes legal tender, that is, currency in the full sense of the word.[3]

The new medium of exchange proved, despite later abuses and inflation, to be a more successful short-term answer to the government's financial needs than most economic historians were once inclined to admit. The liquidation of the *biens nationaux* also had important results, in that countless middle-class farmers and businessmen, who had bought confiscated property at relatively low prices, found themselves the beneficiaries of a revolution they could ill afford to see reversed. These developments, however, heightened the tension already existing between the constitutional monarchy and the Catholic Church. The Assembly, in seizing church lands, had accepted responsibility for supporting at least the secular clergy. Monks and nuns, on the other hand, were strongly urged by the government to renounce their religious vows. On 12 July 1790 the Civil Constitution of the Clergy became law, providing for the selection of priests by district elec-toral assemblies, the abolition of the old episcopal dioceses in favour of new ones corresponding to departmental boundaries, and direct payment of bishops and priests out of public funds. All papal jursidiction in France was terminated. Within a year Pope Pius VI formally condemned the Civil Constitution and, indeed, the entire Revolution. In France itself, while many 'constitutional' clergymen accepted their new status, 'refractory' priests were now classified as public enemies and in some instances, with the support of pious laymen, behaved accordingly.[4]

In addition to its other problems, the French government had serious military and diplomatic worries. The Constituent Assembly, by removing the army and navy from royal control, had created a situation in which military advancement depended on a curious mixture of elections and seniority. The establishment of the National Guard, a militia in which every man who claimed to be an active citizen must enrol, further confused the organiz-ation and distribution of armed power in the country. Even members of veteran units, uncertain about lines of command and embittered over irregular pay, were sometimes influenced by contacts with civilian agitators in garrison towns. In August 1790, the three regiments stationed at Nancy in Lorraine, two of them

French and the other Swiss, joined forces with a disorderly mob in a wild mutiny put down by other troops only after a pitched battle which killed 400 men of the loyal units alone. A parallel naval mutiny occurred the following month at the Atlantic port of Brest. The emigration of nobles inevitably decimated the corps of trained officers, while commanders still willing to serve France were in despair at the disorder confronting them.

The military confusion helps both to explain the indecisiveness of the National Constituent Assembly in foreign affairs and to emphasize the bravado (some said foolhardiness) displayed by its successor. Early in 1790, Spain requested French help against England in the Nootka Sound dispute over rights of navigation and settlement on the Pacific coast of North America; and Louis XVI, conscious of the family ties between French and Spanish Bourbons, felt obliged to offer naval aid. The Assembly, however, amid speeches to the effect that treaties not originally approved by the people through their representatives could not be viewed as binding, postponed a decision until Madrid despaired of French assistance and yielded to the British terms. In the course of the debates that spring orators in Paris soared away from the question of Nootka Sound to renounce all warfare designed to reduce the liberties of other peoples. This was unquestionably the high point of revolutionary pacifism, which yielded only by degrees to a frankly crusading spirit. Even in September 1791, when the expiring National Assembly voted to annex the former papal principality of Avignon in southern France, it insisted that this was not a conquest but the welcoming of fellow Frenchmen who had rebelled against a foreign tyrant. Still, the very nature of the distinction suggested ambiguities for the future.

The crux of the foreign situation appeared to the National Assembly, and still more alarmingly to the Legislative after it, to be the threat of invasion by the armies of anti-revolutionary dynasts. In late August 1791, King Frederick William II of Prussia and Emperor Leopold II met in person at Pillnitz in Bohemia. On parting they issued what both considered a restrained assurance that while concerned about the safety of Louis XVI, neither of them would move against France without the concurrence of England and the other powers. The French, however, found little comfort in a statement which implied that, in certain circumstances, they *might* be attacked. It was also known in Paris that Leopold's son, who became Emperor Francis II on his father's

death early in 1792, was much more bellicose than his predecessor. Quite apart from foreign threats, culminating in the new
Austro-Prussian alliance of 7 February 1792, some of the most
eloquent political leaders in France were becoming convinced that
war could both unite the nation and strike down its enemies
abroad. Men such as General Dumouriez, a foe of Austria, and
the Girondin chieftains, Roland and Brissot de Warville,
demanded action against foreign tyrants. The Girondin party,
which had not yet split off from the mass of Jacobin deputies, was
in fact the most consistently aggressive influence throughout the
period which ended on 20 April 1792 with the Legislative
Assembly's declaration of war on Austria and Prussia.

THE FALL OF THE MONARCHY

With the outbreak of formal hostilities, the monarchical experiment entered its final phase. Although that experiment had
almost from its inception alienated many aristocrats and ecclesiastics who rejected the changes taking place, a still more potent
source of political dissatisfaction lay in the opposite conviction,
namely, that the Revolution was not being pushed far enough.
In particular, the network of local political clubs that took their
lead from the Society of Friends of the Constitution in Paris and
their famous nickname from the old Jacobin monastery in which
it met, provided an ample hearing for radical critics of limited
monarchy. Not only in their clubs but also through the press, the
speeches of orators such as Maximilien Robespierre and the
discussions of communal councils, the more extreme Jacobins
kept up a running fire upon 'aristocrats' (whether titled or not),
refractory clergymen, pro-Austrians and other alleged enemies of
France.

By the summer of 1791 the acridity of political debate belied
the official agreement between the king and the National
Assembly over the constitution then being completed. It was in
this tense situation, on the night of 20–21 June, that Louis XVI
took the fateful step of attempting to escape from the 'protection'
of Paris. Slipping out of the Tuileries with his family, the king
was driven eastward in a heavily curtained coach, only to be
recognized and stopped at Varennes-en-Argonne. It has never

been clear whether the flight to Varennes was intended only to place the monarch among loyal troops in Lorraine or whether Louis meant to claim asylum in Luxembourg with the Austrian forces of his imperial brother-in-law. In any case, the king was brought back to Paris and temporarily shielded from public wrath by the rather lame announcement that he had been kidnapped but happily rescued from his abductors.

Despite this official version, for many knowledgeable people the flight to Varennes doomed the constitutional monarchy even before its constitution went into effect. Loyalist army officers, for example, began to emigrate in sharply increased numbers. Radical politicians in general and the more extreme Jacobins in particular became openly republican, hinting broadly that the king should be viewed as a traitor. For one more year, however, the appearance of parliamentary–royal compromise was maintained. The Legislative Assembly, elected that summer and convened on 1 October, had no aristocratic-clerical wing; but it did have a moderately conservative group on the right, called the *Feuillants*, while a clear majority in the centre still rejected the anti-royalist demands of the Jacobin left. The latter, be it noted, was deprived of Robespierre and several of its other parliamentary spokesman by the enactment which prevented deputies in the National Consituent Assembly from being elected to the Legislative.

It was in local government, above all in the forty-eight wards or *sections* of Paris, that the republican agitators found their most solid base for action. As the assembly of one section after another fell under Jacobin control, conservative elements became either too frightened or too discouraged to take much part in Parisian politics. On 30 July 1792 Danton's own section announced that it would henceforth disregard the distinction between 'passive' and 'active' citizens, as defined by law. This obvious effort to attract support from residents too poor to meet the property requirement for voting was of course an unabashed violation of the Constitution. The next day, another important ward meeting scheduled a march to the Legislative Assembly for 5 August and invited other sections to join in demanding that Louis XVI be stripped of his royal title.

The violence that marked the end of the monarchy came in two waves. During the night of 9–10 August, a new revolutionary Commune elected by the sections threw the members of the existing Paris Commune out of their meeting room at the city hall, placed a Jacobin in command of the National Guard and launched an armed mob in the direction of the royal residence, the Tuileries. In the early morning hours, though the king had fled to the protection of the Legislative Assembly and had ordered his Swiss guards to withdraw, the crowd smashed into the palace and in a frenzy of rage massacred the Swiss troops, numerous courtiers and even some of the servants. The Assembly, its deputies terrified by this slaughter, took the king into protective custody, turned executive power over to a committee of six ministers led by Danton and ordered that a new legislature under the name of the National Convention be elected by a wide manhood suffrage (though domestic servants were still denied the vote).

Before the Convention could be constituted, a second orgy of violence drowned the expiring monarchy in blood. News of military defeats in the north and east continued to arrive, merging with rumours of aristocratic treason at home – rumours which produced so many arrests that the prisons were bursting with suspects. During the first week of September, with the tacit complicity of the revolutionary city government, mobs began a series of gruesome murders of prison inmates. Jail after jail was broken into and emptied of suspected aristocrats and monarchists, as well as many petty criminals. Most of those dragged from their cells were butchered on the spot. The September Massacres, claiming over 1,000 lives by the lowest estimate, foretold the coming of the Terror.

THE BIRTH OF THE REPUBLIC

A total of 782 deputies having been elected, the Convention was called to order on 21 September 1792 and immediately declared the monarchy dissolved. Seventy-five veterans of the National Assembly, including Robespierre, and over twice that many ex-members of the Legislative were returned. It was among the hundreds of 'new men', however, that some of the most extreme revolutionaries were to be found: Danton, the Cordeliers Club's leader, for example, and the radical editors, Marat and Desmoulins. The right, as previously represented by the *Feuillants*, had been swept away in the elections. Such moderate opinion as survived was represented by the group around Jacques Pierre Brissot, sometimes called *Brissotins*, but more familiar to history as *Girondins* because many of their spokesmen came from Bordeaux in the Department of the Gironde. That the Girondin faction, which had been the war party of the previous spring and had not fully detached itself from the Jacobins until the summer of 1792, should now appear relatively conservative was a clear indication of the direction in which the political tide was running. On the opposite side of the meeting hall, in the high seats whence came their nickname, 'The Mountain', sat Robespierre, Danton and their Jacobin cohorts. Between these two positions stretched the expanse of initially uncommitted deputies, 'The Plain', for whose support Girondins and Jacobins would soon be locked in mortal combat.

The proclamation of the Republic on 22 September 1792 seemed to many a positive act, freighted with joy and optimism. Under the slogan, 'Liberty, Equality, Fraternity', the French people were invited to take the future into their own hands, at the same time offering aid to all other peoples who might yearn for freedom. No clearer expression of the messianic sense of a new dispensation can be imagined than the French Republican Calendar. Henceforth, time would be measured from the birth of

The French Republican Calendar*

Revolutionary month	Reference	Gregorian Calendar equivalents
Vendémiaire	Vintage	22 September–21 October
Brumaire	Fog	22 October–20 November
Frimaire	Frost	21 November–20 December
Nivôse	Snow	21 December–19 January
Pluviôse	Rain	20 January–18 February
Ventôse	Wind	19 February–20 March
Germinal	Buds	21 March–19 April
Floréal	Flowers	20 April–19 May
Prairial	Meadows	20 May–18 June
Messidor	Reaping	19 June–18 July
Thermidor	Heat	19 July–17 August
Fructidor	Fruit	18 August–16 September
Sans-culottides	National Holidays	17 September–21 September

* Gregorian equivalents shown above hold true only through 1795. Thereafter, failure to make consistent adjustments for leap years progressively altered the correlation.

the Republic, the first day of the Year I. Since that date falls near the average autumnal equinox, it was easy to divide the year into quarters roughly equal to the astronomical seasons. Each month was allotted thirty days, divided into three ten-day weeks and given a name which referred either to its characteristic weather or to its place in the cycle of farm life. The five days thus left over in September were called *Sans-culottides*, in honour of the long-trousered enemies of aristocracy, and were reserved for patriotic festivals. The months' names, chosen by the poet Fabre d'Eglantine, have considerable beauty and rationality, the same final syllable being employed for all three months of each season. But unlike the metric system of weights and measures – grams, metres, litres, etc. – adopted by the National Assembly in 1791, the Convention's calendar failed to win lasting acceptance. Perhaps this was because, unlike the metric system, which had brought much-needed order out of the previous chaos of varying measures and introduced convenient decimal divisions, the new years and months had to compete with well-established and internationally recognized notions of time. In any event, the Republican calendar was formally abandoned by the Emperor Napoleon in 1806 (the Year XIV).

Far grimmer questions lay before the revolutionaries in the winter of 1792–93. The negative side of founding a republic was the liquidation of the monarchy, which in turn involved a decision about the person of the king. Throughout Louis XVI's trial for treason, which occupied the Convention that December and January, numerous Girondins and deputies of the Plain urged imprisonment or submission of the entire matter to a popular plebiscite. They were defeated by the implacable orators of the Mountain, in particular Robespierre and the young Saint-Just. On 15 January 1793 overwhelming majorities voted for the king's guilt and against any appeal to the people. The next day, 361 of the 721 members present, a majority of precisely one vote, favoured immediate execution, though thirty-nine others endorsed the death sentence subject to various reservations. On 21 January the king perished, with dignity, under the blade of the guillotine on what is today the Place de la Concorde. He was followed to the same scaffold by Marie Antoinette some nine months later.

To ask how the Convention was transformed from a new constitutional assembly into a long-term legislature, controlled by mobs outside and by dictatorial executive committees within, is in effect to ask how the republican experiment evolved into the Terror. To answer that question in turn demands an understanding of several forces which were carrying France beyond the reach of common parliamentary solutions. One of these forces was the brutalizing effect of bloodshed itself. The beheading of the king, only a few months after the September Massacres, seemed to herald a departure from ordinary humanity, whether to soar above it or to plunge below. 'Politics', in any familiar sense of the term, was on its way to becoming a hopelessly inadequate label for public affairs in France.

In 1789 defeat in the struggle for power had meant silence for a time and possibly retirement. In 1791 it had been more likely to mean emigration or exile. By the later months of 1793 it meant almost certain death under the great knife which Dr Guillotin had hoped would render fast and less discriminatory the cruel executions of the Old Régime. A statistical analysis of over 14,000 executions between March 1793 and August 1794 – not including local lynchings, some of them amounting to massacres – shows that in each of the first seven months of that period about 500 formal death sentences were carried out. Then the monthly figure began to climb rapidly, finally reaching a high of over 3,500 judicial killings in January 1794.[5] While such statistics, like the infinitely greater human toll exacted by mass terror in our own century, are all but incomprehensible, it is important to bear constantly in mind the fact that the chill of death, like the heat of believing that one's opponent was a traitor who must die, conditioned almost everything a Frenchman might say or do under the reign of 'Madame Guillotine'.

The apprehension born of war against foreign powers fed the demand for the extirpation of secret enemies at home. On 1 February 1793, 'throwing down the head of a king as a gage of battle', the Convention added England, Spain and the Dutch United Provinces to a list of foes which already included Austria, Prussia and Sardinia. As we shall see in Chapter 7, the hostile coalition concerted its efforts very poorly. Nevertheless, after General Dumouriez had overrun Belgium, an Austrian counter-offensive recaptured Brussels. Early in April Dumouriez himself, as ambitious as ever but now frightened by the Convention's suspicious questioning, slipped across his own battle lines and became one more émigré in the Habsburg camp.

From then until August 1793 the Republic's armies were on the defensive almost everywhere. It was on 23 August that the government formally announced the *levée en masse*, the general mobilization which was one of the most important symbolic acts of the Revolution. 'Young men will go to the front,' read the decree, 'married men will forge arms and transport foodstuffs; women will make tents, clothes, will serve in hospitals: children will tear rags into lint [for gun wadding]; old men will have themselves carried to public places, there to stir up the courage of the warriors, hatred of kings and unity in the Republic.' The tremendous hammer of revolutionary France began to rise over an older Europe it soon would shatter into unfamiliar fragments. Meanwhile, however, the French nation was gripped by hatred and uncertainty.

Its rulers during this period included members of the Convention, of course, and of its judicial arm, the Revolutionary Tribunal. Executive authority, however, was centred in the Convention's Committee of General Security and Committee of Public Safety. Danton was a member of the latter from the day it was formed, 6 April 1793; but when Robespierre was added to it in July, a new leader began his march towards what for a time would be unchallenged power. Another of the Committee's important figures was Lazare Carnot, already concentrating on the military measures which were to earn him the title, 'Organizer of Victory'. One more agency which wielded such great influence that it was actually a major organ of the national state was the reorganized Commune of Paris, where the violent and abusive journalist, Hébert, was the dominant force. It was these bodies that formed the true government of France, despite the new Constitution, ostensibly democratic but suspended for the duration of the war and never in fact put into operation.

INTERNAL THREATS TO THE REPUBLIC

The most serious issues confronting these rulers, apart from foreign attack, were (1) economic difficulties, (2) counter-revolutionary uprisings and (3) the vicious struggle among groups represented in the Convention, in other words, among the revolutionaries themselves. Poverty remained seemingly irreducible.

Official plans for seeing that humble sans-culottes and poorer peasants shared in the distribution of the confiscated lands of aristocratic émigrés did not significantly alter the pattern set by the sale of the earlier, ecclesiastical portion of the *biens nationaux* – citzens already prosperous gobbling up the newly available property.[6] Adding to lower-class resentment were the mounting inflation of the assignats and severe new food shortages, traceable to uneven distribution made worse in some areas by military requisitions.

The response of the government involved in particular two measures, both designed to bring relief – albeit at the cost of repudiating the Revolution's earlier devotion to a free market economy. The first of these measures, the so-called *maximum*, actually developed out of a long series of partial expedients dating from 1792; but the comprehensive Law of the Maximum was passed only in September 1793. It fixed commodity prices all over France at levels set by adding one-third to local figures for 1790, while wages were also pegged to the norms of 1790, in this case increased by one-half. Secondly, a ration-card system was instituted to control the distribution of meat, the coarse 'equality bread' and other foodstuffs. These steps were frankly authoritarian and, in eighteenth-century terms, distinctly illiberal; but they served the French war effort by saving the assignat as a viable currency for the time being, and they almost certainly forestalled paralysing hunger riots.

Meanwhile, another internal crisis, this one involving the government's hold on a number of key areas of the country, added peril to the war situation. Revolts against the Jacobin Republic, generally supported by its foreign enemies and partially dependent for leadership on French royalists and other émigrés who had slipped back into the country, broke out in 1793 from the Channel to the Mediterranean. In March the farmers of the Vendée in western France, with the connivance of certain ruined noblemen and a number of irreconcilable priests, erupted in a furious rebellion which expressed a combination of monarchist, clerical and socio-economic motives.[7] It was followed that summer, especially after the fall of the Girondins enraged their supporters outside Paris, by risings in Normandy, Bordeaux and the big city of Lyon, much of whose National Guard joined forces with a royalist brigade commanded by one Count de Précy. Almost simultaneously, the Mediterranean ports of Marseille and

Toulon revolted. In the former, enemies of the government executed numerous Jacobins and launched a military assault on the Convention's forces in the region. At Toulon, local insurgents opened the gates to a landing party of British, Spanish and Sardinian troops put ashore on 28 August from Admiral Hood's warships.

The Committee of Public Safety struck back hard at all these monarchist, Girondin and 'federalist' (i.e., anti-centralist) elements. Army officers who had been born noble were abruptly deprived of their commissions – an obvious, if costly, precaution – while political agents of the Convention, called 'representatives on mission', were sent into the provinces to coordinate the work of military units and Jacobin committees in crushing resistance. One by one, the defiant cities fell to the republican armies. Bordeaux, like Rouen and Caen in Normandy, capitulated without heavy fighting. Other places had to be taken by storm: Marseille in late August 1793, Lyon in October after a two-month siege, Toulon only on 18 December in an attack which earned young Captain Napoleon Bonaparte a swift promotion to the rank of brigadier general. The very names of these three munici-palities were stricken from the rolls of the Republic. A wrathful Convention rebaptized them, Marseille as Ville-affranchie (Freed City), Lyon as Ville-sans-nom (Nameless City) and Toulon as Port-la-Montagne (Port of the Mountain).

Only in the stubborn Vendée and inland Britanny did rebellion smoulder on. Even after their great defeat by republican forces at Chollet in late October 1793, and despite the massacre of thou-sands of dissidents which was organized at Nantes by Represent-ative-on-Mission Carrier, the embittered Vendéans and the Breton guerrillas called 'Chouans' kept up a series of intermittent raids on government posts. Distracting as this particular insur-rection proved to be, however, the general epidemic of uprisings against the Republic, like the most extreme danger from foreign invasion, had been overcome by the end of 1793.

THE PEAK OF THE TERROR AND ROBESPIERRE'S FALL

Why then did the Terror, with its denunciations, mass trials and staggering total of executions, not subside at that point? Part of the answer doubtless lies in the force of panic become vindictive. Though the regime had won some great victories, the popular fear of enemies both within and outside France's borders took months to lose its hysterical intensity. Equally important was the political struggle to the death among the principal revolutionary leaders. To appreciate the growing fanaticism with which this struggle was conducted, one must read countless speeches, including those of Robespierre in the Convention and of Prosecutor-general Fouquier-Tinville before the Revolutionary Tribunal. One should also bear in mind that Hébert's Cult of Reason was officially proclaimed in place of Christianity in November 1793, only to be replaced at the festival of 8 June 1794 by Robespierre's Supreme Being, an uncommonly pitiless god of anger.

Among the countless individual condemnations, we can distinguish four successive stages in the crescendo of the Terror. The first struck down thirty-one Girondin leaders, including Brissot and Mayor Pétion of Paris, who were arrested on 2 June 1793 by vote of the Convention and beheaded the following October. Though the alleged moderation of the Gironde had been under growing attack from the Jacobin Mountain and Parisian demagogues such as Hébert and Marat (the latter assassinated by Charlotte Corday soon after the June crisis), it was the treason of Brissot's friend and military collaborator, General Dumouriez, which had provided extreme patriots with the chance to brand all Girondins enemies of the Republic.

With its former opponents in the Convention delivered to the guillotine, the Jacobin leadership became increasingly hostile to the noisy faction around Hébert and its ceaseless agitation within the Paris city government. Some members of the Committee of Public Safety appear to have been sincere in their distrust of these radical 'ultras' who periodically denounced the Committee itself as lukewarm in its devotion to revolutionary principles. Others in the national administration may have felt nothing more elevated than political jealousy. Whatever the motives involved, the Convention was suddenly advised by the Robespierrists that the ultras were not patriots at all, but conspirators who intended to turn the Paris mob against the central government. Indicted before the Revolutionary Tribunal on 17 March 1794, Hébert and nineteen of his associates were executed within a week.

Danton had spent the winter in close collaboration with the Robespierrist bloc. Despite his own misgiving about the uncontrolled ravages of the Terror, in a sense *because* of those misgivings, he had been in full accord with the crushing of the Hébertists. It is nevertheless clear that even before the Parisian radicals were denounced, the leaders of the Mountain had marked the Dantonists too for destruction. On 30 March Saint-Just, young, handsome, icy – 'the angel of the Terror', as he has been called – presented to both of the great Committees a report prepared by Robespierre and purporting to show that Danton had been guilty of secret machinations against the Republic, conspiracy with England, pro-Girondin sympathies and a host of other crimes. That night a number of alleged Dantonists were arrested, and the next morning a thoroughly frightened Convention bound these newest culprits over to trial. Before the Revolutionary Tribunal, Danton's powerful oratory seemed for a time to be swinging the gallery's feelings and perhaps the hard-pressed court itself his way, but a rumour was hastily launched to the effect that the defendants were plotting a general insurrection. Convicted on 5 April, Danton, Camille Desmoulins and a dozen others were rushed to their deaths on the scaffold.

The Revolution was now devouring its own at a bewildering rate. Girondins, Hébertists, Dantonists had disappeared in turn, and most members of the Convention were uncertain who might be next. For over three months after Danton's fall, however, Robespierre, in appearance still the fastidious little lawyer who had come to Paris from Arras in 1789, ruled the Convention and its agencies with a certitude that belied any notion that he too might fall. In the best tradition of Greek tragedy, it was a gesture of supreme self-confidence that led to Robespierre's undoing. On 22 Prairial of the Year II (10 June 1794), he forced through the Convention a law which subdivided the Revolutionary Tribunal into four panels for the more expeditious handling of cases, established a vague new category of criminals known simply as 'enemies of the people', denied the accused all right to counsel and gave the two committees (Public Safety and General Security) the power to indict even a deputy of the Convention without need for formal action by that body.

At a time when the guillotine was taking more than 1,000 lives per month, the Law of 22 Prairial could be passed because no one dared speak against it. This very prevalence of fear, however, produced the secret plot which finally destroyed Robespierre. The deputy Fouché, who knew himself to be suspected of Hébertist leanings, concerted the action with several apprehensive members of the Committee of Public Safety. These included not only Carnot but also the ferocious Collot d'Herbois, who had the special advantage of being the Convention's presiding officer. When Saint-Just rose to speak on 9 Thermidor (27 July), he held in his hand a new list of victims, but he never was able to read their names. Instead his voice was drowned out by an uproar of hostile shouts. From the pandemonium there finally emerged an indictment of Robespierre himself, together with a number of other officials accused of sharing his misuse of public power for selfish ends. During the night that followed, it still appeared that a popular insurrection by the sans-culottes of Paris might save the Jacobin chieftains, especially since Robespierre was not actually imprisoned and could have harangued the populace before the city hall. He declined to do so, however, possibly because he felt sure that he could win a triumphant acquittal before the Revolutionary Tribunal – and the crowds slowly melted away. Meanwhile, Robespierre's enemies in the Convention seized the excuse to change the charge against him and his followers to one of insurrection against the Republic. The vote outlawing the Robespierrists also eliminated the need for a formal trial, and they were seized after a brief scuffle in which the Incorruptible himself either was shot, or shot himself, in the jaw. Next day, with Saint-Just and twenty of their associates, he was guillotined.

The fall of Robespierre marked the beginning of the end of massive Terror, but the end itself was a bloody one. Almost 1,400 people were executed in July, first by Robespierre's régime before the 27th and then by his foes in the hectic days that followed. The Thermidoreans, as the new masters of the Convention were called, did not willingly abandon wholesale decapitation as an instrument of rule; but they could not long disregard an unmistakable shift in public opinion. Once the Paris Commune had been liquidated and the Jacobin Club in the capital destroyed, indictments before the Revolutionary Tribunal shrank to a relatively insignificant number. (The court was itself abolished within a year.) Numerous former outlaws, including Girondins who had survived in hiding, were pardoned. By early 1795 not only political trends but also social developments – the revival of wigs and colourful dress, the reappearance of an argumentative press and a libertine theatre, the renewed toleration of prostitutes, even the return of certain avowed aristocrats – all showed that the more (or less) than human demands of the Republic of Virtue had lost their force.

The Republic, despite considerable easing of the tension at home and a series of reassuring military victories in the Low Countries and the Rhineland, still faced severe difficulties. Late in 1794 the *maximum* was repealed in a spirit of loosening controls, and a new inflation began at once. The following spring two bread riots shook Paris, with the indirect result that the Convention wiped out the last veterans of the Mountain, beheading six deputies, exiling Collot d'Herbois and several others. In July 1795 the suppression of a new, British-backed revolt by the Chouans in the west led to over 700 official executions, while the rebels in their turn butchered about 1,000 republican prisoners. Finally, on 5 October, a rising of monarchist elements in Paris, known to history as the Thirteenth Vendémiaire, had to be put down by cannon – the 'whiff of grapeshot' that brought the Convention's artillery commander, General Bonaparte, once more to public notice.

By the time this final insurrection was crushed, the Convention was nearing the end of its stormy three-year life. Its deputies, however, did not propose to fade out of politics. The Thirteenth Vendémiaire was in part a demonstration against the terms of the newly adopted Constitution of 1795; for the rightist rebels in that affair, though they welcomed the restoration of property qualifications for voting, were outraged by the provision that two-thirds of the first Council of Ancients and the Council of Five Hundred should be chosen from among the members of the Convention. In October the decimated assembly held its final session, then dissolved itself to make way for the bicameral legislature and five-man Directory which together inherited the reins of national power.

THE GOVERNMENT OF THE DIRECTORY

The Directory's structure and powers are worth considering, if only to define its place in the evolution of executive responsibility from Louis XVI through the several revolutionary régimes to Napoleon. The five members, who had staggered terms so that the two Councils would elect a new Director each year, exercized sweeping authority over internal, military and foreign affairs, subject only to the control over public finances vested in another group of five key officials, the Treasury Commission. The Directory's power over the administrative hierarchy, in particular, was direct and virtually unlimited. The original members – Barras, Carnot, La Révellière-Lépeaux, Letourneur and Reubell – were all veterans of the Convention. All had voted for the execution of the king, and all took office hoping for the support of a wide spectrum of republican, including Jacobin, opinion. But not one one of them was any longer an idealist, as the next four years would amply demonstrate.

The story of the Directory, from 1795 until its overthrow in 1799, is heavily dominated by military and diplomatic events, and for that reason, much of it belongs to the next chapter. As for domestic affairs, the Directory's performance was no better than might have been expected from a combination of world-weary politicians. Certainly, however, it was not the chronicle of sloth and corruption evoked by many historians whose hearts have lain with either Louis XVI, Robespierre or Napoleon, and who have agreed about almost nothing aside from their condemnation of this administration.

By the mid-1790s there was no denying that military success was essential to the government's prestige, a hint of things to come. In Director Carnot France possessed an able builder and supplier of armies. In Hoche, Jourdan, Masséna and Bonaparte, it found a set of energetic generals. Not only on distant battlefields but also in France's own western provinces, where Hoche crushed the last concerted onslaught by Vendéans and Chouans in 1796, did the military prove equal to its many assignments. Meanwhile economic difficulties persisted. The assignats, despite repeated attempts to save them, continued to depreciate until in 1796 the government at last withdrew them from circulation, redeeming those still outstanding at one-seventieth of their face value, payable in coin. Even this painful and unpopular conversion was made possible only by the foreign stores of gold and silver captured by French armies in the field. Yet the embattled Treasury Commission had averted financial disaster, in the process restoring a measure of public confidence in the nation's credit.

Why, then, was Napoleon able three years later to overthrow this government so easily? Part of the answer may lie in the fact that the Directory was just not very exciting. It did not attract the passionate loyalty of anyone; and especially in a nation at war year after year, the felt need for charismatic leadership can become a political force in its own right. Many of the directors at one time or another displayed a thinly veiled cynicism with respect to the Directory itself – and if even they did not believe in its merits, who else could? Meanwhile, the dashing young generals on the battlefields of Germany and Italy had the opportunity to appear more glamorous in the eyes of the public than could any civilian functionary arguing over currency or taxes.

Above all, the Directory's weakness stemmed from its inability to overcome the splintering of French political life which followed the collapse of the Terror. In May 1796 the threat seemed to come from the left, specifically from the protosocialist demands of Gracchus Babeuf's Society of the Pantheon. This 'conspiracy of the Equals', which included a plan for a lower-class revolt, was easily exposed by the government, and Babeuf went to the guillotine.[8] In September 1797 circles loyal to the regime became convinced that right-wing plots now represented the most pressing danger. A number of conservative politicians and generals, some frankly monarchist in outlook, were rounded up and two of the directors, one of them the capable but disillusioned Carnot, packed off into exile. There were many other political crises during the years we are considering, but Babeuf's conspiracy and the fall of Carnot suffice to illustrate the range of challenges faced by the Directory.

The final *coup d'état* brought together several kinds of dissatisfaction, and in so doing it destroyed the political compromise of 1795. Since the end of 1798 and the creation of the Second Coalition, the alliance of Russia, England and Austria had inflicted a series of reverses upon a French nation grown unaccustomed to military setbacks. At the same time, a combination of economic and financial troubles, some of them quiescent for several years past, flared up once more. In politics, Jacobin resurgence was bringing demands for a more broadly based republicanism, and the elections of May 1799 produced a majority in the Council of Five Hundred openly hostile to the incumbent directors. The latter were compelled to accept a change of membership, with the result that the Directory itself henceforth contained at least two men, Sieyès and Roger-Ducos, who made no secret of their distaste for the existing situation. In a sense, the most acute and the most understandable misgivings were those felt by political moderates who feared either a reactionary uprising or a revival of Jacobin Terror. At the same time, one should not underestimate the extent to which distrust of the populace as a whole led even veteran revolutionaries to heed demands for an end to 'civilian mediocrity'.

Here was a situation charged with confusion but also rich in possibilities for an ambitious soldier. Into it stepped General Bonaparte, most lionized of the army's field commanders, celebrated as the hero of the Italian campaign of 1796–97, and now just returned (early in October 1799) from an Egyptian expedition which still touched the imagination of Frenchmen who had not yet learned of its disastrous outcome. It was Sieyès, the old constitutional debater of 1789, who played the most ironic part, that of conspiring with two of the other directors, Roger-Ducos and the more reluctant Barras, to destroy the Republic as a parliamentary régime. On 18 Brumaire of the Year VIII (9 November 1799), these three, who had been in touch with Bonaparte for several weeks in Paris, announced that they were resigning from the Directory under the threat of a Jacobin revolt. The next day, as arranged in advance, Napoleon appeared before the two legislative Councils and asked for the authority to save the nation. When this manoeuvre miscarried, he did what Louis XVI had failed to do ten years before, simply ordering troops to clear the building. A few hours later, selected representatives of the Ancients and the Five Hundred, using, if not misusing, their right to choose directors, voted emergency powers to three 'consuls', Bonaparte, Sieyès and Roger-Ducos. In circumstances suggestive of a comic opera, the revolutionary era faded into the Napoleonic.

INTERPRETING THE REVOLUTION

When we pause to look back over the entire period from the meeting of the Estates General in 1789 to the Eighteenth Brumaire a decade later, certain aspects of the French Revolution stand out. Some emerge, almost of their own volition, from the narrative as such. Others, by contrast, serve only to raise further questions to which even now no categorical answers can be given. But all help to explain why the Revolution has remained a favourite testing ground for social psychologists no less than for economists, for ethical as well as for political philosophers.

We observed, for example, how a broad coalition of interests displayed its power in the summer of 1789 – anti-royalist nobles and clergymen joining forces with middle-class reformers in the Assembly and, somewhat less willingly, with popular agitators in the streets of Paris. Thereafter, we saw the revolutionary front undergo two successive changes. The first, which continued until the summer of 1793, entailed a steady *shift* of the parliamentary spectrum towards the left. One by one, through defection or physical destruction, groups which represented conservative, or at least relatively moderate, views on certain issues disappeared (liberal monarchists from the National Assembly, Feuillants from the Legislative, Girondins from the Convention), while on the other side more radical elements increased their strength.[9] Then a second change began, a marked *narrowing* of the revolutionary front itself, as Hébertist ultras and Danton's faction within the Jacobin movement fell victim to the Robespierrists. When even Robespierre fell, all that remained was a corps of administrators, facing a set of disparate factions – Babouvists, diehard Jacobins, believers in the constitutional monarchy, impatient soldiers. The Directory was able to preside over the Republic for four years, but it steered no course determined by a national consensus or even by a well-defined minority. In this sense, Bonapartist enthusiasts have some excuse for arguing that by 1799 there was no longer any revolutionary momentum for Napoleon either to reverse or to maintain, that the question was not whether the first consul should either *continue* or *suppress* the Revolution, but instead whether or not he should *resume* it.

This problem of revolutionary momentum or energy touches on another matter of importance, namely, the puzzling record of mass behaviour. What (or who) gave direction to the Parisian crowds that stormed the Bastille, brought the royal family back from Versailles three months later and in 1792 massacred the Swiss guards in the Tuileries? Why did certain town populations, such as those of Bordeaux, Lyon, Marseille and Toulon, rally to the standard of federalism in 1793, while many others upheld the Jacobin central government?[10] How near were the Paris *sections* to rioting in order to save Robespierre on the Ninth Thermidor?

These and related questions will yield answers, if at all, only to meticulous local studies aided by every social and psychological insight the historian can bring to bear. Recent interest in the revolutionary mobs has already produced useful findings. Police records reveal, for instance, that many of the individuals who fought on the celebrated 'days' of the Revolution were quite comfortable shopkeepers and professional men. Hatred born of poverty and panic rooted in superstition were by no means the only contributing motives. At the very least, two other forces may be seen at work. One is the influence of apparently sincere, rational convictions about liberation and progress. The second resides in the often unpredictable power of contagious emotion when large numbers of people come together under conditions of nervous strain in an atmosphere charged with rumours and accusations.[11]

Since the Revolution was violent, it is not uncommon to find those who deplore it, as a whole, citing its brutality as conclusive proof of its essential inhumanity in all respects. Conversely, for others, who sympathize with many of the revolutionaries' aims, there persists the tantalizing thought that it should have been possible to stop short of the Terror, whose bloody means ultimately compromised worthy ends. The figure of Robespierre poses the issue in perhaps its sharpest form.[12] Despite his often wearisome self-righteousness and his refusal to let either sympathy or humour restrain the ferocity of his message, the Incorruptible did embody a consistent belief that the Revolution would prove to have been both a fraud and a failure unless it brought a new standard of justice and security to *all* Frenchmen, including the most disadvantaged. He was correct in asserting that there were many who wished to stop short of that goal, though not all of them for such egoistic reasons as he alleged. But how could justice and security be given to a people at the cost of hundreds, eventually thousands of executions each month?

No attempt will be made here to solve all the dilemmas implicit in the mixture of enlightened reform and cynical opportunism, of foreign crusade, rapacious conquest and demagogic tyranny that was the French Revolution. A few brief suggestions, however, may help to keep the problem in perspective. One is that the eighteenth century, though it had seen a considerable quantitative decline in cruelty, was still an era in which suffering and death stood close to nearly everyone. The society of the Old

Régime had been familiar with not only the physical but also the psychological anguish of unexplained disease, as well as with the judicial cruelty that occasionally broke men on the wheel for having violated religious taboos and sent mere youngsters to the gallows for petty theft. How then could one who was intent on destroying that society object to the swift decapitation of any number of people he or she was sure were plotters against the emerging nation and the beckoning triumph of reason over injustice? Throughout history deep conviction, whether religious or social or political, has shown itself capable of triggering human actions which in themselves appear repellent. Tolerance, respect for the rights of individuals, kindness itself all demand a certain leavening of good humour, perhaps fortified at times by some sceptical doubts. And whatever else the French Revolutionaries were, there were neither good humoured nor sceptical!

At the other extreme from considerations of mass emotion and the violence it supported stands the question of individual roles. Generations of historians have argued, for example, over the nature and even the reality of the choices open to Louis XVI. Should he have struck down the National Assembly when it defied him, or should he have accepted its proposals more wholeheartedly than he did? Could he have made himself a national symbol by leading French resistance to foreign intervention, instead of attempting to flee from Paris? Although later historians have tended to attach less importance to the moderating roles of men such as Lafayette and Mirabeau than was once customary, the enigma of Robespierre and Danton, their personal relationship and their respective influences on the Terror, has lost none of its fascination. Or again, had Bonaparte found no Sieyès to help him in 1799, we may still ask, would a different member of the Directory have served the turn? And if there had been no Bonaparte, would another soldier, Jourdan perhaps, have been jobbed into power?

One factor to be considered when seeking answers to difficult questions is what some political scientists call 'executive discretion'. However intricate the causation of the Revolution's crucial developments, no matter how deep their roots in conditions which had developed over the course of centuries, the fact remains that at every point either one man or a small group of men had the authority to initiate specific responses. In other words, the way in which issues were presented to the public view, the tone in which they were discussed, even the order in which they were taken up depended in part on individual judgements and personal styles. The French monarchy might have been destroyed regardless of who was the king from 1789 to 1792; but if Louis XVI had possessed the supple cynicism of England's Charles II, the ferocity of Russia's Peter I or the cold intelligence of Prussia's Frederick II, the story of its destruction would have been different. There might well have been a Terror without Robespierre, but it would not have been precisely the same Terror. The Directory might still have collapsed in 1799 or thereabout; but without a Sieyès and a Bonaparte, can anyone seriously maintain that it would have collapsed under exactly the same circumstances, or with identical implications for the future? That much we do not have to concede to historical determinism.

It remains only to reflect upon the essential meaning of the Revolution, as assessed from different points of view. For Edmund Burke, in his *Reflections* of 1790, its meaning lay in what he considered the tragic misapplication of mechanical principles to an organic problem, the tearing apart of a basically sound society by innovators who mistook the body politic for a machine and who thus destroyed what they should have sought to heal. For Count Alexis de Tocqueville, writing in 1856, it lay in a no less tragic perversion of a vision of liberty into a delusive quest for equality, ending in tyranny under a successful demagogue. For Karl Marx and Friedrich Engels, developing their Communist doctrine in the 1840s and 1850s, it lay in the selfish, though historically 'necessary', seizure of formal control by the entrepreneurs of business, who had already displaced the old feudal class as the possessors of the decisive means of production and who were now ready to reshape the political system, indeed the entire culture, in their own interest. For the Italian sociologist, Vilfredo Pareto, writing at the turn of our own century, it lay in the violent displacement of a soft, tired aristocracy by a new élite of ability and ruthless ambition. And so on through a wide range of other theories and theorists.

My own estimate takes as its point of departure the several categories and levels of conflict we have encountered repeatedly since our initial look at the European society of the 1780s. So far as *orders* of men were concerned, their primacy seemed to be vindicated by the convening of the Estates General; but in fact the assault on a structure thus conceived began almost at once.

Neither nobles nor clergymen could assert the right to legal privileges after the night of 4 August 1789. The Law of Municipalities (abolishing restricted lists of hereditary bourgeois), the Civil Constitution of the Clergy, the repudiation of a legally recognized nobility, indeed the undifferentiated nature of the title 'citizen', all struck at the very idea of orders so dear to the Old Régime. None of these measures escaped later modification, and some were actually reversed; but after the Revolution, Frenchmen would never again accord to human differentiation by order the reverence it had enjoyed for centuries before 1789.

Classes, on the other hand, could no longer be dismissed as a figment of some troubled imagination. The debates over property qualification for voting and office-holding, the espousal of poor men's interests by Robespierre and other leaders, the institution as well as the subsequent repeal of the Maximum, the attack on existing economic relationships by Babeuf and his followers, the fear of a Jacobin resurgence that gripped the well-to-do men in 1799, these and other evidences of class struggle abound in the Revolution's narrative.[13]

In the same narrative, *status* struggle also occupies an important place. The glorification of the sans-culottes, the denigration of aristocrats, the decline of leisure and international culture as badges of social honour, these constituted basic elements in the revolutionary overthrow of traditional values. By the end of the 1790s, a new status system was emerging, one which attached more significance to wealth than to birth and emphasized service to the nation, especially military duty. These changes, like many others already noted, were destined to be watered down by the compromises of the Napoleonic and Restoration eras. What was true of other categories, however, can be said here as well, namely, that there would be no full return to the Old Régime.

Finally, we should now be able to appreciate the importance of *parties* as yet another type of grouping; for neither orders nor classes nor status groups – nor all three combined – would suffice to explain all of the Revolution's pivotal conflicts. Those categories would not, for example, permit us to distinguish between the opposing factions around Mounier and Sieyès in the National Assembly, nor to differentiate Girondins from Hébertists or Dantonists from Robespierrists in the Convention. No, these were genuine parties, held together not by a sense of legal or social or economic identity, but rather by certain shared political assumptions and by the ambition of their members to wield power in the state. The sequence of attempted coups against the Directory after 1795 reflected no less clearly the influence of rudimentary party interests.

The Revolution thus operated at many levels, impelled as it was by many types of motivation. It destroyed much, and it created much, though sometimes only to destroy again. It crushed old enemies of change and others who had seemed the very prophets of change. It excited generous hopes and sanctioned brutal solutions. It made of France, for better or for worse, a nation unlike any the world had previously known. In the process, both through the agency of France and through the direct effect of the revolutionary example, reaching across borders into other lands, it inaugurated a transformation of Europe that in turn has transformed the world.

NOTES AND REFERENCES

1   *The Coming of the French Revolution* (Princeton, 1947).

2   C. Brinton, *A Decade of Revolution 1789–99* (New York, 1934), pp. 1–63.

3   S. Harris, *The Assignats* (Cambridge, Mass., 1930).

4   P. de La Gorce, *Histoire religieuse de la Révolution française* (Paris, 1912–13), esp. vols. I and II.

5   D. Greer, *The Incidence of the Terror during the French Revolution* (Cambridge, Mass., 1935), p. 165. For further discussion of this subject, see below Chapter 10, in particular pp. 255–9.

6   The best regional study of this phenomenon is G. Lefebvre, *Les paysans du Nord et la Révolution française* (Paris, 1959).

7   P. Bois, *Paysans de l'ouest* (Le Mans, 1960); also C. Tilly, *The Vendée* (Cambridge, Mass., 1964). Among the increasing number of newer works devoted to questions of local dissent, see L. A. Hunt, *Revolution and Urban Politics in Provincial France, 1786–1790* (Stanford, 1978); R. Cobb, *Paris and Its Provinces, 1790–1802* (Oxford, 1975); and G. Lewis and C. Lucas, eds., *Beyond the Terror: Essays in French Regional and Social History* (New York, 1983).

8   E. Wilson, *To the Finland Station* (New York, 1940), pp. 71–9.

9   P. Beik, *The French Revolution Seen from the Right* (Philadelphia, 1956).

10 The problem engages R. M. Brace, *Bordeaux and the Gironde, 1789–1794* (Ithaca, NY, 1947).

11 Examples of important work in this field include G. Rudé, *The Crowd in the French Revolution* (Oxford, 1959); M. Bouloiseau, *The Jacobin Republic, 1792–1794*, trans. Jonathan Mandelbaum (Cambridge, 1983); A. Soboul, *Les Sans-culottes parisiens en l'An II* (Paris, 1958), available also in an abridged translation (Oxford, 1964); K. Toennesson, *La défaite des sans-culottes* (Oslo, 1959); and R. Cobb, 'The revolutionary mentality in France, 1793–1794', *History*, vol. XLII (1957).

12 Apart from various sections in the works of Mathiez, for whom Robespierre was the hero of the Revolution, two excellent short analyses are J. M. Thompson, *Robespierre and the French Revolution* (London, 1952); and M. Bouloiseau, *Robespierre* (2nd edn, Paris, 1961).

13 A. Souboul, 'Classes and class struggles during the French Revolution', *Science and Society*, vol. XVII (1953).

7

THE REVOLUTION BEYOND FRENCH BORDERS

Several recent historical works have pointed out that the term 'French Revolution' casts a false light upon the European situation at the end of the eighteenth century. There was, so the argument goes, a general ferment of ideas and discontents, not all of which can be explained by a simple theory of contagion from the French source. We are reminded that when Edmund Burke chose to devote his famous book to 'the Revolution *in France*', it was precisely because his reflections concerned what he knew to be only the most startling instance of a widespread phenomenon. The problem thus becomes one of balance, that is, of giving due weight to international aspects of the crisis without belittling the French drama as a generator of both examples and physical challenges to the rest of Europe. In the present chapter we shall observe not only the impact of the new France upon other lands but also the ways in which conditions indigenous to those lands helped to determine the nature and extent of the crisis experienced by each.

FIRST REACTIONS TO THE REVOLUTION

The revolutionists lectured other peoples through journalism, tracts and published state papers – the Declaration of the Rights of Man, for example, or the Constitution of 1791 – as well as through correspondence between Parisian and foreign political clubs. In addition, many non-Frenchmen learned of new developments in France from the written and spoken words of compatriots who had visited there. Arthur Young's account of his travels, extending up to January 1790 and quickly published not only in English but also in numerous translations, has remained the most famous of such reports; but those of the Russian historian Nicolai Karamzin, the English surgeon and radical journalist Sampson Perry, the Berlin Opera's director J. F. Reichardt were scarcely less influential at the time. After the French armies began to spill across Europe, the gospel of the Revolution was directly, not to say forcefully, broadcast; but before that happened, another kind of French invasion had for several years been carrying abroad some strong impressions of events at home. This was the emigration.

Beginning on the night in July 1789 when the Count d'Artois, brother of Louis XVI, left Versailles and headed for Brussels, the stream of émigrés became broader almost by the month. They went at first to the Low Countries, Germany, Switzerland, northern Italy, Catalonia in Spain. Then, when these areas were threatened or actually overrun by the Republic's forces, seemingly safer havens beckoned: England, Prussia, Austria, Russia, and even European settlements across the seas. In the course of the next five years their numbers swelled to an estimated 130,000. In terms of their social backgrounds, they were far less homogeneous than the long-accepted image of exiled noblemen and priests might suggest; for the Revolution was an immense civil war in which people of widely differing stations and callings could find themselves impelled to leave their homes in France. Of the 90,000 émigrés whose status has been established, over 27 per cent, it is true, were clergymen, while another 18 per cent were members of the nobility. But note that émigrés belonging to the first two Estates together accounted for less that one-half the total figure. The remainder comprised persons identified as upper or lower middle-class (19 per cent), working-class (15 per cent), peasants (21 per cent).[1]

For this and other reasons, the prevailing response to the Revolution on the part of foreigners was anything but unanimous. In nearly every country there were enthusiasts, some of them highly placed, who believed that a new and better age was dawning for mankind. To understand the evolution and in many cases the abandonment of such attitudes, it is necessary to survey European reactions by periods. Let us begin by looking first at the years between 1789 and the outbreak of formal hostilities in 1792, turning thereafter to developments dominated by war and by the French internal Terror through 1794 and finally to the course of the continuing struggle in which France under the Directory found itself embroiled from 1795 to 1799.

In the case of England, as we saw in Chapter 5, the news from across the Channel broke upon a political scene already agitated by debates over the need for basic changes at home. Pitt, as prime minister, had ceased to press for parliamentary reform. Nevertheless, certain eloquent voices could still be heard demanding the reorganization of the legislature and of municipal governments, civil equality for Protestant nonconformists (if not yet for Catholics) and abolition of the trade in African slaves. By an accident of chronology, 1789 fell only one year after the centenary of England's own 'Glorious Revolution', an occasion which had called forth numerous speeches and pamphlets attacking abuses which the reformers insisted made a mockery of the constitutional 'principles of '88'. The names of Horne Tooke, John Jebb and Major Cartwright are famous in this connection; but those of theorists such as Jeremy Bentham and Joseph Priestley or of prominent politicians including Shelburne and Fox should not be forgotten. It was Fox, after all, who greeted the fall of the Bastille as 'much the greatest and the best event that ever happened'.

In 1791 Horne Tooke and his circle revived the Society for Constitutional Information; and early the next year a Corresponding Society was established in London for the stated purpose of achieving constitutional reforms. Even after the grisly September Massacres of 1792 in Paris some English groups went so far as to send formal congratulations to the National Convention on the founding of the French Republic. At that time, British subjects still felt free to discuss what Sir James Mackintosh, in his *Vindiciae Gallicae* of 1791, had called 'a grand experiment to ascertain the portion of freedom and happiness that can be created by political institutions'. Tom Paine's *Rights of Man*, published the same year, was far more explicit in its scorn for British monarchy and in its glorification of revolutionary France.

Meanwhile, a very different attitude had been taking shape. Burke's *Reflections*, though not published until the autumn of 1790, had begun to crystallize in the author's mind the previous year, when he heard of the October Days and the march on Versailles. His understanding of French history was very imperfect, and his knowledge of existing conditions across the Channel, if anything, faultier still. On the other hand, he wrote passionately and sometimes beautifully of the deep roots of governmental institutions, the importance of the past, the responsibilities of trusteeship for the future and the perils arising from ill-considered change. His sense of impending tragedy in France seemed to belie all the hopes of a Mackintosh or a Paine.

In the short run, Burke's famous tract probably influenced British public opinion less than did the mounting bloodshed in France, though the essay deserved high marks for having warned of the coming Terror. Apprehension engendered by republican agitation in Ireland also played its part. The founding of Wolfe Tone's United Irishmen in 1791 launched a sequence of events which brought growing alarm to England. At the highest political level, Pitt himself had by early 1792 abandoned his earlier noncommittal attitude and was expressing his anti-revolutionary sentiments in no uncertain terms. In May of that year, the government solemnly directed local authorities to take sterner action against sedition, by which it meant specifically pro-French propaganda. Yet Fox clung to his earlier position: the cataclysm would bring much that was good, whatever violence might occur at the outset. With Britain's two leading statesmen aligned on opposite sides of the great debate, the stage was set for a decisive test. The only thing that could sharpen the question any further would be war between England and France.

In the Low Countries no less than in the British Isles, early reactions to the crisis were clearly conditioned by existing political tensions. As we saw in Chapter 5, Emperor Leopold II's troops were able to reoccupy the Austrian Netherlands in 1790. Although he allowed the Vonckist exiles to return to Belgium, he was in other respects deferential towards their conservative enemies in the the Estates party. Whatever the Vonckists might think, the power of religious and social traditions in their country was such that a majority of Belgians seem from the first to have been suspicious of revolutionary France. Yet the coming of the Republic's armies meant that more and more would be heard from a vocal minority who insisted that humanity's future was being shaped in Paris.

The arrogant behaviour of the stadtholder since his – or, more accurately, the Prussian army's – victory over the Dutch Patriots in 1787 made pro-French sentiment stronger and more widespread in the United Provinces than it was in Belgium. Unlike Leopold II in the Austrian Netherlands, William V had not let Dutch democrats return after his military control was assured. Hence, there were numerous observers reporting from France to various 'literary' clubs in Amsterdam, Leyden and other cities. As a recent work on the subject makes clear, the relationship between events in Paris and aspirations in Holland was far from simple: 'Much of what happened in France,' its author writes, 'had the most direct bearing on the fate of the Netherlands and was watched by Dutchmen . . . with attentive anxiety. But few of them, especially among the Patriots who remained at home, looked to the French Revolution for instruction. They were more interested in seeing in its progress the vindication of views they already held.'[2] Perhaps for that very reason, several thousand Dutch volunteers marched northward with Dumouriez in 1792. Both inside and outside the country, enemies of the stadtholder and of the regent families alike were organizing themselves.

German reactions to the revolution in France have been more thoroughly studied than have those of most other Europeans, often with heavy emphasis on the response of intellectuals. We are constantly reminded, for example, that most of the leading figures of German philosophy and literature then living greeted the early tidings from Paris with an approval sometimes bordering on rapture. Kant, Wieland, the aged Klopstock, Herder, Hölderlin, Schelling, Hegel, Schiller and, to a lesser degree, Goethe all, at least at the outset, saluted a new dawn. Exceptions to this chorus included certain important lawyers and scholars, including Niebuhr, the historian of ancient Rome. Friedrich Gentz, after a brief period of supporting the Revolution, read Burke's *Reflections*, which he translated for publication in 1792, and embarked on his own career of conservative advocacy. There can be no doubt, however, as even Gentz's case illustrates, that the stagnation of the empire's political life during the seventeenth and eighteenth centuries had made a large majority of the most thoughtful Germans initially receptive to notions of sweeping change.

The fall of the Bastille and the subsequent march on Versailles touched off some insurrections in German principalities, especially in the Rhineland, where French influence was most immediately felt. At Trier, in October 1789, the local burghers met to declare all noble and ecclesiastical privileges abolished. This action was promptly nullified by the arrival of imperial troops whom the archbishop-elector felt compelled to call in, thus inaugurating a period of reaction destined to last until the coming of the French. Something quite similar happened at Mainz in 1790. There the urban deputies in the hastily revived estates demanded of the ruling archbishop-elector an immediate end to special tax exemptions. As in the case of Trier, the answer was repression, but agitation continued elsewhere. Only a few months later, the dissident liberals of the south-western duchy of Württemberg, in avowed imitation of French ceremonies, assembled on the banks of the Neckar River to plant a 'liberty tree'.

Responses to the Revolution in other German states varied widely. The free city of Hamburg, greatest of the Empire's North Sea ports, witnessed a celebration on 14 July 1790 in honour of the first anniversary of the Bastille's capture; and the speeches and poetry recited there in praise of French liberty were printed and widely distributed throughout Germany. In Berlin, on the other hand, many critics of Frederick William II's régime somewhat puzzlingly decided that what was happening in France was a laudable experiment in enlightened despotism, according to the principles of Prussia's own Frederick the Great. Needless to say, after some initial indifference the Prussian royal government, by implication charged with having strayed from those principles, directed a more and more baleful glare at the unfolding drama.

In Switzerland we encounter much the same mixture of official hostility and private sympathy extended by members of the citizenry. The nationalistic Helvetic Society, founded in 1762 to reach beyond narrow cantonal loyalties, welcomed the centralizing tendencies of the Revolution. Pro-French clubs appeared in Basel, Zurich, Bern and other Swiss cities. In many places, Genevan fugitives from the Black Code of 1782 fed the agitation, while democratic elements in Geneva itself nurtured their resentment and their plans, after the fashion of similar groups in Holland and Belgium. At the opposite extreme, the cantonal governments, supported by much of the religious peasantry, greeted news of the events in Paris with mounting consternation; and when the French Republic was proclaimed in 1792, the Swiss Federal Diet refused to grant it diplomatic recognition. Only France's distractions elsewhere postponed for the time being a military showdown.

The regional diversity of Italian responses was fully comparable to that encountered in Germany. The king of Sardinia, father-in-law to both of Louis XVI's brothers, quickly offered the larger towns of Savoy as asylums for French royalist émigrés – and incidentally, by so doing appears to have made the resentful inhabitants more friendly towards the Revolution than they might otherwise have been. In Tuscany, at the other extreme, both Grand Duke Peter Leopold (who did not begin to fear the new situation until after his accession as Holy Roman emperor in 1790) and the court councillor, Manfredini, were outspoken admirers of the experiments taking place in France. In the Papal States, as well as in Naples and Lombardy, official reactions to those same experiments were blankly hostile and the public reaction, largely uninformed. Throughout most of Italy, in fact, including the relatively cosmopolitan republics of Venice and Genoa, judgements of French affairs, whether favourable or the opposite, were for several years restricted to a tiny minority of officials, scholars and journalists.

If this was true of Italy, how general an awareness could one expect to find in Spain, long ruled by a powerful and autocratic monarchy? In September 1789, the coronation of the new king, Charles IV, at Madrid was marked by an absence of references to contemporary affairs in France not wholly attributable to tightened governmental censorship. With almost reverent approval, the Prussian minister wrote to Berlin: 'The Spanish people are good, noble and peaceable.'[3] Simultaneously, the highest legislative body in Spain, the Cortes of Castile, opened a two-month session which produced absolutely no challenge to royal authority. However apprehensive the chief minister of state, Floridablanca, may have been about revolutionary contagion – he took the trouble to have the Inquisition ban all foreign newspapers – the general public showed no enthusiasm for the godless innovators north of the Pyrenees.

Apart from a few shortlived political clubs in Portugal, the only source of potential sympathy for the new France within the Iberian countries consisted of a handful of veteran reform ministers of Spain's late Charles III. Not even these men, however, became as excited over the fall of the Bastille and the Declaration of the Rights of Man as did Fox in England or Grand Duke Leopold in Tuscany. The principal minister Floridablanca himself seemed initally to see no need for any repudiation of Spain's own commitment to enlightened despotism, assuming that foreign influences were carefully excluded. Nevertheless, as the new king became more hostile to a French government which had, among other things, betrayed the Family Compact in the Nootka Sound dispute (*see above*, p. 120), his distrust of reform-minded administrators became more marked. In 1791 Campomanes were unceremoniously dismissed from membership in the Council of Castile, and shortly thereafter Jovellanos was exiled to his native province on the Bay of Biscay. One of Burke's shrewdest insights, to wit, that the Revolution would make harder the lot of moderate reformers everywhere, was confirmed in Spain, as in many other lands.

Farther from its centre, the initial shock of the western European crisis tended to be less profound. Poland's historic Four-year Diet completed a draft constitution at roughly the same time as did the National Assembly in Paris; but the Polish document, as we have seen, owed much more to British and American models than to that of Revolutionary France. While a Czartoryski or a Kollontay might admire French patriots, Polish conservatives certainly did not; and King Stanislaw came increasingly to share their misgivings. Poland, after all, was racing to overcome threats peculiar to its own position, not to take part in an international revolution.

Austria produced a few enthusiasts. The poet Johann von Alxinger reacted like many of his north German counterparts; and Joseph II's old minister, Baron Joseph von Sonnenfels, until long after his country was at war with France, clung to views closely resembling those of Fox in England. The bulk of the ruling class, however, was anxious to see that the autocratic reform programme of the late 'revolutionary emperor' did not return under a democratic disguise; and his successor, Leopold II, was until his own death in 1792 deeply apprehensive concerning doctrinaire agitation in his sprawling dominions. Leopold's fears were scarcely borne out by any mass excitement on the part of either Austrian or Bohemian commoners. Only in Hungary – where old claims for national autonomy, for the official use of the Magyar tongue and for Protestant emancipation all became entangled with issues being raised in French terms – did a real crisis show signs of persisting despite the pacification of 1790.

Reactions in other parts of the Continent naturally varied with each local situation. In Denmark a remarkably popular reform administration already held power under Crown Prince Frederick (regent for his father, Christian VII, who had been declared insane in 1784). In Turkish-occupied Serbia, on the other hand, and still more in Greece, the heady news from Paris set small groups of literate radicals to talking heatedly, if for the moment ineffectually, about independence from the Ottoman Empire, itself agitated after 1789 by the administrative reform projects of the new Sultan Selim III.[4] Sweden's autocratic ruler, Gustav III, despite having subdued his own nobility in 1789, roundly condemned the calling of the French Estates General and went on to denounce the National Assembly in still stronger terms. First among European rulers, he proposed a general crusade against revolutionary France. Ironically, only his murder by a Swedish nobleman in 1792 prevented this anti-aristocratic reformer from seeking allies for a great campaign whose chief beneficiaries, had it succeeded, would have been the old privileged orders of France!

As for Russia, the ageing Catherine II, having granted much to the nobles of her own realm, while maintaining an unwaveringly autocratic stance, could lay claim to somewhat greater consistency than Gustav III in flatly denouncing the revolutionary changes in France. Like the pope, she almost immediately condemned the National Assembly and all its works; and by the time her *Memoir on the French Revolution* appeared in 1792, she too was talking of a league of monarchs to save Louis XVI. A handful of her highest-born subjects showed a fleeting sympathy for the French experiment, but many more shared their tsarina's horror. The great mass of Russian subjects, if we may judge from contemporary accounts, had little knowledge and less understanding of what was occurring in western Europe.

REVOLUTIONARY FRANCE AT WAR

Who started the long war that from 1792 onward pitted France against much of the rest of Europe? Many parties, for many different reasons. In Paris the king appears to have believed that war would *force* other powers to scatter his domestic enemies as a prelude to treating with him in the old way. Marie Antoinette confidently assured her imperial brother in Vienna that the revolutionaries would prove both disorganized and cowardly. Noblemen such as the Count de Narbonne, named war minister in December 1791, and the Marquis de Lafayette, who was initially in command of over half the French land forces, saw an international crisis, even after the flight to Varennes, as an occasion for reviving aristocratic leadership. Roland, Brissot, Dumouriez and their fellow Girondins, convinced of the political advantages to be gained by war, accepted what turned out to be a fatal alliance with courtiers of the doomed monarchy. Only Robespierre and certain other Jacobins at first denounced this 'betrayal' and the diversion from the Legislative Assembly's proper tasks they were sure would follow from it.

On the other side, it must be said that Austria and Prussia, while ostensibly seeking only to protect the rights of the French ruler, of the pope and of German princes who had lost fiefs in Alsace, moved by stages to direct intervention against the Revolution as such. In this regard, the death of the pacific Emperor Leopold II early in 1792 proved decisive. Thereafter, despite the cautious tone of their earlier pronouncements and their obvious concern over the Polish situation, the German powers hardened in their intent to attack France. Hence the Legislative Assembly's declaration of war against Austria on 20 April – the first of a long series – was perhaps more justified than Robespierre was willing to admit at the time.

What was not justified was the blithe self-assurance with which the Girondin–court coalition approached the test of arms. We have noted earlier the disruption of the French military establishment resulting from emigration and reforms aimed at its hasty 'democratization'; yet the Assembly was assured that 300,000 men stood prepared to hurl back the enemy. Instead, fully four months after war was declared, and after Prussia had joined its unfamiliar Austrian ally, French forces numbered fewer than 80,000 men stretched along the entire frontier from the Channel to Switzerland. Fully half of the officers on active service in 1789 had already left the country. Before the war was more than a few weeks old, Dumouriez's plan to invade Belgium had collapsed because of poor morale and incompetent or disloyal leadership at various critical points. No fewer than three line regiments changed to the Austro-Prussian side under orders from their officers. By July, when the Allied commander, the duke of Brunswick, issued a contemptuous manifesto against the Revolution, the French appeared helpless to withstand the coming offensive.

The failure of that offensive has been variously attributed to heavy summer rains in northern France, to the inability of the Allies to concert their efforts and to an almost miraculous recovery of will power on the part of the French armies, for whom Lafayette's defection to the enemy in August symbolized the elimination of half-hearted leadership. No doubt the weather did delay the Germans' advance. The Allies, for their part, did not exploit very effectively such victories as the capture of Verdun in early September. And it seems clear that French troops had gained some seasoning by the time the energetic Dumouriez took charge in the field. On 20 September Brunswick's army, pushing westward into Champagne from Verdun, encountered a large French force encamped on a fog-covered hill at Valmy. The artillery exchange was heavy, the infantry fighting very light; but once it was clear that the previously unreliable French regiments were holding firm, the Allies first broke off the attack, then went into a mystifyingly swift retreat.

The 'miracle of Valmy' was a tribute to unexpectedly stout defence. During the ensuing six weeks, however, with Custine's pursuit of the Prussians into the Rhineland, Dumouriez's long-cherished invasion of Belgium after his victory at Jemappes in November and the French occupation of Nice and Savoy at the king of Sardinia's expense, the Revolution for the first time passed to the offensive. It was unable to maintain this momentum indefinitely, especially after Britain, Holland and Spain entered the war in the spring of 1793. Yet despite the loss of Brussels, Mainz, Alsace and Toulon to foreign foes, combined with widespread anti-Jacobin revolts at home, the Republic fought for its life with a grim desperation having nothing to do with the spirit in which the Girondin–royalist ministry had entered the war. By the end of the year, the ruthless discipline imposed by Robespierre's regime and the success of Carnot in marshalling new resources through the *levée en masse* had stiffened the armies once more. In December, the Allies left Alsace and retreated again across the Rhine.

What was then beginning, though no one could have been sure of it at the time, was a two-year period of French victories. The Republic's forces, steadily replenished with recruits, maintained heavy pressure on all fronts. During 1794 Pichegru's defeat of the British at Tourcoing in April and Jourdan's and Kléber's of the Austrians at Fleurus in June once again opened the Low Countries to invasion. Belgium was cleared of Allied forces; and by January

1795 Pichegru's veterans entered Amsterdam while Stadtholder William fled to England. At the same time Jourdan had wheeled about and was sweeping south-east through the German Rhineland, taking Coblenz, Cologne and Mainz on the left (i.e. west) bank, then Mannheim on the great river's opposite side. Simultaneous victories over the Spanish in Catalonia and on the Biscayan coast were matched by continued onslaughts against the Austrians and Sardinians in northern Italy. It took Hoche and his Army of the West less than one month to crush the ill-conceived English effort in June 1795 to support the Chouan rebels by landing an army of émigrés on the coast of Brittany.

By that time the First Coalition was clearly falling apart. Under the terms of the treaty signed at Basel on 5 March 1795, the Prussians, discouraged about the western front and eager to concentrate on Poland, had withdrawn from the war, confirming as they did so French possession of the entire left bank of the Rhine. Several other north German states followed suit. In July, also at Basel, Spain made peace, ceding France San Domingo in the West Indies. In December, on both the Alsatian and the Italian fronts, the Austrians concluded local cease fires with the all-conquering Republic, though Vienna, like London, insisted that the general struggle must go on.

THE FINAL PARTITION OF POLAND

It may be well to pause for a reminder that, even in the 1790s, not all the issues confronting the European state system centred around revolutionary France. Prussia and Austria went on bargaining over possible annexations and exchanges of territory: the Netherlands, Bavaria, Bohemia and perhaps – here the French war did impinge – the lost province of Alsace, assuming it could be reconquered. The Russian–Turkish duel and the struggle in the Baltic area still made incessant demands on the attention of eastern capitals. For that matter, they also involved London, at least until March 1791, when Pitt's effort to make England the sponsor of a Swedish–Prussian–Polish–Turkish coalition to restrain Russia foundered on the suspicious isolationism of a majority of the House of Commons. Beyond question, however, the most important non-French focus of concern was the ill-fated constitutional monarchy of Poland.

Even before concluding peace with Turkey in the first days of 1792, Catherine II had suggested to Berlin that Prussia and Russia should ignore Austrian objections and proceed with a further division of Polish lands. Once the Turkish war ended, the tsarina turned her full attention to the problem. In March 1792, she secured Frederick William II's willing agreement to the principle that Prussia was entitled to compensate itself in Poland for the expenses of the impending war against France, and by late April, the Confederation of Targowice, a league of reactionary Polish nobles, had been formed under her sponsorship – its formal compact was actually signed at St Petersburg. On 18 May over 100,000 Russian troops, ostensibly answering the appeal of Poland's own aristocracy, launched a full-scale invasion. For two months, King Stanislaw and his generals, including the American war hero, Kosciuszko, led a brave and, it appeared for a time, not entirely hopeless defence. Then the king's determination simply melted. Abjectly, he rescinded the Constitution of 1791 and awaited the pleasure of Russia and its Prussian ally. Austrian hopes that England might join in opposing a second partition of Poland, which in Vienna's eyes represented dangerous aggrandisement for two major rivals, proved groundless. By the treaty of 23 January 1793 the tsarina took the rest of White Russia and a major slice of the Polish Ukraine, while Prussia received some long-coveted prizes: Danzig, Thorn and Posen (*see* Map 3).

The third partition proved to be scarcely more than an epilogue. Kosciuszko's patriotic rebels of 1794 were no match for the massive Russian forces under Suvorov. By the following spring, the Polish state had virtually disappeared as a political entity. With the Prussians disengaging themselves from the war against France, Austria no longer dared to stand aside from a final settlement. On 24 October 1795 a treaty among the three great eastern powers obliterated what was left of the Polish kingdom, Russia taking the rest of historic Lithuania and in the south, Volhynia; Prussia, the Warsaw region; Austria, all of western Galicia, including Cracow and Lublin. The death of Poland forms one of those chapters of late eighteenth-century history which must be understood as distinct from the French crisis. The two were not, however, unrelated; for it seems inconceivable that this atypically 'total' denouement in the east could have occurred had the western powers been free to intervene.

EUROPE TAKES STOCK

The year 1795, when the Convention gave way to the Directory in Paris and when many of the Revolution's foreign enemies abandoned hostilities, offers a convenient point from which to survey the changes which had been taking place in Europe. Most obvious, aside from Poland's obliteration as a sovereign state, had been the extension of French control to include a number of neighbouring areas. Belgium, invaded in 1792, evacuated the following year, retaken by Pichegru and Jourdan in 1794, became, under a decree of 1 October 1795, an integral part (nine new departments) of the Republic. To the north, the former United Provinces, after ceding a strip of border territory to French Belgium, had by this time been organized into the first of many revolutionary satellites, the Batavian Republic. The entire left bank of the Rhine, though its two 'central administrations' in Aix-la-Chapelle and Kreuznach were largely staffed by obedient Germans, was formally annexed to France. On the Alpine and Mediterranean fronts, the annexation of mountainous Savoy and the former county of Nice, first voted by the Convention in Paris as early as November 1792, would become 'definitive' by virtue of a decree of 1796. The pattern of revolutionary imperialism revealed itself more and more clearly.

Beyond the borders of this expanding France and its dependencies, other countries showed the strain of war, internal unrest and official repression. In England the first clear sign of political reaction had been the decline in parliamentary support for Charles James Fox. With the outbreak of war against France in 1793 numerous Whigs had begun to shift their allegiance to Prime Minister Pitt; and by 1794 a whole new party of Whig leaders around the duke of Portland, named home secretary that July, had joined forces with the Tories in support of the war effort.

Meanwhile, the government was treating avowed or alleged Francophiles with growing severity. From the beginning of 1793 individual arrests for sedition had been increasing in number. The following year Parliament suspended the Habeas Corpus Act (thereby authorizing detention of prisoners without trial), defined disloyal behaviour more broadly through the Treasonable Practices Act and, by passing the Seditious Meetings Act, outlawed unlicensed assemblies of more than fifty persons. The Scottish courts, led by Lord Braxfield, were particularly harsh, imprisoning or transporting to penal colonies overseas a number of persons on charges of having sought to undermine the constitution. Even in England, though thirteen accused revolutionaries – including Horne Tooke, the Corresponding Society's Thomas Hardy and John Thelwall, a co-founder of the Society of Friends of the People – escaped conviction when tried in 1794, free discussion was in danger of vanishing. The knowledge that, despite Parliament's hasty grant of voting rights to the Catholics of Ireland in 1793, Wolfe Tone and other Irish leaders were in Paris to negotiate with the French government added an element of fear to the outlook of British Tories and Whigs alike.

The government of Spain, soon after Charles IV's accession in 1788, had adopted what appear to have been unnecessarily stringent limitations on freedom of the press and public expression. As in several other Catholic countries, notably including the kingdom of Sardinia and the Austrian dominions, Spanish administrators revealed a marked tendency to identify Jacobinism with religious dissent, so that foreign residents were compelled to swear allegiance not only to the Crown but also to the Roman Church. It was the war with France, initially greeted with public enthusiasm in 1793, but increasingly unpopular as the military news from the Pyrenees became worse and worse, that first led some small groups of Spaniards to express a cautious sympathy for the Revolution. In spite of exaggerated rumours at the time, however, nothing approaching Jacobin Clubs appeared. After the ageing Aranda succeeded Floridablanca as first minister in 1792, Manuel Godoy, duke de la Alcudia and lover of the queen, became the dominant figure, destined within two years to oust Aranda altogether. Godoy, as shrewd as he was ambitious, was never popular, even after the welcome Basel agreement of 1795 earned him the resounding title, 'Prince of Peace'. But at least the Spanish monarchy had weathered its first clash with the Revolution and could now reverse its foreign policy, accepting a French military alliance without apparent fear of insurrectionary contagion.

Portugal's royal government, at war with the French since 1793, and in 1796 attacked by the Spaniards as well, hunted down radicals with extreme severity; for these were the 'years of Manique', the dreaded intendant of police. In both Italy and Germany, some states, including Tuscany in 1794 and Prussia,

Saxony and Hanover the following year, had withdrawn from the armed struggle. Others, such as Bavaria and the two Italian kingdoms of Sardinia and of Naples, still remained allies of Austria against the French Republic. But whether at war or not, all continued to feel the menace of French power and the stirring of dissatisfied elements at home. The latter, be it noted, ranged from lower-class admirers of the Jacobin sans-culottes, through businessmen impatient for the end of feudal privilege, to the sort of idealistic young aristocrats whose advanced views brought them death upon scaffolds in a dozen Italian and central European cities. Within these threatened lands, as in Switzerland, where such men as Peter Ochs in Basel looked to France to destroy the old order, an uneasy peace was maintained only by police vigilance. In Austria and Hungary conspiratorial stirrings began to be uncovered by the oppressive régime of Francis II's minister, Baron von Thugut. At Budapest, for example, in May and June 1795, seven convicted 'Jacobins' were beheaded. They included the former Franciscan monk, Martinovics; the writer, Hajnóczy, son of a Protestant pastor; the gentleman officer, Laczkovics; and the learned Count Jaco Zsigray.[5] Despite the disillusioning shock of the Terror and certain disquieting reports about occupation practices in Belgium, the Rhineland and Savoy, French armies could still rely on support from sizeable minorities almost everywhere.

There were some exceptions. The Danish government's pursuit of domestic reforms had kept even the small Jacobin Club in Copenhagen explicitly loyal to the Crown. Sweden, after the anti-revolutionary Gustav III's assassination, was administered for four years by a pro-French regent, the duke of Sudermania, under whom the Swedish press recovered its freedom to report news from Paris; but in 1796, young King Gustav IV attained his majority and promptly swung, if not quite back to his father's vehement hostility towards France, at least to an isolationist policy accepted by his subjects with scarcely a murmur. In Russia Catherine II, who never wavered in her hatred of the new French order, had the social critic, Radishchev, condemned to death in 1790 for writing his indignant *Journey from St Petersburg to Moscow* and his much more emotional *Ode to Liberty*. Although this draconian sentence was commuted to exile in Siberia, no further commentaries in Radishchev's vein were permitted to appear. Catherine refrained, it is true, from military intervention in the west, while exploiting her Polish opportunities; but at home her government prevented any organized expression of interest in the Revolution. The only republican discussions of any importance took place in absolute privacy between her grandson, the future Alexander I, and his Swiss tutor, the Francophile classicist F. C. La Harpe – and even these came to an end when La Harpe returned home in 1795. The old empress died the following year, to be succeeded by her still more violently anti-French son, Paul I, a tsar prepared to plunge at once into the struggle against the Revolution.

THE EMERGENCE OF BONAPARTE

Even before Russia became involved, that struggle had grown infinitely broader and more complicated than the warfare of the years before the Directory. In order to appreciate these changes, it is necessary to recall that by 1795 France had come through the first phase of its military crisis and had clearly recovered the initiative in the game of power politics. The Pyrenean and Flemish frontiers had been made secure, and since the treaty of Basel with Prussia, there was no fear of a major attack from northern Germany. When Carnot and his fellow directors looked about them and began to plan operations against the two principal enemies of the Republic, it was with a sense of considerable freedom in choosing the time and place to do battle.

In order to weaken England, the war of privateers would be pushed to the limit, with American help at sea if that could be obtained, while Irish rebels such as Wolfe Tone and Napper Tandy were to receive direct support through the landing of an invasion force under General Hoche. Against Austria and its allies, the directors agreed upon three massive land strikes. Jourdan and the army of the Sambre and Meuse should drive along and beyond Germany's Main River to join Moreau's army of the Rhine and Moselle pushing eastward through Baden and Württemberg for a junction in Bavaria. Meanwhile Bonaparte would advance from Nice along the Mediterranean coast, with the aim of defeating Austrian–Sardinian forces in Italy and then turning north through the Alps to take part in a coordinated assault on Vienna itself.

It was a magnificent plan, destined to be revived and adapted several times in the next ten years; but on the first application, all but one feature of it miscarried. The United States would not collaborate against England, choosing instead to engage French naval raiders in a three-year undeclared war. In December 1796 Hoche's army, transported from Brest to Bantry Bay, Ireland, was unable to reach the shore because of storms. The following year some 1,400 French troops who had landed in South Wales were promptly rounded up by the English local militia, and Humbert's small landing on the Irish coast in 1798 met no better fate. By this time the Directory's armies in Germany were painfully aware that Austria had at last found a general. Francis II's brother, Archduke Charles, defeated Jourdan at Würzburg on the Main in September 1796, then turned south to drive Moreau back through the Black Forest to the Rhine. For a number of reasons, including the unsuspected ability of the archduke and a lack of cooperation between the jealous French commanders, the northern arm of the great pincers had been broken.

Against this background, it is easy to see why Bonaparte's Italian campaign seemed so dazzling. Advancing south-east in the spring of 1796, the once ragged and discouraged army of Italy under its young general knocked the Sardinians out of the war in a matter of weeks, crushed an Austrian force at Lodi on 10 May and entered Milan five days later. On the 16th, the conquered city was proclaimed capital of a new satellite of France, the Lombard Republic. Stalled for months by the siege of Mantua, Bonaparte finally took that stubborn fortress early in February 1797 and reluctantly (since he was eager to invade Austria) yielded to orders from Paris that he march against Rome. Once satisfied by the terrified pope's cession of Bologna, the Romagna and other territories, the French commander in March wheeled his hardened troops about once more, driving northward into the Austrian Alps to engage Archduke Charles. Here he was frustrated by anti-French revolts in Venetia and the Tyrol, as well as by the failure of the French offensive in Bavaria. Nevertheless, on 18 April, barely a year after the start of Bonaparte's whirlwind campaign, the Austrians found themselves compelled to accept a truce pending final negotiations.

In the six months between this 'preliminary peace' of Leoben and the treaty of Campo-Formio, signed on 17 October 1797, the dominant figure in all these events was anything but idle. In May his army occupied Venetia, which he held as a pawn for dealings with Austria. By July he had fashioned two new satellite republics: the Ligurian, around Genoa, and the Cisalpine, comprising Lombardy, the Bolognese and the Romagna. All this Austria had to accept at Campo-Formio, where Napoleon performed the first of his many prodigies of territorial shuffling. The Habsburgs recognized French annexation of Belgium, the left bank of the Rhine and a former Venetian possession, the Ionian Islands between Italy and Greece. In return, Austria was given the city of Venice and most of its mainland territories, a promise of the archbishopric of Salzburg with a strip of southern Bavaria and the secret assurance that France would allow Prussia no territorial compensation for its losses in the Rhineland. Since this provision directly violated the terms of the treaty of Basel, signed two-and-a-half years before, while the clause touching Bavaria struck at Vienna's principal German ally, Campo-Formio could scarcely be called a model of good faith. Deceitful or not, the treaty was signed by representatives of Francis II, in his capacity not as Holy Roman emperor, but as ruler of Austria. France had still to negotiate with spokesmen for the Empire in a peace conference to be convened at Rastatt in Baden.

1798 witnessed a new series of French tours de force. Early in the year, Rome was occupied, a Roman Republic proclaimed and Pope Pius VI carried off to France, where he shortly died. Simultaneously, the Directory, at the instance of La Harpe and other Swiss exiles in Paris, as well as the Basel revolutionaries around Peter Ochs, gave formal recognition to the creation of a Helvetian Republic. French armies overran large portions of Switzerland to enforce the new order, at the same time annexing outright the previously independent city-state of Geneva. In May Bonaparte embarked from Toulon with over 30,000 troops on his dash to seize Egypt and open the road to India. Landing near Alexandria, he struck at the Mameluke forces of the Egyptian *beys* (vassals of the Turkish sultan) and on 21 July, in sight of the pyramids, he defeated them in a pitched battle. Next day, his army of the East entered Cairo. This was without question one of the high points in an astounding military career, yet the disaster that doomed the expedition occurred only a few days later. Admiral Horatio Nelson's British naval squadron, after weeks of dogged pursuit, finally overtook the French fleet in Aboukir Bay near the mouth of the Nile and on 1 August 1798 virtually destroyed it. Bonaparte himself campaigned for another year in both Egypt and Syria, then slipped back to France, leaving the army of the East under Kléber's command, to survive for as long as it could without naval support.

In Europe too, from the Directory's point of view, events had taken an alarming turn. By December 1798, while a French army was advancing into southern Italy, a new alliance against the Republic was taking form. This Second Coalition's chief members were England, Austria and Russia; for Tsar Paul was now ready to strike *his* blow, and Vienna eagerly resumed hostilities scarcely more than a year after its capitulation at Campo-Formio. Throughout most of 1799 the Allies pressed the French backward on widely separated fronts. Archduke Charles won new victories over first Jourdan and then Masséna on the upper Rhine. From April through June Suvorov's Russian veterans, with Austrian aid, drove the French out of most of northern Italy, while in the south the shortlived Parthenopean Republic was destroyed in a vengeful blood bath by the restored king of Naples. For a time the Russians seemed to be everywhere at once, contributing 17,000 troops to the British expedition against Holland, sending a naval squadron with the Turks to seize the Ionian Islands off Greece. In August Suvorov crossed the St Gotthard Pass from Italy into Switzerland, there to join another Russian force which had recently traversed the Habsburg domains from Poland.

At this point, however, the French, though still weakened by the diversion of Bonaparte's seasoned troops to Egypt, reasserted their capacity for defensive warfare close to home. The Russian–Austrian advance was halted at Zurich, and Masséna, by taking Constance in southern Germany, made an advance across the Rhine too risky for the Archduke Charles to undertake. In Holland the commanders of the British–Russian force, after months of unsuccessful manoeuvring, finally settled for an exchange of prisoners and left the mainland. By the end of October general fighting had subsided; and Paul I, angered by what he considered the bad faith of his allies, abruptly recalled his Russian expeditionary forces and withdrew from the coalition.

As the century approached its end, the military situation, viewed from Paris, justified a renewal of confidence. The newborn Consulate had inherited some dangers, to be sure. Especially in Italy, where Genoa was for the moment the only major base under revolutionary France's red, white and blue flag, the Tricolour, another series of victories would be necessary to restore the situation. In Egypt the army Bonaparte had abandoned in order to become first consul fought on without hope of anything better than a negotiated withdrawal. British sea power continued to claw at French trade and communications, while the collapse of the Rastatt Congress early in 1799 meant that the Holy Roman Empire of German states still did not recognize French conquests. On the other hand, the 'natural frontiers' of France – Rhine, Alps, Pyrenees – appeared secure, the first two made so by annexations, the third by the Spanish alliance. Important buffers such as the Batavian and Helvetian Republics had not been wrested from French control, despite strenuous efforts by the Allies. Russia, Prussia and Sweden, meanwhile, were moving towards a new League of Armed Neutrality, at least as disadvantageous to Great Britain as to France. Under the circumstances, First Consul Bonaparte could choose his own battlegrounds, much as the directors had done in 1795.

FRANCE AND ITS CONQUESTS

Let us now try to arrive at some general estimate of Europe's relations with revolutionary France on the eve of the Napoleonic adventure. Two of the aspects involved, political echoes in various countries and military hostilities, we have followed in alternating sequence through the decade ending in 1799. Still another factor, however, must also be taken into account, because of its powerful influence on foreign attitudes towards the Republic. This is the record of the French in territories which came under their control as a result of military action.

The picture is far from simple, not only because there were substantial differences between the revolutionary conquerors of 1793–94, for example, and those of 1796–98, but also because at any given time a wide variety of policies were being pursued in separate regions. Certain areas, of course, after varying periods of exploitation were incorporated into the *Grande Nation*: Avignon (1791), Belgium (1795), Nice and Savoy (1796), Geneva and the former free city of Mulhouse in Alsace (1798). The left-bank Rhineland, annexed but not fully integrated, remained under what amounted to continuing military occupation. Other areas, Dutch,

Swiss and Italian, submitted to the organization of satellite republics under constitutions worked out by local admirers of the Revolution, with the peremptory advice of French officials.

Practically everywhere they went, from Amsterdam to Mainz and from Basel to Naples, the armies of France could count on immediate support from critics of the Old Régime in each locality. Some of those who hailed the invaders as liberators were, as earlier noted, individuals educated to demand reform under the aegis of the Enlightenment. Others had belonged to revolutionary clubs which stepped forward to claim political power once the French arrived. There is no question that in encouraging these elements, often reinforced by the return of former democratic exiles, the occupation authorities created a situation which made possible an unattractive settling of personal scores. A newly erected guillotine in Brussels or Geneva could not fail to excite both fear and disgust among established social groups. In addition, the conquerors often imposed constitutional reforms which, although reasonable enough in themselves, struck many of their intended beneficiaries as unnatural importations from abroad. If certain arrangements, notably the creation of neat geographical districts on the model of *départements*, had lasting effects all the way from Holland to the Ionian Islands, many others, including reorganized judicial systems, proved viable only so long as the French forces were on hand to enforce them. This mixture of artificial support for radical minorities and doctrinaire insistence on historically rootless institutional reforms created an impression that Jacobinism bloomed under the Tricolour – even after France had thrown its own Jacobins out of power in 1794.

The religious policies of the Republic in occupied or satellite areas have been the subject of considerable misunderstanding. It is natural to assume, for instance, that a France which had confiscated the Church's property at home *must* have been consistently and violently anti-Catholic everywhere its legions marched. A natural assumption, however, is not necessarily an accurate one. The fact is that in only two of the conquered territories, Belgium and Rhenish Germany, did the Roman Church suffer any sustained pillaging of its belongings or mistreatment of its clergy. The erstwhile Austrian Netherlands were invaded first in 1792 and again in 1794, precisely when the two most extreme outbursts of anti-clericalism were taking place in France itself. Yet even here, in both Flemish and Walloon (French-speaking) provinces, the

Convention's decision in 1795 to insist upon the separation of Church and State seems actually to have brought an easing of tension, however unhappy some Belgian Catholics may have felt over the equality accorded Protestants and Jews. Catholic principalities in the Rhineland also witnessed numerous acts of confiscation; but the priests of this region – as distinct from the bishops and other prelates, practically all of whom had fled – suffered much less than their stubborn resistance to the new order would have led one to expect. In Italy the cautious approach of General Bonaparte is particularly striking; for in the big Cisalpine Republic he demanded nothing more than freedom for religious minorities, and elsewhere he did not challenge the dominant position of Catholicism to even that limited degree. It should be added that his solicitude for Muslim sensibilities when he invaded Egypt revealed this same reluctance to outrage subject populations over questions of faith.

In general, of course, the Revolution did bring with it relief for Protestants and Jews in occupied states. For example, 1797 saw the ghetto gates of Venice and several other Italian cities destroyed in formal ceremonies. A further point which merits some attention is the liberalizing effect of French occupation on *non-Catholic* ruling groups – for bigotry and intolerance had not been monopolies of the Roman Church. The Dutch, for all their vaunted toleration, had excluded Jews and Catholics from many key positions. The Batavian Republic, on the other hand, became the satellite state whose degree of religious equality most nearly matched that of its patron, revolutionary France. Protestant states in Germany west of the Rhine and Protestant cantons in Switzerland also had to extend religious freedom to Catholic and Jewish citizens. In the Ionian Islands it was not the wish to see an end to persecution of religious groups that assured the Russians such a warm welcome in 1799, but rather the resentment of the Eastern Orthodox majority against the equality granted Catholics and Jews during the two-year French occupation.

Political favouritism, constitutional innovations and anti-denominational religious policies all made France some enemies, of course. At the same time, these features of occupied or satellite status attracted the support of important local groups. The general impression made by French conquerors might have been more positive, therefore, and their place in the historical memory of a number of other countries considerably higher, had another factor not come to assume overshadowing importance. This was the conquerors' increasing reliance on material exactions, including both military requisitions for use in the field and financial tribute to be sent to Paris. A sober analysis of the subject fixes the total monetary value of such demands for the eight years, 1792 to 1799, at a figure equivalent to slightly more than one-half the French government's average budget for *one* of those years or about 6 per cent of the Republic's revenues from all sources.[6] Expressed thus, the amount involved does not appear crushing. However, the constant demands of the armies and the seeming avarice of the Directory contrasted mockingly with the Republic's gospel of fraternity and a better life for all men everywhere. Bear in mind as well the inequities arising from uneven distribution of the burden among various localities. At specific times and in particular places, the exactions were unquestionably onerous. Finally, they were imposed with little warning, often in arrogant terms which led many an erstwhile friend of the Revolution to complain that the French had come as liberators, only to stay as rapacious invaders.

From the autumn of 1792, when Dumouriez entered Belgium and ordered Tournai to supply his troops with 12,000 rations of bread per day, 6,000 pounds of meat and large quantities of fodder, to be paid for later in assignats, the roll of requisitions and tributes grew steadily longer. Belgium was released from the status of a conquered country when it was annexed by France in 1795; but that same year the new Batavian Republic to the north was assessed, for the cost of maintaining 25,000 French troops, the sum of 10 million *florins* annually until further notice, plus an impossible indemnity of 100 million for hostile acts committed by the previous Dutch government. About 50 million florins were actually collected over the course of the next two years. (By 1797, it should be added, the continuing Dutch contribution had been scaled down to the more realistic figure of 3 million per year in wartime.) In the German Rhineland, meanwhile, though precise computations are impossible, the level of requisitions remained high. Before launching his drive eastward in the spring of 1796, for instance, Jourdan collected 13,000 metric tons of various cereal grains, huge supplies of meat and one-thirtieth of the civilian-owned horses in his sector of the left bank.

As for Italy, most systematically plundered of all the occupied territories, it has been estimated that by the end of July 1796 over

53 million *lire*, then interchangeable at par with French *livres*, had been assessed against Italian states occupied or threatened by Bonaparte. Of that sum, 32 million had been collected and perhaps 15 million already shipped to France in an effort to buttress the Directory's new currency, the silver *franc*. A formal treaty with the young Cisalpine Republic, signed early in 1798, provided for a yearly tribute of 18 million lire, to be paid in monthly instalments. The same year, the treasures of Switzerland were opened to the Helvetian Republic's French 'brothers', and Masséna promptly extorted 800,000 francs apiece from Zurich and Basel. Even the Francophile La Harpe could not hide his consternation.

REACTIONS ELSEWHERE IN EUROPE

Disillusionment with the Revolution on the part of many elements within the geographical limits of French control was matched by shifts of attitude outside those limits. The Terror, the aggressiveness of the French armies and their behaviour in occupied areas, especially when exaggerated by hostile reports, all contributed to the change. There is evidence, for example, that well before Hoche sailed for Bantry Bay in 1796 many Irish rebels, who yielded none of their hatred of the English on this account, had begun to question the benefits of help from an 'atheistic republic'. The following year Tyroleans fought Bonaparte in the Alps with a fervour which temporarily replaced their longstanding grievances against the Habsburgs in Vienna.

The danger of sketching this reaction too simply is that one might be misled into assuming all dissension had vanished within the borders of countries hostile to the Directory. The truth is quite different. Unrest still growled just below the surface of the restored kingdom of Naples after King Ferdinand had overthrown the Parthenopean Republic. In Austria, Bohemia and, above all, Hungary, signs of resentment against Thugut and his police methods were if anything increasing. Most of the German states maintained their nervous measures of surveillance and repression, inevitably accompanied by popular complaints. But at the end of the 1790s, none of these quarrels involved such explicit admiration for or rejection of the *French* model as had dominated most local confrontations only a few years before.

This phenomenon of continuing tension in a changing context was nowhere more striking than in the British Isles. Early in 1798 fighting broke out in Ireland between the English army and rebel forces containing not only Protestants but also growing numbers of resentful Catholics. Pitched battles were fought by these United Irishmen at Wexford, Ballinahinch, Vinegar Hill, while the reciprocal slaughter of prisoners introduced an element of savagery unknown on the island for several generations past. With no firm assurance of French aid and no widespread belief in its desirability, the rebels gambled on victory in their own cause. They failed miserably. Fresh royal forces under the new viceroy, Lord Cornwallis, crushed the United Irishmen, captured the small French landing party under Humbert and arrested Wolfe Tone, who had come ashore with it. (He killed himself in jail after having been convicted of treason.) Yet neither the Catholic emancipation of 1793 nor the military victories of 1798 had brought Pitt's government closer to a solution of the Irish question. Within three years the prime minister was to try a very different expedient: the full political union of Ireland with England, Scotland and Wales.

In England itself the behaviour of the revolutionary clubs reflected ever more strongly both disillusionment with events in France and fear of prosecution for sedition. The House of Commons, it is true, under Fox and his younger collaborator, Charles Grey, resumed debates over parliamentary reform in 1796; but in the face of Pitt's stubborn insistence that this was no time for constitutional tinkering, Grey's Reform Bill lost in 1797 by a vote of 256 to 91. The response of Foxite Whigs expressed the temper of their time – they simply withdrew from active political life, beginning the long interruption in liberal pressure for change. Meanwhile, the government moved to tighten still further the bonds of political discipline. Naval mutinies at the Nore and Spithead in 1797, though alarming in themselves, had no apparent link with pro-Jacobin feeling, the sailors being motivated instead by their own bitterness over low pay, poor quarters and lack of medical care. The Tory ministry, however, was taking no chances with any type of opposition. In 1799, despite the Corresponding Society's prudent discussion the previous year of an enlistment of volunteers to help fend off any French invasion, that body and several other clubs were suppressed by law. At the same time, Parliament passed the first of a series of Combination Acts against organizations which were seeking to promote higher wages and shorter hours for labour.

The shift of emphasis from the fear of a French landing to that of indigenous rebellion in Ireland was thus matched in England by a swing from primarily anti-Jacobin to more specifically anti-labour and anti-reformist measures. These changes, like related ones occurring in Germany, the Habsburg lands and Italy, were extremely important. Political, social and economic unrest had by no means disappeared in countries threatened by France. But a transformation in the way such unrest expressed itself had occurred during the decade of turmoil we have been following.

The French Revolution began amid excited applause from Whig reformers in Britain, supporters of the Josephine programme in Austria and the men around Grand Duke Leopold in Tuscany, not to mention the democrats of Holland and Belgium, the Germanies and Switzerland. Down to 1792, principles enunciated from Paris had exercised a strong appeal over wide areas of Europe. With the coming of war and the Terror, this identification of progress with Francophilia began to evaporate. After Thermidor, the Directory's apparent opportunism at home and rapacity abroad damaged still further the image of France as the 'homeland of all who love freedom'. When the century ended it was possible for an Englishman, a Neapolitan or a Transylvanian to feel highly critical of the government under which he or she lived, yet support that government against the French national enemy.

Up to a point this could be taken to mean that 'the Revolution' had already been assimilated as a shared experience and that no single country was any longer its sole sponsor. The issues of 1789 and 1791 – to say nothing of 1793–94 – in France were destined to become part of a spreading European debate, subject to diverse formulations in different lands. For the time being, however, the military crisis was blanketing these issues, making identification with the Revolution more and more unpopular as the intensity of conflict with France increased. By 1799 war had become the dominant theme of European life. At just this point the rulers of France installed a dictator who would discipline the Revolution at home, while extending the war over distances unparalled since the days of Genghis Khan.

NOTES AND REFERENCES

1 D. Greer, *The Incidence of the Emigration during the French Revolution* (Cambridge, Mass., 1951).

2 S. Schama, *Patriots and Liberators* (New York, 1977), p. 143.

3 Quoted by R. Herr, *The Eighteenth-century Revolution in Spain* (Princeton, 1958), p. 241.

4 B. Lewis, 'The impact of the French Revolution on Turkey', *Journal of World History*, vol. I (1953).

5 C. Benda, 'Les jacobins hongrois', *Annales historiques de la Révolution française*, vol. XXXI (1959).

6 Godechot, *La Grande Nation*, p. 565. Illustrative figures given in the ensuing paragraph are also derived from Chapter XVI of this work.

8

BONAPARTE FROM CONSUL TO EMPEROR

NAPOLEON THE MAN

At the end of 1799 the soldier who had become first consul of the French Republic was thirty years old. Born the son of a minor nobleman on the island of Corsica, shortly after it had been sold by Genoa to France, he was christened Napoleone Buonaparte; but at the age of ten, upon crossing to the mainland and entering the military academy of Brienne, France, he adopted the French spelling of his name. Commissioned a lieutenant in 1785, he began what promised to be a routine army career; but the events of 1789 changed all that. Over the next four years he alternated between active duty with his regiment and pro-French agitation in Corsica during several home leaves. Then, in September 1793, having attracted the favourable attention of the Committee of Public Safety by writing a strongly pro-Jacobin pamphlet, *Le Souper de Beaucaire*, he was promoted to the rank of captain and placed in command of the artillery facing rebellious Toulon. In capturing the great port from the royalists and their allies, Bonaparte won his first victory for the Revolution and with it the rank of brigadier general.

He still had far to go, however, on the uncertain road to power. Arrested in the Thermidorean reaction after Robespierre's fall in 1794, the young officer spent a month in jail, then was released and ordered to prepare what proved to be an abortive expedition against the Corsican separatist régime. British naval forces posed a serious threat to any such project, but it seems to have been Bonaparte's own mixture of political curiosity and calculation that made him find excuses for staying around Paris all through the following year. Hence, in October 1795, he was on hand to supply the 'whiff of grapeshot' needed to scatter the royalist insurgents in the Rue Saint-Honoré. The expiring Convention and the Directory after it shared a natural interest in this energetic tactician, who was shortly named commander of the Army of the Interior and then, in 1796, of the 30,000 discouraged troops who at last, under its new commander, set out to justify its grandiose title: the Army of Italy. We have already followed his rise during the years of the brilliant first Italian campaign, the thrust at Egypt, the hasty return to France and the overthrow of the Directory on the Eighteenth and Nineteenth Brumaire.

Behold this thirty-year-old Corsican immigrant, become first citizen of the mighty and mercurial nation that had slain Louis XVI, Danton and Robespierre in turn and driven out Dumouriez, Lafayette and Carnot! Yet the most amazing portions of his career still lay ahead. Victorious maker of peace and the Concordat of 1801, consul-for-life in 1802, emperor of the French in 1804, victor over the two rival emperors, Austrian and Russian, at Austerlitz the following year and then over the once dreaded Prussian army at Jena in 1806, Napoleon at Tilsit would unfold before the tsar his plan for a new European order. Invader of Spain in 1808, in 1810 husband of the Habsburg emperor's own daughter, leader of the Grand Army's gigantic assault upon Russia in 1812, the one-time artillery lieutenant would at last meet defeat on a narrowing spiral of fronts: Russia, Germany, Spain, southern France and finally the Seine itself. Exiled to Elba in 1814, back to try one more throw of the dice during the next year's 'Hundred Days', defeated at Waterloo, exiled this time to St Helena in the South Atlantic, he would spend the last six years of his life creating the material and sketching the scenario for the Napoleonic legend. It was the legend of a Promethean hero, as he saw himself, chained to a rock by the gods he had defied – and more immediately, according to his version, by the human tyrants he had challenged.

Let us pass over the legend in favour of the history of Napoleon, as accurately reconstructed as the limits of knowledge and space will permit. For detractors no less than for admirers, that history has exercised an inexhaustible fascination, partly because of its implications for the later experience of all the European peoples, but partly too because of its own dramatic form. No other career in modern history seems to embody quite so strikingly the dynamism of what Oswald Spengler was to call 'Faustian man' – tireless in his activity, at once intelligent and amoral in his choice of means, ruthless in his egoistic will to power. Thus, the personality of the first consul of 1799 is uncommonly significant for an understanding of the hectic decade-and-a-half we still refer to by his name.

The pale, arresting countenance, with its luminous eyes, sharp nose and tight-drawn mouth above a deceptively soft, dimpled chin, is known to us from countless portraits. In an age which saw many elaborate coiffures even for men, Napoleon brushed his hair smooth. That feature, combined with the clean-shaven face he chose over the mustachioed bravado of his own Imperial Guardsmen, only added to the classic severity of his appearance. He was short of stature and, from his late thirties onward, increasingly thickset. It should be added, however, that in his time a height of barely five feet was less likely to be seen as a physical disadvantage than it might today.

To reach a confident judgement about his mind is not easy. He was a rapid, voracious, but highly selective reader, preferring history to abstract philosophy, caring little for *belles lettres* as such, despite his not very convincing expressions of admiration for the counterfeit Scottish folk poetry of Ossian. He could be articulate, even eloquent in his own writing; and his published battle reports, as well as the much-quoted orders of the day addressed to his troops, played no small part in advancing his political fortunes. As a speaker, he was effective in presiding over commissions and small councils. Yet he could become strangely tongue-tied before large audiences, as when he faced the Five Hundred in 1799 – and having failed to move the legislators with haltingly delivered arguments, had to resort to military force instead. On balance, however, no other great general known to history, save Julius Caesar, has possessed such . verbal facility. Combined with a powerful memory and a gift for selecting the relevant detail, those skills made Napoleon an effective administrator and diplomat.

Certain of his other traits are either baffling or distinctly unpleasant to contemplate. His lavish treatment of relatives – he made kings or princes of four brothers and three brothers-in-law – bespoke a stubborn refusal to admit their marvellously consistent incompetence, a refusal difficult to reconcile with his generally cold-blooded insistence on efficiency. It seems scarcely plausible that in his vanity he assumed that there must be great abilities in everyone related to him, even by marriage. The traditional clan allegiance of Corsica may come closer to supplying an explanation, but some element of mystery remains.[1]

More easily understood, though less sympathetic, was Napoleon's contempt for the highest among human motives: generosity, devotion to an ideal, self-sacrifice, respect for the truth as near as one may see the truth. He was willing cynically to exploit these motives in people whenever the opportunity arose; but there were others – self-esteem, fear, greed, lust – on which he preferred to base his calculations. He was no monster of personal cruelty, as some kings and dictators have been; but he was indifferent to the suffering of individuals or of entire armies. Other men were pawns to be sacrificed, or obstacles to be crushed without pity, all according to the dictates of his literally boundless ambition, the projection of an admittedly remarkable ego.

One thing else was Napoleon: a liar, sometimes calculating and sometimes self-deceived. He often dissembled quite consciously, leaving unblinkable evidence of mendacity in his written instructions to subordinates and in his characteristic disavowals of unpopular acts which were in fact his responsibility but the blame for which he let devolve upon underlings. To object that self-interest and 'reason of state' have made many other men behave in a similar fashion does not alter the case. It is difficult to imagine that anyone with whom Napoleon ever dealt, in any capacity, would have been justified in trusting him completely.

In addition, as already remarked, he suffered from that standard malady of the vain, namely, self-deception. He appears at times to have believed absolutely preposterous things about the nobility of his own motives. During the last half-dozen years of his life, when from St Helena he lectured posterity on his inspired battle against tyranny, he often achieved a tone of real conviction in the apologetic fiction he was writing in the form of memoirs.

His relations with women were no less suffused with false piety. As promiscuous as most other army officers and high officials of his day, he had his share of erotic adventures, though only one, with the Polish Countess Walewska at Schloss Finckenstein in 1807, deserved to be called a love affair. The others, as a French biographer has remarked, 'smacked of the garrison'. Yet he never publicly acknowledged mistresses; and especially after he became emperor, his entourage strove to maintain a façade of petty bourgeois respectability, smugly presented as an improvement over the nonchalant sensuality of eighteenth-century court life.

A resourceful and often inspirational military leader,[2] a brilliant executive, an eloquent visionary the mere scale of whose projects captures the imagination, yet at the same time a climber, a perverter of humane values, a deceiver of others and of himself as he exploited men and women for his several purposes – what simple characterization will encompass such a being? It is equally difficult to classify Napoleon Bonaparte in terms of the various historical prototypes with which he has been compared, or with which he compared himself. Should he be seen as a latter-day Caesar, wresting unlimited authority from a republic whose armies had carried him to fame? Or ought we instead to consider him a precursor of twentieth-century dictators, claiming to divine the masses' needs by intuition and to serve them without accountability? Was he perhaps something less foreign to his eighteenth-century background, an enlightened despot like Frederick the Great or Joseph II, determined to base his own power and his subjects' prosperity upon rational estimates of the public good? Or was he after all simply an Italian adventurer, a *condottiere* displaced from the Renaissance with a stock of Machiavellian prescriptions for seizing and holding a crown? Doubtless a full picture of Napoleon must include some traits found in all these models, others characteristic of any revolutionary leader and still others peculiar to his own personality.

THE CONSTITUTION OF THE EMPIRE

Lacking the means for retrospective analysis of public opinion, no one can say with confidence to what extent Bonaparte's reorganization of the French state, his efforts to force society into a matrix of centralized order, served as a response to popular desires. His admirers naturally hail steps taken after 1799 to overcome the financial confusion, widespread brigandage, chaotic religious situation and formlessness of legal relationships they associate with the era of the Directory. His critics just as emphatically insist that he robbed Frenchmen of their liberty, offering in its place the exhilaration of martial glory, but at the same time restoring social distinctions contrary to the very spirit of the Revolution. On one point, all commentators agree, to wit, that Napoleon imposed his will upon the entire mechanism of what became his empire, if not completely – he ended, like most other dictators, by overestimating his ability to control events – at least sufficiently to have left a lasting impression of energy, ambition and intelligence.

The new political structure first took shape in the Constitution of the Year VIII, promulgated in December 1799 by two commissions created for this purpose by the Councils of Ancients and of Five Hundred. Their work, fleshed out during the ensuing months in a series of 'organic laws', was subsequently altered in the summer of 1802 by the Constitution of the Year X, after a national plebiscite had endorsed Napoleon's assumption of the title 'consul-for-life', and again by a decree of May 1804, commonly referred to as the Constitution of the Year XII, which superimposed the Empire upon the Republic. Despite this succession of documents and the evolution of Bonaparte's own position to which they corresponded, many principles were retained and amplified from 1799 down to the Empire's collapse in 1814.

The pattern of executive power was one of authority dispensed downward through the ranks of the administrative hierarchy, not upward through levels of election as in the revolutionary constitutions. Napoleon, supreme war lord and ceremonial chief of state, was also, by virtue of his tireless scrutiny of governmental operations, the supreme bureaucrat. The second and third consuls of 1799, Sieyès and Roger-Ducos, were replaced by Cambacérès and Lebrun when the Constitution of the Year VIII went into effect, but none of the four ever posed as a rival to the real master of France. The ministers, including at the outset Talleyrand for foreign affairs, Lucien Bonaparte for interior, Fouché for police and several less prominent figures, formed no cabinet and were individually responsible to the Council of State. This body, in turn, was under Napoleon's direct control. It was, in fact, his favourite instrument for deliberation and policy-making. Here sat the men whose judgement interested him most, twenty-nine of them in 1799, always thirty-five or more after 1805, as many as forty-six by 1811, divided into five working sections: war, navy, interior, legislation and finance. They included lawyers and judges, veteran administrators, scholars and generals, some of them returned émigrés, others convinced republicans, but no Jacobin extremists and no nostalgic adherents of the Bourbon monarchy.

The same preference for efficient technicians of not too pronounced political views was apparent in the recruitment of prefects. Handsomely uniformed in their silver-trimmed blue jackets and white trousers or breeches, surrounded by considerable pomp in their own right, charged with wide-ranging responsibilities and endowed with great authority in their respective *départmentes*, these regional officials were nonetheless kept fully aware of their dependence on the minister of interior, who nominated them, and on Napoleon, who appointed and could at any time remove them. Nowhere was the autocratic nature of the régime more apparent than in the direction from above to which the prefects were subject, instead of being accountable to the departmental councils as in the 1790s. The councils remained in place, but were henceforth assigned only an advisory role.

Just as ministers, councillors of state and prefects were subordinated to the will of Bonaparte, so too were the three branches of the national legislature. The Senate was composed of sixty (later eighty) men, initially selected by the consuls in 1800, but thereafter supposedly kept up to strength by co-optation. In theory, that is, the incumbent senators themselves filled each vacancy by electing a new colleague for life. In fact, however, every such choice was made under the close surveillance of the first consul. Many distinguished Frenchmen were so honoured – generals such as Kellermann, for example, and scientists including Laplace and Berthollet – but their vague mandate to uphold conservative interests should not be confused with real power to make laws.

The Legislative Chamber (*Corps Législatif*), whose 300 members were elected for five-year terms by the Senate, was purposely made junior to that body. The minimum age for senators was forty, while legislators could be as young as thirty; and individual salaries were fixed at only 10,000 francs for the latter, as opposed to 25,000 for the former. Nearly all those elected to the Chamber in 1800–277 out of the first 300 – were veterans of earlier assemblies; but shrewd observers noted that experience had left most of them not so much self-confident as wearily cynical and exceedingly cautious. Renewed at a rate of sixty members chosen each year thereafter, the body remained an almost invariably obedient sounding board for Napoleon's projects. It had no right to initiate legislation, instead being restricted to the formal enactment of laws submitted to it by the government and discussed, supposedly in critical terms, by orators designated by the Tribunate.

This third arm of the Napoleonic legislative mechanism was grandly described in the Constitution of the Year VIII as the voice of 'national representation'. Yet a tribune was elected to his five-year term by the Senate, scarcely a representative body in any broad meaning of the term. He need have reached only the age of twenty-five but had to be drawn from the list of 6,000 national 'notables' (later 'electors'). Of the original 100 tribunes, nearly two-thirds had been members of the Ancients or the Five Hundred before 1799. A few of them, including the writer Benjamin Constant, began by trying to defeat certain bills before the Legislative Chamber, only to discover that they were risking disgrace, or worse, if they took too seriously their duty as critics. The first consul, as a matter of fact, never expressed any genuine enthusiasm for the Tribunate, despite its rapidly acquired docility. In 1802, he reduced its membership by half, announcing that the remaining fifty would henceforth confine their activities to the unpublicized discussion of decisions reached by the Council of State.

The conception of 'notables', just mentioned in connection with the recruitment of tribunes, deserves a word of separate comment, for it is characteristic of the precautions written into the Constitution of the Year VIII in 1799 to counteract any tendency towards participatory democracy. The French electorate remained very broad in appearance, including as it did all adult males who were not domestic servants and who had resided in the same district for at least one year. However, the voters of a locality chose just 10 per cent of their number as communal notables, who in turn elected 10 per cent of *their* group to the list of departmental notables. The latter than picked a final 10 per cent of their membership to be national notables, subject to review by the Senate. At each level, communal, departmental and national, both government officials and recipients of various ceremonial honours could be named only from the appropriate list of notables. The fact that men of some wealth and education tended to dominate these lists showed how far France had moved away from the era when radical *sans-culottes* had swept the administration before them.

Hand in hand with this carefully regulated selection of legislative and administrative personnel went a further tightening of the central government's hold on judicial institutions. A law of February 1800 suppressed the elective principle for all judges except the purely local justices of the peace. Hereafter, members of the highest tribunal, the Court of Cassation, would be named by the Senate. Judges of all other civil, criminal and appellate courts would be selected by the first consul, always from among the notables of the region and the level involved.

At the same time Bonaparte appointed a commission of four legal experts whose work, debated in over 100 sessions of the Council of State with the first consul himself often presiding, led in 1804 to the great Civil Code, in 1806 to the Code of Civil Procedure and in 1810 to the Code of Criminal Procedure. These three, together with a more fragmentary compilation of commercial law promulgated in 1807, made up the famous *Code Napoléon*. It was a structure of law designed to favour order and stability in interpersonal relations, reasonably prompt court action, national uniformity as opposed to variegated regional customs, civil equality, freedom of religion and, of course, the power of the state. In criminal procedure, torture was reintroduced on a limited basis, and a jury, selected by the prefect, could convict by majority vote. The Code as a whole was an intellectually impressive effort to reconcile the laws of the Old Régime with those of the Revolution, as well as with abstract standards of justice not to be found in either, but it was also a powerful instrument of authoritarian rule.

The fact that Napoleon had a special minister of police, Fouché, until 1802, and then in 1804 revived the office under Savary, reveals his concern with strict surveillance. His personal impulses were clearly expressed after the bomb attempt on his life outside the Opera on Christmas Eve of 1800. He first rushed through the deportation to the French penal colony in Guiana of some 130 republican critics, calling them 'the general staff of the Jacobins'. Then, when Fouché identified the real culprits as royalists, the first consul saw to it that these were promptly executed. He did not, however, release any of the men already deported, as he put it, 'for all they have done, and all they still might do'. From that point onward, increasingly harsh censorship was matched by widespread use of police spies and *agents provocateurs* against suspected enemies of the state. More secure than Robespierre had been, and perhaps less convinced of his opponents' wickedness, Napoleon committed many fewer victims to the guillotine. Nevertheless, his government kept the jails full and the prison ships busily occupied on the dangerous run to South America.

THE INTERNAL ECONOMY

Napoleon never displayed any profound understanding of economic and financial problems nor, for that matter, any strong interest in them except as they touched his conception of national greatness and his struggle against Great Britain. The latter aspect, that of economic warfare, we shall take up in Chapter 10. Here we need only remark certain other general developments within the French economy. Progress was made in tax collection, an area where conditions could scarcely have grown worse than they had been before 1800. The greatly increased power of the government, in particular the energetic action of many prefects, made evasion more difficult than it had been during the hectic decade of the Revolution proper. Even so, the great expense of seemingly endless military operations simply devoured available funds, including exactions from occupied foreign lands. The exalted Court of Accounts, ranking just below the Court of Cassation, struggled ponderously, but in vain, to eliminate waste and corruption from the administration of public moneys. War profiteering, often on a massive scale, was prevalent throughout the period of the Consulate and the Empire.

By 1805, with the national deficit soaring to new heights, a major crisis developed. It was made worse by the fact that the Bank of France, founded in 1800, had issued paper money so far in excess of its metal reserves that in the space of only a few weeks that autumn its bills depreciated by 15 per cent. The emperor's personal intervention, when he rushed back to Paris from central Europe's battlefields in January 1806, brought large confiscations of funds from several incriminated financiers, the reorganization of the Bank under a state-appointed governor and a temporary restoration of public confidence in the franc. Napoleon's own financial vision, however, remained curiously limited. He stubbornly refused, for example, to resort to official bond issues, because he objected to having *his* credit discussed on street corners. Despite further improvements in record-keeping, the long overdue standardization of the national coinage and the adoption of increasingly sophisticated budgetary procedures, the economic structure of his régime was never fully secure. In 1810 a new and greater crisis erupted, involving poor harvests, an industrial decline after three years of relative boom and a resurgence of monetary problems. The Empire's military and political collapse four years later found this set of difficulties still unresolved.

The principle of authority was strikingly apparent, though in different ways, throughout the fields of industry, commerce, agriculture and urban labour. A law of 1803 created a hierarchy of local and regional consultative chambers of manufacturers, each composed of six businessmen elected by their peers to deliberate under the chairmanship of the *maire* of their town or the prefect of their department. The textile industry, in particular, enjoyed a somewhat artifical efflorescence because of the trade war against English products. By the end of Napoleon's reign, France had some 2,000 cotton mills, employing close to 40,000 workers, while linen production occupied an estimated 58,000 home or factory labourers. Iron mines and forges were kept occupied striving to meet the demands of war, as were beet sugar refineries and the establishments of the young chemical industry. It cannot be shown, however, that French manufacturing as a whole expanded more than it might have done under peaceful conditions – nor that it grew as rapidly as it had in the last decades before 1789. Indeed, if one considers many important products, including metals other than iron, one arrives at the opposite conclusion.

Commercial activity too had its set of officially supervised consultative boards and local or departmental chambers, culminating at the national level in the General Council of Commerce under the minister of interior. Such institutions had come and gone repeatedly during the Old Régime, but their number and the elaborateness of their graduated relationships had never approached the pattern established under the Empire. Napoleon expected French merchants to profit from his victories and their own exertions – but only for the greater glory of France, the strengthening of his war machine and the weakening of immediate or potential foes. It is possible to paint a relatively favourable picture of Napoleonic commerce, if one concentrates on certain inland centres, such as Lyon and Strasbourg, which served as trading hubs for the continental domains of the Empire. There is no question that the era also witnessed a new surge of highway, canal and bridge construction. However, the French and captive seaports, Marseille, Bordeaux and Nantes, Rotterdam, Antwerp and Genoa, paid the price in stagnation for the struggle against British naval power. In desperation, many of their traders turned to smuggling, often through secret arrangements with the English in direct violation of Napoleon's explicit prohibitions. As the years passed illicit trade to avoid excise payments spread to the inland trading centres as well. Involving not only private merchants and shippers, but also numerous government officials, smuggling became the greatest single instance of corruption behind the Empire's proud façade of patriotic rectitude.

Agriculture was encouraged by the official societies, publications and prizes for successful innovations (the improved sugar beet, better fertilizers and feed crops, increased output of grain, new veterinary techniques). Wheat, potato and beet production rose swiftly. Flax and hemp, on the other hand, declined, while the effort to raise home cotton was disappointing. Taking all crops into account, agricultural production under Napoleon seems to have no more than held its own in proportion to the growing population. In fairness it should be added that given the insatiable drain of manpower into the armies of the Empire, the fact that agriculture could even hold its own speaks well for French energy and ingenuity in the face of serious difficulties.

The manual labourer was for Napoleon merely another resource to be organized and exploited. The penal code, for example, established far more severe penalties for collusion among workers than for illegal agreements among manufacturers. From 1803 onward each labourer was required to possess a *livret*, or work book, and to present it to his employer when entering upon a job. This document both identified its holder for police purposes and showed the conditions under which he had left previous payrolls. Non-possession of a work book was considered proof of wilful vagabondage. Despite the promising advent of local arbitration boards and the existence of certain fraternities of labourers (the *compagnonnages*, tolerated by the régime for limited social purposes but kept under close official surveillance), French workers remained essentially isolated from one another, at the mercy of their employers and of the state.

RELIGIOUS POLICY

No single area of Napoleonic statecraft has generated livelier or more enduring disagreement than that of religious affairs. Part of the problem is that the several lines of policy pursued by the government, though each was clear enough in itself, were never perfectly coordinated. Bonaparte did not destroy the gains made by Protestants and Jews during the Revolution, so far as civil equality and freedom of worship were concerned. Everywhere, however, the familiar pattern of state supervision was in evidence. Each Calvinist synod or Lutheran general consistory met under the eyes of a prefect or his representative. Rabbis, unlike ministers, were not considered salaried public functionaries; but all the Jews of a given district were taxed to pay their clergy. Every local synagogue and regional Jewish consistory was administered with the participation of wealthy laymen selected from the proper list of notables. Non-Catholics were, in short, both protected and brigaded by the irreligious general who was their ruler.

Napoleon's dealings with the Church of Rome followed a much more tortuous course. His instinct for religious conciliation, which we have already seen at work in Italy and Egypt, led him to open his term as first consul with a series of gestures toward the 'recalcitrants', priests who had never accepted the Civil Constitution of the Clergy. On the other hand, he applied himself to effecting a settlement between the papacy and the 'constitutional clergy' who had sworn the required oath to the Republic in the 1790s. On 15 July 1801 a new Concordat was signed, at Paris, between representatives of the Vatican and of the Republic. Henceforth Catholicism was recognized, if not as the state church of France, at least as 'the religion of the great majority of Frenchmen'. The first consul was empowered to name archbishops and bishops, who would swear allegiance to his government; but only the pope could bestow the canonical 'institution' which consecrated them in their sacred functions. Cathedrals, chapels, seminaries and local churches not already secularized were returned to the direct control of the ecclesiastical hierarchy.

For the moment, it appeared that Pius VII had won a great victory over the Revolution. In some respects, including his new right to depose bishops who defied him, the pope now enjoyed greater power in France than his predecessors had possessed even under the old monarchy. The proud Gallican tradition of autonomy for a national Catholic church seemed to have been sacrificed to the needs of diplomacy. Actually, however, the first consul was about to launch a long series of impositions which would make the remainder of his reign an increasingly humiliating trial for the Holy See and its occupant.

As early as April 1802 the Legislative Chamber adopted a set of 'organic articles' purporting to give legal effect to the agreement of the previous summer. Instead, they reversed a number of assumptions which had seemed to underlie the Concordat. No papal legislation could be published in France, nor could any nuncio or legate be sent there without governmental approval. Prefects were to report any disloyal behaviour on the part of churchmen. The latter, indeed, were explicitly equated once more with salaried state officials. The pope protested, to no avail. Then in 1804, Pius was induced to come to Paris for Napoleon's coronation as emperor of the French, only to have the agreed ceremony in Notre Dame altered without prior notice: at the climactic moment, Bonaparte placed the imperial crown on his own head. Less than two years later, in 1806, the government in Paris announced a new catechism, to be used as the basis for all Catholic religious education throughout the Empire. The seventh lesson in particular, though approved by the docile nuncio to France, Cardinal Caprara, nevertheless outraged more deeply devout church leaders. Every true believer, it stated, must pledge to 'Napoleon I, our Emperor, love, respect, obedience, loyalty, military service . . . because God . . . whether for peace or for war, has made him the minister of His power and His image upon earth'.

By this time it was clear that Napoleon's conception of the agreement between France and the Vatican was distinctly one-sided. For the Catholic Church and for its spiritual head, however, the worst still lay ahead. In 1809, after a long sequence of mounting encroachments upon Rome and the surrounding Papal States of Italy, Napoleon finally proclaimed their annexation to the Empire, under rights derived from 'Charlemagne, our august predecessor'. Pius VII, who had become more and more hostile since the coronation farce, now responded by excommunicating the 'despoilers'. The pope was thereupon seized, carried off to Avignon and finally installed as a virtual prisoner at Savona on the Italian Riviera. Rome, officially styled the Second City of the Empire and designated as the seat of Napoleon's future heir, was to be a dynastic and political stronghold, not a religious capital. Only in 1814, after five years of exile, was the pope permitted to return to the Vatican, at the behest of Austria and its victorious allies.

Napoleon's treatment of Protestants, Jews and Catholics alike reflected personal indifference to matters of faith, coupled with steady insistence upon political obedience. Because Catholicism was at once the majority religion of France and an international force, it raised special problems and offered special temptations. In his dealings with the Church of Rome, therefore, the emperor showed himself fully alive to the possible value of the hierarchy's support, achieved at first by sweet words but increasingly, as time passed, by coercion. What he could scarcely have foreseen was that his persecution of the papacy would give it a new spiritual appeal, even for Gallican churchmen, and thus would form the background for an ecclesiastical resurgence in the nineteenth century rivalling that of the Counter-Reformation in the sixteenth.

RESHAPING EDUCATION

In the field of education, Napoleon's actions were conditioned by the effects of a prolonged civil and military upheaval. Under the Directory, the government had been content to rely on non-compulsory elementary schools, financed entirely by student fees, offering an uninspiring combination of the 'three R's' plus a fourth – republican morality – and staffed by ill-paid teachers who were apt to be ignorant and reportedly, in some cases, depraved. Public secondary schools had fared rather better, but they had continued to charge fees so high that many promising students were excluded from their combination of mathematical, literary and historical courses, the last two categories generally much inferior to the first. After the old universities were shut down in the early 1790s higher education had lagged badly, this despite the revolutionaries' efforts at constructing a new network to replace that of the Ancien Régime. The reopened medical schools at Paris, Strasbourg and Montpellier, the Museum of Natural History, the Central School of Public Works (renamed in 1795 the *Ecole Polytechnique*), the Observatory, the 'Normal' schools for the training of teachers, and the other special foundations culminating in the National Institute of Arts and Sciences, did not fully replace the universities, the national and provincial academies, the endowed scientific and scholarly centres of the monarchy.[3]

Bonaparte's reorganization was announced early in 1802. The cost of elementary schooling was declared to be henceforth a joint responsibility of local treasuries and of the pupils' parents. Restrictions on the establishment of private schools were at the same time relaxed; and the Catholic teaching orders were encouraged to resume full activity. Local secondary schools were restructured around a utilitarian curriculum emphasizing the French language, mathematics, history and geography. A more élite echelon of schools for pupils between the ages of ten and fifteen, the *lycées*, stressed all these subjects plus science and classics of antiquity as well, though the inculcation of military virtues constituted an additional, seemingly at times an overriding, aim. The state made clear its direct interest in lyceans by granting over 1,000 scholarships a year to gifted candidates and to needy sons of heroes who had died fighting for France. At what had previously been the university level, a general creation of new institutions waited several more years after 1802, notwithstanding the resurrection of such traditional degrees as the doctorate in letters and the successful launching of a dozen law schools capable together of handling some 2,000 students at time.

Then in 1806 a much more sweeping project was announced: the establishment of an Imperial University. As amplified by subsequent enactments down to 1810, its charter had nothing to do with a 'university' in the older sense. Instead, it provided for a single, monolithic structure in the form of a pyramid, presided over by the emperor's representative, the Grand Master, and charged with the supervision of education throughout the Empire, private as well as public, from the primary grades through the highest levels of training. At the elementary and secondary stages the results proved disappointing, in part because the original time schedule was unrealistic and in part because military demands kept draining the country of adequate teaching personnel. Napoleon had set a goal of 100 lycées by 1813, but when that year arrived there were still not fifty in existence.

In higher education the results, at least on paper, were considerably better. The overarching university was divided into twenty-seven academies, each responsible for higher education within the jurisdictional district of a court of appeals. Under the control of every academy and its rector was a faculty of letters. In addition, scattered through various French, Italian, Swiss, Belgian and Dutch cities were thirteen faculties of law, fifteen of sciences, seven of medicine, ten of Catholic and three of Protestant theology, each subordinate to the regional academy. The size and quality of these faculties varied greatly from the outset; and in the deteriorating situation of the later Empire, few if any achieved a pattern of operation one might call normal. The elaborate system, however, was sketched for all to ponder. (Even in America it provided a model for the University of the State of New York, as initially conceived.)

Napoleon appears to have treated education as he did any other activity within his purview: as something to be centralized and administered from above according to a clear chain of command. There can be no doubt that he wanted his subjects well trained, in the interests of military efficiency, public service and material productivity. At the same time, he appreciated the importance of schools for the propagation of pride in the nation and loyalty to his régime. Not surprisingly, he was less interested in the value of free inquiry. As matters turned out, his other undertakings, both at home and abroad, so vitiated his educational programme as to leave it just one more truncated monument to an intelligence at once sharp, orderly, and ungenerous.

THE CONTROL OF CULTURE

The same intelligence shaped the government's attitude towards information, art and letters. The master policeman, Fouché, and after him Savary, took pains to have their press bureau scrutinize all periodicals. In January 1800, scarcely a month after the Consulate was established, a decree suppressed no fewer than sixty newspapers in Paris and its suburbs, accusing them of being 'in the hands of the Republic's enemies'. Only thirteen political journals were permitted to go on publishing, and even they were threatened with confiscation if they printed articles critical of the public authorities. The first consul himself reviewed censors' reports and press summaries with great care. Year by year his régime grew harsher and more suspicious until finally, in 1811, a new edict reduced to just four the number of authorized newspapers in the capital – the now entirely official *Moniteur* and three other banal sheets – each one receiving the undivided attention of a censor assigned to it by the minister of police.

When it came to the production of books, the Napoleonic formula combined monetary rewards to properly admiring authors with the suppression of volumes the proofs or advance copies of which betrayed seditious tendencies. As a matter of fact, the full development of official screening machinery, like so many other expanded controls, came rather late in the history of the Empire. Not until 1810 was the Directorate General of Printing and Bookselling created, with a staff of over sixty readers, inspectors and border guards. Long before that happened, however, countless writers had felt the sting of official displeasure expressed through fines and confiscations. One of the first sufferers under the organization established in 1810 was the famous Madame de Staël, daughter of the former royal finance minister, Necker, and herself one of Bonaparte's early admirers. In the first months of its operation, the new Directorate General called to the emperor's attention her recently completed book, *Concerning Germany*. Enraged at the sympathy the work expressed towards a people whose growing nationalism was already causing him serious trouble, Napoleon ordered the edition seized and its author banished to Switzerland.

Faced with the difficulty of policing a soaring number of French theatres, the government in 1807 at last resorted to its favourite principles of reduction and rigid classification. That year, all but eight of the thirty-three theatres in Paris were ordered closed. Those allowed to continue were distinguished as four 'grand' ones (the *Comédie Française*, the *Opéra*, the *Opéra Comique* and the *Odéon*) and four vaudeville houses. Other cities were simultaneously restricted to one or, in a few instances, two stationary troupes apiece. Both in the capital and in the provinces, each company had to limit itself to a fixed repertory of productions, and even these could be performed only in the presence of police officers.

In art as elsewhere the principle of hierarchy was the guiding rule, however uneven its application may have been. Early in 1800 Jacques-Louis David was named 'painter to the government' and given authority over all paintings undertaken in France. Two years later, a veteran diplomat, Vivant Denon, was made director general of museums, in effect a minister of fine arts with sweeping powers. After 1804 the Opéra was also entitled the Imperial Academy of Music and Dance, though in these fields even the emperor seems to have been unable to detect much political meaning, to say nothing of danger.

THE REBIRTH OF SOCIAL HIERARCHY

One of the several features of Napoleon's rule which have continued to agitate, and often to confuse, observers was the so-called 're-aristocratization of France'. That a professional soldier, a general, should feel kindly towards a pyramid of ranks and honorific distinctions, with himself at its summit, is not surprising. Merely to say, however, that Napoleon left Frenchmen their *civil* or *legal* equality, while abandoning the Revolution's ideal of *social* equality, is to leave unanswered several important questions.

To what extent did this policy represent an attempt to restore the old pre-1789 aristocracy, as distinct from the creation of new privileged groups? Bonaparte did not wait long before explicitly encouraging the hordes of émigrés, including substantial numbers of former nobles, to return to France. It is true that an article in the Constitution of the Year VIII (1800) pledged the government to uphold 'the irrevocability of the laws against émigrés'. As early as April 1802, however, the Senate acceded to the first consul's demand that this article be annulled and the exiles welcomed back on condition of sworn allegiance to his régime. Unfortunately we have no such detailed figures for returnees as we do for the emigration itself. Nevertheless, the *ralliés*, old enemies of the Revolution who came home from abroad to live under Napoleon, were henceforth an important element in the French population, prominently mentioned in contemporary records, their names encountered with increasing frequency on lists of civil and military appointments.

Complicating this picture is the fact that the return of formerly noble *ralliés* did not in itself reconstitute the pre-revolutionary nobility. It was not uncommon for such a returnee to go on using his title as a social adornment, but he was generally referred to by his fellow citizens as the *ci-devant* ('the erstwhile') marquis or count or chevalier. Furthermore, he recovered no special tax exemption, no special privileges in any court of law, no rights of ceremonial precedence at public or religious functions. Even after the Senate's action of 1802, it cannot truthfully be said that the old noblesse fastened itself once more on French society. Its members became noblemen in a newer and more meaningful sense only if they were assimilated, as individuals, into the Napoleonic hierarchy of honorific distinctions conferred in recognition of public services.

It is important to recognize, beneath the titles and ornate uniforms of this hierarchy, a principle of advancement quite foreign to the notions of the Old Régime. This was the requirement that the individual honoured must himself have demonstrated heroism in battle, administrative capacity, diplomatic skill or the ability to make money. Had the system survived for two or more generations, the original rewards for personal achievement might, of course, have become the basis for just one more hereditary caste. At the outset, however, the offer of personal dignity to soldiers, bureaucrats, diplomats and rich men, regardless of their birth, sought to reconcile aristocratic honours with the dream of careers truly open to talent, with 'a marshal's baton in every soldier's knapsack'.

Bonaparte's first constitution, that of the Year VIII, rested on a rather curious mixture of democratic and elitist principles. We have seen that 'notables' were chosen by their peers at the local, departmental and national levels. The result was a graduated series of rosters, culminating in the national list of 5,000 to 6,000 names supposedly identifying the most 'considerable' Frenchmen fit to be entrusted with a wide range of legislative, judicial, administrative and even religious responsibilities. Nevertheless, these notables *were* elected and served for fixed terms. In 1802, when a new law abolished the earlier lists in favour of electoral colleges, several features of a more explicitly aristocratic nature were introduced. First, the members of these colleges were chosen for life. Second, the voters of each locality could henceforth select their primary assembly or *collège d'arrondissement* only from a list of 600 citizens nominated by the government as 'most imposing', which in practice generally meant wealthiest. Third, the consul-for-life could now appoint ten members to each local and twenty to each departmental assembly, in recognition of public services rendered.

Subsequent modification of the electoral colleges tended to make them only more clearly privileged, predominantly appointive bodies.

The same year that brought the adoption of this system saw the realization of Napoleon's plan to create a standardized set of rewards for military valour and for other civic virtues. This was the Legion of Honour. On 18 May 1802 the Legislative Chamber passed the law establishing the new institution, placed it under a Grand Council, with Napoleon as president, and endowed it with lands the revenues from which would provide pensions for all members. The national organization was subdivided into sixteen cohorts, each under its own administrative board. A legionnaire was named, for life, by the Grand Council in Paris, and was originally assured an annual stipend ranging from 250 francs up to 2,000 for a commander and 5,000 for a grand officer. Despite ostensibly strict rules governing the choice of members, including an eligibility requirement of twenty-five years' distinguished service to France, the Legion's size grew at a startling rate. By 1808 its numbers had surpassed 20,000, posing obvious financial difficulties. Finally, in 1811, the monetary payments were abolished. Nevertheless, titles and decorations of the Legion of Honour remained public reminders that France counted certain of her sons and foreign friends as far more praiseworthy than the rest.

There were many other examples of honorific designations and attendant benefits. The *senatories*, for instance, were endowments of land and income which the ruler could confer for life on especially favoured members of the Senate. There were fifteen such recipients in 1804, and in the course of the ensuing ten years this total rose to thirty-six. Another case of conspicuous distinction, this one copied in part from the expiring Holy Roman Empire and in part from the old French monarchy, involved six 'grand dignitaries' with whom Napoleon in 1804 surrounded his imperial throne. They included the emperor's brothers and designated heirs, Joseph and Louis Bonaparte, as grand elector (titular head of all the electoral colleges) and grand constable, respectively; his brother-in-law, Murat, as grand admiral, without duties at sea; his stepson, Eugene Beauharnais, as arch-chancellor of state; and his two previous consuls, Cambacères as arch-chancellor of the Empire and Lebrun as arch-treasurer.

Most revealing of all these innovations was the Imperial

Nobility founded in 1808. This, far more than the welcome home extended to nobly born émigrés, more even than the founding of the Legion of Honour, expressed the emperor's rejection of social equality among his subjects. Each grand dignitary now became a prince of the Empire – 'his most serene highness'. Ministers, senators, councillors of state, archbishops all became counts. Presidents of departmental electoral colleges, higher judges, bishops, mayors of thirty-seven large cities became barons. Ordinary members of the Legion were henceforth chevaliers.

It would be easy to conclude that with this action Napoleon 're-aristocratized' France once and for all, but we must be careful to note that even in 1808 he did not restore the *order* of nobility as the Bourbon monarchy had known it. Like the *ralliés* from the Old Régime who came back to France as citizens, the imperial nobility enjoyed none of the legal and financial immunities that had been the very substance of *noblesse* in the eighteenth century. Furthermore, the emperor not only established a whole new set of honorific titles, identified with specific forms and grades of public service, but also tied the *hereditary transmission* of such titles to financial requirements which would have utterly outraged the earlier possessors of rank acquired by birth alone. A prince of the Empire could be sure that his eldest son would be a duke, able to pass that rank on to future generations, only if he could bequeath as well an estate made indivisible by entail (*majorat*) and yielding an income of at least 200,000 francs per year. The title of count might be inherited only if accompanied by an assured income of 30,000 francs; and the figures for a baron and a chevalier were 15,000 and 3,000, respectively. Napoleon's nobility was intended to remain an 'upper class' in the strictly economic sense.

INNOVATIONS – EPHEMERAL AND PERMANENT

Looking back over the full range of projects and policies, we should ask ourselves to what extent Napoleon's institutional reforms were fundamental and to what extent ephemeral, that is, destined to fade from sight in a relatively short time. Many of his innovations clearly failed to take root. The lists of notables and the electoral colleges that replaced them, the solemn fraud of the Tribunate, the archaic role of the grand dignitaries and indeed, save for its revival by his nephew in the mid-1800s, the imperial title itself were all rejected by later French constitution makers. The imperial catechism for Catholics, like the essentially military organization of the schools and the elaborate censorship of everything from imaginative paintings and foreign books to provincial comedies and speeches made at workingmen's social evenings, also proved incapable of outliving the Empire.

Not everything that proved temporary perished because it lacked vitality or promise. It would be a mistake to ignore the deep changes in French intellectual life which *might* have resulted had the superstructure of the Imperial University, as constituted in 1810, lasted not four but forty years. Similarly, the imperial nobility of 1808 survived only until the Bourbons returned to the throne, but its potential effect on social attitudes and organization became manifest even during that short time. Many of the Napoleonic creations disappeared, in other words, not because they had shown themselves incapable of reshaping society, but because the régime that had instituted them was itself destroyed by military action from without before any such reshaping could take permanent effect.

When all is said and done, however, the greatest significance still attaches to institutional changes which were *not* reversed in 1814–15; for these continued to affect French life – and in many cases European life more generally – long after their instigator was dead on St Helena. In government, to cite one example, the prefect's wide powers in the implementation of regional policies, combined with his direct subordination to the central ministry of the interior, where policy was determined, became a hallmark of French administration from 1800 onward. The judicial system would never again be staffed by owners of venal offices, as under the Old Régime, nor made dependent on the political election of judges, as during the 1790s. The Code Napoléon, needless to say, remains the foundation of modern French law (even after the recodification undertaken in 1958).

In other spheres of human activity, the far-reaching influence of the Napoleonic expedients, modified and adapted by later generations, is not difficult to perceive. The Concordat of 1801, despite occasional challenges, remained throughout the nineteenth century the charter which defined relations between successive French governments on one side and the Roman Catholic Church on the other. Not until 1904 was it abrogated by French legislation aimed at achieving total separation of church and state. That year also saw the abandonment of Napoleon's system of financial support for the Protestant clergy and official supervision over Jewish synagogues. The organization of lower schools, the prestige of the lycées, the unparalleled centralization of French higher education, all survived the *Université Impériale* when it died with the Empire. So did the technical excellence of the 'Polytechnique' and the other specialized *Grandes Ecoles*.

Turning to yet another field, one encounters the aura of official authority still surrounding such theatres as the Comédie Française and the Opéra. Finally, in view of the not very laudatory judgments expressed earlier regarding the Empire's economic institutions, it is only fair to add that one of them, the local arbitration board (*conseil de prud'hommes*), today according workers more of a voice than they were allowed under the Empire, has remained a flexible and valuable feature of modern French industrial relations. Whether or not all the innovations mentioned here, as well as countless others which might have been cited, strike a modern observer as changes for the better, their combined importance is scarcely open to question.

Let us return briefly to where this chapter began, with Napoleon Bonaparte himself. His almost frenetic energy and the range of his personal activism help to explain why historians have found it so difficult to agree in classifying and characterizing him. He was in fact at various times an imaginative revolutionary statesman and a demagogic dictator, an enlightened despot after the letter and an unscrupulous outsider come from Corsica to make his own and his family's fortune. Yet the figure of the latterday Caesar remains most compelling of all: the successful and articulate general, quick to smash all republican obstacles in the way of his own thrust towards power, but then anxious to give the state and society a formal structure which would restrain other ambitious men from aspiring to his high place.

Seen thus, Napoleon appears neither as the betrayer nor as the executor of the Revolution. There is no evidence that he was determined to perpetuate all the trends of the decade that had ended in 1799, nor that he was intent upon systematically reversing them without exception. He was as anti-Jacobin as he was anti-royalist, determined to suppress criticism and opposition on both flanks. Whether he revived a specific feature of the Old Régime or embraced some characteristic of the Republic he had overthrown, he acted without admiration for the avowed principles of either. *He*, after all, was now the system.

To some extent, of course, whether one considers Napoleon a 'man of the Revolution' or just the opposite, depends on how one evaluates the Revolution itself. If its essential aims were personal liberty, social equality, dignity of the independent spirit, then assuredly it was betrayed by Napoleon Bonaparte (though liberty, dignity and social equality had scarcely been delivered intact into his hands by the régimes that ruled Frenchmen from 1793 to the Eighteenth Brumaire). If, to take another position, the Revolution's own momentum had been not towards liberty, but towards governmental efficiency and the *legal* equality of all citizens, Napoleon can reasonably be portrayed as it greatest continuator.

Even if a judgement of the man's career becomes meaningful only in terms of a judgment of the times, the career itself retains a kaleidsocopic character at once baffling and fascinating. How, but for the immense variety of elements to be found in it, could his record have appealed, after his death, to both anticlerical liberals and conservative French nationalists? How else can we explain the fact that in our own century his political legacy has been claimed by radical democrats and by militarists, including fascists? To adherents of each group, certain of Napoleon's measures have appeared to mark him as 'their' man. This disagreement over his historical significance has beset not only Frenchmen but also foreigners whose countries still bear the marks of his passage. It therefore seems natural to turn now to the events of the Napoleonic era in Europe as a whole, to the mixture of collaboration, imitation and violent resistance that filled the age with fury and confusion.

NOTES AND REFERENCES

1 Desmond Seward, *Napoleon's Family* (New York, 1986).

2 O. Connelly, *Blundering to Glory: Napoleon's Military Campaigns* (Wilmington, Del., 1987), emphasizes Bonaparte's many strategic errors throughout a long career and concedes only the ability to improvise as partial justification for his reputation as a military genius.

3 *See* R. R. Palmer, *The Improvement of Humanity: Education and the French Revolution* (Princeton, 1985).

9

NAPOLEON AND EUROPE

The fifteen-year segment of European history we call the 'Napoleonic era' possessed, like the career of its central figure, a structure at once epic and theatrical. Its story is one of tremendous French victories turning at last to over-extension and crushing defeat. The same story features several pauses or breathing spells in the tumultuous narrative, points at which one is tempted to ask: Why did Napoleon not stop here, consolidate his gains and ask no more of Europe? Whether or not there ever was a real chance of his drawing rein, the times when he appears, in retrospect, to have had that opportunity – 1802, 1807, 1810–11 – punctuate the drama of the age, dividing it almost as intermissions divide a stage production.

The present chapter will review the military and diplomatic events that constituted each of these 'acts'. While doing so, we should bear in mind that save for a single year one nation, Great Britain, was continuously at war with Bonaparte's France. The stubborn conflict between these enemies facing one another across the Channel might upset the division into subperiods justified by events on the Continent. Even in the Anglo-French struggle, however, the sequence of European crises and relative lulls revealed itself clearly enough to justify our taking up the account as a whole in chronological segments.

It would not be enough merely to chart the wars and temporary pacifications between 1800 and the peace of 1815. We need also to follow the principal internal developments within various European states during successive periods, admitting the while that to keep all the nations constantly in view would be impossible. Our goals will be, first, to observe the widening impact of the Napoleonic offensive on an entire civilization and, second, to distinguish the variety of responses, country by country, which in due course will help to explain the new map, the new Europe of 1815.

There is another problem, a significant one for the student who tries to place the Napoleonic wars in relation to other careers of conquest, Louis XIV's in the seventeenth century, for example, or Hitler's in the twentieth. This is the question of 'French hegemony' – how it was conceived by Napoleon, how close it came to being realized under his leadership and, to the extent it ever approached realization, why it finally collapsed. Hegemonial struggles and, indeed, changing conceptions of what hegemony is or might be, as distinct from a balance of rival powers, are among the most important themes of European history.

TO THE TREATY OF LUNÉVILLE

As was pointed out in Chapter 7, the French military situation at the end of 1799, when Bonaparte became first consul, bore the scars of Austro-Russian victories the previous spring and summer. On the other hand, it had improved markedly as a result of the Allies' withdrawal from Holland, the tsar's disgusted abandonment of the coalition, and Masséna's victories in Switzerland – all events of the weeks preceding the Eighteenth Brumaire. During the winter France's enemies suffered further reverses. Russia exchanged its recent military partners, Austria and England, for a northern cluster of diplomatic allies, the armed neutrals, Prussia, Sweden and Denmark. Britain angrily condemned this Russian 'betrayal', while on his side Paul I found cause for resentment against London in the Royal Navy's apparent designs upon the island of Malta. That Mediterranean stronghold, between Sicily and Africa, had a garrison made up of French troops put ashore in 1798 by Napoleon's expedition en route to Egypt. The wily first consul, however, was now issuing hints that he might cede the island to the tsar, who was Grand Master of the Knights of St John, the international Maltese Order. As a result, the Russian government was openly hostile to the British blockade and to the Admiralty's undisguised plans for an assault.

It was Austria, however, that attracted Bonaparte's special attention as he sought an inaugural series of victories. In part, this was because the Habsburg dominions constituted a land power, accessible to French military action, while any serious onslaught aimed at Britain would require a costly mobilization of naval forces. In addition, his determination to strike at the Austrians was a response to the pressure which Habsburg forces were applying on the Italian front. Here the French clung only to Genoa, plus the coast stretching westward to Nice. Early in April 1800 an Austrian army under General Melas suddenly fell upon and split in two the column which Masséna had recently led into Italy. One set of survivors retreated towards Nice, to shield southern France against invasion. The other fragment, under Masséna, dug in at Genoa to face a siege by the Austrians on the land side and by Lord Keith's British squadron at sea. For two months the stalemate continued, under conditions of mounting horror for the Genoese population and its French 'defenders', until 4 June, when a capitulation on honourable terms was concluded.

While this was going on, the first consul in Paris, with no immediate concern for the unfortunate regiments trapped in Genoa, moved deliberately ahead with his own offensive preparations. In April General Moreau was given command of a large army and directed to cross the Rhine into southern Germany, which he succeeded in clearing of Austrian units without a pitched battle. Having taken Munich in July, Moreau concluded a temporary armistice and stood by for further orders. Bonaparte himself, meanwhile, reviving the two-pronged strategy adopted by the Directory five years earlier, took command of a new Army of Italy and in mid-May 1800 led it over the Alps via the pass of Great St Bernard. Proceeding by forced marches into the Po Valley, he entered Milan on 2 June, proclaimed the rebirth of the Cisalpine Republic and began operations designed not only to reverse the decision at Genoa, but actually to drive the Austrians completely out of Italy.

It is conceivable that no other battle prior to Waterloo was so crucial to Bonaparte's career as that which decided the outcome of this second Italian campaign. In order to justify his assumption of control over the French war effort, the first consul *had* to win – and he very nearly lost. Bonaparte had dispersed many of his units to block supposed Austrian lines of retreat, when on 14 June, near the village of Marengo, the energetic Melas appeared with an army of 30,000 Imperials, confronting only about 18,000 French. By mid-afternoon, the battle seemed certain to end in victory for Melas and defeat for Bonaparte. Nevertheless, the outnumbered French units kept up a desperate resistance until General Desaix arrived with one of the brigades earlier sent away by Napoleon. Desaix charged immediately, leading 6,000 fresh troops onto the field; and though it cost him his life, he saved the day. The discouraged Austrians, having lost 9,000 killed or wounded as against 7,000 French casualties, asked for an armistice. As for Bonaparte, the 'victor of Marengo' returned to Paris amid scenes of patriotic jubilation.

Before a general peace could be imposed on Vienna the decision of arms had still to be reached in Germany. This was especially true since Emperor Francis II, in return for a subsidy of £2,500,000, had just promised the British government that he would continue hostilities at least until 1 February 1801. French and Austrian diplomats began preliminary negotiations at Lunéville in Lorraine, but as the summer dragged into autumn Bonaparte became convinced that another great victory was required. Consequently, early in November he formally terminated the armistice applying to both Germany and Italy. Moreau's powerful command in Bavaria, numbering fully 120,000 men, began to roll towards the Inn Valley, gateway to Austria. Slowed at first by the tactics – confusing because confused – of Archduke John, who had replaced his abler brother Charles, the French finally caught the Austrians in the snow and mud around Hohenlinden and there on 2–3 December 1800 inflicted over 20,000 casualties on their shattered foe.

The combined disasters at Marengo and Hohenlinden left the house of Austria no choice but to sue for peace. On Christmas Day, with Moreau's army only sixty-five miles from Vienna, a new armistice was signed. It was followed some six weeks later, 9 February 1801, by the formal treaty of Lunéville (*see* Map 4). Under the latter's terms, Austria confirmed the provisions of Campo-Formio (*see* above, pp. 161–2), agreed to the loss of Tuscany as a Habsburg principality, recognized France's satellite republics as sovereign powers and accepted the *Talweg* of the Rhine (its central trough or channel) as the boundary between France and the Empire, thus guaranteeing the former a full share of all navigational rights on the great river.

The effects of all this within the Holy Roman Empire took two more years to reveal themselves, but meanwhile Bonaparte was pushing ahead on other fronts in an effort to achieve his 'pacification of Europe'. In March 1801 the king of Naples came to terms, promising to close his ports to British ships and to maintain 15,000 French troops in several southern Italian towns until peace was fully restored. At the same time, the first consul revived the Ligurian Republic in Genoa and created a new Kingdom of Etruria out of Tuscany and Parma for the benefit of the latter's duke, a puppet of France. That summer, it will be remembered, also witnessed the signing of the solemn Concordat between Paris and the papacy. Within the space of a year, Italy had to all intents and purposes been reconquered, though in an almost contemptuous gesture on the part of the French Caesar, Austria was allowed to keep Venetia. As for Spain, its nervous monarchy was about to launch a war against Britain's ally, Portugal, on Napoleon's behalf, despite his having forced the Spaniards to sell him Louisiana in America for a pittance the preceding year.

BRITAIN AND THE WAR

The great question mark in 1801 hung over England, the only power still at war with France. Eager for the title of triumphant peacemaker, but determined to trade away none of the Republic's trophies of war, Bonaparte in March opened cautious negotiations with London. British willingness to make terms agreeable to the first consul obviously depended on a number of considerations, domestic as well as foreign. On the latter plane, His Majesty's government were facing a number of difficulties which might well induce them to cease hostilities. Lunéville in February had deprived the British of their last major ally on the Continent. The treaty signed at Florence between France and the Neapolitan monarchy threatened to close them out of southern Italy; and by the end of the summer, Portugal would accept the treaty of Madrid, repudiating all ties with England.

Despite these reverses, Britain's government could point to certain assets which, as the months of haggling wore on, seriously complicated Bonaparte's diplomatic offensive. Trinidad in the

West Indies, Ceylon in the Indian Ocean, the Cape of Good Hope at the southern tip of Africa, all had been seized from their former rulers, Spanish in the first instance, Dutch in the other two. In September 1800 the French on Malta capitulated, with no chance to hand the island over to Tsar Paul. A year later in Egypt, the last soldiers in Napoleon's abandoned expeditionary army of 1798, their general, Kléber, having earlier been slain by a Muslim assassin, laid down their arms on the promise of being shipped home as exchanged prisoners of war.

Even in the Baltic, where England's position had seemed so precarious in 1800, the events of 1801 were running in London's favour. The second League of Armed Neutrality (Russia, Sweden, Denmark, Prussia) lost its chief sponsor on the night of 23–24 March 1801, when Paul I was murdered by court conspirators. His son and heir, young Alexander I, soon showed himself to be less anti-British than his father; but even before he had a chance to express his views, the Royal Navy struck an unexpected blow at the northern allies. On 31 March, only a week after the assassination in St Petersburg, an English squadron under Nelson sailed through the Sound into the Baltic. On 2 April, still with no declaration of war, it battered the Danish fleet to pieces in the harbour of Copenhagen. Thereafter, Nelson was ordered scrupulously to avoid hostilities, while Tsar Alexander, as a conciliatory gesture of his own, gave up the Grand Mastership of the Knights of Malta and with it all claim, on Russia's behalf, to that key island. By June, with the Danish navy eliminated for the foreseeable future and with Russia no longer a potential belligerent, the League of Armed Neutrality collapsed. Behind her reasserted naval might, Britain appeared secure.

Yet there remained powerful motives for seeking peace with France. The war-weariness of Englishmen found clear expression at the highest level of government, where Pitt had left office virtually on the eve of the treaty negotiations. Ironically, it was not policy towards France but disagreement with George III over the treatment of Ireland that brought down the prime minister. Since 1798, when the Irish rebellion failed and Wolfe Tone killed himself, the affairs of the troubled island had continued to plague Britain's war leadership. A separate, subjugated Ireland posed a continuing threat to England's security, both as a scene of recurrent uprisings and as an inviting target for French military intervention. But what was to be done?

Pitt's answer had been the dual policy of Union and Catholic emancipation, that is, a series of projects by which the Irish Parliament would be abolished, Irish members elected to an enlarged British House of Commons and Irish Catholics allowed to serve there as they had been serving in Dublin since 1795. To Catholics, he pointed out that it was in their interest to support the Union, since only on those terms would Protestant opinion accept granting them the right to vote as British subjects. On Anglo-Irish Protestants, he urged the commercial and political advantages of amalgamation, adding that Catholic representation in Parliament would lose its terrors, inasmuch as Catholic voters, though 75 per cent of the Irish electorate, would be only a minority in the United Kingdom as a whole. Without this concession to the Catholic population, he argued, union with England could only plunge the Irish countryside into a new and terrible civil war. When someone asked the son of Lord Cornwallis who he supposed would follow his father as viceroy and commander-in-chief at Dublin if Catholic emancipation were rejected, the young man, who clearly agreed with Pitt, replied: 'Bonaparte'.

Unfortunately for the prime minister (and for Britain), only half his policy was adopted. In the spring of 1800 the Irish Parliament voted itself out of existence; and that August the Act of Union was passed into law at Westminster, where Ireland would henceforth be represented as part of the United Kingdom. Pitt, however, found himself unable to keep his promise of Catholic emancipation. Many Protestant leaders, English and Irish alike, continued to oppose it. Still more serious, the king himself considered any appearance of Catholics in the House of Commons a deadly threat to the Anglican Church, a violation of his coronation oath, in short, as he called it in January 1801, 'the most Jacobinical thing I ever heard of!'

Faced with George III's intransigence, Pitt resigned in February 1801, after seventeen years as prime minister and in the very week when the treaty of Lunéville was being signed on the Continent. Though the fallen giant of British politics continued to advise and support his friend, Henry Addington, the former speaker of the House who formed a ministry in March, both the prestige and the resolve of the war government had undeniably faded. The new prime minister was not the insignificant quantity suggested by a contemporary jingle: 'Pitt is to Addington as London to Paddington'; but he was a cautious, at times a timid man. From

Napoleon's great victories over the Austrians, combined with the spectacle of Britain's own economic problems (serious food shortages, a national debt risen to £500 million and an annual budget which had tripled in eight years), he felt unable to draw any conclusion save that peace was essential. Increasingly, Pitt's own voice seconded this view.

EUROPE AFTER AMIENS

The discussions which finally produced the Franco-British settlement lasted for a full year, until March 1802, when the formal treaty was signed at Amiens in northern France. During that year, as we have seen, England had important successes in the Baltic and Egypt; but Bonaparte's trump cards were more impressive still. Furthermore, the first consul and his foreign minister, Talleyrand, played those cards with great ability. The result was a treaty whose terms filled most British subjects with disgust, however fervently they welcomed peace as such. Egypt, though lost to the French, was handed back to Ottoman Turkey. Malta was promised once more to the Knights of St John. All Britain's conquests in the Mediterranean and even Capetown in Africa had to be returned to their former owners, leaving only Trinidad and Ceylon as lasting acquisitions. France, on the other hand, merely evacuated the Papal States and the Kingdom of Naples, at the same time recognizing the new Republic of the Ionian Islands under joint Russo-Turkish protection. Otherwise, not a single conquest of the Republic or the Consulate was surrendered. As seen from Paris, the treaty represented full acceptance of French primacy by the power which had so long and so stubbornly opposed it. As seen from London, the settlement offered nothing more than a chance for financial and perhaps diplomatic recovery. In England there was little confidence that the peace would endure, but a great willingness to make the most of it while it lasted.

Whatever Addington's weaknesses as a political leader, he was a tidy and by no means unintelligent administrator. He moved swiftly to cut armament costs, released 70,000 of the navy's 130,000 wartime personnel, sharply reduced the regular army (though he kept 95,000 men in uniform, twice as many as had been serving on active duty in 1784), abolished Pitt's 10 per cent income tax of 1799 and resorted to a new loan, simultaneously establishing a sinking fund designed to pay off the government's debts over a period of forty-five years. Thus far, his reforms appeared essentially conservative, and as such they were greeted enthusiastically by the landed and commercial classes. In addition, however, the prime minister took other measures which showed how strongly the example of revolutionary-consular France was beginning to influence even its most nearly irreconcilable enemies. Without regard to political principles, whether democratic or dictatorial, it was clear that the terrible Republic had developed administrative mechanisms for harnessing national power which no rival could safely ignore. Thus, Addington instituted an annual budgetary study of public accounts, induced Parliament to take over direct responsibility for official salaries, including many previously paid by the king, and pushed further the cabinet's control over pensions and other charges on the Civil List. Most striking of all, as soon as war broke out again in May 1803, he restored the income tax, this time with an unprecedented provision for collection at the source and with such sharply improved methods of assessment that though the rate was only 5 per cent, half that of Pitt's earlier tax, the net yield to the Treasury equalled four-fifths of the old amount.

While Great Britain was striving to put its house in order, other European states reacted in various ways to the unaccustomed lull in international conflict. France's satellite republics, as well as the Etrurian Kingdom in Italy, quickly discovered how little heed Bonaparte would pay to his solemn assurance, given at Lunéville, that they would be fully independent. In September 1801, for example, the first consul had announced a new constitution for the Batavian Republic, vesting power in an executive council, with only a limited role reserved to a thirty-five man consultative chamber. In the ensuing plebiscite fewer than 17,000 Dutchmen voted in favour of the constitution, while over 52,000 opposed it; but Napoleon blandly announced that the nearly 340,000 eligible voters who had abstained from casting any ballot at all should be recorded as 'not opposed' and hence as supporters of his authoritarian reforms! In Italy, meanwhile, where the Ligurian Republic was being converted into what amounted to a cluster of new French *départements* around Genoa, the Cisalpine or, as it was now entitled, the Italian Republic was being reorganized under the presidency of Napoleon Bonaparte himself. The satellite system, whatever the treaty of Lunéville might say, was in fact being revealed as an increasingly cynical façade for direct French control. Its conversion into an openly imperial constellation awaited only the first consul's pleasure.

Among the other continental states, the most docile ally of France was the kingdom of Spain, victorious over Portugal in 1801, but exhausted by the six years of war against Britain that ended at Amiens. The weak, ageing Charles IV and Prince Godoy, with his interesting dual position vis-à-vis the king and the queen, clung to their policy of repression at home and deference to the now gratifyingly anti-Jacobin French régime in Paris. Knowing Bonaparte only through his suave, cordial messages, they could assure themselves that a mixture of prudence and Anglophobia would suffice indefinitely to shield the monarchy from outside interference.

Prussia, despite its ill-concealed desire for the British ruler's German domain, Hanover, joined most other states after Lunéville and Amiens in a noncommittal watchfulness. Neither the Prussian nor the Austrian nor any other continental government yet showed much interest in administrative reforms on the French model – here they lagged behind England for the time being, though some would eventually go much further. Leaving aside for the moment the special case of the Holy Roman Empire, it must be said that only one great power on the mainland underwent a major political change during the era of Bonaparte's consulship. This was Russia, where Tsar Paul I had moved from his violently anti-French sentiments of 1799, through furious resentment of his Austrian and British allies in the Second Coalition, to a literally wild enthusiasm for Bonaparte after learning of Marengo in 1800. We have already seen how the tsar's assassination spared the British the threat of a Baltic maritime league directed against them; but domestic no less than external considerations lay behind his murder in St Petersburg's Mikhailovsky Palace on a March night in 1801. The important point is that this was no democratic uprising, nor even a revolt by aristocratic liberals. Rather, it was a cabal of powerful officials, Count Panin, General Bennigsen, Count Pahlen (army commandant in the capital) and several other co-conspirators. They strangled their ruler out of desperation over his insane outbursts, his capricious changes of policy and his atrocious behaviour towards subordinates, including the military hero, Suvorov, which led all men to fear for their own lives. Having killed the father, they installed his twenty-four-year-old son as Tsar Alexander I.

With the exception of Russia, the leading powers remained essentially static. Not so the smaller states of the Holy Roman Empire. The treaty of Lunéville had stipulated that German princes deprived of territories on the left bank of the Rhine, through cession to France, should be compensated on the right bank, primarily through the secularization of church lands. Theoretically, it was the Empire's own Diet, at Regensburg, which was to work out these indemnities. In fact, however, that body became hopelessly divided, the ecclesiastical delegations and those of most of the free cities violently opposing any juggling of boundaries, which most of the secular princes saw as filled with the promise of spoils. It was Napoleon himself who virtually dictated the final settlement.

The first consul's German policy had several different aims. He wished to isolate Habsburg Austria, to keep Prussia friendly without letting it become a powerful rival, and to reduce the number of west and south German states, increasing their size enough to make alliance with them more meaningful yet keeping this buffer zone of principalities clearly dependent on France. On 5 February 1803 the imperial commission on territorial adjustments presented to the Diet a comprehensive resolution, or 'Recess', endorsed by Napoleon and by Tsar Alexander, rapturous over his role as mediator. This document was the *Reichsdeputationshauptschluss*, whose very title has numbed generations of history students. Pushed through the Diet by the secular princes, it satisfied the French dictator's requirements. It also destroyed whatever substance the Holy Roman Empire had retained through the eighteenth century.

The losers within Germany were the prelates and the imperial free cities. Of the latter, forty-two out of forty-eight lost their independence by being absorbed into larger principalities, leaving only the three Hanseatic ports of Bremen, Hamburg and Lübeck, plus Frankfurt-on-Main, Nuremberg and Augsburg in their old relationship to the emperor. Two of the three electoral seats held by archbishops, those of Trier and Cologne, simply disappeared, though the archbishop of Mainz, while he lost his diocesan city, survived as a territorial ruler by virtue of having been ceded lands on the right bank of the Rhine. Most of the other ecclesiastical microcosms were gobbled up by neighbouring secular principalities, of which Bavaria and the new electorships of Württemberg, Baden and Hesse-Cassel were the most lavishly rewarded. Prussia had already received a number of bishoprics and abbeys under a separate agreement with France in 1802; but Bonaparte still withheld the most coveted prize of all, Hanover, on the convenient grounds that he was currently at peace with the latter's ruler, King George of England. No matter, the first consul had little to fear from resentment in a Germany most of whose princes were now his henchmen, bought and paid for. Already the ruler, in one way or another, of France, Belgium, Holland, Germany west of the Rhine, Switzerland and much of Italy, as well as patron of Spain, he had shown that he could even, as one bemused diplomat expressed it, 'redraw the map of the Holy Roman Empire and send it to Regensburg to be stamped "official"'.

THE WAR RESUMED: 1803 TO THE TREATY OF TILSIT (1807)

While Bonaparte was engaged in his reorganization of Germany, the brief interval of general peace was already expiring. Just as England in the spring of 1802 had been the last power to come to terms with France, so it was the first to resume hostilities a year later. Napoleon had shown, almost from the day the treaty of Amiens was signed, that he did not propose to be hampered by its terms and that he continued to view Great Britain as at best a temporarily non-belligerent adversary. His actions in the Holy Roman Empire, his annexation of Piedmont and his tightening of controls in the Dutch, Swiss and Italian tributary states showed London that no lasting stability or balance had been achieved on the Continent. Furthermore, rejecting the advice offered by at least some of his councillors, who favoured reviving Anglo-French trade, the first consul proceeded to exclude British exports from France and then, in December 1802, proclaimed the ports of Holland and Italy likewise closed to England's merchants. At the same time, he let it be known that the French battle fleet was to be increased by over 50 per cent, to a strength of sixty-six ships of the line. Such a step could only have been taken with one adversary in mind.

Faced with a combination of threats, particularly in the Mediterranean, Addington's government kept postponing the evacuation of Malta. Napoleon pounced upon the delay in fulfilling this clause of the Amiens settlement as clear proof of London's bad faith in other respects as well. His treatment of the British ambassador during the winter of 1802–3 became so abusive as to suggest that he considered a virtual state of war to exist once more. There can be no doubt that British refusal to return Malta to its Knights was a violation of a treaty commitment; but it was a violation to be judged in the light of the first consul's own contempt for numerous other promises made and hopes aroused at Amiens and Lunéville. On occasion Napoleon spoke as though tiny Malta were the hinge of Europe, while dismissing complaints about his own behaviour with impatient remarks suggesting that Piedmont, Switzerland, Holland were mere trifles.

It has never been clear whether or not Bonaparte sincerely hoped to remain at peace with Great Britain, assuming he could move freely in his own vast sphere of influence and bluster with impunity at all who angered him. What does seem clear is that his policies, which drove even the mild and cautious Addington back to formal hostilities, were scarcely those of a man attempting to relax tension. On 17 May 1803, determined to mobilize its own resources before France achieved prohibitive advantages, England abruptly declared war. Two months earlier, at a reception in the Tuileries, Napoleon had snarled at Lord Whitworth: 'You will be the first to draw the sword; I shall be the last to sheath it!' The first half of his prophecy had now come true.

Warfare was not at once resumed on the Continent, save for the swift French occupation of Hanover in Germany. The Royal Navy, of course, resumed operations at sea, while Bonaparte in turn began to assemble a huge invasion force on the Channel coast around Boulogne. For fully two years, however, other powers hung back, unwilling to commit themselves to a new alliance against the formidable power of France. During this interval, Britain turned once more to Pitt. Addington's personal hold on the Commons had never been very secure, and as a prime minister in time of war he was thoroughly uninspiring. After months of hesitation, during which King George III complicated matters by suffering another of his recurrent fits of madness, Pitt finally agreed in May 1804 to form a new government. It was a ministry of national defence in which he would have included even his old opponent, Charles James Fox, had the king not objected violently. The French 'army of England' was building all that year; and in December Spain obediently declared war on Britain, bringing an ominous increment of fighting ships to Bonaparte's growing naval armada. As seen from London, the sky was darkening.

If the first consul hoped to keep England isolated by ingratiating other nations, however, he did not show it in 1804. Apprised of a new internal conspiracy against himself in February, he executed several highly placed suspects. General Moreau, the hero of Hohenlinden, barely escaped to America. So far, of course, only French internal affairs were involved. In March, however, Bonaparte ordered the arrest of the young duke of Enghien, an émigré prince of the Bourbon-Condé line, who was living quietly in German Baden, across the Rhine from France. This arrest was effected by sending French cavalry into the territory of the Holy Roman Empire, an arrogant affront to Vienna. More serious, Enghien was summarily executed at Vincennes outside Paris, after a court martial had convicted him, without specified proof, of being an English agent. A thrill of disbelief and horror ran through every princely court in Europe. Indifferent to the shock created by the Enghien affair, the first consul in May had himself proclaimed Napoleon I, emperor of the French, by the Senate and the Tribunate. A national plebiscite approved this action by the remarkable margin of 3,572,329 to 2,569; and on 2 December the coronation, with Pope Pius VII in attendance, though scarcely officiating, took place at Notre Dame in Paris. Small wonder that foreign statesmen who knew their Shakespeare were asking, 'On what meat doth this our Caesar feed?'

The last hesitations of Austria and Russia began to crumble in March 1805, when Napoleon announced that the Italian Republic would henceforth be the kingdom of Italy and that he would himself accept the crown, as in fact he did at Milan in May. The following·month Genoa and the rest of the Ligurian Republic were formally incorporated into the French Empire. Meanwhile, on 11 April Russia and England had signed the treaty of St Petersburg, pledging a joint effort to restore the European balance. On 9 August Austria joined this Third Coalition, promising, unrealistically, a total of 315,000 troops. Though Sweden also adhered, Prussia hung back, in the hope that the French would treat Hanover as a suitable reward for Berlin's neutrality. By the autumn, however, the lines were drawn for the supreme struggle of Napoleon's 'middle years' in power.

The first beneficiary of the vastly expanded conflict was England. To meet the new forces arrayed against him Napoleon wheeled the invasion army back from Boulogne and sent it east towards Germany under forced march. The naval tension remained, however, with control of the Mediterranean at stake. Horatio Lord Nelson, now forty-seven, had arrived off Cadiz, Spain, in late September 1805 to take command of a British squadron consisting of twenty-seven vessels, including his own flagship, *HMS Victory*. On 20 October the French–Spanish fleet of thirty-three units under Admiral Villeneuve came out of Cadiz; and on the following day, at Cape Trafalgar, Nelson wrecked it so completely in the 'pell-mell battle' he had sought that eighteen enemy ships of the line were sunk on the spot and the remaining fifteen never saw action again. The price of Trafalgar was the life of England's greatest naval hero, killed on his own quarterdeck by a sniper's bullet. The reward was to be more than a century of naval supremacy. When the exhausted Pitt died three months later, in January 1806, that much he could hand on to the 'Ministry of All the Talents' which succeeded him.

Elsewhere, however, the enemies of Napoleon were involved in a two-year nightmare. At the very time when Nelson was closing in on Trafalgar, French armies struck their first blow against the coalition, surrounding and forcing the surrender of General Mack and some 50,000 Austrians at Ulm in south-western Germany. Marching straight down the now weakly defended Danube valley, Napoleon entered Vienna in November and on 2 December, the anniversary of his coronation, confronted the main Austrian–Russian forces near the Moravian town of Austerlitz, seventy-five miles north of the Habsburgs' fallen capital. When the terrible battle was over 25,000 Allied casualties and 7,000 French lay dead on the field. Before the end of the month, Austria abjectly signed the treaty of Pressburg, surrendering Venetia and the Dalmatian coast of the Adriatic to Napoleon's kingdom of Italy, as well as various Habsburg lands in Germany to Bavaria, Württemberg and Baden, the former two now elevated to the rank of kingdoms. Before the next year was over, on 6 August 1806, the Holy Roman Empire itself expired, Francis II renouncing its crown in favour of the hereditary title, 'Francis I, emperor of Austria'. Meanwhile, in December 1805, French victories in Italy having vitiated the meaning of Trafalgar in that quarter, Napoleon proclaimed from Vienna the dethronement of the Bourbons of Naples and the accession of his brother Joseph as its new king.

Russia, of course, was still at war, but for the moment it was Prussia which suddenly assumed a crucial role. The vacillating government of Frederick William III, ruler since his father's death in 1797, had come close to joining the Third Coalition before Austerlitz. After the great battle, however, Berlin scrambled to make terms with the victor, giving up additional lands in the west to France and the Hohenzollerns' Neuchâtel in Switzerland to the puppet Helvetian Republic. In return, with Napoleon's permission, Prussia occupied Hanover, in the first weeks of 1806 and formally annexed it, an act destined to poison relations with England long after the Prussians had themselves become enemies of France.

Ironically, the suspicion that Napoleon planned to return Hanover to the British king, as part of a possible peace settlement, was one of Prussia's two main reasons for turning against him that summer. The other was fear of his aggressive German policy, especially the founding, on 12 July 1806, of the French-sponsored Confederation of the Rhine, comprising Bavaria, Württemberg, Baden, Hesse-Darmstadt, Nassau and a cluster of smaller states. The emperor's troops now held garrison rights in over half of Germany. By September the Prussian monarchy, more nervous and exasperated than rationally committed, was mobilizing to back up its demand that the French withdraw west of the Rhine. The expiration of this ultimatum, instead of signalling a Prussian advance, found Napoleon with 160,000 men in northern Bavaria, poised to drive north into Thuringia where his newest enemy was concentrated with its Saxon allies. On 14 October he routed one Prussian army at Jena while Davout crushed another at nearby Auerstädt. Never before had even Bonaparte knocked out a serious opponent so quickly. On 17 October he entered Berlin while fortresses capitulated on all sides and Frederick William III fell back into East Prussia with the remnants of his forces. Within two months, Saxony, its duke rewarded with the title of king, made a separate peace and joined the Confederation of the Rhine.

Russian support postponed, though it could not prevent, Prussia's collapse. The French, having cleared Silesia and taken Breslau, turned north against the coalition partners, who fought their pursuers to a bloody stalemate at Eylau in early February 1807. After several months for rest and regrouping, Napoleon's army resumed the offensive, took Danzig on the Baltic in May and finally caught the Russian–Prussian forces in a murderous battle of attrition at Friedland in mid-June. Having occupied historic Königsberg and all East Prussia within the next few days, the emperor stood at the tsar's own frontier. Stubbornly though the Russian troops had fought, their field commander, Bennigsen, now felt that he had no choice but to beg his ruler to seek an armistice. On 25 June, with the shooting stopped, Napoleon and Alexander held their famous meeting on a raft in the Niemen River.

The treaties signed at Tilsit, 7–9 July, purported to settle all differences between France on the one side, and both Prussia and Russia on the other. Out of deference to the tsar, Napoleon allowed Frederick William III to retain about two-thirds of his kingdom, but limited his army to 42,000 men. The treaty also sheared away all Polish lands taken by Prussia since 1772, in order to form a grand duchy of Warsaw under French protection, with the king of Saxony on the throne. The Prussians further agreed to close their ports to British trade and acknowledged France's right to dispose, as its emperor saw fit, of all German territory on the Rhine's right bank as far eastward as the Elbe. Finally, Frederick William recognized Napoleon's brothers, Joseph, Louis and Jerome as kings, respectively, of Naples, Holland and 'Westphalia', a synthetic Hessian–Hanoverian German state created that summer as part of the Confederation of the Rhine. The former system of satellite republics was being rapidly converted into a dynastic complex of puppet monarchies.

Russia at Tilsit likewise recognized the three Bonapartes in Naples, Amsterdam and Cassel (Westphalia's new capital), together with the Saxon grand duke of Warsaw. In return, the tsar received the Bialystok region of what had been Prussian Poland. On the surface, Napoleon's mediation was welcomed to help end the year-old Russo-Turkish war, while Alexander graciously volunteered to supply the same good offices as between France and England. Actually, the French emperor gave a secret promise that he would desert the sultan (whom he had himself induced to attack the Russians) and would not object to the Rumanian principalities' permanent separation from the Ottoman realm. The tsar also secretly agreed to declare war on England if the latter did not, as it surely would not, accept French terms within two months.

Napoleon had already instituted the 'Continental System', a general embargo on British goods, the previous November by the Berlin Decree. The programme was to be made more sweeping and more explicit by the Milan Decree of 17 December 1807. Before that happened, Foreign Secretary Canning in London had guessed, correctly, that Denmark was under heavy pressure to join the hostile alliance and would soon either close the Baltic to all English shipping or see its navy taken over by the French for the same purpose. In the first days of September, therefore, a British flotilla again, as in 1801, descended on Copenhagen, this time putting ashore landing parties which commandeered no fewer than thirty-three ships, including the entire Danish battle line. All were sailed off to England. This stroke, not surprisingly, brought neutral Denmark into the war on Napoleon's side. Tsar Alexander too declared war, as promised; but during the next five years of technical hostility, the Russians gave Napoleon no more actual help against Britain than he gave them against Turkey – which is to say, none at all. For the moment, the only serious new reverse, from London's point of view, was the occupation of its ally, Portugal, by a French army striking through Spain in November 1807.

NAPOLEONIC EUROPE: IBERIA AND AUSTRIA

The 'pacification of Tilsit', stately in appearance but superficial in fact, opened a five-year period during which the Napoleonic Empire continued to wage war on many fronts, but without having to face any simultaneous array of forces comparable to the Third Coalition of 1805–7. It was also a period which saw the Empire, as such, expand greatly, at the cost of numerous states treated heretofore as semi-independent vassals. Finally, it was a period of varied responses, on the part of Bonaparte's enemies, to the French administrative and military techniques which deserved much of the credit for the emperor's victories.

What historians tend to consider Napoleon's most fateful decision, one which set his course away from the peaceful consolidation of past gains and towards seemingly limitless conquest, he reached in the first weeks of 1808. The Spanish monarchy, having ceded him Louisiana (which he resold almost immediately to the United States), had suffered at Trafalgar and elsewhere for its naval alliance with France. More recently still, it had permitted Junot's army to cross its territory in order to invade Portugal. Even such abject submission, however, had not satisfied the emperor. For one thing, he seems to have brooded over the incongruity of collaboration with Spain's King Charles IV of the house of Bourbon, a dynasty long since driven from France and in 1805, by Napoleon's own action, dethroned at Naples as well. It may be that the emperor also rightly distrusted a government led by an ineffectual monarch, whose queen was the mistress of his chief minister and whose son, Ferdinand, was at once hostile towards his mother and critical of the king himself. Finally, it is essential not to lose sight of Napoleon's virtually unbounded family pride, expressed this time as determination to place his brother Joseph on the Spanish throne.

The tactics employed to achieve this goal were as simple as they were brutal, though their complex aftermath mocked the foresight of the man who adopted them. During the winter and early spring of 1808, more and more French regiments, ostensibly en route to Portugal, remained encamped in Spain until the northern half of the country was effectively under foreign occupation. In March a political crisis erupted, when a series of popular revolts against Charles IV, the queen and her lover led the king to announce his abdication in favour of the *Infante*, Ferdinand. Temporizing in order to keep a grip on all parties, Napoleon first refused to recognize this change of rulers, then in late April invited the king, the queen and their rebellious son to meet with him at Bayonne, on the French coast of the Bay of Biscay, there 'to compose their differences'. Instead, in a humiliating scene, Prince Ferdinand yielded to French threats (supposedly justified by the queen's admission that Charles IV was not his father) and abandoned his hereditary rights to Napoleon, who promptly bestowed them on Joseph Bonaparte, then still king of Naples. A hand-picked *junta* or council of intimidated Spanish notables, summoned to Bayonne expressly for the purpose, ratified this act of dynastic extortion.

The Spanish people, proud, devout, suspicious of outsiders and fiercely loyal to their legitimate royal family, proved to be less accommodating than the Bayonne junta. On 2 May 1808 the populace of Madrid launched a bloody uprising which French troops put down with a savagery calculated to discourage any future resistance. What the shooting of insurgents produced, however, was a surge of popular hatred against the invader, expressed in the warcry 'Dos Mayo!' and in Goya's great series of sketches, 'The Horrors of War'. The situation in Spain was obviously deteriorating into a serious civil conflict, the more ominous from Napoleon's point of view because British armed forces had entered the Iberian arena in their first serious land commitment since the Dutch fiasco of 1799. Arriving in Portugal with some 10,000 troops, Sir Arthur Wellesley marched towards Lisbon and at Vimeiro on 21 August 1808 overwhelmed the French forces under Junot. Only a foolish set of changes in the British command, the result of personal rivalries and the thirty-nine-year-old Wellesley's lack of seniority, saved the French from a disastrous pursuit. Even so, while the Convention of Cintra (30 August) allowed Junot to retire in good order, Portugal had become a base from which Napoleon would be attacked almost without respite until his final defeat. That autumn a British army under Sir John Moore pushed forward into Spain, only to be driven back to La Coruña, where in January 1809 it was picked up by the fleet. The gifted and courageous Moore died in action, but this early offensive served notice that the Spanish rebels could fight on in the expectation of growing support from abroad.

The spring of 1809 brought new defiance against Napoleon in central Europe. Austria, heartened by French troubles, its army reorganized by Archduke Charles and its government incited by the foreign minister, Count Stadion, to resume hostilities, declared war and undertook an April offensive into Bavaria. Events quickly demonstrated, however, that Napoleon's claws had not yet been blunted by his recent difficulties. Racing from Spain to the Danube, as he had from Boulogne in 1805, the emperor, relying heavily at first on German troops of the Confederation of the Rhine, drove the Austrians back across their own frontiers. On 13 May he entered Vienna and, pursuing Archduke Charles northward towards Bohemia, crushed the main Habsburg forces in a series of engagements which culminated at Wagram on 5–6 July. By the treaty of Schönbrunn, signed that October,

Vienna once more capitulated, ceding Salzburg and surrounding
territory to Napoleon's Bavarian puppet, western Galicia to the
grand duchy of Warsaw, part of eastern Galicia to Russia and
further segments of the Dalmatian coast to the French Empire
itself. In April 1810, having divorced the childless Josephine,
Napoleon married Francis I's daughter, the Archduchess Marie
Louise, in solemn rites at St Cloud. When their son, a future
Napoleon II immediately designated 'king of Rome', was born
in March 1811, Europe beheld a prince half-Habsburg and half-
Bonaparte.

This dynastic triumph was in a sense the culmination of a
process of imperial aggrandizement which had advanced by stages
ever since the coronation at Notre Dame in 1804. We have already
seen how, by the time of Tilsit in 1807, the Batavian Republic
had become the kingdom of Holland under Louis Bonaparte; the
earlier Parthenopean Republic, the kingdom of Naples under
Joseph; and portions of Hanover, Hesse-Cassel and other German
territories, the kingdom of Westphalia under Jerome. After 1808,
of course, Joseph was king of Spain, while his and the emperor's
brother-in-law, General Murat, had replaced him in Naples as
King Joachim. The kingdom of Italy and the grand duchy of
Warsaw were other principalities controlled from Paris.

Still more striking than this substitution of monarchical for
republican satellites, however, had been the growth of the French
Empire by direct, formal annexations: Piedmont in 1802, Genoa
and the rest of the Ligurian Republic in 1805, Tuscany and Parma
in 1807, the Illyrian provinces across the Adriatic from Italy in
1809 and the Papal States that same year. When in July 1810 King
Louis abdicated rather than impose on Dutch commerce the
ruinous embargo demanded by his brother's Continental System,
the kingdom of Holland disappeared by virtue of its incorporation into the Empire, an action followed that December by the
annexation of northern Germany's coastal plain, including the
Hanseatic cities, which brought to more than 130 the swelling
total of *départements*. Finally, in 1812, Catalonia in north-eastern
Spain was absorbed. The dominions of the *Grande Nation* now
stretched from south of the Pyrenees to the Baltic Sea at Lübeck,
from the Hook of Holland to Ragusa (Dubrovnik) in what today
is Yugoslavia. In addition to Rome, officially styled its second
city, this empire of almost 43 million subjects contained Barcelona
and Amsterdam, Hamburg, Turin and Florence, to mention only

a few of its non-French centres. Not since Roman times had so much of Europe been subject to a single ruler (*see* Map 5).

NAPOLEONIC EUROPE: THE NATIONS' INTERNAL AFFAIRS

Outside the Napoleonic domains other nations struggled against the spread of French power or remained uneasily neutral, while shoring up their domestic structures as best they could. In England the death of Pitt in 1806 had ushered in the 'Ministry of All the Talents', with Lord Grenville as first lord of the Treasury (i.e. prime minister), Charles Grey as first lord of the Admiralty and Charles James Fox as foreign secretary. Fox too, however, was nearing the end of a life which had carried him from the youthful adventures of a Georgian rake through eloquent enthusiasm for the French Revolution at its beginning to bitter enmity towards the authoritarian France of Bonaparte. He died in September 1806 at the age of fifty-seven, the last of the great eighteenth-century parliamentarians. Two other men were meanwhile moving into the centre of British public affairs. One was George Canning, the able and aggressive young foreign secretary in the duke of Portland's ministry, 1807–9, and author of the surprise attack on Copenhagen during his first months in office. The other man, for the time being still more influential, was Spencer Perceval, chancellor of the Exchequer under Portland and himself prime minister from 1809 to 1812. A politician of no dramatic gifts but considerable courage, Perceval clung stubbornly to the policy of war against Napoleon, while steering a difficult course between the king, now sinking into his last, long mental illness, and George III's profligate heir, the prince of Wales, who became regent in 1810, but assumed full powers only two years later. By that time Perceval's career was approaching its tragic and unexpected end. On 11 May 1812, while walking through the Commons' lobby, he was shot down by a vengeance-crazed businessman, ruined by the war. It was a senseless murder, history's only case of assassination of a British prime minister.

Through years of fiscal strain and dragging military operations the British political system had ample opportunity to demonstrate its unique resiliency and ability to provide a consensus in wartime, even among jealously antagonistic factions. There was on the scene no charismatic figure, no Pitt the Elder or the Younger, no Lloyd George and certainly no Churchill. There were, however, merchants and bankers who, as we shall see in Chapter 10, had evolved some effective techniques of economic warfare – and of economic survival while at war. There were also soldiers and civil administrators who pushed hard for a reorganization of the British army along lines which gave it new hope against the French. Finally, there were politicians including Grenville and Grey and the 'Saints' around the Yorkshire MP, William Wilberforce, who among them in 1807 steered through Parliament the act abolishing the slave trade everywhere British rule extended. It was a fitting memorial to Fox, who had long fought the battle of persecuted groups. It was also a timely indication that Napoleon was not truly the champion of freedom against the antique tyranny of all his foes.

In Russia, at the other extreme of Europe, the fact of war was no less central than in England. Even after Tilsit, the armies of Alexander I continued to struggle against the Turks, with growing success, until May 1812, when the spectre of French invasion forced the tsar to make peace. Meanwhile, in 1808–9, Russia had wrested Finland from Sweden, with consequences for the latter country to be noted shortly. Amid these military exertions, complicated by the increasingly ominous clashes between Russian interests and those of France, the government of the tsar managed to display considerable interest in domestic reforms and innovation. Innovation, it should be emphasized, did not extend to any real liberalization of the political system. For example, the much discussed plan for enacting a bill of rights for all subjects never got beyond discussions within Alexander I's entourage, where men like Novosiltsev and Prince Czartoryski (veteran of Poland's Four-year Diet), Counts Stroganov and Kochubei sought without much effect to filter primarily English liberal principles through a screen of Russian traditionalism. In the field of administrative reorganization, however, western influences were clearly apparent. As early as 1802, eight specialized ministries of a familiar 'European' kind were substituted for the unwieldy old system of governmental boards called colleges.

After Tilsit in 1807 open imitation of Napoleonic France was the order of the day, as witness the tsar's appointment of the able, though ruthless, Arakchev to the post of war minister, with sweeping powers. Still more important, in 1808 the gifted young political philosopher and executive, Michael Speransky, a student of French governmental practices, became Alexander's chief personal adviser. Some of Speransky's projects, including his draft constitution of 1809, patterned after Bonaparte's of 1799 and designed to provide both local and national elective bodies, remained dead letters. However, his creation of a Council of State, composed of the country's highest administrators, went into effect in 1810 as another major step on the course set eight years before when the ministries had been established. It would be a mistake to exaggerate either the strength or the consistency of the tsar's own commitment to reform; but at least, before turning his attention to foreign affairs from 1812 onward, Alexander presided over these and other efforts at that defensive modernization into which the French onslaught drove some of Europe's most conservative societies.

In Sweden a dramatic political episode produced surprising results. The Russians' seizure of Finland and their invasion of the Åland Islands, threatening Stockholm itself, led to a violent crisis within the Swedish government. On 29 March 1809 King Gustav IV, still demanding greater military exertions against Russia and Denmark than his country could support, was arrested by his own army commanders and forced to abdicate. The nobility within the Estates as a whole reasserted the rights it had lost in Gustav III's coups of 1772 and 1789 (*see above*, pp. 36 and 99). As king the insurgent aristocrats chose an uncle of Gustav IV, an elderly gentleman who was crowned as Charles XIII and who promptly made peace with the Russian-Danish alliance, surrendering Finland to the tsar and agreeing to exclude British cargoes from Swedish ports, in deference to Napoleon's Continental System.

Since Charles XIII had no son, the Estates first designated a Danish-German prince, Christian of Augustenburg, as his heir. In May 1810, however, Christian suddenly died, leaving the Swedes confronted by Denmark-Norway's king as a possible claimant to their throne as well. To prevent that unpopular solution, the Estates and King Charles decided to install one of Napoleon's marshals, as yet unnamed, in the position of heir apparent. Their choice, announced in August 1810, was Jean-Baptiste-Jules Bernadotte, prince of Ponte Corvo, a tall, dignified Gascon and a veteran of both fighting and diplomacy in Germany. Napoleon, who incidentally disliked this particular marshal of

France, was both surpised and disconcerted. The emperor was no friend of Sweden, as he had shown not only by urging the Russians to invade Finland after Tilsit but also by 'inviting' them to take Stockholm as well. On the other hand, the invitation was flattering to French pride, and there were possible advantages in having one of his former subordinates in line for the Swedish throne. The imperial permission, which Bernadotte had made a condition of his own acceptance, was somewhat grudgingly given, accompanied by a demand that the new prince royal promise never to take up arms against his French homeland. Bernadotte quite properly refused to impose limits on his new allegiance and, also properly, proceeded to renounce his title and pension as a prince of the French Empire. Though destined not to become king until Charles XIII's death in 1818, Prince Charles John, as he was now styled, immediately assumed control of Swedish diplomacy and military affairs. In a sense, Napoleon had given Europe yet another king, though not one who was to prove at all satisfactory from the emperor's point of view.

No portion of the Continent, including France itself, underwent greater or more lasting changes during the Napoleonic era than did the German lands. The successive treaties of Lunéville, Pressburg, Tilsit and Schönbrunn, like the deliberations of the *Reichsdeputation* from 1801 to 1803, revolutionized the map of what had been the Holy Roman Empire. The number of German states was greatly reduced, through the annexation by secular principalities of countless bishoprics, free cities and imperial fiefs. However, the states that remained, generally enlarged, in several instances raised to the status of kingdoms and in several others made grand duchies, were even more jealous of one another than the units of the old *Reich* had been.

French influence appeared in several different forms. From 1807 onward, the kingdom of Westphalia, ruled by Napoleon's brother, Jerome, and possessed of a constitution 'made in France', was at once a member of the German state system and a show window for Bonapartist principles of rule. Certain of Napoleon's south German allies, notably Württemberg under King Frederick I and Bavaria and Baden under their energetic ministers, Montgelas and Reitzenstein, introduced reforms aimed at rationalizing bureaucratic control, making church officials essentially civil servants, reducing caste privileges in law and taxation. Even Austria, once Stadion became in 1805 not only its foreign minister but its leader in domestic affairs as well, did honour to hated France by borrowing some of its institutional forms. The creation of a *Landwehr* or militia in 1808, with all adult males made liable to call, showed the belated impact of the *levée en masse* upon Austrian thinking. Ironically, false confidence inspired by this Landwehr led to the disastrous war against Napoleon in 1809, which forced Stadion to retire in favour of the former ambassador in Paris, Count Clemens von Metternich. Hence Austria's reform period was cut short before the fallen minister's other projects, administrative, judicial and fiscal, could have much effect. Yet the pressures of change had been created and had to be acknowledged, not least in Hungary where Napoleon had taken great pains to stir up an anti-Habsburg revolt.

It was Prussia, however, that witnessed the most general effort to reorganize a state battered into temporary submission by the French Empire. The name commonly associated with this programme of regeneration after the military disaster of Jena and the diplomatic humiliation of Tilsit is that of Karl, Baron vom und zum Stein, born an imperial knight near the Rhine in Nassau but already a veteran of the Prussian civil service when he was appointed minister of home affairs in October 1807. Other figures, however, played major roles in Prussia's Reform Era: War Minister Boyen, Generals Scharnhorst, Grolmann and Gneisenau, the philosopher and educator Wilhelm von Humboldt and a man who was both Stein's colleague and his successor in office, Karl August von Hardenberg. Stein himself was driven into exile by Napoleon's wrath in September 1808, after the interception of a letter in which the minister had praised the Spanish rebels and prophesied a new war between Austria and France. Nevertheless, his own activities during that year in office, plus the subsequent efforts of the men who followed him, made the period after Jena and Tilsit one of the most significant in Prussian history.

The reforms enacted at Stein's own instigation included the liquidation of serfdom throughout the kingdom, effective as of 1810, and its *immediate* abolition on the royal domains in October 1807. This Edict of Emancipation also put an end to the old prohibition against individuals' moving among noble, burgher and peasant occupations. Finally, it obliterated the former distinction between noble and non-noble lands and permitted free sale to any buyer, without reference to his legal or social status. In

1808 Stein also promulgated the important Municipal Ordinance, which gave town governments a new dignity and autonomy in fiscal administration, authorizing the election both of aldermen and of the executive councillors who would henceforth share with the crown the right to choose mayors.

Meanwhile, the Prussian military reformers were introducing a Great General Staff to co-ordinate operations, founding the War Academy for advanced study, opening careers as officers to non-noblemen of proven ability and planning a system of universal reserve service which, like its Austrian counterpart, reflected the dread inspired by France's *levée en masse*. Prussia, they argued, must have highly trained officers and cadres of regular troops; but in addition, it must have patriotic citizen-soldiers, prepared to fight for a cause which commanded popular allegiance. In another area of reform, that of education, the drive to create a more open, more practical and at the same time more competitive system of public schooling reached its culmination with the founding of the University of Berlin under Humboldt's leadership in 1810 and the University of Breslau in Silesia the following year.

There has long been dispute over the source of inspiration for these programmes. Was Stein, the country gentleman from the Rhineland, guided by his admiration for England's local and national institutions, which he had observed at first hand during his travels? Or was his ministry dominated by the wish to imitate post-1789 French models? Actually, it would appear that English, French and indigenous German themes are so thoroughly inter-twined in the record of Prussian reform as to defy all efforts to disentangle them. One dominant impulse, however, does merit special notice, for it alone lends unity to an otherwise disparate array of administrative, socio-economic, military and educational measures. This was the desire to train and then to mobilize the energies of a new kind of Prussian citizenry, committed by rational understanding and enlightened self-interest to a patriotic struggle against the foreign oppressor and, by the same token, against old injustices at home. In this respect, Stein and his collaborators were responding, at the level of public policy, to the same challenge which called forth the philosopher Fichte's *Addresses to the German Nation* (delivered at Berlin in the winter of 1807–8), the anti-French poetry of the Rhinelander Arndt, the patriotic vehemence of the Moral and Scientific Union, or *Tugendbund*, founded at Königsberg in 1808, and the efforts, gallant but doomed, of Major Schill and others to launch Prussian revolts against Napoleon in 1809.

The reform programme, as such, was by no means triumphant over all obstacles in its path, including the resistance of many Prussian aristocrats. Most of the freed serfs, for example, instead of becoming the class of independent farmers Stein had dreamed of, lost out in the scramble to acquire property in land and tended to sink to the status of hired hands on large *Junker* estates. There is no question, however, that local administration, public education and military organization all benefited from the impulse to reform. Prussia emerged with certain assets it was to exploit throughout the nineteenth century and far into the twentieth.

FROM THE INVASION OF RUSSIA TO WATERLOO

We must now return to the great international struggle of Napoleon's era, as it entered its final phase. Earlier, we observed that after Lunéville and Amiens in 1801–2 and again after Tilsit in 1807, there seemed to be some chance of a peace devoted to consolidation within the various power blocs. Both times the hope faded, in the first case because of British reactions to renewed commercial and naval pressure on the side of France, in the second because the emperor turned to an extension of the policy of force, this time directed against Spain. By 1810–11, however, while the Spanish battle lines continued to sway as Wellesley duelled with Masséna and Soult, there again appeared to be a possibility that by concentrating his immense military resources on the Iberian peninsula and by capitalizing on Britain's economic difficulties, Napoleon could obtain a favourable, general settlement. His marriage to a Habsburg heiress, the accommodating attitude of Metternich in Vienna, the impotence of Prussia, the fawning solicitude of most German princes, the quiescence of Italy, Switzerland and the Low Countries, all suggested that Europe was ready to accept the Empire on existing terms. It was with a total disregard for any such possibilities that in June 1812 the Grand Army of some 430,000 French veterans and allied troops crossed the Niemen River, launching the invasion of Russia.

Exactly when Napoleon reached the decision to attack the empire of the Romanovs is not clear. Immediately after Tilsit, it is true, he had begun to send secret encouragement to the Turks in their struggle with the Russians, meanwhile complaining bitterly of Tsar Alexander's failure to take effective military steps against England or even to enforce the Continental System against British cargo vessels entering Russian ports. The gala Erfurt Congress in September 1808, which was supposed to seal the friendship between the two rulers in the presence of nearly forty German kings and princes, in fact produced the first serious indications of reciprocal mistrust. At St Petersburg, with émigrés such as Stein on hand to feed the tsar's suspicions, French plans for Poland and Napoleon's noncommittal reaction to Alexander's demand for Constantinople were viewed with special hostility. It was Bonaparte, however, and not the Russian ruler, who by the summer of 1811 was actively preparing for the great assault he believed would knock out his only remaining rival on the Continent.

Russia, for its part, hastened to assure itself of freedom to meet the attack with undivided energies. In May 1812 peace was concluded with Turkey, and a few days later with Great Britain as well. Sweden was already an ally; for Bernadotte had decided that spring to defy his former emperor, to end the Swedes' costly war against England and to support the tsar in the coming struggle, in return for a Russian promise that Norway would become a Swedish possession. The British were distracted by the opening stages of a two-and-a-half-year conflict with the United States, the 'War of 1812', a long-delayed but probably inevitable result of various frontier disputes, compounded by the Royal Navy's actions in restraint of neutral commerce. Nevertheless, English attacks on French ships at sea and on French armies in Spain offered the Russians some hope in a long struggle. One of the great questions in 1812, of course, was: how long *would* the war last?

The army of French, Austrian, Prussian, Saxon, west German, Italian and other satellite troops which swept eastward during July and August was the most powerful military force the world had ever seen in action, or would see again until 1914. It took Smolensk on 18 August. On 7 September, at Borodino, the emperor destroyed a third of Kutuzov's opposing army, at a cost of one-fourth of his own. On 16 September he was in Moscow, a metropolis largely deserted save for the small groups of civilians and disguised soldiers who that night began burning the place around its conquerors' ears. For well over a month, technically triumphant but actually frustrated and seemingly confused, Napoleon remained in the outskirts of the ruined city, vainly hoping that the tsar would come to terms. Finally, on 19 October, amid the first warnings of the terrible Russian winter, the Grand Army was ordered to fall back across the scarred countryside towards friendlier territory.

Thus began the long torment of the retreat from Moscow. It has been estimated that of the troops which had crossed the Niemen in June 1812, only 50,000 managed to recross it and that of the 380,000 casualties, almost half died of freezing, hunger and disease on the desperate winter march.[1] Early in December, leaving what remained of the army under Murat's command, Napoleon hurried back to Paris to crush the most recent of several conspiracies against him. He also extracted from the Senate a pledge of 350,000 more troops to be raised and equipped without delay. These troops were urgently needed, for the Russians, now openly supported by Bernadotte's Swedes, were pushing into Germany. Furthermore, while the Austrians withdrew into watchful neutrality, Prussia, having made peace with Russia in December, declared war on France and its allies in March 1813. Before the end of that month, Prussian troops entered Dresden, driving Napoleon's Saxon henchmen before them.

Meanwhile, with Soult and his forces transferred from Spain to Germany, the marquess of Wellington, as Wellesley had become (he was made a duke in 1814), pushed north-east until on 21 June he caught and smashed the army of Marshal Jourdan at Vittoria. During this same period, English subsidies were being hurriedly granted to a dozen central European partners, to increase the pressure on Napoleon. In August cautious Austria at last declared war on France, joining Russia and Prussia in a formal alliance at Teplitz in September. Even Bavaria left the Confederation of the Rhine to enter the coalition against the French. Finally, in four days of violent fighting around Leipzig, 16–19 October, the allies defeated Bonaparte in what was soon christened the Battle of the Nations. King Frederick of Saxony, the emperor's last major German sympathizer, was taken prisoner; King Jerome fled from his Westphalian realm; and the other west German states hastened to leave the sinking ship. As Napoleon dropped back from the Rhine in November, Wellington crossed the French frontier at the western end of the Pyrenees and successfully attacked Bayonne. From Holland came news of a general revolt and the expulsion of imperial officers, both military and civil. Everywhere the great structure, built in victory, was buckling in defeat.

Napoleon's chief hope of salvation lay in the chronic jealousy and suspicion among the powers attacking him. In addition, there was some chance that he might capitalize on their monarchs' uneasiness in the face of patriotic demands for mass risings against the French Empire, demands which might threaten other kinds of authority as well. Austria, in particular, had reason to stop short of a total victory likely to benefit its old rivals, Prussia and Russia, while releasing nationalistic passions among the various groups of Francis I's subjects. In 1813 Metternich could still perceive advantages in maintaining Bonaparte, linked as he was to the Habsburgs by marriage, on the throne of a France reduced to manageable size and made less belligerent by adversity. Early in November, therefore, the Austrian foreign minister stole a march on his allies by making a peace overture which guaranteed France its natural frontiers, that is, the Rhine, Alps and Pyrenees as permanent boundaries. This would have acknowledged the erstwhile Republic's conquests through 1796, leaving Belgium, the German left bank and Nice-Savoy under French rule. These terms, however, the emperor curtly refused. On 21 December the armies of the coalition crossed the Rhine, beginning the invasion of northern France.

Local victories in February 1814 so exhilarated Napoleon that he again brushed aside peace offers, this time reduced to the boundaries of 1792. As a result, the British foreign minister, Castlereagh, was able to secure an Allied agreement, signed 9 March at Chaumont in Champagne, that the war should be fought out, in concert, to a clear decision. For the next three weeks, the French fell back, losing one encounter after another. On 31 March their enemies entered Paris. Simultaneously, in southern France, Wellington was ending the long struggle that had carried his soldiers from Portugal to Bordeaux on 12 March and a climactic victory over Soult at Toulouse on 10 April. A week earlier Napoleon had abdicated. On 11 April he accepted the treaty of Fontainebleau, which gave him sovereignty over the tiny island of Elba, off the Italian Mediterranean coast near

Piombino, an annual pension of 2 million francs from the restored Bourbon monarchy and the right to retain the title of emperor.

The fears and criticisms of some observers who found this treatment excessively mild were justified by events within a year. Napoleon reached Elba on 4 May 1814; on 1 March 1815 he landed on the southern coast of France once more, determined to rally his former subjects against the foreign powers and King Louis XVIII, one of Louis XVI's younger brothers, whom those powers had placed on the French throne. The oft-told story of the 'Hundred Days' that followed need not be repeated in detail. As he proceeded north towards Paris, collecting troops around him as he went, Napoleon had several assets still working to his advantage. His name and military reputation had not lost their magic. The Bourbon restoration had been accompanied in many parts of France by a White Terror or persecution of suspected anti-monarchists, who consequently turned in anger and disgust to welcome the emperor back from exile. Ex-officers, in particular, found themselves intoxicated by resurgent memories of past glory. Marshal Ney, who had promised Louis XVIII that he would bring back the outlawed Bonaparte in an iron cage, met the culprit at Auxerre – and threw himself into his old commander's arms. The Allies, stunned by the turn of events, reacted with a predictable lack of coordination. Not until 25 March, five days after the former exile had entered Paris, did the Austrian, Prussian, Russian and British governments agree to contribute 180,000 troops apiece to a coalition army under Wellington's command.

Yet despite the euphoria surrounding his reappearance, the odds against Napoleon's gamble remained prohibitive. At no point in this final campaign did he control more than 150,000 troops, in the face of all Europe rearming against him. Allied forces immediately available totalled almost three-quarters of a million men, some 225,000 of them already poised in the Netherlands. The only considerable force supporting the emperor outside France was Murat's Neapolitan army, which invaded the Papal States and pushed north through Italy, only to be routed by the Austrians in the first days of May. The emperor now had no hope save in a smashing victory which would split his enemies and rally all Frenchmen behind him. On 12 June he hurried north from Paris to join his army for the showdown in Belgium. On the 16th, at Ligny, he won a tactical decision over Blücher's Prussians. Two days later, however, on the fog-enshrouded ridge of Waterloo, a few miles south of Brussels, the steadiness of Wellington's forces and the timely arrival of Prussian reserves destroyed over half the French army – and with it the last possibility that Napoleon might reverse the outcome of nearly a quarter-century of warfare. Abdicating for a second time on 22 June, he surrendered on 15 July to the commander of the English warship *Bellerophon* in the Breton port of Rochefort, in time to escape almost certain execution by the pursuing Prussians. In October the British vessel carried him to his final place of captivity, comfortable but escape-proof, on the remote South Atlantic island of St Helena. There, six years after his Empire's collapse, he died in 1821 before his fifty-second birthday.*

THE NATURE OF THE NAPOLEONIC EMPIRE

Thus laconically must the writer of a general history turn from a career which has inspired countless multi-volume works. So too must end the chronicle of international events which swirled about the figure of the Corsican cadet who became an emperor. The next two chapters will examine, respectively, the role of violence in the era and the diplomatic settlement that marked its close. The story of Europe and Napoleon, however, as it concerns the shifting alliances with and coalitions against him, as well as the political changes occurring in countries outside France during the long struggle, we can here pursue no further.

There remains only the question posed at the start of the present chapter. What was 'hegemony' as visualized by Napoleon and resisted by his enemies? Some French historians have argued that all their country has ever sought, even under the imperial eagle,

---

* Although several recent books, including that by Ben Weider and David Hapgood, *The Murder of Napoleon* (New York, 1982), have sought to prove that the ex-emperor was assassinated by poison administered on St Helena by a royalist secret agent, the balance of available evidence still appears to favour the view that his death resulted from cancer of the stomach. Traces of arsenic identified in his remains when they were transferred to their present resting place, the Invalides in Paris, can be plausibly accounted for by the frequent use of that chemical as a specific for internal pain used throughout the nineteenth century. For further discussion of this controversy, (see F. L. Ford, *Political Murder: From Tyrannicide to Terrorism* (Cambridge, Mass., 1985), pp. 409–10.

was security within its 'natural frontiers'. The other annexations, whether in Italy or Spanish Catalonia, Germany or Holland or the Dalmatian coast of the Adriatic, were required, according to this view, in order to protect the *Grande Nation* itself. And all the battle lines, from Egypt to Portugal to the freezing plains before Moscow, had to be stretched so far because other powers, England above all, would not accept Greater France.

Proceeding from their own assumptions and sentiments, apologists claim that Napoleon could not call a halt to his rampaging armies so long as the United Kingdom remained at once hostile and unreachable. The Continental System and the coercion required to consolidate it are justified by the thesis that, confronted by England's sea power, the emperor had no choice but to organize all Europe in pursuit of victory. Even his betrayal of Spain in 1808 appears in some treatments as a necessary effort to 'free the Iberian shoulder' for the final struggle against Great Britain.

However, presented with this moving image of an organizer of France who only yearned for peace and stability, yet was compelled by defensive considerations to undertake ever more ambitious struggles, the thoughtful student is apt to feel misgivings. *Did* Napoleon in fact see all his wars as part of a master plan to bring England to its senses, if not its knees? We have no evidence that he did. The Spanish venture, for example, he seems to have embraced out of a mixture of dynastic pride and rather petulant distrust of his Bourbon allies in Madrid. Still more difficult to explain away is the aggressive, unbridled tone adopted by the emperor towards Russia in 1812. True, he accused Alexander of failing to support the common front against Britain; but still more vehemently, he denounced Russian ambitions in the Near and Middle East, thereby revealing his own. Furthermore, this allegedly wistful defender of French frontiers proposed, whatever the tsar might feel, to reorganize Slavic Europe around his expanding grand duchy of Warsaw. Even if the British Isles had not existed, it seems unlikely that Napoleon could have long endured Alexander I as a co-arbiter and rival in continental affairs.

Hegemony in Europe has meant different things to different individuals at different times. French hegemony, as Napoleon conceived it, was no doubt a less repellent vision than the German hegemony, at once pitiless and vulgar, envisaged by Adolf Hitler. It was also, however, something more ambitious than the kind of paramount power or leadership among a constellation of weaker, but nonetheless comparable states that would satisfy Bismarck, as for that matter it had satisfied Louis XIV of France in all his pompous pride. Year by year Napoleon seemed to lose the capacity for dealing with other governments or even tolerating their independent existence. Not surprisingly, he ended with virtually all such governments arrayed against him. Even in 1813 he was not willing to accept the natural frontiers so dear to French nationalist historians. As the final tides of defeat washed in, when the Allies offered precisely those frontiers, the emperor refused what he considered an insolent and demeaning proposition. By now, it was all or nothing. Or almost nothing – St Helena covers forty-seven square miles.

NOTES AND REFERENCES

1   G. Bodart, *Losses of Life in Modern Wars* (Oxford, 1916), pp. 214 ff.

10

THE DIMENSIONS OF VIOLENCE

An age of conflict demands of its students a willingness to consider many forms of violence indulged in by *homo sapiens* from the latter's beginnings as the earth's most dangerous species. Because the age of the Great Revolution and Napoleon was one of war, it seems best to begin here with the evolution of formal warfare. To do that and that alone, however, would be insufficient.

Beginning around 1790, and continuing for some three decades thereafter, Europe was swept by waves of actually or potentially violent behaviour by no means confined to military action. Personal crimes, mob violence and harsh judicial penalties all retained their places in European life. In addition, the purposeful killing of politically significant individuals – in other words, assassination narrowly defined – resumed an importance it had lost during the latter stages of Europe's pre-revolutionary history. Finally, we shall need to consider the economic and ideological weaponry whose use went hand-in-hand with the battles fought on land and sea from the outbreak of formal hostilities in 1792 to their thunderous climax at Waterloo.

THE SIZE AND EQUIPMENT OF ARMIES

A twentieth-century American historian has seen in this era the beginning of modern man's experience with total war, fought by greatly expanded armies, using weapons supplied by increasingly

232

efficient technology, in pursuit of aims defined by entire peoples' will to conquer.[1] According to his view, the marriage of war and industry goes back at least as far as the fifteenth century; but until about the middle of the eighteenth religious restraints, combined with the traditional caution of princes, had prevented the full realization of this military–industrial combination's potential for destruction. Increasingly, so runs the argument, the late 1700s brought into view the motives, the techniques and the implements of modern carnage. It then remained for the French Revolution to unleash the requisite popular passions to make such havoc a reality. Whether or not one agrees with this vision in all respects, there can be no doubt concerning the military significance of the almost quarter-century-long struggle that opened in 1792. It witnessed not only the involvement, on an unprecedented scale, of armies and navies but also the marshalling of economic and psychological weapons in the service of vast projects.

As we have already seen, most eighteenth-century armies had been small by later standards. Prior to the 1790s, a major strategic plan or military treaty might call for no more than 18,000 or 24,000 troops – the familiar reckoning in units of 6,000, traditionally associated with the size of a Roman legion, having survived until the end of the Old Régime. It is true that by the time of Frederick the Great's death in 1786, the Prussian army could boast a mobilizable strength of some 200,000 men, as compared to 90,000 at his accession in 1740; yet even in Frederick's bitterest wars, on only two or three occasions did he commit more than 50,000 men to a single action. A contemporary French general too might find himself in command of at least that many; and Russia had raised still greater numbers for action on its sprawling Turkish, Polish and Baltic fronts. These exceptional cases, however, did not alter the prevailing reliance on small, highly trained armies of long-term regulars.

A new level of expectations regarding military manpower began to emerge with French levies of 1792, theoretically composed of volunteers but actually fixed by quotas assigned to all the territorial *départements* and filled by lot wherever necessary. The results were not immediate. In the first campaign, leading to Valmy, some 70,000 Prussians and Austrians faced at most 52,000 French defenders, of whom only the 16,000 men of Kellermann's *Armée du Centre* appeared ready for battle. By January 1793, however, the combined forces of the Republic on the northern frontier alone came to about 112,000.[2] In the course of that year, a more startling increase resulted from the *levée en masse*, the nationwide mobilization destined to raise an estimated 450,000 recruits during Lazare Carnot's four years as war minister.

Concentrations of military manpower varied considerably in size throughout the Napoleonic era. The differences separating Bonaparte's 30,000 troops in the first Italian campaign, Moreau's 120,000 at Hohenlinden, the 430,000 with which the Grand Army assailed Russia in 1812 and possibly 150,000 for the emperor's last, Belgian, campaign make it difficult to generalize about the 'normal' size of even French armies during those two decades of campaigning. Napoleon had perhaps 65,000 men under his direct command at Austerlitz, 85,000 or more at Jena, nearer to 165,000 at Wagram, 135,000 at Borodino, 190,000 at Leipzig. In themselves, these figures may suggest no radical increase over those of pre-revolutionary armies, but note that they refer only to specific engagements. In 1808, on the eve of the campaign that would end at Wagram, the former Corsican cadet disposed of some 300,000 troops stationed in Spain, 100,000 in France, 200,000 in the Rhineland and 60,000 in Italy.[3] Heavy conscription at home and in occupied (especially German) lands had by that date produced armed masses which dwarfed any in Europe's past. One expert has calculated that between 1800 and 1815, the number of Frenchmen alone called to the colours reached 2 million, of whom an estimated 400,000 died either during or as a result of their military service.[4] Though Napoleon's enemies, in combination, were obviously capable of matching, and eventually surpassing, the armed might of his Empire, a persistent lack of enthusiasm and co-ordination prevented their actually doing so until the final campaigns of 1813–15. In 1812 even the Russians were outnumbered in several key battles. Throughout that same year Wellington in Spain never controlled more than 80,000 troops at any one time, while Marshal Soult's Iberian command, although dispersed and constantly harassed by the Spanish irregulars who introduced the term 'guerrilla' into common usage, still totalled over 200,000. Only after the campaign in Russia ignited the War of Liberation were overpowering Allied forces assembled in central and eastern Europe. By the time of the Hundred Days, as pointed out in Chapter 9, France's enemies were able quickly to remobilize three-quarters of a million men, 225,000 of whom would converge on Waterloo.

No such numbers could have been attained without conscription on a scale sufficient to match the tremendous French levies. Russia had long raised its regiments by the drawing of lots in villages, the young peasants thus selected being enrolled for terms of twenty-five or even thirty years. In the Slavic and Hungarian regions of the Habsburg empire, similar methods were used, though the terms of service were generally shorter and the dependence on compulsory service was less nearly complete than in the territories under Romanov rule. The Hungarians in particular seem to have enlisted with notable enthusiasm. Austria, under Archduke Charles's leadership, and Prussia, under that of the post-Jena reformers, led the German states in the formulation of orderly rules covering recruitment, active duty and service in the reserves. As for Britain, while the government never imposed conscription for active duty abroad, local military units were frequently replenished by the drawing of ballots; and the War Office sought with considerable success to induce militiamen thus enrolled to transfer into regiments of the line bound for Spain, the colonies or, later, Flanders.

During this period, a number of interesting and by no means irrelevant changes took place in military uniforms. Perhaps the most important was an increase in uniformity itself within a particular army. During most of the eighteenth century, standardization had remained limited to a relatively few crack regiments. Nevertheless, certain general features of European military costume were widespread on the eve of the Revolution. Headgear ranged from the turned-up tricorn and other forms of cocked hat through close-fitting leather helmets and the Russian common soldier's cylinder of soft wool to the high, stiff 'grenadier's cap' suggestive of a bishop's mitre. Some form of cutaway coat was frequently seen, usually adorned with flaps, facings, epaulets, buttons and frogs. Since the creation of the Black Watch in 1739, Scottish troops in His Britannic Majesty's service had been authorized to retain their traditional kilts; but most other European infantrymen wore short breeches and either high boots or, more often, tightly buttoned gaiters.

As a result less of the revolutionaries' aversion to old-fashioned costumes than of the need to attire large new armies more simply and less expensively, military dress by about 1800 had in many countries lost much of its earlier character. Hard campaigning had led to the abandonment of unessential adornment. Comfortably loose-fitting trousers over shoes or low boots were becoming far more popular than breeches and long leggings. The tall grenadier's mitre had by this time all but disappeared, though the cocked hat and the snug helmet of leather or metal both retained favour with some armies.

In the years that followed, Napoleon's troops and the principal forces opposing them displayed a somewhat puzzling tendency to move back to more elaborate, even pretentious uniforms. Perhaps this development can be explained by a combination of imperial pomp in France and the long period of militarization of European life in general. Whatever the cause, by 1815 there had evolved a characteristic set of costumes destined to remain in general use for a half-century or more: trousers or long, close-fitting pants, low boots, high-collared jackets with crossing shoulder belts and stiff, cylindrical visored hats modelled on the Hungarian *shako*. There were of course many exceptions: plumed helmets and breastplates worn by the cuirassiers (heavy cavalry), the towering fur headgear of Napoleon's Imperial Guard, the loose tunics and round caps of Russia's Cossacks. In a number of armies, an entire family of special units were born of romantic enthusiasm for the dashing cavalrymen of eastern Europe. These *uhlans* and *hussars*, whatever their actual nationality, affected the ornate boots, richly braided jackets, capes and fur hats associated with Hungary and Poland – and their swagger bespoke the elitist arrogance that often accompanies the exotic. The degree of uniformity achieved by 1815 was nonetheless remarkable.

Weapons underwent relatively little modification between 1792 and 1815. At first glance this may appear surpising; but it becomes less so when one recalls the very considerable changes in the tools of war immediately preceding the Revolution. The famous artillery of Napoleon, for example, was essentially the product of Gribeauval's reforms in the 1770s and 1780s: standardized field pieces for four-, eight- and twelve-pound balls; light howitzers for close bombardment; prefabricated cloth bags containing powder charge, ball and wadding; four- and six-horse teams paired in spans; gun carriages and limbers made both stronger and lighter by increased use of thin iron frames. By the 1790s all these developments were available to any army wishing to copy them, as was the growing reliance on interchangeable parts (wheels, pins, bolts) and the cannister of round antipersonnel shot recently invented by an Englishman, Lieutenant Shrapnel.

One new form of artillery, the explosive rockets developed by Colonel William Congreve in imitation of weapons first encountered by British troops in India, made its appearance in Europe during the Napoleonic period. 25,000 of these projectiles are supposed to have been fired upon Copenhagen during the British attack of 1807, and some use was made of them by the Allies at Leipzig in 1813. Napoleon expressed no interest in this development, however, and even his enemies seem to have relied only sparingly on 'Congreve's rockets', best known to Americans through the words of their national anthem.

Basic categories of infantry weapons were already well established before general fighting broke out in the century's final decade. Smoothbore flintlock muskets, firing heavy lead bullets from two-thirds to four-fifths of an inch in diameter, albeit with no claim to accuracy beyond a hundred-yard range, had been widely adopted by major armies early in the eighteenth century. Longer muskets with spiral grooves (rifling) in the barrel were by the mid-1700s already prized for their greater range and accuracy. Rifles were especially popular for hunting in the German and Scandinavian countries, and during the American Revolution the British had found them dangerous implements in the hands of frontiersmen serving as skirmishers. At the same time, long-barrelled hunting pieces were both fragile and unwieldy in bayonet encounters, while calling for more careful priming than service muskets demanded. Not until 1800 did the British army create a full brigade equipped with Baker rifles, and continental commanders were more cautious still. Official conservatism also greeted the Scotsman Forsyth's percussion charge, a small quantity of potassium chlorate capable of replacing the flint-sparked ignition of gunpowder. Though the inventor perfected a percussion lock in 1805, it was to be another ten years before a separate, self-contained percussion cap became available.

SUPPORTING SERVICES

What today would be called 'service forces', responsible for military supplies, construction, medical care, communications and intelligence, in Napoleon's time lagged far behind the combat arms. Quartermaster functions, for example, were in most armies relegated to the status of temporary duty for soldiers assigned to foraging details and to the protection of supplies pending their distribution. French revolutionary armies, noted for their willingness to live off the country in which they were operating, had only contempt for the ponderous supply trains of the eighteenth century; and Napoleon himself, despite his alleged remark that an army travels on its stomach, paid little attention to the organized services of supply. In relatively prosperous territory, such as northern Italy, the Rhineland or the Low Countries, troops could indeed support themselves by foraging and were the more mobile for doing so. In the emperor's later campaigns, however, especially in barren reaches of Spain and the frozen expanses of Russia, part of the French armies' woes stemmed from the exhaustion of local resources.

In contrast to Bonaparte, British military leaders showed themselves singularly determined to have needed supplies accompany the army. 1794 saw the creation of the corps of Royal Wagoners, resplendent in red jackets, yellow cuffs, blue breeches and leather caps. This body was reorganized in 1799 to form the Royal Wagon Train, familiar to readers of Kipling and other chroniclers of nineteenth-century campaigns. Wellington, at once meticulous and conservative in this as in other matters, insisted that supply columns, equipped with light, high-wheeled carts, accompany his forces on the long marches of the Peninsular War. In the event, this form of mobility, less obvious but more reliable than that of the rampaging French legions, helped to bring final victory.

In military engineering, on the other hand, France under both the Republic and the Empire could justly claim to lead all Europe. The proud *Génie*, as every student of military history knows, had held a secure place in the French army under the Bourbon monarchy as well. However, until the revolutionary government created the Central School of Public Works (renamed in 1795 the *Ecole Polytechnique*), no nation had ever accorded so high a priority to training in fortification, demolition, bridge construction and related skills. Only by learning from the enemy did Napoleon's foes bring their own engineering services up to the level they had attained by the Waterloo campaign.

Medical care for troops in action remained, in all armies, dependent on the good offices of the wounded's own comrades and the possible, though largely fortuitous, presence of one of the pitifully scarce field surgeons. A serious wound was almost certain to result in, at worst, death or, at best, amputation and lasting disability. Field hospitals were seldom more than cellars, garrets or farm buildings commandeered for this purpose. Despite rudimentary improvements in sanitation and control of epidemics, the loss of life caused by disease during the long Prussian retreat from Jena in 1806–7, for example, or Napoleon's Russian campaign in 1812 is terrible to contemplate. The filth, neglect and inefficiency reported by Florence Nightingale in the 1850s had of course been accepted parts of the military scene long before her exposure of the Crimean horrors.

In the related areas of communications and intelligence gathering, the revolutionary-Napoleonic period brought certain technical advances, but surprisingly few of major significance. The British system of naval flags denoting letters and numbers which had been developing for some time, was both expanded and refined by Sir Home Popham in the 1790s. Armies and navies alike relied heavily on hand semaphore signals. However, French experiments with a mechanical semaphore telegraph – signal towers strung across the countryside from hilltop to hilltop – failed to produce a revolution in military communications. Napoleon, never an enthusiast where technological innovation was concerned, derided the system as costly and, much worse in his view, susceptible to easy interception of its messages by hostile observers. Hence the most important such chain proved to be the one operated by his British enemies between Portsmouth and the Admiralty in London.

It was doubtless this same distrust of gadgetry that led Napoleon to quash another innovation: the use of ground-anchored observation balloons. This experiment had been launched with considerable fanfare in 1794 but was abandoned by French forces when Bonaparte came to power. The gathering of most military intelligence remained thereafter, as it had been before, dependent upon espionage, reconnaissance by cavalry patrols, interrogation of enemy prisoners and sightings through the light, collapsible telescopes not replaced by binocular field glasses until the mid-nineteenth century.

ORDER OF BATTLE

As remarked in Chapter 4, the Old Régime's long debate over tactics – thin line versus solid phalanx, *ordre mince* versus *ordre profond* – was still in progress when war broke out in the 1790s. It was doubtless inevitable that the first military efforts of the new French Republic should be based on a violent, largely undisciplined onslaught of masses of men; for the hastily recruited armies of the Revolution possessed neither the precision of movement nor the coolness in musketry required by the *ordre mince*. Their counterbalancing asset was the wild *élan*, the enthusiasm of troops who began by defending what was for them a holy cause and who came to believe, after victories such as Jemappes and Fleurus, that no force on earth could withstand their bayonets.

In this collision between the armed hordes of French recruits and the well-drilled but generally dispassionate regiments of the Allies, both sides started by proclaiming the virtues of their respective tactics. Actually, however, each began almost at once to take steps which betrayed some recognition of the other's capabilities. Robespierre himself sponsored the shortlived School of Mars in 1794, hoping that young Jacobins could be taught sound tactical principles in a fifteen-week course without losing their zeal for the headlong attack. After Thermidor this particular experiment was dropped, but Carnot perceived too clearly the value of operational discipline not to insist on increasingly careful training of the Directory's armies. Conversely, by the end of the 1790s the enemies of France were translating their concern over the revolutionary style of assault into specific tactical adjustments. Unfortunately for the Allies, none among them developed a coherent new system of defence – still less of attack – until the roll of French victories had begun to appear endless.

In certain respects Napoleon's preferred tactics recalled the mixture of discipline and temerity, of manoeuvre and impact, which had been Guibert's ideal before 1789. This, however, is only a part of the story. On the one hand, Bonaparte's reliance on swiftness of movement, his willingness to employ thin screens of infantry to conceal the disposition of his main forces, his use of cavalry probes and harassment by teams of snipers did mark him as an heir of the *ancien régime*. On the other hand, in his insistence on the decisive charge, relentless pursuit and wholesale carnage as an end in itself, he revealed his debt to the Revolution.

It is a fact worth noting that the armies responsible for overthrowing the French Empire owed their ultimate success to two sharply opposed principles of action. On the one hand, the Russians had relied heavily on the mass assault long before the

French, and nothing about the latter's military record after 1792 inclined the tsar's commanders to make significant changes. Similarly, Prussian military recovery after 1806 was to a considerable extent achieved by abandoning the precise movement of files in favour of a more dashing, if less disciplined 'onrush of patriots'. The battle of Leipzig in 1813 may be seen as the climax of this development; for in that four-day melee of savage bayonet charges and confused retreats, central and eastern European forces simply wore out Napoleon's army, beating it at its own game.

At the the other extreme, the British had by this time transformed the eighteenth-century *ordre mince* into a set of tactics which succeeded in Spain and soon would share much of the credit at Waterloo. Wellington was no blind traditionalist. He reduced the old three-rank formation to a more efficient double line able to deliver rapid, alternating fire over a wide front. He employed skirmishers to punish advancing columns before the latter reached his infantry. Above all, he used terrain with a skill rivalling Napoleon's own, in order to shield that infantry until its fire power could have full effect. Basically, however, he remained wedded to the proposition that an unshakeable line of well-trained men, often formed into a square, could withstand and eventually disperse the most furious charge. In part, this strategy was determined by the very nature of his forces, which had to compensate in precision for what they lacked in sheer weight of numbers. The problems of overseas supply, combined with Parliament's refusal to impose conscription, set stringent limits on British manpower available for operations on the Continent. Even at Waterloo, the Redcoats totalled fewer than 30,000. At the same time it must be said that Wellington's system was also the product of his own cold, orderly mind and his estimate of potential French weaknesses.

Given the scale and complexity of warfare during this period, important developments in command organization were doubtless inevitable. In 1793 Britain revived the office of commander-in-chief, a position earlier included among other functions of the king but now entrusted first to Lord Amherst and then, in 1795, to Frederick, duke of York and Albany. Much criticism has been directed at this second son of George III for his alleged shortcomings: inability to keep his mistress out of matters of army administration, unrealistic strategic views and personal vacillation in combat. More recent studies, however, have brought at least a controlled reaction in favour of the duke of York, crediting him with having laboured conscientiously to overhaul his country's military organization.

Under his aegis the adjutant-general's department was expanded, training regulations were modernized, financial accounting was improved, provisioning of troops was brought under more centralized control and the chain of command was somewhat better defined. Not that the diligent duke, from his office at the Horse Guards in London, succeeded in coordinating field operations to the liking of everyone. For several months in 1808, to cite one example, he left the brilliant General Moore in a subordinate position under the two senior nonentities technically commanding British forces in Portugal. The demand for increased paper work, a by-product of the effort to improve accounts and records, was anathema to many officers including Wellington, who wrote from Spain in 1810 to the under-secretary of state for war: 'My Lord, if I attempted to answer the mass of futile correspondence that surrounds me, I should be debarred from all serious business of campaigning.'[5] Despite Wellington's angry contempt for 'the futile drivelling of mere quill-driving', however, he owed more than he would admit to the duke of York's efforts as commander-in-chief.

Napoleon, as France's chief of state and at the same time her supreme war lord, had distinct advantages in seeking to maintain centralized control over military planning and operations. Even he, of course, encountered periodic frustration born of poor intelligence reporting and communications, the vanity of subordinate commanders or some unforeseen change of circumstances. But despite his subsequent complaints about slow or faulty obedience to his orders, Napoleon's strategic oversight set a new standard for European armies.

The emperor's continental opponents, be it said, were not notably successful in meeting that standard in his own time, despite widespread efforts to strengthen the machinery of command. Austria's best general, Archduke Charles, was never quite sure what to expect from his brave but mercurial regiments. Tolstoy's brilliant caricature of Napoleon and Kutuzov in *War and Peace* – the former convinced that he was directing a great army, the latter aware that he was merely being swept along in front of one – is misleading in that it underestimates Bonaparte's actual power, but it may well contain a valid comment on the Russians' own experience. In Prussia, though the army reformers unquestionably began to work great changes for the future through their expansion of the General Staff, Scharnhorst himself had to admit that once operations began, an old warhorse such as Blücher would go where his experience and his hunches dictated.

OFFICERS AND MEN

All armies at the start of the nineteenth century were striving to find the best strategic unit, large enough by itself to offer decisive weight in specific engagements, compact enough to react swiftly to changing threats and opportunities, small enough to be readily assimilated into more complex formations. By the end of that century there would be widespread acceptance of just such a self-contained battle unit: the *division*, its three or four infantry regiments and cavalry components accompanied by their own supply train, artillery, engineers and signals, its commanding general entrusted with considerable discretion in the conduct of local operations. In the period we are considering, however, variation and lingering confusion were still the ruling characteristics. The division, to be sure, had been tried as an experiment in the French army as early as the 1770s, and Napoleon frequently used such units for specific tasks. The British 'Light Division', which won fame in the Peninsular War, was formed in 1803 out of three regiments superbly trained by Sir John Moore. Last but not least, the Prussian leaders sought briefly, in 1813, to impose a standardized divisional structure on their renascent army. Nevertheless, the great wars ended with all armies still organized primarily on the basis of regiments, constantly regrouped into shifting patterns of brigades and corps.

Under these circumstances, a major burden inevitably fell on officers of company and field, i.e. regimental, grade. Just who the colonels and majors, the captains, lieutenants and ensigns of the period were, where in society they came from, how they were selected and how trained, are questions which have never to my knowledge elicited broad, comparative inquiry. We do know that the French officers' corps suffered serious decimation of these ranks in the early 1790s, through defection and emigration, that the promotion of non-commissioned officers from the old army and of promising recruits subsequently built able new cadres and that the latter's heavy casualties, especially in the Russian campaign, may have been the most damaging single blow suffered by Napoleon's Empire.

In most other countries, some commissions were regularly granted in the field, for valour in action, but many more were conferred upon landed gentlemen (considered the natural leaders of peasant levies) or were purchased by aspiring young men of wealth. The duke of York, though critical of Britain's system of venality and favour, never attempted to do more than mitigate its worst effects, noting as he did so that the old methods had, if nothing else, permitted the rapid advancement of Wellington. In the Habsburg lands, the county rolls of landed titles determined, almost alone, what military rank a young man might initially receive – and in many an instance, how high he could rise. Needless to say, the Russian Empire looked to its nobility for officers.

Prussia's case is the most complex, for the Prussian army of the eighteenth century had been noted for the near monopoly enjoyed by its landed gentry, or *Junkers*, in the matter of access to commissioned ranks. After Jena, however, General von Scharnhorst and his colleagues in the Military Reorganization Commission quickly concluded that able young men of middle- or even lower-class origins must be permitted to rise in the service. Training schools for new ensigns were established in three cities; and in order to provide more advanced officers' training, the old Military Academy was revived and shortly renamed the War Academy. By the time it resumed hostilities in 1813, the Prussian army boasted an officers' corps which, for the time being at least, could rival the French in its openness to talent.

Before leaving the subject of land warfare, we should ask how the common soldier saw this long period of struggle. A great deal, of course, depended on the army to which he belonged. As for the troops of Napoleon, despite terrible casualties (indeed, perhaps in part because of the rapid promotion resulting from them), fighting spirit seems to have remained extremely high to the very end. Even the screams and curses of dying men along the emperor's road back from Moscow did not echo so loudly as to drown out the cheers that greeted his return from Elba in 1815 or the defiant shouts of French regiments at Waterloo. Napoleon offered glory, spoils, preferment and those ringing exhortations which marked him as one of history's true masters of the technique known in modern jargon as 'opinion control'.

Here again, the Prussian reformers after 1806, bent as they were on mobilizing the patriotic devotion of citizen soldiers, were frankly imitative of the French model. In place of brutal floggings, they insisted that troops be accorded decent treatment under fair discipline. The abolition of corporal punishment for minor offences was in fact one of the handful of unqualified victories scored by Scharnhorst, Gneisenau and their associates over the enemies of change. When Napoleon himself said of the Prussians at Waterloo, 'these animals have learned something', he must have recognized that they were no longer the kind of troops he had routed at Jena nine years before.

Elsewhere, cruelty and contempt on the part of officers in their dealings with enlisted men remained a depressingly common pattern. Russian soldiers were serfs of the state and were treated accordingly, a rough paternalism being the best they could hope for. Austrian, Italian and Spanish practice was little better; and a Saxon colonel in 1812, even while serving as an ally of the French, regularly spoke of his regiment with ambiguous possessiveness as 'my swine'. British commanders, having no conscripts in their charge and necessarily cognizant of the 'scarcity value' of English, Scottish, Welsh and Irish soldiers, seldom permitted themselves the excesses of brutality displayed by many of their continental opposites. Corporal punishment nevertheless continued to be meted out in His Majesty's forces, and innumerable dispatches, notably including those of Wellington, breathe aristocratic scorn for the lowborn rabble in the ranks. It is necessary to call to mind an enlightened trainer of men like General Moore or visualize the genial militia colonel, riding a 'low pony' and hence dubbed 'Punch on a pig' by Private Wheeler and his comrades, if one is to understand how some troops retained as much liking for the service as they apparently did.[6]

NAVAL FORCES

Men who fought at sea tended to be very different from the soldiers on land, not only in background and training, but also in appearance. The enlisted seaman's uniform common to most navies until well after the end of the Second World War – short jacket or middy, bell-bottom trousers, neckerchief and small round cap – was already making its appearance among the British in Napoleonic times, although the old broad-brimmed hat was still more commonly worn. Naval officers of all nations tended to cling more tenaciously than did their army colleagues to costumes of a traditional, eighteenth-century style, including cutaway coats, silk knee breeches, white stockings and cocked hats.

That this formal, conservative look should have been especially characteristic of the Royal Navy was in one sense paradoxical. For to a much greater degree than her army, England's sea forces offered an opportunity for advancement to men of humble, or at most quite modest, origins. The same cannot, however, be said of other European navies. Even the French, after severe decimation of titled officers during the Terror, quickly turned once more to former noblemen such as Villeneuve, Magon de Clos-Doré and Ganteaume to fill most of the senior maritime commands. As for the Spanish and the Russians, their admirals and senior captains were almost without exception high aristocrats.

All the more striking, therefore, is the roster of British commanders who served under Nelson, himself one of eleven children of a Norfolk country clergyman. Though some of these men were of the gentry – and one of them at Trafalgar was a Scottish lord, the earl of Northesk – many more sprang from families of traders, seamen, farmers or parsons. Without exception, however, they had shared a rigorous training, ordinarily beginning as midshipmen when only twelve or thirteen years old and thereafter working their way up. It may be that the formal attire of these officers and their punctilious etiquette served an important purpose in ironing out differences of social rank, while creating the *esprit de corps* needed for the success of a ship or a squadron. For whatever reason, the Royal Navy seemed to build its own aristocracy.

Crews were still put together by a combination of enlistment and impressment, the latter amounting to the abduction of potential sailors ashore, having them transferred to the fleet by jail officials or even taking them from merchant ships at sea. The work of the press gangs went on continuously, in France no less than elsewhere, for the patriotic zeal that filled land regiments seems to have been only rarely found on shipboard. Once a naval vessel sailed, with a crew at least half of whose members were likely to have been impressed, it might remain at sea for several years, bringing supplies aboard from lighters even when it anchored in port. Wherever it finally docked there were sure to be desertions, in spite of threatened penalties and the dangers facing penniless seamen in a strange place. Discipline was brutal under the lash and the cat-o'-nine-tails, a wicked little many-stranded whip; quarters were cramped; the work was hard and dangerous; medical care was primitive; the food comprised a mixture of weevil-infested biscuits, maggoty gruel and dried meat of rocklike consistency.

A modern observer is understandably puzzled to find that common seamen recruited thus, living under such conditions and led by haughty, sometimes tyrannical officers, could bring themselves to fight as bravely as most did in countless engagements of the period. Why, one may ask, were the British naval mutinies at Spithead and the Nore in 1797 not frequently repeated instead of remaining, as was in fact the case, quite isolated events? In seeking an answer, we should bear in mind that for many of these men – unskilled labourers, vagrants, convicts – life on land had been even harder than life at sea. If the meals aboard ship were bad, they were at least regular. Naval justice was ordinarily no more savage and was generally less capricious than that of criminal courts ashore. Existence among the crowded hammocks below decks was preferable to shivering in city hovels or prison cells; there might be material windfalls in the form of prize money, and the crews themselves often developed a rough cama-raderie of danger, a share in the pride which the sea has always imparted to its own.

One more category of naval manpower deserves mention: the marine infantry or, more simply, 'marines'. Most eighteenth-century navies carried units of soldiers aboard warships, the British and Dutch having actually begun doing so as early as the 1660s. The age which concerns us, however, witnessed further expansion and still more regularization of this practice. By the end of the long struggle, all naval powers had companies of marines, attired in distinctive uniforms of army cut and assigned, some-times for long terms, to specific vessels. After 1802, Britain alone had some sixty companies, operating out of four major ports. Marines were used to deliver musket fire at enemy ships from decks and rigging, to carry out occasional landings (usually small ones) and, significantly, to enforce discipline upon their own ships' crewmen.

The sailing vessels that fought the era's battles were essentially those of the eighteenth century: tall-masted ships of the line, plus the smaller, faster frigates and sloops. These naval craft did not change significantly in size or fire power between 1792 and 1815. Nelson's flagship, HMS *Victory*, for example, with its displacement of 3,500 tons, an overall length of 186 feet and a crew of 660, was considered, deservedly, a powerful instrument of war. Possessed of 102 cannon able to fire twelve-, twenty-four- and thirty-two-pound balls with reasonable accuracy up to one mile, plus a pair of the deadly short-barrelled carronades for sweeping enemy decks at close range with sixty-eight pounds of grape shot per charge, a powerful instrument it certainly was. At Trafalgar no more than two of the other British ships were its equals in size and armament or manpower, most of them carrying from seventy to eighty-four guns. As for other European men-o'-war, only Spain's huge *Santissima Trinidad*, with its 130 guns and its crew of over 1,000, and Russian's ponderous 110-gun *Rostislav*, left over from Catherine the Great's naval building programme, could have been considered serious rivals to *Victory*. Yet the latter had been launched in 1765.

There were, to be sure, certain novel projects advanced during the protracted duel at sea. Napoleon's army of England, poised on the Channel coast from 1803 to 1805, was supposed to be equipped with hundreds of long, shallow-draught galleys, in which the French invasion troops were supposed to row themselves across to Kent and Sussex during a calm when the Royal Navy would lie helpless under empty sails. A few such galleys were actually built, but only a few – the emperor had too much else on his mind.

Far more dramatic, as well as more prophetic, were the American Robert Fulton's offers, first to the Directory and then to Napoleon, of both steam-propelled barges and underwater warships. In July 1800 Fulton's submarine, the *Nautilus*, was launched at Rouen; and the next year it successfully exploded a submerged mine which it had affixed to an abandoned hulk in the port of Brest, both impressing and horrifying the French officers for whom the demonstration was conducted. Napoleon having remained, as usual, unconvinced by mechanical ingenuity, the impartial inventor set off for Britain with his plans in 1805. The Admiralty apparently recognized the danger to conventional vessels which submarine attack might constitute; but it saw no reason whatever why a navy with the world's greatest surface force should help to develop this form of warfare. So Fulton went home to more peaceful achievements with his paddle-wheel steamer on the Hudson River, while in Europe the great, square-rigged ships of the line sailed on unchallenged – for the time being.

OPERATIONS AT SEA

As with the forces employed, so with strategy and tactics, naval wars of the Revolutionary-Napoleonic period produced little outward change. Powers with possessions overseas continued to detach warships from home squadrons in order to accompany or (depending on its nationality) to seize shipping en route to and from the colonies, protect distant outposts and attack enemy settlements. This last is what the British did in 1802 when they wrested Capetown from Napoleon's Dutch allies.

The distances covered in these forays were astounding considering the technical problems involved, not least of which were the weeks of waiting for orders and reconnaissance reports brought by messenger sloops. In 1805 Lord Nelson's 'great chase' took the British Mediterranean fleet from near Toulon, France, to Egypt (February), thence to Malta and back to the waters off Toulon (March), to Sicily and Gibraltar (April), across the Atlantic to the West Indies (11 May to 4 June), and back to Gibraltar once more before the admiral's return to England, where he arrived in mid-August for what proved to be less than a month of home leave. During all that time, while the Admiralty waited anxiously for news, Nelson never sighted the French-Spanish squadrons he was pursuing. Only in October, after the enemy had assembled at Cadiz and sailed forth as the Combined Fleets in an attempt to reach Gibraltar, was he able to close for his 'pell-mell battle' off Cape Trafalgar on the south-west coast of Spain.

Such a battle, once joined, might begin as a contest between lines of warships, with the opposing admirals exercising, at least at the outset, a degree of tactical control through the use of signal flags. Inevitably, however, the developing action became a mêlée of individual vessels, each seeking to deliver its salvos for maximum effect. The damage inflicted by such fire was often ghastly, for a broadside might be fired at the bow or stern of an enemy ship from only yards away, sending a deadly hale of cannon balls and grape shot, mixed with flying splinters from the victim's own timbers, the entire length of the hull below decks.

Trafalgar, history's last major battle between fleets under sail, deserves a moment's special attention. For, as numerous commentators have pointed out, it was a puzzling victory. The Combined Fleets of France and Spain lost twenty-three of their thirty-three ships, sunk or captured, with casualties amounting to an estimated 4,400 dead and 2,500 wounded. The British lost their admiral, 448 others dead and 1,214 wounded – but not one of their twenty-seven vessels. What Nelson had done was to sail into the strung-out enemy line with two parallel columns of ships, his own division and Admiral Collingwood's, breaking the line at two points as planned. Until those penetrations were achieved, however, the oncoming British, slowly approaching at right angles to the enemy line before only a light wind, had to take head-on a long series of French and Spanish broadsides directed at their own bows. Even with all three segments of the Combined Fleets' line scattered after contact, with individual ships trading cannon fire and boarding attempts, it is not immediately clear why the toll should have been so one-sided. The French and Spanish had some of the world's best-designed ships, handled by crews which fought stubbornly under a number of brave and able officers.

It seems likely that at Trafalgar, as in other battles of the period, the British advantage lay partly in superior equipment, especially cannon, but still more in experience. Since this in turn was the product of England's overall naval superiority, the explanation is of necessity a circular one. While would-be opponents spent months at a time penned up in various ports, ships of the Royal Navy were constantly at sea in large numbers. Hence, at Trafalgar and elsewhere, they were better handled in the scramble for position, their salvoes were fired more rapidly, and their gunnery was more accurate.

There was also the matter of leadership. What Nelson brought to naval warfare – at Cape St Vincent, the Nile, Copenhagen, as well as in sight of the Spanish coast on the last day of his life – was not an elaborate set of new theories, but rather a clear awareness of British assets and his own ferocity, an almost frantic impatience to get at and smash the enemy. He visualized every battle as one of annihilation. In his demonic intensity, supported by the skill and experience of his forces, he was to the war at sea what Napoleon was to the war on land. Together, these two commanders embodied the changes in war's very spirit occurring beneath the surface of apparent continuity in weapons and tactics.

AMPHIBIOUS WARFARE

Setting aside for the moment the matter of blockades, we have still to consider one more topic having to do with ships: sea–land operations. The transporting, disembarking and, where necessary, re-embarking of bodies of troops can have crucial strategic importance, as the Second World War emphatically revealed – and as the increased use of marine infantry reflected even in Nelson's time. Such actions, however, require especially elaborate preparation, carefully timed execution and adequate provision for a continuing flow of reinforcements and supplies to the forces once ashore. Judged by such requirements, large-scale landings attempted during the Revolutionary-Napoleonic wars were for the most part unimpressive affairs.

For one thing, marines were not yet conceived of as a service trained and equipped for *sustained* sea-to-land action. As earlier noted, marine companies were parcelled out to individual ships of the line, primarily to discharge shipboard duties. Hence, amphibious forces, such as they were, tended to be unprepared and often recalcitrant infantry regiments, marched aboard crowded vessels for movement to some ill-prepared assault. That picture holds true for the British landings on the French west coast in 1795, at Ostend in 1798, with the Russians against Holland in 1799, against Cadiz in 1800, on Walcheren Island at the mouth of the Scheldt in 1809 and a number of less ambitious actions. It holds equally true for French efforts to launch effective operations in Ireland and Wales during the 1790s. Napoleon's initially successful invasion of Egypt in 1798 can fairly be called a triumph of daring and luck over existing conditions – and the luck ran out very quickly. As for the joint Russian–Turkish conquest of the Ionian Islands in 1798–99, the inability of the small French land forces there to offer any serious resistance made the campaign militarily unimportant.

Apart from the Peninsular War, a vast land campaign partially supported from the sea, there were only two actions during the entire period which to modern eyes appear genuine amphibious victories. One was the disembarkation of some 5,500 British troops under Abercrombie and Moore at Aboukir Bay, near Alexandria, in March 1801. Here, the generals had made reasonably careful plans, covering among other things the initial movements of the troops after they were ashore. The result was a victory, over stiff opposition, the first step towards eventual defeat of Napoleon's abandoned army of Egypt. The other successful landing was the hit-and-run British assault on Copenhagen in 1807. In general, however, interservice rivalry in the field – navy officers' prejudices in the British case, matched by the contempt of army men for admirals in the French, Spanish and Russian – completed the work of lethargy and inexperience back at headquarters.

The era's greatest amphibious operation, of course, was never carried out. From 1803 through the summer of 1805, Napoleon's first Grand Army crouched along the Channel coast, while intricate plans for the invasion of England were prepared, revised, discarded, replaced by others. French cities and army regiments gave funds for men-o'-war and troop barges to be named in their honour. The emperor more than once ordered ships of the line to assemble off Brittany and to wrest control of the Channel from the Royal Navy long enough for his legions to 'jump the ditch'. At other times he seemed to be counting on oared galleys. In England, alarm beacons were prepared, militia were drilled, small forts of heavy brickwork (called Martello towers) were constructed along the south-east coast, and the Admiralty watched nervously for any threatening signs of a French or French–Spanish naval concentration.

But no invasion came. Weeks before Trafalgar ended the danger that Britain might lose, if only briefly, her naval supremacy, the French 'army of England' was dismantled, its components tramping towards the Danube to smash the continental partners in the Third Coalition. It may never be known whether Napoleon was serious about his invasion plans. He insisted repeatedly that he was; but he also framed the requirements for a successful landing in England in such a way that he could easily avoid the showdown, yet place the blame on his admirals' incompetence or timidity, or both. Perhaps, as some have argued, he merely used the Boulogne encampment to train a host for use elsewhere, welding it into a force wholly committed to himself in his new role as emperor. However that may be, the largest army ever assembled for a seaborne attack prior to the Second World War never set sail. Instead, it marched out of the naval sphere altogether, to become the army of Austerlitz and Jena.

THE SIGNIFICANCE OF THE PERIOD

Up to this point, nothing has been said concerning the development of general military *theory*, despite the important intellectual efforts of such commentators as the Prussian, Karl von Clausewitz, and the Swiss, Baron Antoine de Jomini. The reason for their omission is that these theoretical reflections were a part not so much of the age itself as of its legacy to later times. Napoleon applied calculation of a high order to his operational plans and decisions in the field. So did Carnot, John Moore, Wellington and, if I read the record correctly, Suvorov. There is a great difference, however, between the experienced pragmatism of such men and the elaborate conceptual structures created by even the most brilliant observers. For the years we have been examining only the former had immediate reality and meaning.

There is also, throughout most of the present chapter, a deliberate concentration on the principal contenders. This does not bespeak indifference to the armies of Turkey or Spain or Bavaria, the Danish or the Portuguese navy, the place of Holland or Sweden in the mercantile struggle. It is essential, nevertheless, to recognize in the progressive concentration of power in a few major states one of the period's chief characteristics. In the cold-blooded reckoning of force, the only armies that ultimately made much difference were the French, the Russian, the Prussian, the Austrian and, for reasons unrelated to numerical size, the British. Similarly, naval interest must be focused primarily on England and France, secondarily on Spain and, to a still lesser degree, on Russia. Economic warfare, in turn, involved all of Europe, but at the centre of the struggle were France, Great Britain and, increasingly in the later years, Russia. If those three powers alone seem to demand attention under all of the above headings, that is no illusory impression. For they were in fact the antagonists whose struggles did most to determine the outcome of the entire drama.

A final question has to do with our period's place in the long chronicle of organized war. As has been noted, the amount of technical innovation was surprisingly limited. Many novelties were advocated by individuals or small factions; but most of them either, as was true of steamships, submarines and military balloons, were not adopted at all or received only the grudging, partial reception accorded rocketry and the semaphore telegraph. As for tactics, it should be observed that the era's two climactic battles, Trafalgar at sea and Waterloo on land, were old-style victories, won by still recognizably eighteenth-century rules.

Yet there remains something more to be considered, something that transcends tactical and technological aspects to give the epoch its true significance for anyone pondering war and human history. What I have in mind is the brutally obvious combination of mass and intensity. As noted earlier, the wars dealt with here brought into conflict hundreds of thousands instead of tens of thousands; and these hosts were armed with the products of existing technology, developed in the eighteenth century but never before produced and put to work on such a scale. Whole peoples went forth to kill and be killed, under commanders the ferocity of whose conceptions of victory or annihilation outsoared the bounds of previous imagination.

NON-MILITARY VIOLENCE: CRIMES, MOBS AND PUNISHMENTS

One of the most serious errors we could make in approaching the record of violence not directly attributable to warfare would be to underestimate the incidence of purely personal crimes both before and after 1789. Felonies such as murder, rape, looting, armed robbery and kidnapping for profit were committed under the Old Régime as they have been, with varying rates of frequency, in all times for which judicial records survive.

Common sense and documentary evidence alike suggest that less violent offences, including various forms of thievery and fraud, were much more numerous still; and some modern critics insist that the period's special quality of harshness lay in its failure to distinguish as sharply as it should have between major and minor crimes. A society that hanged a sneak thief with no greater compunction than it brought to the execution of a murderer had much to answer for at the bar of Reason. What the French Revolutionary leaders, like countless other revolutionaries after them, were eloquent in offering was a double improvement: an overall reduction of crime, due to the burgeoning of civic virtue, and more even-handed treatment of those unfortunates who still ran afoul of the criminal courts.

Lethal action by crowds was also much more familiar to the eighteenth century than misleading suggestions of the latter's quiescence or lethargy might suggest. The Saint Bartholomew's massacre in Paris (1572) and the lynching of the brothers De Witt in Holland (1672) may have faded from memory with the passage of time, but the threat of mob violence still muttered ominously beneath the surface of public life before the Revolution. In England, as recently as 1780, it had broken into the open with shocking force in the notorious Lord Gordon riots (*see above*, p. 88). The question confronting leaders of the French populist movement was whether or not they could keep the tactics of protest, which were essential to their purposes, from deteriorating into mass butchery.

To a society accustomed to barbarous punishments for heresy, treason or lese-majesty, the altered modes of public slaughter under a new flag were not at first repugnant. France had after all been witness to the sadistic execution of a pitifully incompetent regicide, Damiens, literally torn apart before a large crowd at Paris in 1757 (following the pattern of execution laid down by the judges of Henry IV's assassination almost a century-and-a-half before). The very next year, in Portugal, the Marquis of Pombal had defended his hold on ministerial power by sending an entire family of aristocratic opponents – the Tavoras, father, mother and sons – to hideous deaths on a single public platform. Still fresher in the minds of Frenchmen in 1789 was the fate of Jean Calas, a Protestant falsely charged with having murdered his own son for religious reasons and broken on the wheel in 1762 by order of the Parlement of Toulouse before Voltaire could launch his famous campaign of exoneration. The welcome accorded the French Revolution by its admirers abroad as well as at home owed much to the mistaken idea that it would bring with it a new standard of criminal justice, born of a humane spirit and governed by rational restraint.*

Instead, after only a short respite, it brought the opposite. To be fair, one must concede that Dr Guillotin, in proposing to the National Assembly (of which he was a member) the adoption of the decapitating mechanism that bears his name, believed the step to be a progressive one. First, the guillotine could scarcely be so painful as the means applied to Damiens or Calas. Second, it promised to wipe out class distinctions, since under the previously existing system only noblemen were beheaded, whereas henceforth all condemned prisoners, regardless of social rank, would be entitled to suffer death by the same means. So French revolutionaries, at least for a time, endorsed the sanguinary programme of Robespierre's dictatorship. After all, as the Incorruptible himself so confidently asserted, betrayers of the Revolution were everywhere – communicating with royalist émigrés abroad, profiteering in the midst of war, arguing for political moderation while true patriots fought to achieve a final solution.

The psychology of the Terror remains in many ways the most familiar feature, as well as the most persistent enigma, of the French Revolution. This is so because the psychology has resurfaced so often in our own century, not only under Hitler and Stalin but also in the impatient tactics of ruling régimes in many other parts of the globe today. It is a psychology containing elements of ritual and dramatization of group identity social scientists are better equipped to explain than are most students of history. Historians in turn must ask themselves whether the

---

* It is important not to confuse the surviving, albeit greatly diminished, recourse to slow executions in· the mid–eighteenth century with the legal employment of judicial torture, whose abandonment *preceded* the French Revolution in almost every European nation. As its most recent historian has pointed out: 'Prussia all but terminated judicial torture in 1740; it was used for the last time in 1752 and authoritatively abolished in 1754. In 1770 Saxony abolished torture; in 1776 Poland and Austria-Bohemia; in 1780 France; in 1786 Tuscany; in 1787 the Austrian Netherlands; [and] in 1789 Sicily.' J. H. Langbein, *Torture and the Law of Proof* (Chicago, 1977), p. 10. England and Scotland had done so much earlier.

claims of purges past, with their assurance of better conditions once the culprits had perished, were justified by their results.

Whatever standard is applied to the French Terror's achievements, its ability to take human lives cannot be denied. In the opening stages of the great insurrection, destruction wrought by crowds did not exceed that inflicted in the Dutch Netherlands during the 1670s, for instance, nor in England during the Lord Gordon riots of 1780. The summer of 1789, it is true, brought death to members of the Bastille's garrison and to rather more insurgents, there and elsewhere, fired upon by royal troops. Less prophetic as things turned out, but considered sensational at the time, were attacks by peasants against unpopular rural landowners, and more especially their resident overseers, in response to the Great Fear (*see above*, pp. 112–13). Even these local revolts, however, recalled well-known precedents, the *jacqueries* that had erupted periodically for hundreds of years prior to the Revolution.

Two genuinely new departures resulted from the Revolution's national scope and emotional intensity, fuelled by what its leaders saw as ever-growing threats from their opponents. One was the persistence of mob violence *not* in the countryside but in the cities. The other was the greatly increased use of politically motivated death sentences, handed down by the Revolutionary courts in numbers simply unheard of under any judicial system known to Europe. This judgement reflects no sympathy for the often capricious cruelty of penal justice under the Old Régime, only a reminder of the staggering growth in frequency of executions under the new dispensation.

Regarding mass applications of lynch law, not a great deal can or need be added to what has been said in Chapter 6 about the September Massacres of 1792, which involved at least a thousand killings of alleged enemies of the Revolution inside and outside Paris prisons. It should perhaps be emphasized that during the ensuing years this lurid episode was not repeated in any other country. Even in France nothing quite like it took place under the Republic or Empire, the nearest thing to a recurrence coming only after 1815 in the 'White Terror' which for a time envenomed the Restoration. One other reflection suggested by the illegal Terror of 1792 is that in the eyes of its perpetrators, those who paused to reflect at all, it *did* have precedents in the worst cases of royal repression, especially the crushing of regional revolts under Louis

XIV a century or more in the past, when scores of insurgents were hanged and hundreds sent to the galleys. That memory, coupled with more recent examples of brutal arrogance by privileged individuals, led some sympathizers to defend the 'September murderers' as others called them.

Less obvious than crowd action, but more ominous in its implications, was the connection between political homicide carried out by mobs on the one hand and, on the other, ostensibly legal capital punishments handed down in thousands by the courts of the Republic. Local tribunals in more than a hundred cities and towns equipped with guillotines or other means of execution aped the practices of the central authorities in Paris; but figures showing formal death penalties that resulted by no means reflected the full extent of the slaughter. Also to be considered are the executions ordered by delegates 'on mission' and military commissions sent out by the Convention, armed with extraordinary powers to try suspects before summary panels and to inflict such penalties as the gruesome mass drownings (*noyades*) of hundreds of condemned traitors and 'aristocrats' in the Loire River at Nantes.[7]

One is tempted to say that revolutionary proscription and summary execution represented little more than the institutionalization of mass lynching, and in a sense this is true. At the same time, one would miss an important aspect of Jacobin Terror at the height of Robespierre's power during 1793 and the first half of 1794 if one overlooked the underlying force of its claim to legality. After all, its proponents argued, revolutionary justice was better than uncontrolled mob violence, in form if not in substance. And more important still, it represented the indispensable purge, without which freedom could never be secured. As the Jacobin anti-hero of Anatole France's novel, *The Gods Will Have Blood*, exclaims: 'At last we shall be happy, pure and innocent, if the traitorous scoundrels permit it.'[8] Obviously, the ever-growing number of such scoundrels – aristocrats, turncoats, deviationists, profiteers – would be sure to 'permit it' if all of them were dead.

The question arises whether this tremendous increase in the use of capital punishment was a phenomenon limited to France under the Terror or a more widely dispersed response to feverish times in Europe as a whole. Some evidence of the latter tendency does exist, as for example in the Habsburg 'Jacobin trials' of 1795, which produced seven executions at Budapest, and in the demands by British authorities for harsher treatment of defendants charged with sedition. However, neither Baron von Thugut's campaign in Austria and Hungary under Emperor Francis II nor actions by the English and Scottish courts even in their most repressive period resulted in anything approaching the scale of the French bloodbath.

For a full appreciation both of lynch justice and of its institutionalized extension, the death penalty for political prisoners, attention must be focussed on the home of the Revolution. Only there did mortality figures reach five figures. To say that they were imposed by the conditions of war and threats of treason in 1792 and 1793 is common but wholly inaccurate. As a brilliant French historian has recently written, 'The "Great Terror" did not coincide with the greatest distress of those terrible years: it arose instead in the spring of 1794, just as the military situation was improving. . . . It was the fantasy to compensate for the political impasse that had been reached, the product not of real struggle, but of the Manichaean ideology that would separate the good from the wicked, and of a pervasive social panic.'[9] This judgement, though it may concentrate too much on the final stages of the experience, helps to explain why only in France did major political figures perish on the scaffold of the guillotine: the king and queen, Brissot, Hébert, Danton, Desmoulins, Saint-Just, Robespierre, to mention only a few of the most prominent. One name, however, is missing, that of Jean Paul Marat, stabbed in his bath by Charlotte Corday. His death takes us to a category of political violence we have thus far not considered: purposeful, individual homicide inspired by political motives.

ASSASSINATIONS

For approximately 150 years prior to the outbreak of the French Revolution, Europe had been passing through one of those never easily explained intervals between epidemics of rampant political murder. This is not to say that there were no instances of assassination during the remission, to borrow a medical term. Plotters tried to kill King William III of England in 1694, and an aristocratic Hungarian opposition leader was fatally stabbed as he sought to address his country's Diet in 1707. The following decades witnessed a scattering of other episodes including the abortive attacks on Louis XV of France and Joseph I of Portugal in the 1750s, previously mentioned in connection with the frightful executions of their perpetrators. Most sensational of all had been the slaying of Tsar Peter III of Russia in 1762, with the knowledge and approval of his consort, Catherine the Great.

Yet the number of such acts, either consummated or only attempted, over so long a time was amazingly small when compared with the scores of sensational killings during the Wars of Religion before the 'early modern interlude' began, or the many more that followed in the nineteenth and twentieth centuries, after it ended. Historians are still far from agreement over an explanation for this near-eclipse of assassination. Did it occur because in Age of Reason, low in both religious and secular 'causes', lacked both the popular fervour and the theoretical defense by intellectuals needed to promote political murder? Or does the answer lie in the *relative* absence of mass warfare, capable of dulling people's repugnance toward bloodshed, until almost the end of the 1700s? Whatever the cause, or combination of causes, there can be no doubt that the Revolutionary epoch brought dramatic changes, in this as in many other regards.[10]

Given its time and location, the fatal stabbing of Jean-Paul Marat by a deeply anti-Jacobin young woman, Charlotte Corday d'Armont, at Paris on 13 July 1793 brought assassination most dramatically into the centre of the Revolution. Corday saw herself as the avenger of friends in her native Normandy proscribed and executed by the Robespierrian regime to the accompaniment of Marat's journalistic applause – and she went to the guillotine showing neither fear nor regret while the Convention solemnly mourned her victim, the first politically prominent Frenchman to be slain in more than 170 years.

In purely chronological terms, however, not the Parisian drama but a different one, unfolding in distant Stockholm, signalled the end of the Old Régime's escape from murder as a common feature of politics. For it was there, in March 1792, that a Swedish nobleman named Anckarström, acting on behalf of a sizable coterie of disgruntled aristocrats, shot King Gustav III while both were attending a lavish costume party in the royal opera house. The monarch's death would eventually provide the inspiration for Giuseppe Verdi's opera, 'A Masked Ball'. Its immediate importance, however, lay in removing from the European scene one of the last enlightened despots, a ruler who had brought his own country's nobility to heel by dint of methods at once harsh and courageous, but who by 1792 had made himself the most outspoken among crowned enemies of the French Revolution. Events in Paris, needless to say, had little if anything to do with Anckarström's own motivation.

Elsewhere, the turn of the new century brought a cluster of new attempts to assassinate major power figures. One victim, the unquestionably demented Tsar Paul I, perished in the palace coup of 1801, carried out by a group of high officers who gladly exchanged the father's unpredictable cruelty for the as yet unknown qualities of his son, Alexander I. Although this event in St Petersburg constituted the only successful attack on a ruling monarch during the Napoleonic era, others aroused almost as much excitement. One of them, aimed at King George III, had occurred in May 1800 at London's Drury Lane Theatre when an unbalanced army veteran fired a shot at the royal box, striking one of its pillars and inspiring the distinguished playwright Richard Sheridan, who was present that night, to add another stanza to the national anthem:

> From every latent foe,
> From the assassin's blow,
> God Save the King![11]

Although George III, after forty years on the British throne, was actually at or near the zenith of popularity with the mass of his subjects, the shooting at the Drury Lane (preceded by a couple of less serious incidents in previous years) seemed an ominous portent for crowned heads. Not only rulers but also their generals and ministers for a time were threatened with violent death. One of France's most prominent military men, Marshal Kléber, left in command of the army Bonaparte had abandoned in Egypt (*see above*, p. 202), was slain by a zealous Muslim at Cairo in June 1800. Then, near the Paris Opéra on the following Christmas eve his old commander barely escaped death in a bomb explosion that took the lives of thirteen bystanders. Napoleon seized the excuse for deporting to Guiana more than 100 surviving Jacobins (not in fact involved in the explosion), while as part of the same purge he condemned to the guillotine the handful of royalist conspirators who had been the real culprits.

Other would-be assassins are believed to have plotted Bonaparte's murder after he became Emperor of the French. The best authenticated of such episodes was the effort in 1809 by a youthful German patriot, Friedrich Staps, to stab the victor of Wagram, then sojourning in Schonbrünn Palace on the outskirts of Vienna. Not long thereafter, in May 1812, Spencer Perceval became the only British prime minister to die at the hands of an assassin, a ruined businessman who shot him as he crossed the lobby of the House of Commons. By this time a substantial body of opinion was convinced that another great wave of political murder was breaking over Europe.

In point of fact, however, no massive revival of assassination took place until about the mid-point of the nineteenth century. Instead, although the post-Napoleonic Restoration was to witness several lurid crimes of this sort, notably the Kotzebue killing at Mannheim in 1819 (*see below*, p. 317) their rarity and the horrified response they elicited in most quarters suggests that the Restoration brought with it a conscious return, by governments and subjects alike, to the values and manners of the Old Régime. Not even the recent attempts to prove that Napoleon himself was assassinated on St Helena in 1821 have altered the probability that he was simply allowed to die a prisoner in exile, the victim of his own long-standing infirmities.[12]

Assassination was indeed destined to play an increasing part in modern politics, but its growth was not continuous between the 1790s and the present day. Instead, as we have seen, political homicide assumed renewed prominence during an age of revolution and mass warfare. When they subsided for a term, it too receded, if only for a few decades.

ECONOMIC WARFARE

Far from being a separate aspect of the Revolutionary and Napoleonic wars, the economic struggle, in which belligerents sought to cripple their enemies' trade, financial strength and supply of vital commodities, was closely bound up with the course of military events. No sooner had war broken out in 1792–93 than the money power of Great Britain in particular emerged as an important weapon. Promises of financial support from London bought allies and sometimes kept them in action even after punishing setbacks.

It cannot be maintained that such confederates offered much hope of defeating revolutionary France – that had to await later outbursts of popular patriotism in Spain, Russia and central Europe. Nevertheless, financial grants kept the fight going year after year, without Britain's having to raise and maintain large land forces of its own. If it is true that British subsidies between 1793 and 1815 amounted to approximately £52 million, expenditures under this heading amounted to less than 6.5 per cent of the kingdom's total war disbursements.[13] Not the least remarkable feature of the long conflict was the fact that when it finally ended, Great Britain's public debt was almost twelve times that of France – the latter having been offset by confiscations and indemnities from conquered lands, but no doubt still more by expedients available only to a highly autocratic regime. Yet King George III's credit, as even French bankers had to admit, was infinitely stronger than the Emperor Napoleon's. The answer lay in trade.

The commercial warfare of the 1790s saw hundreds of British ships taken as prizes by French privateers. Nevertheless, the average attrition suffered by England's merchant marine, including the East Indiamen plodding home from the orient, remained quite steady at around 2.5 per cent per year from 1793 to 1800, certainly no crippling loss. Contrast this result with the systematic sweeping away of French maritime commerce. By 1799, the Directory admitted officially that 'not a single merchant ship is on the sea carrying the French flag'.[14] Small French coastal vessels continued to slip from port to port, but for exports from overseas the Republic had come to rely on American and other neutral ships.

A good indication of the part played by commercial warfare in Europe's general conflict is the striking increase in its importance during and after the crucial years 1805–7. For those years not only saw Trafalgar clinch Britain's naval supremacy, guaranteeing British invulnerability to direct naval attack, but also witnessed Napoleon's defeat of the Austrians, Russians and Prussians, followed by his diplomatic triumph in the Tilsit settlement. Now, as Admiral Mahan would later explain, the struggle entered a new phase:

The battle between the sea and the land was to be fought out on Commerce. England had no army wherewith to meet Napoleon; Napoleon had no navy to cope with that of his enemy. As in the case of an impregnable fortress, the only alternative for either of these contestants was to reduce the other by starvation. On the common frontier, the coast line, they met in a deadly strife in which no weapon was drawn. The imperial soldiers were turned into coastguardsmen to shut out Great Britain from her markets; the British ships became revenue cutters to prohibit the trade of France. The neutral carrier, pocketing his pride, offered his services to either for pay, and the other regarded him as taking part in hostilities.[15]

It is easy, when one is studying Napoleon's Berlin and Milan Decrees of 1806–7 on the one hand and, on the other, Britain's Orders in Council of 1807–9, to develop a misleadingly neat picture of the struggle thus joined. On *paper*, the emperor's Continental System closed every European port either directly or indirectly controlled by France to all British ships and all other ships that had touched the British Isles. Furthermore, such vessels were defined as legitimate prey for any marauding French sea captain. The aim was theoretically unlimited – to starve England into submission – though few French officials seem to have considered that a real possibility, preferring to rely instead on general economic depression to exhaust their enemy's will to fight.

As for retaliation from London, beginning with the famous Order in Council of 11 November 1807, it amounted to a formal blockade of all continental ports not open to British ships. Neutral vessels might still visit French-controlled ports in Europe, provided they stopped in England both going and returning, to submit to inspection, reload and pay the prescribed duties. Otherwise, they were subject to confiscation as blockade runners. All this represented a particularly heavy blow to the American carrying trade, and was so intended. For while American shipments to Europe from the West Indies and elsewhere had been a supplementary resource for England, they had been incomparably more valuable to France.

What of the realities behind this stern exchange of threats and prohibitions? First, note that both sides had declared blockades so vast as to be unenforceable (and hence, under international law, not legal at all). Every month numerous ships defied the prohibitions of the French emperor and His Britannic Majesty alike. American and other blockade runners could almost always be seen anchored in Brest, Nantes and Amsterdam. At the same time, Napoleon's government proved incapable of preventing the British from smuggling goods into Europe on a massive scale. The islands of Malta in the Mediterranean and Heligoland in the North Sea became especially convenient depots for this contraband trade. Anxious to maintain the supply of precious timber from Sweden and Russia, the Royal Navy for several years offered a regular convoy service by warships in the Baltic, to escort 'neutral' merchantmen (often British vessels carrying false registration papers) past the hostile Danish coast on their way to ports in England.

A bizarre aspect of the trade war was the principal adversaries' purposeful circumvention of their own rules. Great Britain often permitted neutral cargoes to evade its 'stop and reload' requirements – for a price or for political advantage in Holland, Russia or other nations. Napoleon, on his side, was prepared to relieve temporary surpluses at home and to accumulate gold by permitting specially licensed exports to England. Following the harvest of 1809, which was plentiful on the Continent but nearly disastrous in England, the imperial government licensed the shipment across the Channel of over 1,300,000 quarters of wheat, or about five-sixths of the United Kingdom's total wheat imports for 1810.[16] In certain other years, to be sure, the emperor applied his restrictions rigorously, hoarding foodstuffs for his armies. But the picture is scarcely one of a sustained, coherent effort to starve a foe.

Is it safe to assume, then, that the economic war was a farce, winked at in all knowledgeable circles? Certainly not. Most of the concessions and exceptions were made not out of indifference to advantages they might bring the enemy, but out of a recognition that the home economy, be it French or British, urgently required the stimulation or relief that only a partial easing of restrictions could provide. Blockades and embargoes, after all, are notorious for cutting two ways. Hence both sides occasionally eased controls in their own interest. The basic determination to break the other side nevertheless remained until the end as constant as it was savage.

It should also be borne in mind that certain very real consequences flowed from the economic struggle. In Britain's case, if the threat of starvation was never deadly, given the increase in home production and a generally high level of imports, the hardships accompanying a crop failure such as that of 1809 constituted a serious political factor. Still more significant was the financial strain of the seemingly endless war, a strain that wore out many of the men responsible for public credit and tax revenues during financial crises such as those of 1808 and 1810–11. As for British exports, Napoleon's tightening of the Continental System dropped their value from a high of £66 million in 1809 to £44 million in 1812, this despite the ingenuity of London's businessmen in finding new markets, especially in Latin America.[17] It should be added that the costly distraction of war with the United States in 1812–14 was a direct outgrowth of the European struggle as a whole, a struggle that in many respects ended none to soon for England.

Within the French Empire, the danger of starvation was even more remote than in Britain; for Europe is a productive continent and the supply of most foodstuffs remained secure. The officially sponsored exploitation of sugar beet was an intelligent, but not essential, response to the reduction of imports from overseas, in this case, West Indian cane sugar. The issue was quite literally one of frosting on the Frenchman's cake.

Several other results of the economic conflict were particularly serious for the Republic and the Empire. That conflict never ceased to jeopardize the fiscal credit of a succession of French governments all of which lacked the recuperative promise based on large-scale foreign trade. It brought depression to industrial centres such as Lyon and to great seaports from Genoa and Marseille to Hamburg and Amsterdam. As for political complications, those imposed upon Britain, in America and elsewhere, paled by comparison with the troubles it stirred up for Napoleon. In order to maintain his Continental System he outraged influential groups in France, the Germanies, Switzerland, Italy and the Low Countries. To plug serious leaks in the System, he deposed his own brother, the defiant King Louis of Holland, then annexed the Dutch and north German coasts, stretching his Empire all the way to Lübeck on the Baltic Sea. Whether or not the tsar's refusal to bar British-sponsored neutral shipping from Russian ports was a principal cause or only a pretext for the invasion of 1812, it was unquestionably the issue that signalled a final rupture between the erstwhile allies. One may argue that Napoleon could have treated all these problems differently, but there is no denying that they were at once real and intractable.

Perhaps the best balance can be struck by observing that when all was said and done commercial and fiscal warfare remained basically Great Britain's rather than France's game. Napoleon could diminish his enemy's access to the European market, but he could not deny such a sea power the markets of the world beyond. And since one inevitable result of blockades and embargoes was a reduction in neutral shipping, the chief loser was sure to be the party more dependent for vital imports, commercial stimulation and foreign markets on the carrying services of other countries. That party was France and its land-locked Empire.

THE PROPAGANDA WAR

As was to be expected in the midst of fierce collisions between rival political systems and among competing patriotisms, the Revolutionary-Napoleonic era gave birth to propaganda in abundance. Books, leaflets, cartoons, broadsides, orders of the day, speeches, poems, songs all were employed to whip up the enthusiasm of contending masses, while attempting to undermine the confidence of enemies. Unfortunately, we have no reliable way of gauging the effects, whether positive or negative, of such propaganda. Certain features of this warfare of ideas nevertheless deserve attention.

In keeping with the other changes occurring at the time, propagandistic appeals in the 1790s were more general, more systematic, more broadly ideological than those of the Napoleonic era yet to come, when loyalty to one's national state became the dominant public emotion. In this respect, there was an important shift in the arguments used to justify or to motivate group action. The anti-revolutionary powers of 1792 and 1793 regularly announced that 'the crowned heads of Europe', supported by 'all humanity', had no choice but to condemn and to punish the men responsible for the 'horrors unfolding in France'. The 'good, old law' was invoked against these men, who replied by claiming to represent the rights and interests of mankind against 'reactionary tyrants'. In contrast, by 1805 Nelson's signal flags at Trafalgar read simply: '*England* (not God or Humanity or Great Britain or even the king) expects that every man will do his duty'.[18] The next year, seeking to rally the Prussian forces and to inspire steadfastness following the disaster of Jena, General Gneisenau insisted that 'our country deserves no less than sacrificial loyalty'.

Despite changing values, certain techniques showed a high degree of consistency throughout the period. Indeed, allowance made for the evolution of media, such devices had been characteristic of struggles going back at least to the religious wars of early modern times, and in some cases to medieval conflicts. The often shrill assertion, for instance, that God was with one's own legions and against the enemy's rang from British pulpits throughout the tense years of bracing for a French invasion, just as it was heard in the Protestant, Catholic and Orthodox churches of Prussia, Austria and Russia when the War of Liberation began. It had also, of course, been somewhat belatedly appropriated by Napoleon in his Imperial Catechism of 1806.

On a more distinctly human plane, each contending party tried to make sure that its enemies received all the discouraging news that could be reported or, if necessary, fabricated. A colourful English cartoon from the winter following Trafalgar and Austerlitz shows a rotund John Bull on the Dover Cliffs, facing a particularly disreputable looking Corsican on the heights above Boulogne. Through the air across the Channel are seen flying two streams of bulletins, those from England carrying announcements of naval victories (and conveniently labelled 'Truth'), those from the Continent (just as succinctly tagged 'Falsehoods') listing Allied defeats in central Europe. In this case *both* sets of claims happened to be true, but exaggeration and distortion mark countless news sheets and leaflets which survive in various collections.

Along with motives of patriotic pride and hatred for the national foe, appeals to fear played an important part in domestic and foreign propaganda alike. Napoleon believed as firmly as had the Jacobins in terror's paralysing effect on an enemy. He therefore made no effort to suppress accounts of the mass executions carried out by his troops in Madrid after the 1808 uprising. At the same time, French propaganda designed for home consumption portrayed in detail the starvation threatening Europe unless England was defeated, as well as the orgy of murder and rape that presumably would accompany an invasion of *la patrie* by any of her continental enemies. No less explicit were British cartoons showing what life in London would be like under French occupation.

A significant form of propagandistic appeal, by no means novel but reaching an especially high level of intensity during this period, was addressed to actually or potentially disaffected groups under enemy rule. The British fed a steady stream of verbal encouragement, sporadically accompanied by material aid, first to the Chouans and other French rebel elements, then later to dissident Dutchmen, Germans, Swiss, Italians and Spaniards. The French in turn welcomed visits from leaders of Irish, Hungarian and other insurgent movements, sending back with them effusive words of sympathy. Napoleon's proclamation to the Hungarian gentry, dated May 1809 and published in Magyar, German and French, failed to win them to his side, but it represented a masterful attempt to capitalize on old resentments against the Habsburgs.

In all these respects, the era we are considering was merely a segment, albeit an important one, of psychological warfare's long development. At another level, however, it appears in retrospect to have been unique. The great conflicts of history have characteristically given rise to mounting emotional antagonism, increased receptivity to crude propaganda and a readiness to view all enemies as essentially inhuman. With regard to that general pattern the revolutionary–Napoleonic wars constitute an exception. It seems clear that, terrible though the battles from the turn of the century to Waterloo unquestionably were, they were fought by men for most of whom the enemy seemed *less* a member of some alien and repugnant species than he had in the 1790s. The great collision of ideologies, of systems, of quasi-religious zealots was over by the time Napoleon became first consul. Thereafter, contending nations 'smote and shuddered and smote again'; but their armies (save perhaps for Spain's after 1808) tended to look, to act and even, leaving aside specific allegiances, to think more nearly alike than had those in action at Valmy or Jemappes. In this, the soldiers presumably reflected attitudes widely shared by civilian populations. For the propagandist, it was almost certainly more difficult in 1810 or 1814 than it had been in 1793 or 1794 to convince Europeans that the Devil really *was* on the other side, whichever side that might be. The carnage continued. Indeed it mounted. But it was no longer supported by any emotion grander than national egoism and the determination to dictate the eventual terms of peace.

NOTES AND REFERENCES

1   J. U. Nef, *War and Human Progress* (Cambridge, Mass., 1950).

2   R. W. Phipps, *The Armies of the First French Republic* (London, 1926), vol. I, p. 152.

3   *New Cambridge Modern History* (Cambridge, 1965), vol. IX, p. 345.

4   A. Meynier, cited in G. Bruun, *Europe and the French Imperium* (New York–London, 1938), p. 72.

5   E. J. Kingston-McCloughry, *The Direction of War* (London, 1955), p. 38. See also Martin Van Crefeld, *Command in War* (Cambridge, Mass., 1985).

6   *The Letters of Private Wheeler, 1809–28*, ed. B. F. Liddell Hart (London, 1951), pp. 14–16.

7   D. Greer, *The Incidence of the Terror during the French Revolution* (Cambridge, Mass., 1935), pp. 135–43.

8   A. France, *The Gods Will Have Blood [Les Dieux ont soif]*, trans. F. Davies (Harmondsworth, 1979), p. 212.

9   François Furet, *Interpreting the French Revolution*, trans. Elborg Forster (Cambridge–Paris, 1981), p. 128.

10 F. L. Ford, *Political Murder: From Tyrannicide to Terrorism* (Cambridge, Mass., 1985), pp. 194–9.

11 John Brooke, *King George III* (New York, 1972), pp. 314–16.

12 Ford, *Political Murder*, pp. 409–10, note 15. The assassination thesis was advanced by S. Forshufvud in his *Who Killed Napoleon?* (London, 1962) and given greater prominence by B. Weider and D. Hapgood, *The Murder of Napoleon* (New York, 1982). See also Note on p. 229, above.

13 Vagts, *History of Militarism*, pp. 144–5.

14 Mahan, *The Influence of Sea Power upon the French Revolution and Empire*, pp. 223–4 and 229.

15 *Ibid.*, p. 289.

16 W. F. Galpin, *The Grain Supply of England* (Philadelphia, 1925), p. 196.

17 F. Crouzet, *L'économie britannique et le blocus continental* (Paris, 1958), *passim*.

18 Using Popham's signal code, the famous message required twelve flags, one for each of the first eight words and a separate flag for each letter in "duty". D. Pope, *England Expects* (London, 1959), p. 237, n. 1.

11

THE EUROPEAN STATE SYSTEM AFTER 1815

Earlier, in Chapter 4, we surveyed the political map of pre-revolutionary Europe and identified its most important features. Having since reviewed the international drama of the ensuing quarter-century, especially the shocks administered to the old state system by the French Republic and Empire, we should now consider what followed upon the latter's disappearance. In doing so, we shall need to distinguish between those features of the period 1815–30 that had survived from the eighteenth-century pattern (or were restored) and those that were undeniably novel.

This mixture of old and new strikes one immediately in the very conditions surrounding the conduct of diplomacy. As in the eighteenth century so in the nineteenth, Europe's diplomats were an aristocratic corps of urbane practitioners, accustomed to conversing (usually in French) over dynastic interests, boundary changes offset by 'compensations' and a long list of equally familiar issues. Even during the recent turmoil, save for a brief period in the 1790s, and then only in France, neither the personnel nor the procedures of diplomacy had really been revolutionized. Napoleon's own *methods* had been far more traditional than his increasingly ambitious *aims*.

Actuality, however, differed from appearances. While the polite language of negotiation might still refer to kings and princes, it would never again be possible to avoid speaking of peoples as well. Diplomacy remained hidden, in its detailed manoeuvres; but in most countries its results had now to be explained to many more citizens than would have felt either competent or interested before the Revolution. Europe was still generations away from anything approaching open debate over questions of foreign policy. However, the mobilization of entire nations, first France and then her enemies, had by 1814–15 produced a larger and more critical audience than the past had ever known – parliamentary deputies, journalists, businessmen, teachers and students – whom even the coolest diplomat could ill afford to ignore.

Prolonged warfare had wrought another significant change: a hardening of awareness that certain states disposed of preponderant force, and with it the rights and responsibilities of great powers. The latter phrase, be it noted, first came into general use during the conferences at the close of the Napoleonic era. We have seen that, prior to 1789, England, France, Prussia, Austria and Russia had already constituted such an echelon. Nevertheless, the etiquette and the formal language of the Old Régime had taken for granted the sovereign equality of countless lesser polities. Nothing destroys polite fictions so effectively as does the test of head-on conflict, and in the gigantic struggle lasting from 1792 to 1815 precisely this kind of destruction had occurred. However ingratiating might be the tone adopted by the great powers' spokesmen in their dealings with lesser states, men would not thereafter confuse protocol with the realities of unequal might.

THE TWO TREATIES OF PARIS

The necessary precondition for a general reordering of Europe was the dissolution of the superstate created by French arms and French diplomacy over the course of two decades preceding Napoleon's invasion of Russia in 1812. Once the conqueror was at last defeated, the victorious Allies found themselves beset by the difficulties that inevitably overtake a broad coalition as soon as it achieves its initial, essentially negative, goal of victory over a common foe. In the spring of 1814, with the armies of the Grand Alliance occupying Paris and Bonaparte safely – or so it was thought – packed off to his island realm of Elba, the would-be peacemakers faced some hard decisions.

There were sharp differences of opinion over how the French nation deserved to be treated. The Prussians, remembering their humiliation in 1806 and thereafter, were especially insistent on harsh punishment. The British and Austrian foreign ministers,

Viscount Castlereagh and Prince Metternich, on the other hand, favoured generous terms as offering the best hope for Europe's pacification. Closely tied to this question, of course, was the problem of giving France a government to replace that of the Empire. There was no instant unanimity supporting the return of the Bourbons, in the person of the executed king's brother, Louis XVIII.[1] The mercurial Tsar Alexander I, who now saw himself as both the liberator and the arbiter of Europe, skipped lightly from one alternative to another. One moment his solution was a new French Republic for which he would supply a constitution, the next it was Sweden's Bernadotte as king of France, and so on through several other possibilities. However, Castlereagh and Metternich, once the latter gave up hope of a Bonapartist succession, insisted on a Bourbon restoration, while Prince Talleyrand, France's representative, having abandoned Napoleon with characteristically shrewd timing, worked effectively to convince the other victors that only the old dynasty could make his country once again a reliable member of the family of nations.

The treaty of Paris, which emerged from these debates, was signed on 30 May 1814. It provided for the return of the Bourbon monarchy and granted the lenient peace terms deemed necessary to make Louis XVIII secure upon his throne. The French were accorded the boundaries of 1792, including such early conquests as Avignon and certain small areas on the Flemish and Savoyard frontiers. No war indemnity was imposed, and France was allowed to retain the art treasures Napoleon in particular had shipped home as spoils of conquest. For his part, the restored king abandoned French claims to formerly occupied territories in the Low Countries, Germany, Switzerland and Italy (save for the early annexations noted above) while ceding to England the islands of St Lucia and Tobago in the West Indies, together with Mauritius in the Indian Ocean. Despite these relatively minor losses, and the return to Spain of its old share of San Domingo, France had emerged from the long struggle remarkably undiminished.

Other, more general European questions broached at Paris were referred to a great congress to be convened forthwith in Vienna. Before that body could complete its work, however, Napoleon's return from Elba and the renewed violence of the Hundred Days overturned the mild settlement just outlined. Five months after Waterloo, on 20 November 1815, was signed the second treaty of Paris, an agreement embodying much more stringent provisions than had been imposed the previous year. The French now surrendered the slices of Savoy and Flanders left to them by the first treaty, as well as the Alsatian fortress of Landau to the German Confederation and all territory north of the Lauter River in the Rhenish Palatinate to the kingdom of Bavaria. Numerous art objects had at last to be restored to European palaces and museums, and a cash indemnity of 700 million francs was assessed. Lastly, France was called upon to bear the cost of a 150,000-man Allied army of occupation for a period of up to five years.

Although still not reduced beyond its pre-revolutionary boundaries, save on the northern edge of Alsace, the erstwhile *Grande Nation* had nevertheless felt the impact of foreign reprisals. Whether or not that nation could soon resume a major role in European affairs thus loomed as one of the immediate future's most portentous questions. The answer, however, would depend on developments in many places other than Paris and on negotiations the subjects of which often seemed remote from the 'French question' narrowly defined.

THE CONGRESS OF VIENNA

While the last hectic scenes of Napoleon's adventures were being played to their conclusion, broader issues were addressed by the general diplomatic assembly agreed upon in the first treaty of Paris. Never before in history had so many rulers and principal ministers met to hammer out a comprehensive peace settlement. The Congress of Vienna was charged with nothing less than the awesome task of putting Europe together once more and establishing the conditions required to give this work of reconstruction a reasonable chance of survival.

The Austrian capital, into which the august delegations came pouring that September of 1814, was a city of about 250,000 inhabitants. Above its picturesque medieval centre rose the Stephanskirche, Vienna's treasured cathedral, surrounded by a profusion of shops and cafés in the narrow, twisting streets. Scattered through the old city and its early modern neighbourhoods were the princely residences of the Kaunitz, Thurm und Taxis,

Esterházy and other aristocratic families. Some of these ornate mansions were rented or lent to visiting diplomats (Talleyrand, for instance, moved directly into the Kaunitz Palace), while in others the Austrian owners themselves presided over a whirl of receptions, banquets and balls. The most lavish social centre of all, however, was the Habsburgs' imperial palace, the sprawling Hofburg, where Emperor Francis I entertained night after night, at crushing expense. Through all the soirées, dinners, sleigh rides and hunting parties in the surrounding countryside ran the twitter of gossip about the tsar's, Prince Metternich's and other famous men's love affairs. Only slightly more consequential was the whispering of diplomatic secrets, real or alleged, a traffic which kept large numbers of people busy without producing much effect on the actual course of deliberations.

The cast of players was without doubt one of the most remarkable ever brought together under such auspices. Seldom far from the centre of attention was the unstable tsar, one moment generous, the next petulantly self-regarding, consistent only in his unpredictability. With him he had brought three Russian diplomats: Counts Nesselrode (the foreign minister), Razumovski and Stackelberg. More important, however, in influencing Alexander I's views on a wide range of issues were his foreign advisers: the German Stein, the Polish Prince Czartoryski, the Swiss tutor La Harpe, the Alsatian Baron Anstett, the Greek Capo d'Istria from Corfu and another island-born politician, the Corsican Pozzo di Borgo. Small wonder that Russian policy so often proved difficult to foretell or even to discern. Greedy for spoils in the Balkans, determined to write his own prescription for a restored Polish kingdom, loftily claiming a dominant voice in western European affairs as well, the tsar both puzzled and exasperated other national spokesmen.

Among the latter, none seemed at the outset more likely to wield decisive influence than Austria's foreign minister since 1809, Clemens von Metternich. By birth like Stein a German Rhinelander, this enigmatic man was in other respects almost the perfect opposite of that sincere but impetuous reformer. Handsome, witty, voluptuous, oblique in manoeuvre, but tenacious in defence of his central preoccupations – peace, stability and continued aristocratic leadership for Europe as a whole and for the patchwork Austrian Empire in particular – he was, as he himself candidly remarked, 'bad at skirmishes . . . but good at campaigns'. By his side, to assist in the drafting of papers both public and private, hovered the German author (and translator of Burke), Friedrich von Gentz.

Two other figures command immediate attention. One was Robert Stewart, Viscount Castlereagh, the British foreign secretary, who reached Vienna in mid-September and took a modest house where he lived quietly with his wife throughout the months of deliberations. No less handsome than Metternich, this Anglo-Irish aristocrat was quite different in personality: correct in his personal life, coldly polite to strangers, sometimes effective in debate but always strangely clumsy in written expression. Like Metternich, however, he clung stubbornly to a ruling conception of the need to stabilize Europe, in his case not so much by ensuring social and political 'legitimacy' as by creating a durable balance among sovereign powers. 'Balance of power' has been subjected to so much criticism, including blame for starting wars, that it is important to recall the by no means unintelligent calculations that led Castlereagh and the younger Pitt before him to adopt the position they did. Their position rested on a belief that genuine national interests, clearly recognized, could create in Europe an equilibrium of forces capable of rendering war unfeasible for any one power, or even for a coalition unless directed against a single aggressor.

The remaining major protagonist was the French foreign minister, whose right to speak at all had still to be established when the Congress of Vienna began. A secret article inserted in the first treaty of Paris the previous May had reserved to the great powers of the Quadruple Alliance – Russia, Austria, Britain and Prussia – the determination of Europe's future ordering. France, the other great power but also, in 1814, the not yet finally defeated enemy of the Allies, was at that time given no voice in the deliberations. Nevertheless, the French representative at the Congress was not one to accept a passive role, for himself or for his country. The sixty-year-old Prince de Talleyrand-Périgord, though physically crippled since childhood, stands out in history for his truly phenomenal ability to land, figuratively at least, on his feet after each of his many political somersaults. A bishop of the Catholic Church under the Old Régime, revolutionary deputy to the Estates General of 1789, exile in America during the Terror, then foreign minister under the Directory and supporter of Bonaparte when power changed hands, he had served as head of

Napoleon's foreign office until 1807. Thereafter he had gradually detached himself from the emperor, whose abdication he helped to engineer in 1814. Now once more France's leading diplomat, this time in the service of Louis XVIII, he arrived on the Viennese scene with his uncanny sense of timing, the resiliency won through hard experience and the sharp logic of an unsentimental mind.

Other delegates, as personalities, counted for rather less, though the Prussians, led by their uninspiring King Frederick William III, clearly had to be taken into account. The head of their working diplomats was Prince Hardenberg, Stein's old collaborator but never a social, as distinct from administrative, reformer. Accompanying him, and badly needed because of Hardenberg's deafness, was the educator and philosopher, Baron Wilhelm von Humboldt, as well as a bevy of military and technical advisers. For the rest, neither the Swedish spokesmen nor the Vatican's emissary, Cardinal Consalvi, nor Spain's pompous ambassador, Don Pedro Labrador, could do more than clamour to be heard. The sultan of Turkey, rival Italian factions, thirty German princelings, even the Jews of Frankfurt-on-Main were also among the myriad interests represented, but their agents were in fact little more than observers.

Representatives of the great powers met repeatedly with one another and, depending on the issue at hand, with those of other parties. Meanwhile, a total of ten special commissions concentrated on specified questions ranging from the reorganization of Germany and Switzerland to such topics as population statistics, diplomatic precedence and the slave trade. The Congress of Vienna was in fact primarily a combination of such committee hearings and of informal talks among leading delegates, extending over a period of eight months. There was no plenary session of all participants until the signing of the comprehensive treaty or, as it was called, the Final Act.

Going back to the opening of the Congress and to the host of problems that confronted Europe's assembled diplomats, it bears repeating that from the outset a difficult mingling of restoration and innovation had to be attempted. There was no possibility of simply reimposing the pre-revolutionary map – too much had happened in the quarter-century coming to an end in 1814. In Germany, for example, the former 300 states had been reduced in number by the *Reichsdeputationshauptschluss* of 1803 (*see above*, pp. 207–8) and subsequent settlements to only thirty-nine political units. Newly consolidated kingdoms and grand duchies, all counting themselves among the final victors, would brook no discussion of a return to the Holy Roman Empire's welter of political microcosms. A special question centred upon the future status of Saxony, whose king had remained an ally of Napoleon until the battle of Leipzig and now was treated as a defeated enemy of the Allies, his entire realm demanded by neighbouring Prussia.

Tsar Alexander's project for a Polish kingdom, with himself as king, impinged sharply on the German problem. The Russian monarch hoped to recover for Poland all of Prussia's share in the partitions of 1793 and 1795, in return supporting Frederick William III's wish to annex the whole of Saxony. Similarly, if Alexander had his way, Austria would return Cracow and the rest of Polish Galicia, against compensation in Italy and Dalmatia. The Italian situation, be it said, was thoroughly confused, for there were conflicting claims to virtually every square mile of that sundered peninsula. Even the exiled Bourbons of Naples could not be sure of recovering their patrimony from King Joachim (Murat), who was loud in his protestations of devotion to the Allies and whose Queen Caroline, though a sister of Napoleon, was also one of Metternich's former mistresses. Meanwhile, Switzerland awaited a new constitution, the future of the Low Countries remained obscure, and the Scandinavian settlement agreed upon between Sweden and Denmark at Kiel in January of 1814 would be in jeopardy unless ratified by the great powers.

Of all these knotty problems, the two that proved most divisive were those involving Poland and Saxony. By the last days of 1814, in fact, disagreement among the great powers had become so intense that a complete breakdown of relations between Russia and Prussia on the one side and Austria and England on the other loomed as a distinct possibility. A westward projection of Russian power into the large Polish state envisaged by Alexander and the creation of a new north German giant if Prussia were permitted to gobble up all of Saxony stood as prospects neither London nor Vienna would accept. Pitt's old dream, pursued by Castlereagh, the dream of a Prussian–Austrian–British alliance to restrain both France and Russia, had already foundered on the mutual hostility of the two German powers and on Prussia's effort to win great rewards by collaborating with the tsar.

At this point Talleyrand intervened. His achievement was a brilliant *tour de force*, and it was decisive. Having already made himself the spokesman for all the nations excluded from the deliberations of the 'Big Four', he now convinced Castlereagh and Metternich that what they needed above all was more active French participation at the highest level. (Once he had done so, needless to say, he at once ceased to complain about the 'evils of great-power dominance'.) On 3 January 1815 the representatives of Austria, Great Britain and France signed a secret agreement to resist, by force of arms if necessary, the most extreme demands of Russia and Prussia. The Big Four had in reality become the Big Five. Even during the Hundred Days, though the old Allies once again took the field against Napoleonic France, the *Bourbon* France for which Talleyrand spoke remained an active partner in a quite different coalition.

No one can say with complete assurance whether or not the Anglo-French–Austrian agreement to threaten the Russians and Prussians with military action was merely a bluff. It may have been no more than that, for while the French nation proved willing that spring to rally behind Napoleon's final effort, it might well have refused to join with unfamiliar allies in a war over central European boundaries. There can be no doubt that Castlereagh, for his part, would have been hard put to secure approval in Parliament of such a war. If the threat was a bluff, however, it succeeded against what turned out to be no very stern resolve on the part of Alexander I and Frederick William III. These monarchs, both of whom received almost immediate reports of the secret treaty, promptly began to moderate their demands. Within six weeks, the Polish and Saxon questions had been resolved by compromise. Thereafter, the other issues before the Congress were settled with relative ease and with a dispatch which had seemed outside the realm of possibility during the dangerous stalemate of mid-winter.

The Final Act was signed on 9 June 1815, pending Napoleon's final defeat. As already indicated, the Polish arrangement represented a compromise. A kingdom of Poland – 'Congress Poland' as the nineteenth century would know it – was resurrected under Alexander I and ostensibly guaranteed a constitutional régime more liberal by far than that of the tsar's Russian empire. To help form this new entity, Prussia disgorged the Warsaw region, though not Posen, while Austria gave up western

Galicia, allowed Cracow to become a free city, but retained all Polish lands previously annexed by the Habsburgs south and east of the Vistula. In return, the Prussian monarch obtained the northern 40 per cent of Saxony, the last remaining strip of Swedish Pomerania on the Baltic, all of the Hohenzollerns' past holdings in Westphalia, plus a solid, heavily populated tract west of the Rhine from the Moselle valley to the Dutch frontier. Francis I of Austria, for his part, was accorded Venetia and Lombardy in Italy, Illyria and Dalmatia on the east coast of the Adriatic, the Bavarian Tyrol and the former archepiscopal principality of Salzburg. If Russia had moved west, through its extension of control across Poland, so had Prussia and Austria as a result of these compensations (*see* Map 6).

Despite a chorus of objections from liberal and nationalist groups, a loose confederation was the only superstructure accepted by Germany's thirty-five essentially unreformed principalities and four surviving free cities (Frankfurt, Hamburg, Bremen and Lübeck). The political problems facing the new German Diet, established at Frankfurt under permanent Austrian chairmanship, will be discussed in Chapter 12. Meanwhile, the work of political regrouping also went forward in the Low Countries, Switzerland and Scandinavia. The old United Provinces and Austria's former Belgian domain were joined to form a 'kingdom of the Netherlands' under the former Dutch stadtholder, now styled King William I and at the same time grand duke of Luxemburg. The Swiss Confederation was revived and indeed expanded, for its twenty-two cantons would henceforth include the erstwhile republic of Geneva and the principality of Neuchâtel, the latter resuming its ambiguous status as a fief of the Prussian king under the Swiss federal government. Finally, Sweden's Crown Prince Bernadotte obtained confirmation of the cession of Norway by Denmark the previous year, though the Norwegians received a separate constitution purporting to guarantee their traditional rights.

Elsewhere, past régimes declared legitimately reinstalled: in Spain, in Sardinia (which acquired Genoa), in the Italian Papal States (though not in Avignon and its territory, which were left to France), in Tuscany and in Modena. Despite Spanish protests, the north Italian duchy of Parma-Piacenza was awarded to Marie Louise, Napoleon's empress and the daughter of the Austrian emperor, to hold for her lifetime but not to transmit to her son.

Joachim Murat having reversed himself by rejoining the cause of Napoleon in the Hundred Days, a blunder for which he was shot by a firing squad several months after Waterloo, the Bourbon King Ferdinand I was returned to Naples, there to rule what was now termed the Kingdom of the Two Sicilies.

Of all the major powers, England apparently had least to show for its military and diplomatic efforts. It had annexed nothing on the Continent, although Hanover was restored as a personal possession of King George III. The United Kingdom had returned scores of overseas points occupied during the long years of warfare and had failed to secure any effective agreement to abolish the slave trade, a matter of both moral and economic interest in London. On this last point, the Final Act of the Congress included a resolution condemning in principle the traffic in slaves but leaving to future negotiations the question of how its actual suppression was to be achieved. Despite appearances, however, Great Britain emerged with some very considerable advantages. First, there were the islands already ceded by France. In addition, the Dutch flag was not raised again over Ceylon or the Cape of Good Hope, nor did Denmark recover Heligoland in the North Sea, while strategic Malta became a British possession. At Ghent, in December 1814, England's potentially dangerous war with the United States had ended with a return to the *status quo ante*.

Most important of all, when in late February 1815 he turned over to Wellington responsibility for British interests at Vienna and started home to London, Castlereagh took with him the assurance of a restored European balance. It was not precisely the one he had hoped to achieve, involving as it did more reliance on France, and less on Prussia, than he would have preferred. But it offered the promise that his country would not soon again have to face, alone, a giant hegemonial power on the Continent.

CONGRESS EUROPE

To Metternich, Castlereagh, Alexander I, Talleyrand and many others who had joined in the Vienna settlement, that settlement was more than a single act of diplomacy. Each hoped, for reasons of his own, that it would signal the creation of a permanent system of consultation, a genuine 'concert of Europe'. During the next seven years, the powers did in fact convene four additional congresses. The system as such, however, proved incapable of perpetuating itself. In order to judge its brief record and to understand its collapse, we must first identify the several bases upon which different parties believed it should rest.

The earliest, and most obvious, support for collaboration lay in the military partnership that had defeated Napoleon. Castlereagh's anxious efforts to give definite form to the alliance of Britain, Austria, Russia and Prussia had produced the pledge of solidarity against French aggression signed at Chaumont in March 1814. Disrupted by the diplomatic crisis over Poland and Saxony the following winter in Vienna, that agreement recovered full life and vigour during the Hundred Days. Finally, on 20 November 1815, the day they signed the second treaty of Paris, the four major victors solemnly renewed the Quadruple Alliance, each committing itself for twenty years to contribute 60,000 men should there be any further attempt by France to overturn the peace settlement.

Castlereagh never abandoned the view that the Quadruple Alliance was the bedrock upon which to base all other arrangements designed to ensure a balance of power. He welcomed the return of France to peaceful ways, and he had already shown himself willing, at Vienna, to enter into special agreements with Talleyrand. But French energy and French resentment, he believed, would constitute a potential threat to Europe for a long time to come. Thus, whatever efforts were made to restrain other nations, the wartime allies should be sure to keep a cautious eye on their formidable enemy of the preceding quarter-century.

Not surprisingly, the tsar of All the Russias conceived of stability as depending on principles quite different from those of England's foreign secretary – and on a quite different sort of treaty. Having taken no direct part in Napoleon's second defeat, Alexander in 1815 was something less than the conquering hero, the focus of rapt attention, he had been a year earlier. While Wellington and Blücher finished the military business in Belgium and northern France, he sojourned first in the Rhineland and then in Paris, with Baroness von Krüdener at his side. This Latvian-born German woman, an unsuccessful novelist, a veteran of love affairs, but at fifty-one scarcely more than a self-hypnotized religious mystic, helped Alexander to immerse himself in a vague, ostentatious piety. One day in September 1815, he arrayed the entire Russian expeditionary force in France before eight open-air altars, to which the baroness addressed herself in succession, performing before each what apparently was intended as an inspirational dance.

Despite this curious feminine influence, the tsar could justly claim as his own the concept of a personal agreement among monarchs, born of religious sentiments; for he had been discussing such a possibility for more than a decade. The Holy Alliance which he signed with Emperor Francis I and King Frederick William III on 26 September 1815 seems innocuous enough at first reading. The Russian, Austrian and Prussian rulers promised to treat one another in accordance with 'the sublime truths which the Holy Religion of Our Saviour teaches' and to watch over their respective peoples 'as fathers of families'. There was no reference to extirpating progressive movements and no effort to limit the pact to the three eastern autocracies. On the contrary, all other European rulers were invited to subscribe to its terms. Eventually, all did so save three: the sultan, who obviously was not devoted to the religion in question; the pope, who would not join with Orthodox and Protestant monarchs; and the prince regent of Great Britain, who explained that his country's constitution forbade him to enter into any such personal agreement.

Bland and unobjectionable as the tsar's project may appear – and doubtless *did* appear to many of its signers – the Holy Alliance began at once to disrupt the hoped-for concert of Europe. It was, as liberal critics pointed out in speech and in print, a compact among rulers, not among nations or peoples. Furthermore, the grounds for the British prince regent's non-participation suggested an incipient division within the *Quadruple* Alliance itself, as between absolute and constitutional monarchies. But most serious of all, the tsar's brainchild threatened to make the defence of 'decent Christian order' an excuse for repression, aimed at even the most respectable opponents of established régimes. In fairness to Alexander, it must be said that the use of the Holy Alliance for this purpose was less his work than that of a man who scoffed at pious mysticism, Prince Metternich.

The Austrian minister seemed to many observers at the time, as he has to many since, the evil genius of tyranny and reaction, who believed that even if history could not be reversed in all details, it should at least come to what his adviser, Gentz, referred to as 'a full stop'. On the other hand, he has been praised by numerous admirers for having recognized that what Europe needed most was rest and recuperation, for having resisted the divisive, potentially violent force of nationalism and for having sought to keep international affairs in the hands of cultured cosmopolites. Whichever view one favours, it seems clear that Metternich's definition of 'legitimacy' provided an uncommonly persistent principle underlying both his foreign and his domestic policies as Austria's chief policy-maker for almost forty years. The empire he served, if it was to survive at all, required peace without and a respite, within, from the nationalistic agitation of Germans, Italians, Hungarians and Slavs. A man committed to such aims was not apt to be disturbed by charges of repression.

In combination, the tsar's religiosity and Metternich's increasingly negative conception of legitimacy presented the British government with an unwelcome set of problems. Castlereagh clung to the hope that a stable European balance could be arrived at among nations whose internal political systems, within broad limits, remained their own business. Parliament, he felt sure, would never support a policy of recurrent intervention in the domestic affairs of various states. It seemed just as unlikely, however, that the other great powers would agree to refrain from such intervention wherever there appeared to be a threat of renascent 'Jacobinism' – and Jacobinism was fast becoming a scare word for the most moderate sorts of constitutional liberalism. In the years immediately after 1815, London was left with no choice but to pursue a course of uneasy participation in international conferences, hoping for the best.

The first of these meetings, the Congress of Aix-la-Chapelle in the autumn of 1818, actually seemed to augur well for the future of consultation among the great powers. Present for Great Britain were the foreign secretary and the duke of Wellington; for Austria, Francis I and Metternich; for Russia, the tsar, Nesselrode and Capo d'Istria; for Prussia, Frederick William III and Hardenberg; for France, the Duc de Richelieu (Talleyrand having resigned as foreign minister after the Congress of Vienna to become Louis XVIII's royal chamberlain). Richelieu was not admitted to all the discussions, but Aix-la-Chapelle nevertheless marked the end of the postwar treatment of France as a defeated enemy. Although the Quadruple Alliance was reaffirmed, another, Quintuple Alliance was formed, with French participation, 'to protect the arts of peace' and to increase general prosperity. The last details concerning payments of the indemnity of 1815 were settled, after which it was agreed that all occupation forces should leave French soil. In addition, some further progress was made towards a more generous definition of Jewish rights, towards abolition of the slave trade and towards an improvement in Sweden's and Denmark's embittered relations.

Yet the meeting at Aix-la-Chapelle, encouraging as it seemed in many respects, provided the first unblinkable evidence that the congress system itself was endangered by fundamental disagreements among the nations involved. The tsar kept talking of 'sacred principles of order' and the need to create an international army to protect those principles everywhere. At the same time, he urged all monarchs to grant constitutions for the sake of their peoples' wellbeing and tranquillity. That exhortation in itself was enough to make Metternich oppose the creation of an international police force to defend such ill-defined purposes. Far more blunt was Castlereagh's warning that his government condemned all efforts 'to provide the transparent soul of the Holy Alliance with a body'.[2] Even a new revolt in France, he added, would justify intervention only if prudent calculation were to indicate that the disorders threatened the peace of Europe.

Against this background it is not difficult to see why the next two congresses brought a growing alienation between England and the continental powers, especially since both meetings dealt with the issue of intervention essentially on Metternich's terms. The first of them, at Troppau, Silesia, in October 1820, considered the revolutions then in progress against the disreputable Bourbon monarchs of the Two Sicilies and Spain. Castlereagh did not attend, but he sent a British delegation instructed to oppose any project for sending foreign troops into either the Italian or the Iberian peninsula. The English effort to block such action proved unavailing. While the Spanish question remained temporarily in abeyance, the other powers at the congress voted to authorize military action by Austrian forces in Italy and to ask that a Russian army of 90,000 men also stand ready to march there from Poland if needed.

Before these military operations actually began, still another congress met, this one in January 1821 at the Austrian town of Laibach in Carniola. Once more the powers of the Holy Alliance affirmed their determination to intervene wherever a legitimate régime was in danger of being overthrown. Once more the

British spokesman declared that no treaty in existence justified such intervention unless a direct threat to international tranquillity could be demonstrated. This time there was no real effort on either side to reach a compromise. As Sir Harold Nicolson has written: 'The Great Coalition was thus finally dissolved; the Concert of Europe had disintegrated; the Holy Alliance had succeeded in destroying the Quadruple Alliance; the Congress System had failed.'[3]

Within only a matter of weeks after the Congress of Laibach had adjourned, combinations of Austrian and local royalist troops crushed both the revolution in Naples and a shortlived uprising that broke out among Piedmontese subjects of the king of Sardinia in March 1821. The Spanish insurgents, however, still held the upper hand in their struggle with Ferdinand VII. Hence, on 20 October 1822, the five great powers came together at Verona for what proved to be the last of the era's conferences involving all of them.

In many respects, the Congress of Verona was scarcely more than a funeral service for earlier hopes of cooperation between Great Britain and the Continent. Castlereagh, after a long physical and nervous decline, had killed himself that August at his country home. His place as foreign secretary was taken by George Canning, a man quite untouched by any lingering desire to get along with the autocratic governments that ruled in Vienna, in St Petersburg, in Berlin and – since 1820 when the *Ultras* had returned to power – in Paris as well. Under Metternich's prodding the diplomats at Verona moved towards intervention in Spain. This decision, needless to say, was taken against the advice of Britain's delegate, Wellington. The Iron Duke, on Canning's orders, served notice that 'come what may' his government would have no part in such a venture. Nevertheless, the other powers were committed to action. Having managed to fend off an insistent Russian offer of troops, they commissioned France to send an army across the Pyrenees. The victory of French forces over Spanish rebels in the summer of 1823 brought a sigh of relief to most continental ministers, though it enraged their liberal critics. It also put an end to any lingering illusion of Great Britain's possibly moving back into the European system Castlereagh had worked hard to help create.

Mention of Castlereagh and his strivings suggests the need to beware of oversimplification. Because he was a Tory and his eloquent successor a liberal independent, because the two men were personal rivals, because Castlereagh shared in the fashioning of the Vienna settlement while Canning denounced it, an earlier historical tradition saw the one as Metternich's henchman and the other, as Metternich's enemy. In actual fact, the signal change in British policy occurred during Castlereagh's ministry. It began as early as the Congress of Aix-la-Chapelle in 1818 and was accentuated by those of Troppau and Laibach in 1820–21. The course of increasing withdrawal from continental involvements, relentlessly (and rather noisily) pursued by Canning from 1822 onward, no doubt caused him far less sadness than it had his predecessor. It was none the less a course already clearly traced in Castlereagh's lifetime.

As for the other powers, Austria would seem to have come nearest to getting what it wanted from the successive congresses: the snuffing out of potentially contagious revolts in Italy and Spain without a massive Russian re-entry into central and western European affairs. By the same token, Tsar Alexander had been compelled to moderate his more extreme ambitions as self-styled arbiter of Christendom. For the time being, Prussia remained what it had been at Vienna in 1814–15, a weak third among the eastern powers. From certain points of view, France might appear to have made good use of the congresses to recover her international standing. So she had, but her involvement in Spain following the decisions taken at Verona proved expensive, unpopular at home and embarrassing for her ostensibly constitutional government. The irony of a French army fighting Spaniards on the latter's own soil, so soon after Napoleon's disaster there, was apparent to any thoughtful observer. As for the smaller European states, they could only look on, with varying degrees of official approval, as their more potent continental neighbours sought to impose tranquillity not by pondering reform but by seeking to stifle it.

DIPLOMACY AFTER VIENNA: ITALY, SPAIN AND PORTUGAL

It can be argued that the congress system was not defunct, merely because consultation in the form of large and highly publicized colloquies had broken down. Groups of diplomats of various nationalities went on meeting in one or another capital to discuss current issues, and later decades would witness several congresses not unlike those of Vienna and Aix-la-Chapelle – at Paris in 1856, for example, and at Berlin in 1878. To confuse traditional diplomatic procedures with the survival of the experiment begun in 1814–15, however, would be to miss the latter's most important feature. For the central question had been whether or not *all* great powers, definitely including Great Britain, could agree on the conditions for international peace, and then regularly deliberate in common over the maintenance of those conditions. Conceived in those terms, the 'concert of Europe' was moribund by 1820 and dead by 1822. What followed was a resumption of power-political manoeuvring – complex, multilateral and, be it granted, successful for almost a century in preventing a general war – but not truly *conciliar*. After Verona, now one and then another major state took the initiative, employing means and encountering responses most of which would have been familiar to eighteenth-century statesmen.

At the risk of obscuring such critical problems as Russian–Polish tensions and the troubles in the kingdom of the Netherlands, to be discussed later, it is both possible and useful to examine international relations during the 1820s with regard to three primary sources of disagreement. One was the effort of the conservative powers to sustain oppressive, and in several cases grossly incompetent, régimes in the Italian and Iberian peninsulas. The second involved the degree of European influence which could be imposed on colonial settlements overseas. The third was focussed on the 'eastern question', as it developed during the Greek War of Independence.

The first of these issues, despite British opposition, appeared to have been settled by Austrian intervention against Neapolitan and Piedmontese rebels in 1821 and by the French invasion of Spain, to rescue Ferdinand VII, in 1823. The Italian cauldron, however, continued to simmer and occasionally broke into a boil, at one instant in Parma, the next in Modena, the next in the Papal States. None of the sporadic riots and assassinations overturned an established government, thanks largely to the busy Austrian regiments; but Metternich complained that no other power fully shared his determination to uphold legitimacy in Italy. Neither Paris nor Berlin had any material stake there, none at any rate comparable to Vienna's, while Russia, after the death of Alexander I in 1825, showed signs of increasing preoccupation with its own Polish and Balkan interests.

The two Iberian kingdoms, each in its own way, were proving as troublesome as Italy for a statesman committed to order as an absolute value. No sooner had the Duc d'Angoulême's French expeditionary force defeated the Spanish insurgents, which it did in August–September 1823, than King Ferdinand launched a savage reign of terror. Hundreds of liberals were executed in gruesome fashion. Thousands more were imprisoned or driven into exile. Like his relative in Naples two years before, the unbalanced ruler of Spain was encouraged in these measures by the Austrian and Prussian emissaries to his restored court. Angoulême, on the other hand, was horrified at the sadistic excesses of revenge; and from Paris Louis XVIII, indecisive but not inhumane, denounced the aftermath of his army's victory as a betrayal of the honour of French soldiers. In the circumstances, there was little cause for surprise when in October Canning curtly refused even to have England represented at a proposed congress to discuss the future of Spain. For the remaining ten years of his life, however, Ferdinand VII would practise largely undisturbed his own sanguinary version of that fatherly care espoused by the Holy Alliance.

Developments centring on Portugal followed a different but scarcely a more peaceful course. Given the proximity of British naval power and the absence, at first, of sustained fighting among the Portuguese themselves, Metternich found it inadvisable to plead for intervention on the Italian–Spanish model. Conservative governments, however, looked on nervously as King John VI returned from Brazil in 1821 to accept a liberal constitution, applauded when he repudiated it the following year, only to shudder once more at his announcement that some form of parliamentary system was still his goal. When John died in 1826 the same governments noted with approbation the reactionary plans of the new regent, Dom Miguel. This time, however, it was Britain that intervened by sending a military force to the aid of the constitutional party. (Castlereagh's old prescriptions against meddling in the domestic affairs of other countries were, in Canning's view, to be applied selectively!) The English, prematurely reassured by Dom Miguel's suave promises, withdrew in 1827 after sixteen months in Lisbon; and as we shall see in

Chapter 12, the Portuguese regent's almost immediate resumption of attacks on the liberals touched off open civil warfare. Here it need only be emphasized that in this relatively remote kingdom the Holy Alliance failed to make its weight felt in any decisive manner.

THE AMERICAS AND THE MONROE DOCTRINE

Directly related to the troubles in Spain and Portugal was the second dominant issue of the post-congress era. This was the question of the continental powers' right or, more to the point, their ability to reverse the outcome of colonial rebellions across the Atlantic. Here the position of Britain was naturally crucial, and Canning's personal influence proved decisive. In 1825, without waiting for any statement by another European government, he suddenly announced that His Majesty recognized the independence of several republics – initially Argentina, Colombia and Mexico – which had been born, over the course of the preceding decade, out of revolts within the former American empire of Spain. The same year, Canning likewise extended formal recognition to Brazil under its constitutional emperor, Pedro I, eldest son of John VI of Portugal.

The flamboyant foreign secretary did not rely exclusively on British naval power in calling 'the New World into existence to redress the balance of the Old,' as he explained his initiative to the House of Commons. Needless to say, the chief obstacle to any effort by continental powers to reimpose Spanish and Portuguese rule upon Latin America was the Royal Navy, warmly supported in this task by Britain's merchant class. Canning, however, was eager to dramatize both the morality and the political soundness of playing the friend to constitutional liberalism and the self-determination of peoples. It was for this reason that he welcomed messages of thanks from liberators such as Bolívar and San Martín. Ironically, it was also for this reason that he helped to convert an American charter of hemispheric isolationism (admittedly coupled with national interventionism) into an important document of European history.

In Washington, D.C., on 2 December 1823, President Monroe sent to Congress his annual message on the State of the Union.

Contained therein was a lengthy passage reflecting especially the views of the secretary of state, John Quincy Adams, and devoted to the territorial interests of the United States in the Western Hemisphere. The Monroe Doctrine, as this section came to known, comprised two distinct assertions. The first, inspired by Russian settlements pushing down the Pacific Coast from Alaska to what is now the San Francisco Bay area, was that 'the American continents . . . are henceforth not to be considered as subject to future colonization by any European power'. The second had to do less with fresh colonization than with intervention in the treatment of already established settlements. Referring to the possibility that the powers of the Holy Alliance might act against Brazil and the new Spanish American republics, the message read: 'We owe it . . . to candor, and to the amicable relations existing between the United States and those powers, to declare that we should consider any attempt on their part to extend their political system to any portion of this hemisphere as dangerous to our peace and security.'[4]

It would be a mistake to assume that Canning welcomed Monroe's and Adams's sweeping pronouncement as support, pure and simple, for his own opposition to the Holy Alliance. The non-colonization clause was distasteful to Britain at a time when the westward extension of the U.S.–Canadian border had yet to be determined. Furthermore, the Americans, after temporizing, had in effect ignored Britain's offer of a joint declaration forbidding European attempts to restore the lost Portuguese and Spanish colonies. Last but not least, Canning was personally anything but an admirer of the bumptious young nation that had fought two wars against his own country during the preceding fifty years and had now seized as its own a policy he would have formulated rather differently.

Nevertheless, the Monroe Doctrine did in a general way fit into the foreign secretary's scheme of things. British commercial interests – as Canning, who sat in the Commons for Liverpool, was quite aware – rejoiced in the opening of trade with Spanish America, unhampered by the restrictions so long imposed by Madrid. (An independent Brazil, given England's already established influence in Lisbon, seemed less necessary, but not in itself unattractive.) Liberals in both France and England hailed the United States' *démarche* as supplying a programmatic basis for quarantining the New World against the devices of European autocrats. More immediately, it helped to justify British refusal to participate during 1824 in a proposed new congress of powers to consider Latin America. Finally, though he still sought for a time to reconcile Portugal and Brazil, Canning was quite prepared to play upon the danger that the United States might establish control over the former Spanish colonies as a reason for Madrid to see in their full independence the lesser of two evils.

It is not necessary to adopt the foreign secretary's very generous self-evaluation in order to arrive at the conclusion that his five years in office were momentous ones for what we have come to call the Atlantic community. Before an early death ended his career in 1827, he had laid the groundwork for a use of British naval power that would continue throughout the nineteenth century – as a force which effectively (save in the 1860s) separated the United States and Europe from one another, and South America from them both.

GREEK INDEPENDENCE

The third and last great issue to be noted here broke into the open on 2 April 1821 when the Orthodox Archbishop Germanos publicly repudiated Turkish rule and thereby converted Greek unrest into an avowed war for independence. Not only in Greece but in Serbia as well, Ottoman control of south-east Europe had been the object of increasingly sharp attacks since the turn of the century. Political ideals derived from the Enlightenment, the example of the French Revolution, the dawning awareness of distinct cultures and potential nationhood, all had helped to inspire resistance against the existing order in the Balkans. It was the Greeks' outright demand for freedom, however, that first lifted such resistance to the status of a burning question for Europe as a whole.

The struggle thus begun unfolded on several different levels. The military chronicle as such was at once complicated and terrible, for both Christians and Muslims slaughtered their enemies with a ferocity capable of sickening men who had walked on some of the bloodiest Napoleonic battlefields. The spring of 1821 saw the Morea (the ancient Pelopponesus in southern Greece) wrested from Turkish control with remarkable speed and apparent ease. The sultan's forces, still dominated by the corrupt and indolent Janissaries, were no match for the furiously attacking rebels. In the first two years of fighting, not only the south but Attica as well passed into the hands of the insurgents, though the Turks exacted a ghastly vengeance by massacring or enslaving some 30,000 island inhabitants of Chios in the Aegean.

Then a mixture of internal and external difficulties overtook the Greeks. Their commanders in the field often refused to consult one another about strategy or to abide by such battle plans as were from time to time agreed upon. Peasants of the interior showed increasing resentment towards the more sophisticated maritime Greeks, the merchants who dominated the provisional government. By 1824 these two elements found themselves actively engaged in armed conflict with one another.

While the above events were transpiring, Sultan Mahmud II finally resigned himself to paying the price for military aid from his all but sovereign tributary, Egypt's Muhammad Ali. The latter demanded Crete for himself and the Morea as a principality for his son, Ibrahim Pasha; but in return he provided the first well-organized Muslim army to appear in Greece since the outbreak of hostilities. First seizing Crete, the Egyptian forces under Ibrahim crossed to the mainland and began the systematic reduction of rebel strongholds, among them Navarino in 1825, Missolonghi in 1826, Athens in 1827. The brutality of this campaign, combined with indications that Ibrahim meant literally to depopulate the Morea for the benefit of future Egyptian settlers, forced the warring Greek factions back together. In April 1827 they elected the late tsar's old Corfiote adviser, Count John Capo d'Istria, president of Greece for a seven-year term. By that time, however, the chance that anything which could be termed 'Greece' would survive the Ottoman–Egyptian onslaught seemed exceedingly slight.

The turning of the tide and the ultimate failure of the sultan's and Ibrahim Pasha's offensive resulted from a number of simultaneous developments, many of them occurring outside the Balkans and far from the deep blue waters of the eastern Mediterranean. Involved were at least two quite distinct forms of action. One was popular and extended over most of the Christian world: an epoch-making surge of sympathy for the Greek cause. 'Love for the Greeks', or 'philhellenism' as it was called, had its roots in religion (the Cross was at war with the Crescent), in classical education (were the descendants of Herodotus and Thucydides, Plato and Aristotle not fighting for their lives?) and in liberal political sympathy for the heirs of Pericles as they struggled against an alien despotism. Writers as different in other respects as the Vicomte de Chateaubriand, Ludwig Uhland and leading English Romantics lent their literary gifts to the task of convincing Europeans that this was a war to save civilization. Lord Byron actually gave his life for the cause, succumbing to disease at Missolonghi in 1824, after he had contributed thousands of pounds to the Greeks' effort and had organized an auxiliary military contingent at his own expense. Support in the form of money, supplies and volunteers came from America – where town names as well as architecture in upstate New York, the Middle West and many parts of the South recall the power of philhellene sentiment – from the French royal government, from Swiss societies, from German princes. The king of Bavaria even sent a brigade of his regular army.

It was in the midst of this public clamour that important events occurred on the other level, that of governmental decision-making by the great powers. Russia's imperial court, by reflex hostile to the Turks, had at first encouraged the Greek rebels. In 1821 Alexander I permitted General Ypsilanti, of Greek Phanariote stock (*see above*, p. 41), but a tsarist army officer, to launch an invasion of Moldavia-Wallachia aimed at freeing both Rumanian and Greek Christians from their Ottoman masters. Ypsilanti, however, failed miserably, not least because the Rumanian gentry almost without exception hated Greeks more bitterly than they did Turks. Simultaneously, Metternich began a successful campaign to convince the tsar that the radicals of Greece were as bad as those of Naples and Spain, and that they should be left to their fate. England's Castlereagh, and for a time Canning after him, took the position that since a Turkish defeat would only add to Russian power, intervention on the rebels' behalf would be foolish. With France and Prussia both inclined to vacillate, Metternich had no great difficulty in blocking concerted action for Greek independence throughout the first five years of the war.

By 1826, however, popular indignation, sharply increased by the Egyptians' cruelty, was subjecting this policy of aloofness to very strong pressure for change. Perhaps even more important, the views of several leading European figures were hardening in opposition to those of the cool aristocrat in Vienna. King Charles

X of France, certainly no friend of constitutional movements in general, had nevertheless caught the philhellene fever (primarily for religious reasons) and become critical of Metternich. At St Petersburg, 1825 had brought the death of Tsar Alexander I and the accession of his brother, Nicholas I, a ruler who felt no personal obligation to act in concert with Austria and who was determined to exploit every advantage over the Turks that fate might send his way. Finally, the British official attitude, as personified by Canning, had grown increasingly pro-Greek – a transformation reflecting not only .public opinion but also the foreign secretary's growing belief that bland refusal to act would leave the field clear for a unilateral Russian triumph over Turkey.

In April 1826 at St Petersburg, therefore, the duke of Wellington signed a protocol which committed the Russians and British jointly to impose their mediation upon the belligerents, the solution envisaged being an autonomous Greece under the nominal suzerainty of the sultan. As we have already seen, however, the war ground on amid mounting indications that the Turks and their Egyptian allies would win a total victory. It was to prevent such an outcome that on 6 July 1827 France joined the co-signers of the previous spring's St Petersburg protocol in a three-power agreement, the treaty of London, which provided that if either side in the conflict continued to spurn mediation, all three signatories would lend naval and perhaps other forms of support to the more conciliatory party.

A combined British–French–Russian flotilla hovered about the Morea that summer and autumn, its English commander, Admiral Codrington, being under a quite remarkable set of orders to block all Turkish and Egyptian reinforcements, without letting the operation 'degenerate into hostilities'. Ibrahim Pasha was in fact prevailed upon to halt operations for several weeks, pending further negotiations; but on 20 October 1827 Codrington received news at sea that the Muslim armies had resumed their full-scale attack. For a veteran of Trafalgar, and one of Nelson's most loyal disciples, the next move was virtually reflexive: he sailed his ships straight into the harbour of Navarino. Firing began, in circumstances of some confusion, and within three hours the close-packed Egyptian–Turkish fleet was all but annihilated. Before the end of the year the three intervening powers, though still technically at peace with the sultan, had recalled their ambassadors from Turkey.

It was Tsar Nicholas who ended this ambiguous state of affairs and initiated the climactic chain of events. Late in April 1828, against the wishes of Wellington's newly formed cabinet in London but with French approval, the Russian imperial government declared war on the Sublime Porte. During the next few months it still appeared that diplomacy might achieve more than arms; for while the Russians were meeting unexpectedly stiff Turkish resistance in the Rumanian provinces, British and French representatives negotiated the final evacuation of the Greek mainland by the Egyptian army. The next year, however, told a different story. Early in June the Russian general, Diebitsch, won a great victory at Kulevcha, on the Black Sea near the mouth of the Danube, and immediately thrust his army southward across the Balkan Mountains into Thrace. On 20 August 1829 he took Edirna (Adrianople).

Never before had Russian troops stood so close to Istanbul, but they were seriously weakened by disease and exhausted after the long forced marches. Yielding to the advice of General Diebitsch, therefore, the tsar decided to negotiate with the Turks on relatively generous terms. By the treaty of Adrianople, concluded on 14 September, Russia secured the entire Danube delta, the promise of a large cash indemnity and sweeping pledges of Christian religious supremacy in the Rumanian principalities. In return, Russian armies evacuated their other recent conquests.

The same treaty, and the same autumn, brought to a triumphant end the Greeks' battle for independence. At Adrianople the sultan promised to accept the three-year-old St Petersburg Protocol, that is, to confer on Greece what would have amounted to autonomous status under his nominal suzerainty. Before the final terms were signed on 30 November 1829, however, the British, Russian and French representatives had increased their demands to include absolute independence for Greece (minus Crete, which was left to the Egyptians). The Porte was thus compelled to let Europe's diplomats write the conclusion to this chapter in the history of the 'eastern question'. Many more chapters were still to come; but here, looking ahead to later developments, we should perhaps simply emphasize the suspicion between London and St Petersburg that underlay even the momentary collaboration of the two governments and by mid-century would eventuate in the Crimean War.

The ultimate success of the Greeks and their supporters in many lands had one other important aspect. It constituted a more serious defeat for Metternich than had any previous occurrence, not excepting the isolation of the New World from action by the Holy Alliance. Austria had been effectively excluded from great-power negotiations during the last years of the war in Greece, unwilling to endorse the decisions reached, but unable to prevent their implementation. The defeat, however, was not simply a matter of reduced diplomatic influence for Vienna. Its most ominous significance, seen from Metternich's point of view, lay in the emergence of an international public opinion endorsing the national and constitutional goals of the Greek rebels. Liberals and nationalists from Hungary to Belgium and from Poland through the Germanies to France took heart at this triumph of their chosen heroes over an avowed autocracy. By his own lights, Metternich was right to look upon the Greek revolt as a threat not only to the Turks but also to his own domestic and international system.

THE EUROPEAN POWERS IN 1830

Before turning from the story of diplomatic and military relations to that of internal politics, we should perhaps ask to what extent, and in what respects, the European state system of 1830 still resembled and how much it had come to differ from that of 1780. For, as always in the study of history, purely narrative treatment might obscure important elements of both continuity and change.

Up to a point, it seems fair to say that the fifteen years after 1815 brought a full and conscious restoration of earlier relationships. The pattern of roles in the 1820s was more akin to that of the 1780s than to the sprawling chaos, dominated by a singly conquering nation, we observed in the revolutionary and Napoleonic decades. England had resumed a posture of aloofness from any coalition on the Continent, though the United Kingdom was by no means so dangerously isolated as it had been at the end of the American War of Independence. Russia, however assertive it remained with respect to the Balkans, had largely abandoned Alexander I's bid for influence in western and central Europe. Austria, under Metternich as under Emperor Joseph II before him, wielded great influence in many areas but was ineffectual in the south-east. Prussia was again the junior partner in the German dualism, not the standard bearer of reform and national revival it had briefly appeared to be at the end of Napoleon's reign. The situation of France under Louis XVIII and Charles X was similarly reminiscent of the 1780s, when the monarchy's desire to direct the course of foreign affairs had far exceeded its actual ability to do so. Even the fact that there were still five great powers – the same five – suggests that the old order had survived the tempest intact.

Nevertheless, in at least two respects, Europe's state system was far different at the end of our period than it had been at the beginning. One change was geographical, and perfectly manifest: there were many fewer political entities portrayed on the map. During these decades the consolidation of large and medium-sized states, already in progress for several centuries, had taken another giant step forward. The kingdom of Sweden and the kingdom of the Netherlands now constituted the largest indigenous political units yet to appear in Scandinavia and the Low Countries, respectively. Spain's and Portugal's boundaries were unchanged; but France and Prussia had succeeded in absorbing a number of small principalities, free cities and ecclesiastical holdings, while Austria's sway had been extended around the northern and eastern shores of the Adriatic Sea. In Italy, the former republic of Genoa had at last fallen to the House of Savoy's Sardinian kingdom. Even Switzerland had been increased by its incorporation of Geneva.

To be sure, certain minuscule states survived, entitled to manage at least their own internal affairs: Andorra in the Pyrenees, for instance, and Monaco on the Mediterranean Riviera. The sovereign republic of San Marino existed in the heart of the Italian Papal States. In general, however, the progress of consolidation during the half-century ending in 1830 had been relentlessly pursued on many fronts. This was true even of divided Germany. Four free cities and such tiny principalities as Anhalt, the two Lippes and the landgraviate of Hesse-Homburg still figured among the thirty-nine members of the Confederation that had emerged from the Congress of Vienna. But in addition to Austria and Prussia, the new German political structure gave prominence to four other kingdoms (Bavaria, Württemberg, Saxony, Hanover) and a number of sizeable grand duchies (Baden, Hesse-Darmstadt, Hesse-Cassel, Mecklenburg-Schwerin, Oldenburg,

Holstein). Thus, a dozen states controlled about 90 per cent of the Confederation's total area.

Elsewhere, the picture was more confusing and the drift of developments less easy to characterize. In the case of Poland, the kingdom erected in 1815 gave the illusion that the work of the late eighteenth-century partitions had been substantially undone. To a realistic observer, however, the appearance of this Russian puppet, with the tsar as its king, could not hide the fact that one of the larger European nations of 1780 was no more. On the other hand, the birth of an independent Greece at the very end of our period constituted an extremely significant change in the map, one pregnant with meaning for the future of the crumbling Ottoman Empire.

If the reduction in the number of states was one critical change separating the European power-political scene, as we now leave it, from that with which we began, a second was the altered conception of states themselves, viewed simply as actors on the diplomatic stage. Earlier, as pointed out in Chapter 4, what a sovereign power *was*, in relation to others powers, had been little more than its monarch or chief magistrate, its restricted aristocracy and its entrenched bureaucracy, military as well as civilian. The French Revolution, both in its spread and in the conditions that resistance to it called into being, had banished this older, simpler situation beyond recall. Henceforth, not merely *states* but also *nations* would have to be taken into account.

Needless to say, the reality of the 'people's voice' differed radically as between Russia, for example, and either Great Britain or France. Even in the latter kingdoms, public opinion on foreign affairs was still no more than a slowly emerging and grudgingly recognized force. Nevertheless, almost everywhere in Europe, the age of the Restoration was filled with that peculiar tension produced when deeply entrenched habits of thought and action are in conflict with permanently altered circumstances. The tendency of diplomats trained in the old school to behave as though the revolutionary-Napoleonic drama had been an isolated episode, an aberration, ran squarely into the sentiments of countless other individuals for whom it had been an unforgettable experience. How could anyone who recalled the *levée en masse* in France, the rising of the Spanish *pueblo* against Bonaparte's troops or the ferment of the War of Liberation in Germany ever again accept cold dynastic calculation as the sole determinant of foreign policy?

By traditional standards, Metternich, Castlereagh and Talleyrand were unquestionably masters of diplomacy; but it was Canning, with his histrionic gifts, his awareness of public emotions and his solicitude for the interests of not at all aristocratic merchants, who most clearly represented the dawning of a new age.

NOTES AND REFERENCES

1   The former *dauphin*, son of Louis XVI, had been styled 'Louis XVII' by monarchists prior to his death in a Parisian jail cell in 1795.

2   Quoted in F. B. Artz, *Reaction and Revolution, 1814–1832* (New York, 1938), p. 161.

3   H. Nicolson, *The Congress of Vienna* (London, 1946), p. 268.

4   D. Perkins, *A History of the Monroe Doctrine* (rev. edn, Boston, 1955), p. 28. The same author's *The Monroe Doctrine, 1823–1826* (Cambridge, Mass., 1932), is a more detailed analysis of origins and initial effects.

12

RESTORATION POLITICS

The title of this chapter, narrowly construed, would be misleading. For the domestic affairs of European states between 1815 and 1830 were much too complex to fit any simple notion of 'a world restored'. Nevertheless, behind virtually every post-1815 political debate lay memories of the revolutionary–Napoleonic experience and the conflicting lessons it had to offer, depending on whether one saw it as a sickness, now happily cured, or as a season of hope, temporarily frustrated. The drama so recently ended obviously did not offer answers to all new questions, but it had left behind a set of powerful associations and sentiments certain to influence the way in which such questions were posed.

Take the matter of language. It is useless to argue that a fact has exactly the same effect on human behaviour regardless of the words used to express it, or that an event has the same historical meaning whatever its participants are called at the time or however their motives are labelled. The truth is that terminology has power in its own right. In present-day politics, it makes a great difference to all concerned whether a given proposal is identified as liberal, progressive, social–democratic or 'Red'. Still greater is the impact of such terms as 'Bolshevik', 'Fascist', 'neo-Nazi'.

The period we are concerned with echoed to many comparable epithets. At the head of the list stood 'Jacobin'. There remained, to be sure, some avowed Jacobins in Europe after 1794, and even after 1815, but far fewer than the lavish use of the name would suggest. As early as 1801, it will be recalled, George III rather mysteriously concluded that Catholic Emancipation in the United Kingdom was, or would be if enacted, 'Jacobinical' – and rejected it in horror. Time after time, men who favoured even the most limited constitutional or social reforms found themselves being singled out by their opponents as Jacobins, allegedly nostalgic for the Terror and eager to erect new guillotines. On the other hand, the mildest conservative could become in hostile eyes a selfish reactionary, an 'aristocrat' in the usage of 1789 and after. Other evocative words and phrases – Old Boney, *Dos Mayo*, the German Rhine, the Rights of Man, Throne and Altar – inflamed emotions without in most cases doing much to clarify thought.

Another legacy of the recent past lay in several social groups that had counted for little in political life before 1789, but had since come into prominence. Journalists were one of them. Despite elaborate efforts at government censorship, the Fourth Estate had arrived to stay. University students too, especially active in Germany, would henceforth be found at the barricades when rebellion flared almost anywhere on the Continent. The mention of barricades is a reminder that the urban crowd, that mixture of shopkeepers, workers, drifters and idealistic men of some wealth and education characteristic of Paris during the Revolution, would in the course of the ensuing decades take repeatedly to the streets of many another European city.

Perhaps the most significant new political element, however, was 'the military'. Most army officers of the Old Régime had been either professionals, largely indifferent to high policy, or courtiers playing soldier. For better or for worse, Napoleon, his commanders and the commanders who fought against him had given the military almost everywhere in Europe that combination of prestige and self-awareness needed to make it a genuine force in civil affairs. It was a force sometimes progressive, at other times reactionary, but seldom quiescent. We shall observe the results in Spain, in Italy and in Russia, to mention only a few instances.

A characteristic inherited from the recent past was the role of radical societies, heirs of the French revolutionary clubs and of anti–Bonapartist fraternities (*Philadelphes* in France, the *Tugendbund* or 'League of Virtue' in Germany, etc.). These emerged briefly into view in 1815, only to become secretive once more as various governments' security police, itself a notable feature of the period, forced agitators underground. Freemasons in Poland,

Switzerland, Austria and elsewhere, *Carbonari* and *Adelfi* in Italy, members of the student *Burschenschaften* in Germany, United Slavs and related groups in Russia, brethren of the *Philiké Hetaeraea* in Greece and the Greek exile communities, all represented expressions of defiance to established governments.

In Filippo Michele Buonarroti (1761–1837) we encounter a noteworthy product of these societies, their methods and their inter-relationships. Born in Pisa of noble Tuscan parentage, educated as a lawyer and early attracted to Freemasonry, he was expelled from Florence in 1789 for having written too enthusi-astically about the French Revolution. By 1793 he was in Paris, an honorary French citizen, avowed Jacobin and admirer of Robespierre. Upon the latter's fall, Buonarroti continued to dabble in Dutch and Italian affairs, then joined actively in Babeuf's 'conspiracy of the Equals' against the French Directory. Arrested when that plot collapsed, he was at last freed in 1806 and moved to Geneva, where he stayed for some fifteen years, attending meetings of both Freemasons and Jacobins while plotting with the *Philadelphes* in Paris to overthrow Napoleon.

After the emperor's defeat and abdication, this tireless pamphleteer, letter-writer and organizer of rebellion continued his international struggle for egalitarian causes, now directed against all 'restored tyrants'. No one else can have been in touch with so many conspiracies between 1815 and 1830. He spent a great deal of time in Brussels during the 1820s, and disciples of his took leading parts in the eventual Belgian rising against Dutch rule. He quarrelled with Mazzini over the future shape of a free Italy, but agreed that a free Italy there must be. His own secret organization encouraged and advised dissidents all the way from Warsaw to Madrid. In truth, he deserved to be called, as a twentieth-century biographer has called him, 'the first professional revolutionist'.[1]

ECONOMIC CHANGES

Many disputes of the restoration period were avowedly political, in that they turned on questions of national independence, consti-tutional guarantees, voting rights, and so on. Behind them, however, lay a number of other issues – economic, social, religious and administrative – which lent substance to the debates while helping to determine the alignment of forces.

Perhaps the most obvious economic concern after 1815 was that over public finances. We know that by the end of the Napoleonic Wars both France and Great Britain were thought by many experts to be close to national bankruptcy. Such was the resiliency of the two economies that neither in fact suffered this fate, but they escaped only after hard trials. The recovery of the French monarchy was particularly impressive. Under Louis XVIII, two ministers, Baron J.-D. Louis and Count Luigi Corvetto, so effectively overhauled the system of tax collection and official accounting that by 1818 the indemnity of 700 million francs had already been paid in full to the Allies, the principle of honouring the debts of the Empire firmly established and the credit of the Crown assured. Needless to say, this had not been achieved without bitter outcries from all of the interests pinched by fiscal rigour and reform.

In England, the rapid abandonment of war taxes, in the initial euphoria of peace and victory, sharpened the crisis confronting the earl of Liverpool's government. The British national budget for 1815, more than £83 million,[2] had been the largest ever known in any country. Now, with drastically lowered income, and at least momentarily reduced foreign trade, the greatest money power of the age seemed threatened with collapse. Once again, however, the resources and resourcefulness that had made possible the long resistance to Napoleon combined with some good luck to avert disaster. Exports both to the Continent and to the wider world began to climb once more, and industry joined commerce in the revival of Great Britain's national prosperity. It would be wrong to envisage that revival as immediate. By the early 1820s, however, the most acute fears of public bankruptcy had been dispelled. Even the speculation in Latin America, leading to the new crisis of 1825, only shook the Bank of England, it did not topple it.

Other states gripped by fiscal troubles could show little to compare with the French and British recoveries. Prussia in 1815 had an unprecedented public debt of 217 million *Thalers*. Administrative reforms and stern economies could no more than stabilize a parlous situation. To correct it, a major increase in the kingdom's productivity would be required, and that still lay several decades in the future. In Russia, the tsar could maintain a court, with the revenue from his own immense properties, and an army, through conscription and requisitioning. However, the plundering of treasury and people alike by provincial governors, who are known to have pocketed a large share of the proceeds from such taxes as the vodka excise, scarcely permits us to speak of national finances. Austria at long last founded a national bank in 1816; but Metternich characteristically refused to offend the privileged aristocracy by reforming the tax system, preferring instead to borrow large sums from private bankers, notably the brothers Rothschild.

The Italian states, with the partial exception of Sardinia-Savoy, generally appeared oblivious to standards of financial responsibility. They maintained their theoretical solvency only by borrowing and by the use of police power. The kingdom of the Netherlands, its combined deficit more than doubled in 1815 by the Waterloo campaign alone, had recourse to a combination of taxes on grain and meat, making its Belgian subjects more resentful than ever. King Ferdinand's war-ravaged Spain was running an annual deficit of £5 million in December 1816, when Don Martin de Garay was named secretary of the treasury. Garay made a valiant effort at reform. He consolidated personal taxes into a single levy, negotiated increased fiscal support from the clergy as well as from town merchants, and drafted plans to reduce the national debt over a period of years; but his projects made so many enemies that in 1818 he was forced to resign, and the Spanish treasury sank back into the habit of juggling its books.

Régimes with such unstable finances might well have pondered the role played by the threat of national bankruptcy in the French crisis of the 1780s. On the other hand, as noted earlier, each state had its police mechanism for use against critics. Problems of public finance *alone*, it should also be noted, are unlikely to bring down a national government unless accompanied by misfortunes in war or more immediate, tangible kinds of popular grievance. Food, clothing, shelter – these are the wants that can become politically decisive. But why should such wants have been felt after 1815, during years of peace, by a basically rich continent then enjoying increases in both its agricultural and its industrial productivity?

An important part of the answer lies in the persistence, indeed the acceleration, of population growth. That growth, from about

140 million to 187 million in 1800, surged on towards an estimated total for all Europe (including Russia west of the Urals) of 266 million by 1850.[3] Great Britain's roughly 12.4 million inhabitants in 1810 had risen to 14.3 million by 1820 and ten years later, at the end of our period, stood at 16.5 million. Ireland by that time (1830) contained 7.8 million souls, almost three times its population of just sixty years earlier. Between 1800 and about 1850, the tsar's subjects in European Russia increased from 37.5 million to almost 62 million, while Italy's growth in the same years was from 18 million to 23 million and the German Confederation's, 23.5 to 34.5 million. France was rather more stable in numbers, going from something over 27.3 million in 1801 (for the area of 1831) to about 31.9 million by the latter date. The population of Paris, however, doubled in size during the first half of the century, passing the million mark before 1850.

This last statistic deserves to be stressed. Taking Europe as a whole, in the early nineteenth century the rise in population continued to be greater in rural than in urban areas. The dramatic growth of the French capital, however, serves to highlight a major new development, the rush to particular cities: to Brussels (70,000 in 1815, 251,000 in 1850), to Milan (170,000 in 1800, 242,000 in 1850), to Vienna (247,000 in 1800, 444,000 in 1850), to Berlin (172,000 in 1800, 419,000 in 1850). It was the 1820s that witnessed an especially steep rise in urban population figures. During that decade alone, the six largest cities of the English midlands grew in the aggregate by more than 40 per cent. The misery of overcrowded urban centres had particularly ominous implications for political life.

Though several explanations have been advanced to account for this general increase in Europe's numbers, some of them fail to survive close analysis. It cannot any longer be seriously argued, for example, that the death rate declined sufficiently to provide an answer, especially in view of the still appallingly high figures showing infant mortality. Epidemic disease had receded somewhat since the early eighteenth century; but smallpox, typhoid and, periodically, cholera continued to inflict heavy losses of life. Sanitation and preventive medicine had not yet begun the remarkable progress they would make in the later 1800s. A famous essay of the past generation directs attention to two factors which seem more significant in the causal pattern: (1) a substantial decline in the average age of marriage during the late eighteenth and early nineteenth centuries, while the rate of illegitimate births remained very high, and (2) the rapid spread of the humble potato, nourishing, easily grown on small plots and admirably resistant to either drought or frost.[4] So far as political effects are concerned, this addition to the diet of needy Europeans and its contribution to population growth constitute a notable instance of historical irony. For the rise in number of living persons, especially in cities, only heightened the incipient panic sure to greet any threat to the food supply, be it a bad harvest or artifical restraints on edible imports.

Among the most unsettling factors must be counted the effects of early industrialism: the swift making and losing of private fortunes, the *relative* decline of small manufacturing in towns, the gradual decline of the 'putting out' system in village and farm, and the inevitable resistance to the new machines on the part of craftsmen still tied to older ways. Included too were bewildering shifts in supply and demand, as one innovation after another brought sudden increases in this or that category of saleable goods, accompanied by equally sudden shortages of currently needed raw materials. Included, above all, was the imperious presence of the factory. Here was a new entity, social as well as economic, in which workers of narrowly limited skills serviced the tireless machine, a despot who demanded constant attention yet was capable, if superseded by a better machine elsewhere, of suddenly abandoning his own servants to idleness and destitution.

England, as we have seen, had shown the way in factory growth before the French Revolution. By about 1780, certain British manufactures, cotton in particular, were already displaying that combination of reliance on machinery, concentration of labour under supervision and rational planning with respect to the acquisition of raw material and the marketing of finished goods we associate with modern industrialism. The special role played by cotton is not hard to explain. It was, and is, a tough, uniform fibre, admirably suited to mechanical processing and infinitely more plentiful, given the Indian and American sources of supply, than its elegant rival, linen. It addition, the cotton industry was comparatively young and hence could expand without having to overcome all the traditional restrictions still hedging the older crafts. Finally, cotton answered the immense demand of a new market in part created by its own low cost, a market for cool, comfortable summer garments and for underclothing, which most

Europeans began to be able to afford only in the late eighteenth century. Where cottonmaking led – towards increased scale and concentration of production – other industries, such as wool, brewing, soapmaking and metal stamping and casting, rapidly followed.

Great Britain's overall precocity in industrial development is less easily accounted for. Many contributory explanations have been put forward, among them the long accumulation of manufacturing skills in an island kingdom untouched by land warfare and recurrently the haven for continental refugees; comparatively good roads (though less good than those of France) and especially water transport; the unique merging of different forms of capital, making income from landed wealth far more readily available for business investment than it was across the Channel; a well-developed banking and credit system; an active home market, swelled by a rising population which nevertheless felt reasonably safe in spending money on comforts and utensils; a still more active foreign market served by a large merchant marine and guarded by a powerful navy.[5] Doubtless all these and still other reasons must be borne in mind if we are to understand why, with respect to industry, Britain in 1815 was the tutor of Europe.

For the ensuing period, only a few observations and statistics are needed to demonstrate the growth of manufacturing and to suggest its political significance, both in Great Britain and on the Continent. In the United Kingdom, whereas some 2,400 power looms had been weaving cotton in 1813, there were 14,150 in 1820 and no fewer than 55,500 in 1829, while the production of pig iron, only 258,206 long tons in 1806, by 1830 stood at 678,417.[6]

On the Continent, emulation of British techniques, the appearance of further inventions, the gradual improvement of transportation, the expansion of credit and governmental encouragement to meet a growing domestic market brought the first modest evidences of industrialization. French cotton production, to take an important example, climbed substantially, as the industry moved out of Paris to Lille in Flanders, Rouen in Normandy, Mulhouse in Alsace. In the last-named town there were 426 power looms in 1827, but 2,123 just four years later.[7] Prussia, whose Institute of Trades (*Gewerbe Institut*) was established in 1821, also saw a rise in textile production. By 1831 an industrial census of the kingdom revealed 252,000 linen looms in operation, chiefly concentrated in Silesia.[8] During the short lifetime of the United Netherlands, King William I offered generous subsidies, especially favourable to Belgian industry. He brought the English engineer, John Cockerill, to introduce the manufacturing of machinery at Seraing in 1817, sent Roentgen to Britain to study metallurgy in 1821, consulted Omalius d'Alloy on the latter's methods of blending metals and pushed ahead with vast canal projects. What all this meant to Belgian cities is suggested by the fact that in 1830 Ghent alone was estimated to have eighty textile mills of various kinds, employing 30,000 men, women and children.[9] By that time, Belgium had established itself as in many respects the most advanced industrial society on the European mainland.

Admittedly, most of the rest of Europe lagged behind the French–Prussian–Belgian pace. For the Continent as a whole, the period from 1815 to 1830 might in fact best be thought of as one of education and 'tooling up'. Even for the relatively favoured areas just mentioned, with the exception of Belgium, the spurt to overtake Great Britain still lay in the future, around mid-century. Nevertheless, the first decades after 1815 witnessed the emergence of the political problems, the clamour, the dislocations accompanying industrial growth in its early, and highly controversial, phase.

Commerce too constituted an economic concern of immediate significance to public life. The kingdom of the Netherlands, for instance, had a major stake in commercial activity, both the carrying trade long practised by its Dutch subjects and the exportation of finished goods produced by its Belgian ones. For a time, the coal of Belgium, mined in quantities far exceeding the total French production, seemed likely to remain a major export; but the demands of the Belgian iron industry itself rose so rapidly that by 1830 the country was actually beginning to import coal from Great Britain. Note, however, that the European coal trade, whichever way it was moving – including the route from west German mines to French blast furnaces – was a critical factor in national economic growth, including warmaking potential.

Throughout our period, European states kept their tariff barriers high, with one great exception. That was the United Kingdom, which in the mid-1820s began to move towards freer trade in most manufactures. With respect to agricultural interests, however, England's own policy was at least as exclusionary as those of most continental countries. British landowners, encouraged to extend their plantings of grain during the long Napoleonic siege, faced a drastic fall in prices when peace came. To save them (and ostensibly to maintain food production against future war needs), Parliament enacted the Corn Law of 1815, prohibiting all imports of foreign grains unless a domestic shortage pushed the price in Britain above 80 shillings a quarter (eight bushels). Basically Great Britain remained protectionist towards foodstuffs, to the chagrin of both the earners and the payers of industrial wages. Despite mounting agitation, repeal of the Corn Law and its successors would not come until 1846.

The trade policies of other countries tended in general to follow a pattern established by France, which in 1822 pushed its duty on British iron (50 per cent *ad valorem* in 1814) to an unprecedented 120 per cent and in 1826 the French tariff of 1826 set new records for customs charges on textiles. As for grain, the Bourbon monarchy had as late as 1817 been compelled to import wheat and rye; but the growing spectre of Russian competition led French producers to insist on the high protective barriers finally enacted amid bitter debate in 1819. Elsewhere on the Continent, in the Netherlands, in the German, Italian and Scandinavian states, as well as in Spain and Portugal, makers of public policy seemed almost unanimously to favour protectionism.

A partial exception was Prussia. For while its external duties remained high, the Hohenzollern kingdom embarked soon after the liberation on a sweeping consolidation of its own internal market, and then began negotiations designed to expand the free trade area thus created. Frederick William III's tariff decree of 1818 abolished all customs barriers dividing the provinces and other historic subdivisions within his realm. The following year, tiny Schwarzburg-Sondershausen in Thuringia signed a treaty bringing it into the Prussian tariff system. Thus was born the famous customs union (*Zollverein*), which by 1834 would include the bulk of non-Austrian Germany and little more than a generation later would play its part in Bismarck's fashioning of a German Empire ruled from Berlin. In 1819, however, a contemporary would scarcely have seen any deep economic or political significance in the adherence of Schwarzburg-Sondershausen, with its population of 45,000!

RELIGION

Turning from the economic to the religious component in political affairs, we at once encounter evidence that Roman Catholicism was recovering from the losses and humiliations of the revolutionary-Napoleonic crisis. Indeed, this recovery erased even some features of the pre-1789 situation. In 1814 the Society of Jesus, outlawed as early as 1773 by the Vatican because of pressure from numerous secular rulers, was reinstated by Pope Pius VII, allowing the Jesuits to resume openly their mission of education and conversion. As we shall see in the next chapter, Catholic thinkers as diverse as the Savoyard de Maistre, the Frenchmen Bonald and Chateaubriand, the German Gentz and the Swiss Haller (the last two converts from Protestantism) led the intellectual counterattack against the heritage of the 'Godless Revolution'. At the same time, there was a visible increase in church attendance and sacramental observance, not uncommon in the wake of great secular convulsions.

It was doubtless inevitable, under the circumstances, that both the Holy See, under Pius VII and his successor, Leo XII (1823–29), and the prelates in wholly or partially Catholic countries should speak on various subjects with newly recovered confidence. This restored tone of authority, in turn, produced its own reaction from the side of more liberal Catholic leaders, for the most part younger laymen. Both in Belgium and in France 'modern Catholics' denounced the hierarchy's support of political reactionaries, support these critics believed would alienate the Church from the mass of its own followers. In Italy too, their counterparts urged ecclesiastical leaders to repudiate local tyrants.

At the same time, clashes between Catholics and non-Catholics continued to embitter European politics. In Ireland religious hatreds had grown worse since the Act of Union in 1800. And England itself after 1815 saw a mounting demand on the part of Catholics for legal equality join that of Protestants outside the Church of England for repeal of the hoary Test Act. Needless to say, the hostility and fear separating Dutch Calvinists from Belgian Catholics contributed nothing to the unity of the 'United' Netherlands. As for France, Huguenots as well as Jews seemed more secure and less disaffected than under the Old Régime, especially in view of Louis XVIII's confirmation of freedom of worship in his 1814 Charter. Even here, however, the murder of numerous Protestants by royalist mobs during the White Terror of 1815 was a reminder, mercifully brief, that old wounds could still bleed. Despite the small size of its Protestant minority, Italy offered an interesting and significant extension of religion into politics. Resentful of the Catholic hierarchy's political role, introduced to the teachings of the Reformation while exiles in Great Britain or Switzerland, more than a few of the future leaders of the Italian national rising embraced Protestantism under the Restoration.[10]

Europe's Protestants meanwhile faced divisive issues of their own. The seemingly abrupt, though in fact long-matured, decision by Frederick William III of Prussia in 1817 to decree the union of his Lutheran and Reformed (Calvinist) subjects, was promptly denounced by numerous 'Old Lutherans', some of whom eventually emigrated. The mere fact that most Prussian Calvinists and 'modern' Lutherans accepted the Church of the New Prussian Union only increased Old Lutheran hostility. Similar unions were carried out in other German states, notably Hesse-Cassel, Nassau and Baden, with broader popular support; but everywhere civil and ecclesiastical authorities were obliged to make allowances for variety among liturgies and forms of parish organization.

Disagreement over questions of public policy too was widespread among Protestants. In Germany, it is true, the most significant development, an espousal of deep social conservatism by Lutheran leaders, was not to appear until the middle years of the century; but even before 1830 the lack of religious progressivism was apparent in the home of the Reformation. Far different was the case of England, where the Dissenters' political demands on their own behalf merged with their humanitarian assault on slavery and on the Anglican divines' alleged lack of social conscience. It is not easy to identify the specifically religious content of such reformist zeal, as distinguished from the politics of middle-class Englishmen in general, but it is nonetheless important to note that the Dissenters, 'Evangelicals' as well as Methodists, continued to clothe their statements in the sonorous language of faith.

Almost everywhere in Europe, as a matter of fact, religious conflict entered and influenced public life. In Russian-occupied Poland, the Catholicism of the people clashed with the rulers'

Eastern Orthodox beliefs. In Russia itself the westernizing quasi-Protestant views of Alexander I and advisers such as Golitsin and Kiselev drove conservative religious leaders into a mounting frenzy. In the Balkans, where Christian subjects could expect nothing better than contemptuous toleration from their Turkish sovereign (himself beset by Muslim fanatics), the Greek Orthodox clergy voiced its vociferous hatred of all other faiths.

CONSERVATIVE ADMINISTRATIVE REFORMS

Let us pass to one more sign of the times, having little to do with questions of piety. This was institutional reorganization, imposed from above. Between 1815 and 1830 the reforms decreed by established régimes seldom if ever carried the sweeping, potentially revolutionary implications of Napoleon's or even Stein's. Instead, they were selective, limited and explicitly conservative efforts to shore up the structure of authority, with a minimum of threat to existing privileges. Yet despite their authors' motives, these administrative changes inevitably trod on various toes, excited complaints and thus exacerbated the resentment expressed over larger questions of the day. The legacy of the Revolution, like the defensive reflexes it had called forth, continued to agitate a system only lately re-established on shaken foundations.

Some of these technical reforms have already been mentioned in other connections – the tightening of French treasury procedures by Louis and Corvetto, for example, and Garay's revision of Spanish taxes, as well as the new Prussian tariff system of 1818. In the polyglot Austrian Empire, Francis I rejected Metternich's proposal of 1817 to clarify the governmental structure by creating an office of supreme chancellor, with subordinate chancelleries for Austria, Hungary, Bohemia, Transylvania, Illyria-Dalmatia and the Habsburg holdings in Italy. Even in Vienna, however, the long-delayed establishment of a Ministry of Finance in 1816 proved that the impulse to match French innovations of the preceding period had not wholly spent itself.

The relative importance of this phenomenon varied, of course, from country to country. In England, purely administrative reform played only a minor part in these turbulent years. By 1815 there was no doubt that the cabinet was an entity to which only the occupants of key offices belonged, but the immediately ensuing period brought no clearly defined principle of solidarity around the prime minister or of ministerial responsibility to the House of Commons. Treasury practices, like Admiralty and War Office procedures, remained essentially as the younger Pitt had known them. When Englishmen argued over reform, as we shall see, they meant something quite different from the reordering of relationships among officials.

At the other extreme was Russia, where *only* administrative projects offered any meaningful expression of reformist thinking. One project, the military colonies, which by 1816 comprised 750,000 people, was finally suppressed by the tsar in 1831, but not before it had stirred up deep animosity and lent fuel to the smouldering resistance. Alexander's minister, Arakchev, had insisted that this elaborately organized system would produce a stronger army and at the same time bring better food, housing and medical care to masses of Russian subjects. To most of the peasant-soldiers, however, such benefits were not worth the increased work and discipline.[11] On the other hand, in 1822 the governmental and economic reforms enacted in Siberia by Speransky effectively replaced archaic modes of local administration and opened a new land of economic promise.

A final example takes us once more to the newly created kingdom of the Netherlands. There all efforts at administrative rationalization automatically became political questions. This was so because such efforts were aimed at furthering, among other things, the 'amalgamation' of Dutchmen and Belgians. In appearance, William I's reign opened with a return to old forms. The Napoleonic *départements* were renamed provinces once more, and 'prefects' gave way to restored 'governors'. But in fact, neither the geographical areas nor the offices were basically changed. The French model was repudiated in words, but only to be retained in practice. Similarly, the metric system of weights and measures was carried over from the Empire, though the *names* of units were changed to Dutch. The important point is that the king alone decreed all these provisions for his mixed kingdom. Dutchmen who cherished local autonomy thus had cause to grumble, as did Belgians who recalled their struggles with a previous reforming monarch, Emperor Joseph II.

CENTRAL AND NORTHERN EUROPE

Yet despite the importance of socio-economic issues, religious tensions and administrative changes, our attention should not be too long diverted from the explicitly political debates of the restoration years. For politics could not then, and cannot now, be dismissed as mere window-dressing for other interests. Political *parties*, as distinct from homogeneous sects, cliques or court factions, were no longer strange or new. We saw them at work in the French revolutionary assemblies and in many countries divided over the question of how to respond to the Revolution. Even earlier, during the 1780s in Holland, Poland and elsewhere, we identified groups of men of diverse socio-economic backgrounds who nevertheless shared certain opinions regarding the proper functions of government and the direction of public policy. Finally, for anxious Europeans after 1815, the history of English parliamentary struggles combined with the example of the American Revolution to suggest lines of argument and forms of action.

For many of these men, the burning question was how to make the *nation* a focus for its people's highest loyalty, in pursuit of both domestic peace and external power. For others, the central issues involved the legal rights of individuals, rights to be defined and protected by written *constitutions*. For still others, battle was joined over the participation of more citizens in public affairs, especially through increased freedom of expression and the broadening of *voting* rights. Before the end of our period, be it added, social and economic discontent was beginning to produce what we can identify as socialistic demands for greater sharing of economic benefits. For the time being, however, the political stage resounded primarily to the claims of nationalism, constitutionalism and democratic reformism, sometimes in conflict among themselves, but more often merging into a broad attack on traditional forms.

Allowance made for national variations in tone and timing, one may sketch a general pattern of domestic politics within European states during the first years following Napoleon's defeat. At the outset, on all sides were heard optimistic calls for reform, some of them carried over directly from the resistance to Bonaparte, others born of conditions created by the Restoration itself. Conservative régimes, by contrast, braced themselves to defend the old order, using military resources assembled during years of war. Few rulers or ministers were prepared to confront the problems which spawned unrest. Instead, state power was typically applied to the tasks of repression, of crushing the opposition, in short, of attacking symptoms rather than causes.

To understand this swing towards repression we must look briefly at the motives and the forms of reaction, as well as the forces against which it was directed. In the Austrian Empire, for example, patriotism itself, at least the newer, French variety of patriotism, seemed a serious threat to the established order. It is worth remarking that not even Prince Metternich paid such close, continuous and apprehensive attention to that threat as did Emperor Francis I, who gave as his motto: 'Rule, and change nothing.' For who could have felt more acutely than a Habsburg, heir to a dynastic complex of differing ethnic groups, the disruptive force of the hunger for national self-determination? His response was to play off Germans against Hungarians, both against Slavs and all three against Italians. The stationing of regiments far from home, among people whose speech and customs were foreign to the troops, made feasible the use of Austrian army units to crush popular demonstrations of a type they might actually have joined in their native provinces. At the same time, nationalism was not the only doctrine viewed as threatening by the government. Austria's secret police hunted down liberal constitutionalists, tax objectors, violators of religious censorship and many others as diligently as it did spokesmen for the subject peoples.

Metternich's personal influence was most apparent in that other Austrian-led complex: the German Confederation. It is true that the Federal Diet met in Frankfurt, not in Vienna. However, the chief Austrian delegate, always named by Metternich, was president of the assembly *ex officio*, and the powerful minister regularly got his way by dint of parliamentary manoeuvres, diplomatic negotiations with individual German states and occasional threats of military force. Weak as the Diet was, it could be useful in providing an umbrella for concerted, 'legitimate' resistance to demands for reform. That it did so, despite the survival of quite vocal constitutional factions in the governments of several principalities – Bavaria and Württemberg among them – was evidence of the fear affecting even moderate conservatives when confronted with demonstrations of violence (*see* Map 7).

In October 1817, at the Wartburg, the Thuringian castle that had once sheltered Martin Luther, several hundred members of liberal and nationalistic student groups (*Burschenschaften*) assembled to hear speeches and sing songs. Although ostensibly called to celebrate the tercentenary of the Reformation and the fourth anniversary of the battle of Leipzig, the rally was primarily devoted to appeals for German unification under a national constitution. On the final evening, after a torchlight procession, many of the *Burschen* stayed together, built a large bonfire and proceeded to burn a number of symbols of authority: a corporal's cane, a pigtailed military wig, a cavalryman's leather corset and some slips of paper bearing the titles of books by accused reactionaries.

This adolescent display, disquieting though it was to solemn folk, would scarcely have warranted sweeping countermeasures, had it not been followed by a sensational crime, emotionally if not logically linked to the Wartburg Festival. On 23 March 1819 the playwright and journalist, August von Kotzebue, who was known to have supplied newsletters concerning German affairs to the tsar in St Petersburg and whose works had been among those symbolically burned by the Wartburg demonstrators, was stabbed to death in his home at Mannheim. The assassin was Carl Ludwig Sand, an unbalanced theology candidate from the University of Jena who had attended classes given by the fervent nationalist professor, Karl Follen. Sand was beheaded for his crime, but its repercussions continued to influence German politics for many years.

Seizing upon the Kotzebue murder as an opportunity to tighten controls within the Confederation, Prince Metternich first met with the King of Prussia at Teplitz in July 1819. A month later, at another Bohemian town, Carlsbad, he assembled the chief ministers of the nine largest German states. In addition to demanding a federal commission to investigate seditious agitation all over Germany, this group presented the Diet with a series of laws which the deputies in Frankfurt meekly passed that September. The new legislation, commonly referred to as the Carlsbad Decrees, outlawed both the *Burschenschaften* and *Turn-vater* Jahn's gymnastic clubs for patriots, imposed a stringent press censorship and placed university faculties under close police surveillance. The official course of the German Confederation was set: demands for reform were not even to be countenanced, let alone discussed – they were to be crushed as treason.

Prussia's role in all this was scarcely less prominent than Austria's. Ever since 1807 the eyes of German liberals had been turned hopefully towards Berlin, where the ideals of Stein and the Reform Era were assumed to have survived among many high officials. But Frederick William III, at once fearful and petulant, was no reforming monarch. The assassination of Kotzebue, coming close on the heels of the Wartburg proceedings, at which the killer had been present, confirmed the king's deepest misgivings. As a result, he warmly endorsed the Carlsbad Decrees. When the veteran army reformer, Boyen, and the University of Berlin's founder, Wilhelm von Humboldt, tendered their resignations in protest, both were curtly accepted, while certain outspoken patriots, Jahn among them, soon found themselves in prison. Others, including Arndt, were ousted from academic positions. Still others chose exile, which in the case of Napoleon's former adversary, Görres, meant asylum in once-hated France. Stein's colleague and successor as minister president (i.e. Prussian prime minister), K. A. von Hardenberg, though an administrative reformer, had never subscribed to all of the reform movement's social aims; but even his willingness to compromise in 1819 could not save him from the political eclipse in which he lived out the last three years of his life.

Other European governments adopted measures quite consistent with the Austrian-Prussian solution for Germany. In Denmark, the opposition – nationalists enraged by the loss of Norway, constitutionalists embittered by King Frederick VI's disregard for past promises, particularists in the border provinces of Schleswig and Holstein – could only bow before their stern ruler. Charles XIV of Sweden and Norway, as Bernadotte had become upon ascending the throne in 1818, policed the separate assemblies of estates in his two kingdoms with barely veiled hostility. In the United Netherlands, William I's Dutch subjects found the constitution of 1815 less liberal in its application than it had appeared on paper and viewed the compromises with Belgian economic interests as objectionable acts · of a royal autocrat. Still more serious was the discontent of the Catholic Belgians, numerically under-represented in the combined States General and resentful of the Dutch Calvinist officials who administered the kingdom's affairs.

IBERIA AND ITALY

In fairness to these northern monarchs, however, it must be said that neither political resistance nor governmental harshness reached its peak in lands bordering the North Sea or the Baltic. Instead, for the Restoration's bloodiest episodes we must look to the Latin kingdoms in the south. Spain's re-established Ferdinand VII simply ignored his former pledge to respect the constitution drawn up by the national *Cortes* at Cadiz in 1812, while the struggle against Napoleon was still in progress. Resentment against his capricious cruelty, against the selfish courtiers and churchmen around him and against the crown's inept response to the colonial revolts in America finally burst forth in January 1820. The uprising began, appropriately enough at Cadiz, where two regiments of troops revolted under Colonel Rafael Riego and proclaimed their allegiance to the constitution of 1812. Matched by other rebellions in northern and eastern Spain, the Cadiz movement quickly swept Riego to power in Madrid, and on 9 March the king, a virtual captive, swore an oath to the constitution.

The Spanish revolutionaries, though split between the radical majority (*Exultados*) in the Cortes and the more conservative *Moderados*, clung to power for over three years despite the furious objections of aristocrats and bishops alike. In April 1823, however, the French army of the Duc d'Angoulême crossed the frontier to enforce the decisions of the Congress of Verona (*see* Chapter 11, above). Unable to hold their own against disciplined foreign troops, the insurrectionary régime collapsed in a matter of months, its last stronghold, the Trocadero fortress by the Bay of Cadiz, surrendering on 31 August. Riego was publicly hanged, and sections of his dismembered body were displayed in various cities. Hundreds of his supporters, though supposedly protected by Ferdinand's earlier promise of amnesty, were tortured and killed by royal command. For the next ten years Spain would live under a crowned sadist.

In Portugal, where the Spanish uprising evoked an inevitable response, revolt erupted in the summer of 1820. By 1822 King John VI had resigned himself to accepting the liberals' demands, returning from Rio de Janeiro to Lisbon as a constitutional monarch and leaving his son Pedro behind in Brazil as the ruler

319

of an autonomous South American kingdom. Within a year, John felt secure enough to reduce the constitution's liberal features, but that was not enough to satisfy the reactionary party at court. The latter, making the ruler's second son, Miguel, its standard-bearer, continued to press for an end to all constitutional guarantees. When John died in 1826, Dom Miguel assumed all real power in the realm, as regent for Queen Maria II, the daughter of Brazil's King Pedro. Two years later, Miguel was ready to cap his policy of suppressing opposition by formally assuming royal authority. In May 1828 he declared Maria unfit to rule and formally abolished the constitution; and that summer, the young queen having fled to England, he proclaimed himself king of Portugal, as absolute in theory as Spain's Ferdinand was in fact.

Closely related to the Iberian troubles were those of splintered Italy. In the Two Sicilies another Bourbon, Ferdinand I, uncle of his Spanish namesake, also had to face a 'constitution of 1812', this one originally drafted on the island of Sicily with British help. Apart from the public executioner, whom one of Ferdinand's ministers called 'the crown's first servant', the chief props to Neapolitan tyranny were a corrupt court, a bigoted higher clergy and masses of desperately poor, often superstitious subjects. Its principal opponents were to be found in the liberal professions, the small, insecure middle class and groups of disaffected army men (*see* Map 8).

Next to the Two Sicilies, the Italian territory which suffered most from dishonesty and ignorance in government, despite the efforts of certain enlightened churchmen, was the Papal States. At Rome, amid the splendour of monuments to political and spiritual greatness, the reactionary Catholic party (*Zelanti*) proved capable of blocking every proposed reform, whether of education, justice or economic conditions. By comparison, the grand duchy of Tuscany, under its Habsburg archduke, Ferdinand III, seemed almost free and prosperous; but here too the swarms of secret police could never be forgotten. In the other grand duchies of the north, Modena, Lucca and Parma (the last ruled by Napoleon's former empress, Maria Louisa), autocracy and extortion were twin principles of government. Far richer, and somewhat better administered, was the Austrian emperor's own Lombard-Venetian kingdom. There, education, communications and commerce all benefited from Habsburg rule. This remained, however, the rule of foreigners. Whereas Metternich's policies predominated in the

Two Sicilies and the four grand duchies only by virtue of family alliances and military dependence, in Milan and Venice Austrian control was direct, untroubled by even the pretence of indigenous authority.

At the northern extreme of Italy, in mountainous Piedmont and Savoy, the Sardinian monarchy of Victor Emmanuel I also deserved to be contrasted favourably with the Two Sicilies or the Papal States. Though traditionally suspicious of foreign ideas and fearful of change, the government at Turin could at least point to a reasonably honest administration and a tax load kept comparatively light with the help of commercial duties from the newly acquired seaport of Genoa. Nevertheless, as time would show, the fact that this regimented, lacklustre polity could be praised by a visitor from Naples or Rome did not mean that it was free from smouldering discontent.

Against the general Italian background, events occurring in 1820–21 assume their full significance. Early in July of the former year, the garrison at Nola, a few miles east of Naples, broke into open revolt. Specifically, the mutineers were protesting against Austrian influence in the kingdom of the Two Sicilies, especially in its military affairs; but their demands extended to general reform as well. The leader of the spreading rebellion was General Guglielmo Pepe, a disaffected officer who succeeded for the time being in uniting army dissidents with the politically more doctrinaire *Carbonari*. The latter had early that summer begun to emerge from their secret clubrooms for sporadic demonstrations. Somewhat surprisingly, the oath which these insurgents extracted from their momentarily cowed King Ferdinand was not to the Sicilian constitution of 1812 but to *Spain*'s hallowed charter of that same year.

As in the Spanish case so too in the Neapolitan, a determined revolt seemed at first to have triumphed with almost incredible ease. However, on the island of Sicily a further rebellion broke out, this one directed against the revolutionary government – in Sicilian eyes just another expression of the mainland's authority. Meanwhile, in January 1821, blandly stating that he wished to secure international approval for the new constitution, Ferdinand I went off to Laibach with a personal appeal for Metternich's aid. As we already know, the result of that conference was prompt intervention by Austrian troops, the military defeat of the rebels at Rieti on 7 March and the restoration of a vengeful king, now relieved of constitutional restraints. General Pepe made good his escape to England by way of Spain, then still controlled by his fellow revolutionary, General Riego; but most of the other Neapolitan rebels were far less fortunate.

Revolutionary outbreaks flared briefly in the Papal States and in the grand duchies, but none was sufficiently widespread or co-ordinated to avoid being crushed at once by police action. Not so in Piedmont. There, a junta of army officers and professional men, joined by a few liberal nobles, revolted in March 1821. Undaunted by the depressing news already arriving from Naples, these insurgents demanded war against the hated Austrians and a constitutional monarchy under their somewhat embarrassed hero, Prince Charles Albert, nephew of the king. Victor Emmanuel, however, though he abdicated the throne and named Charles Albert as temporary regent, designated as the new monarch his own brother, Charles Felix, then residing in Modena. The young regent hesitantly declared his support for a new constitution, but only pending the approval of Charles Felix. The latter repaid this deference, upon arriving in Turin, by exiling his nephew to Tuscany and immediately calling for Austrian military assistance. On 8 April, 1821, at Novara on the route from Milan to Turin, the rebels were defeated by a combined royalist-Austrian force. With that decision the Piedmontese revolution, like so many others in Italian history, became one more lesson in frustrations, concluded amid executions, imprisonments and sentences of exile.

THE BALKANS AND EASTERN EUROPE

In two great eastern empires, the Russian and the Turkish, historical patterns of rule had suffered no such interruption as the power and the example of France had brought to the rest of Europe. Even the lands of the tsar and the sultan, however, had felt the repercussions of the revolutionary-Napoleonic upheaval and, though peace had returned, the stirrings of political unrest continued.

In 1815, only two years after the first Serbian revolt led by Kara George had been put down by the Turks, a second rising occurred. This time the leader of the Serbs was Milosh Obrenovich, half patriot and half dynast. When Kara George returned from his Austrian refuge to resume the struggle, he was assassinated on orders from his jealous rival. By the end of 1817, the Turks decided to recognize Obrenovich as prince of Serbia – in effect the area around Belgrade – and to leave him considerable independence in his role as vassal of the sultan. For the time being, the vendetta between the two houses was pushed into the background, to await its bloody renewal a few years later. Meanwhile, in his own interest, Prince Milosh imposed upon his fellow-countrymen an oppressive régime of 'order' actually exceeding in harshness the pattern of Ottoman rule.

We have already traced the successful Greek rebellion beginning in 1820, because of its significance for European diplomatic and political history in general. Most other Balkan risings, however, proved abortive. Montenegro, under Prince-Bishop Peter I, was a petty tyranny recognized as independent by the Turks since 1799. Bulgarians, on the other hand, had to await the second half of the nineteenth century for any loosening of the Ottoman grip. The same was true of Rumanians south of the Danube, while those in the principalities of Moldavia and Wallachia, despite interruptions such as the unsuccessful revolt of 1821, continued to obey their *hospodars*, the local rulers who owed allegiance to the sultan but in fact relied heavily on Russian protection. As for Albania, it remained an integral part of European Turkey.

Nevertheless, for the Turkish as for the Spanish monarchy, the crumbling of imperial power created serious problems at home. Sultan Mahmud II (1808–39), seeking to rebuild his dynasty's control over the Balkans and the Middle East, encountered two of the most serious obstacles to that effort in Istanbul itself. One was a reactionary Muslim sect of dervishes, the *Bektashi*, who joined large landowners in opposing every project for administrative modernization as being foreign-inspired, i.e. 'un-Turkish', and sacrilegious as well. The other was the proud military corps of Janissaries, once crack troops recruited in the Balkans and granted sweeping privileges, but now a corrupt order disinclined either to fight for the sultan against his enemies or to countenance any basic reorganization of the army. While the Bektashi and the Janissaries retained their standing, Mahmud's govenment could only be that sorriest of political spectacles, an ineffectual despotism.

In Russia too, as we have observed, the monarch had to contend with religious reactionaries, the Old Believers. On the more distinctly political front, meanwhile, Alexander I was caught between the aspirations of his Finnish and Polish subjects and the resistance of Russian aristocrats to making any concessions where 'conquered peoples' were concerned. In Finland, the tsar did permit a comparatively high degree of autonomy, leaving the Lutheran Church untroubled, sanctioning the continued use of Swedish alongside the native tongue and entrusting the administration for the most part to Finnish officials. While the genuine liberalism of this policy could easily be exaggerated, the amount of self-government permitted the Finns stood as an object of envy for many other nationality groups in eastern Europe.

Unfortunately for all concerned, Alexander's Polish experiment suffered a disillusioning fate. Under the constitution drafted by Prince Czartoryski for 'Congress Poland', Warsaw was to be as clearly the capital of a self-governing state as was Finland's Helsinki. In 1815 the Poles were also guaranteed their own army, their own bureaucracy and their own Diet, comprising a royally appointed Senate and an elective Chamber of Deputies. As matters turned out, however, the Russians kept a suspicious eye and a firm grip on Polish affairs, forbidding the Diet to discuss finances, retaining command of the army under Alexander's brother, Grand Duke Constantine, and dominating the administration through the agency of the tsar's commissioner, Novosiltsev. It is true that as late as 1818 promises of further liberalization came from St Petersburg; but the very next year sharply increased censorship was decreed for Poland, and shortly thereafter, Alexander warned the Diet not to formulate further complaints.

In Poland, as in so many other countries, restrictions gave rise to resistance, which in turn elicited sterner oppression. By the early 1820s several clandestine organizations had been uncovered in Warsaw, and the leader of one of them, Major Valezy Lukasinski of the National Patriotic Society, was packed off to jail with his principal associates. Debate in the Diet was muzzled so effectively as to render farcical its more and more infrequent sessions. At universities such as Warsaw and Vilna, liberal-nationalist professors, not to mention outspoken student leaders, were arrested and consigned to Siberian prison camps. Within a decade after 1815, the dreams of Alexander and Czartoryski, dreams of a contented Polish kingdom under Russian protection, had vanished before the harsh reality of alien rule and the hatred it aroused.

Within Russia proper the tsar's last years were marked by his increasing reliance on a single, ruthless minister, Count Alexei Arakchev, and a fanatical adviser, the monk Photius. Every expression of modernism, whether religious, economic or intellectual, was proscribed. Inevitably some of Alexander I's subjects, including a number of army officers who had served in western Europe, began first to grumble, then to plot. A secret society, the 'Union of Salvation', was formed under Colonel Paul Pestel in 1816, at a time when the tsar was still indulgent towards ostensibly progressive movements. By 1820, now clearly illegal (given the change in Alexander's views), the organization, renamed the 'Southern Society', had embraced a republican programme, as well as a plan for liquidating large estates. Another group, composed of intellectuals and westernized aristocrats around Prince Sergius Trubetskoi and named the 'Northern Society', also espoused freedom for the serfs, in emulation of Baron von Stein's Prussian reforms, but favoured instead of a republic a liberal monarchy under the Romanovs. There were still other secret coteries, including the United Slavs, who longed to develop a solid front with Poles, Czechs and the Russians' other ethnic brethren. Finally, numerous Freemasonic lodges indulged in forbidden political debates. Yet despite this ferment among scattered groups of officers and intelligentsia, the empire of Alexander, on the eve of his death in 1825, offered a picture of oppression calculated to reassure the most apprehensive enemy of change.

FRANCE AND BRITAIN: AUTHORITY VERSUS LIBERTY

France and the British Isles have been intentionally placed at the end of this brief survey of the post-Napoleonic scene. In both cases, reactionary policies typical of the age clashed with western European notions of political freedom and constitutional safeguards which to much of the rest of Europe still seemed novel or academic, or both. Somewhat ironically, therefore, the two great antagonists in the recent struggle now shared the distinction of posing in its most compelling and most difficult form this question: how far could authoritarian rule be pushed, confronting as it did the libertarian principles expressed in parliamentary forums and echoed in the streets?

France's White Terror, which followed the initial defeat of Napoleon in 1814 and was revived with still greater intensity after the Hundred Days, was not, let us remember, a direct expression of royal policy. Louis XVIII, whom the vicissitudes of long exile had lent a degree of restraint and common sense rarely encountered in a modern Bourbon, openly deplored mob attacks upon accused republicans and Bonapartists. Nevertheless, while the government did not condone the riots in Orléans and in Languedoc, the lynchings in the Vendée and Alsace or the murder of Marshal Brune at Avignon, pressure from the *Ultras* (extreme monarchists) did compel the king and his ministers to take certain steps against alleged enemies of 'throne and altar'. Thus, press censorship was tightened, commissions were appointed to expose seditious acts or even opinions and numerous officers were brought to trial for having remained loyal to Napoleon. Among these last was the Bonapartist hero, Marshal Ney, executed by a firing squad at Paris in December 1815.

Louis XVIII nevertheless tried, on the whole successfully, to stand by the constitutional charter he had promulgated upon his return to France. After the first frenzy of vindictive rancour subsided, his subjects enjoyed more legal protection of their rights than did most other Europeans at the time. The king maintained his attitude of firmness and moderation despite the opposition of his own brother, the Count d'Artois, the existence of a clamorous Ultra majority in the Chamber of Deputies elected in 1815, the humiliating presence of 150,000 Allied troops in the country and the near panic engendered by the miserable harvest of 1816. By September of that year Louis actually found it necessary to dissolve the Chamber before its rightist majority could launch an open rebellion.

Though he had scarcely hoped for so much, the new elections turned back the tide of extremism which had threatened to engulf both the king and his charter. The Chamber they produced still contained representatives of both the right (Ultras) and the left (Liberals), but a large centre bloc permitted business to go forward under the moderate ministries of Richelieu, Dessolles (1818–9) and Decazes (1819–20). During those years the government stabilized the food supply, reorganized finances, paid off the war indemnity (thus freeing the country of Allied occupation forces), liberalized the electoral law, eased censorship and broke the reactionaries' grip on the army high command. When one considers that all this corresponded in time to Metternich's Carlsbad Decrees in Germany, Arakchev's repressive measures in Russia and Ferdinand VII's brutal despotism in Spain, the course pursued by Louis XVIII's government appears singularly mild.

Yet reaction came to France as well. It came, like similar developments elsewhere, in the wake of a senseless atrocity. On 13 February 1820, as he was walking out of the Paris Opéra, the Duc de Berri, nephew of the king, was stabbed to death by a demented veteran of Napoleon's armies, one Louvel, who believed he had a mission to exterminate the royal family. Though clearly the act of an individual lunatic, the murder was immediately seized upon by the Ultras as proof of the Liberal menace and of the government's criminal weakness. Decazes was forced to resign in favour of a second Richelieu ministry, this one committed to determined action. Censorship was markedly increased, a new electoral law benefiting large landowners was passed, and numerous officials distasteful to the right were pushed into retirement.

In response to these measures, the familiar undergrowth of secret societies, including French Carbonari, began at once to appear. For a year or two, plots against the government showed up in various localities, especially garrison towns; but every overt display of opposition was crushed, and before long the disorganized resistance lapsed into despondent inactivity. Only their bitterness and the spectacle of police terror remained. As for the royal government, it drifted, or was driven, farther and farther off Louis XVIII's desired course. Amid the ruins of his conciliatory hopes, the old king died in 1824, to be succeeded by the Ultras' darling, d'Artois, as Charles X. Now indeed the Revolution seemed a fading memory, as though history after thirty-five years had come full circle. For on the throne sat the most anachronistic of the French Bourbons, the prince royal who had wanted bayonets turned on the National Assembly at Versailles in 1789 and who seemed to epitomize the charge against his family that 'they had learned nothing and forgotten nothing'.

Finally, what of the United Kingdom? So far as Ireland was concerned, the government of the prince regent carried on where that of George III had ended. With no Catholic representation at Westminster and no parliament remaining in Dublin, the Irish common people toiled in sullen voicelessness. Their quiescence under English officials and absentee landlords was destined to end very soon, but in the first years after Waterloo, an air of resignation seemed to hover over the land.

In England, Scotland and Wales, on the other hand, there was no lack of excitement. The Whig opposition in Parliament, to be sure, was still demoralized by the success of wartime Tory rule and virtually immobilized by its own fear of revolution. Many of the older Whigs frankly embraced the views of such government leaders as the lord chancellor, Eldon, and the home secretary, Viscount Sidmouth (Henry Addington), who saw danger in every suggestion of change. Other men, however – Anglican Evangelicals, Methodist Dissenters, Philosophical Radicals of the Utilitarian school – attacked as outdated and unfair the distribution of seats in the Commons, the over-pricing of poor men's bread under the Corn Law, the corruption and insensitivity of royal officials and the exclusivity of town oligarchies. Some of these critics worked through such organizations as Major John Cartwright's Hampden Clubs. Others, including that most vehement of journalists, William Cobbett, trumpeted their protests with the help of newspapers and pamphlets. Still others shared Henry Hunt's reliance on oratory before mass audiences.

As in many other countries, so too in Britain, a brief interval of governmental hesitancy and relative freedom for dissenters came to an end amid conservative charges that public order was not being adequately defended. In December 1816, excited by the speeches they had heard at an open-air meeting near London, some rioters broke into a gun shop, stole a number of weapons and accidentally shot a bystander. Two months later, while the House of Commons was still discussing this outrage, an unidentified projectile shattered the windows of a coach in which the prince regent was riding. Jolted into action by fear, the squires and merchants in Parliament voted to outlaw public meetings, to close all unlicensed clubs and to suspend for one year the right of Habeas Corpus, which guaranteed anyone under arrest a prompt trial on clearly stated charges. Agitation did not cease at once; for while Cobbett sailed to America, many other would-be reformers continued to register their views. Nevertheless, official pressure was mounting rapidly, as shown by the number of publishers and journalists brought to trial for sedition or even treason.

Such was the tense atmosphere in August 1819, when a vague report reached London of 'cavalry action against a mob' in Manchester. Lords Liverpool and Sidmouth rushed off congratulations to the officials of that Midland city, though when more news came in, the prime minister and the home secretary had reason to qualify their initial enthusiasm. A huge assemblage of people at a protest rally in St Peter's Fields, Manchester, had been waiting quietly to hear 'Orator' Hunt when a nervous officer unaccountably ordered his cavalry squadron, which was standing by, to advance on the platform. The crowd at first gave way before the mounted troopers, then, apparently seized by the notion that an attack was being launched, broke into panicky flight, trampling several persons to death and injuring many more. This was the Manchester Massacre, or, as it came to be sardonically called, the 'battle of Peterloo'.

Despite vociferous criticism of the Manchester fiasco and the contempt expressed by recalling Wellington's historic victory over real enemies, the Portland ministry used the shock of violence to secure additional police powers. That November (1819) Parliament passed the Six Acts, which made the enactments of two years before seem mild in retrospect. Under the new laws, unauthorized parades and other paramilitary demonstrations were forbidden. So were private meetings called to hear political or religious protests. House searches for arms were authorized, as was the seizure of allegedly seditious works by direction of any magistrate. The rights of the defendant in a criminal action were reduced, though certainly not abolished, by the tightening of trial procedures. Finally, newspapers and small journals were subjected to a heavy tax, in order to restrict their sale among the poor. These provisions were enacted over a slowly emerging body of Whig opposition in the Commons, but enacted they were.

One culminating incident, more clearcut than Peterloo, was also, in its way, more shocking than even the murders of Kotzebue in Germany and the Duc de Berri in France. In February 1820, only a few weeks after death had at last freed George III from his lonely world of madness, a plot to murder the entire cabinet was uncovered. Its leader was a well-known radical orator, Arthur Thistlewood, whose rage over the Six Acts and despair at the accession of the prince regent as George IV had driven him to homicidal frenzy. The plan which he and his fellow-conspirators hatched at their secret meeting place in London's Cato Street envisioned the assassination of the Tory ministers at a banquet, seizure of the Bank of England and the establishment of a revolutionary government. The plotters, however, included at least one police spy (who reportedly pressed for wilder and wilder additions to the scheme), and at a pre-arranged signal the constabulary burst in upon the assembled conspirators. Five of them, including Thistlewood, were hanged on 1 May, after a trial which had called forth lurid comparisons with Guy Fawkes and the Gunpowder Plot two centuries before.

Thus Great Britain, its people at once nervous and cowed, entered the new reign under a government which abroad rejected Metternich's vision of an international conservative alliance, but at home embraced an authoritarianism to rival that of many continental states. With Louis XVIII's search for moderation abandoned in France, with Austria and Prussia agreed that historical change was a manifest evil, with Russias's tsar divorced from his erstwhile liberalism, with cruelty and superstition enthroned in Madrid, Naples and the Romagna, with British political wisdom for the time being encased in the Six Acts, a reform-minded European could scarcely view the future with much optimism. On the other hand, to a conservative – who might be such not out of selfishness or ignorance but in response to a well-founded fear of disorder – that same future offered a reassuring vision of stability. The Revolution, once an awesome engine of movement, seemed at last to have spent its force. Repression, whether one hated or welcomed it, appeared triumphant in the mid-1820s. Yet nothing was to be more characteristic of Europe's dynamism, its literally *restless* history, than the sudden collapse of that triumph even before 1830, where our narrative will end.

REFORM IN BRITAIN AND THE IRISH PROBLEM

Any scheme of historical periodization, as we have previously noted, is useful only if it is recognized to be an imperfect approximation. Thus, in the present case, the Greek War of Independence, so important for its effect on liberal idealism in countless

lands, actually broke out· *before* oppression reached its peak in
Spain under Ferdinand VII, in France under Charles X or in
Portugal under Dom Miguel. Conversely, authoritarian rule
remained outwardly secure in some European countries long *after*
signs of movement had struggled to the surface in others. Nevertheless, despite the fact that new forces did not assert themselves
everywhere at once, the mid- and later 1820s brought a series of
changes, helping to explain the brevity of that 'full stop' so fondly
contemplated in official quarters at the beginning of the decade.

With respect to the United Kingdom, it is customary to date
such stirrings from as early as the summer of 1822, when George
Canning came to the Foreign Office following Castlereagh's
suicide. In fact, however, it was not so much the unorthodox
foreign secretary as several of his Tory colleagues who revived
the cause of domestic reform. One of them, Robert Peel, had
entered the government as home secretary several months before
the advent of Canning. It would be difficult to imagine a sharper
contrast in personalities than that between Sidmouth, the tense,
sincere conservative, and his successor, an energetic, self-confident
young administrator, the son of an industrialist, a commoner
surrounded by fellow ministers most of whom were peers of the
realm. Peel was not quite the calm, consistent statesmen his
admirers later sought to portray; but even at the start of his brilliant career there was clear evidence of a quick, inventive intelligence and, most of the time, an engaging generosity of spirit.
Another vigorous recruit from the world of business and finance
was William Huskisson, who in October 1823 became president
of the Board of Trade, the first holder of that office to receive
cabinet rank. A minister of the more familiar aristocratic stamp,
but also a proponent of liberal economic theories, was F. J.
Robinson (the future Viscount Goderich) who became chancellor
of the exchequer, also in 1823.

The fact that men such as Peel, Huskisson and Robinson could
win positions of power so soon after the victory of reaction
suggests that Lord Liverpool, prime minister until 1827, had
never looked upon the Six Acts as a permanent solution to all
problems. It also indicates that George IV, whatever the scandals
of his private life (his reign had opened with an attempt to divorce
Queen Caroline amid sordid recriminations), was no tyrant. It is
true, of course, that the Whigs, in Henry Brougham, Earl Charles
Grey and Lord John Russell, possessed leaders who applied

increasingly effective pressure on the government. Nor should we ignore the activities of the socialist and philanthropist, Robert Owen (*see below*, pp. 360–1), of William Cobbett, home from America since 1819, or of numerous Benthamite Radicals. Nevertheless, the responsible officials who after 1822 spoke for reform were members of the very party that had previously seemed incapable of rising above the fears expressed by an Eldon or a Sidmouth.

What were some of the steps in this new departure? One of the most important came in the field of commercial policy and was the work of Huskisson. His first budget, setting a course which was to be followed with growing confidence from 1823 onward, lowered import duties on textiles, iron, sugar, beverages and a number of other foreign products. Needless to say, the poorest Englishman felt no immediate improvement in his standard of living as a result of these measures. Yet the process begun under George IV was destined one day to give Victoria's England a higher level of comfort, more widely shared, than any the past had known.

Peel, in the meantime, was pushing through legal reforms similarly modest in appearance – and similarly prophetic in their significance. He revised the criminal code, cutting in half the number of capital crimes (which had stood at over 200) and reducing the penalties attached to a number of lesser offences. His motives, be it noted, were not purely humanitarian, surely not visionary; for as home secretary he was concerned over, and hoped to decrease, the number of acquittals traceable less to the defendants' probable innocence than to juries' refusal to endorse excessively harsh punishment. With Huskisson's support, he also sponsored the repeal of the Combination Acts, thus permitting labourers to organize legally. This measure, long advocated by the eloquent Benthamite, Francis Place, was enacted in 1824. The ensuing wave of strikes led to a new law the following year, denying unions the right to order work stoppage; but their right to combine for purposes of bargaining over hours, pay and working condition was henceforth secure in theory.

Down to January 1828 (Liverpool had resigned in April of the previous year, to be followed by Canning and then, on the latter's death in August, by Goderich) the pattern of the Tory government in power had for several years been quite clear. A handful of vigorous young middle-class reformers in the cabinet had faced the more numerous but less self-assured aristocratic wing, with successive prime ministers mediating the struggle as best they could. When Goderich was replaced by the stiff-necked duke of Wellington, however, a major shift seemed unavoidable. For now the prime minister was himself the personification of the conservative peerage, an opponent of Corn Law reform, an outspoken believer in the Combination Acts and a supporter of stern retributive justice for violators of the law.

Yet a recurrent chapter in British history was about to unfold once more. To the surprise of Wellington's anxious opponents, and the rage of his former henchmen, the political clock did not stop. Its hands kept moving. The new prime minister, who had only a year earlier successfully opposed Canning's proposal to lower duties on grain, now found himself obliged by the critical food shortage to steer through parliament (in June 1828) the first substantial reduction in the Corn Law schedule. This modification in the thirteen-year-old legislation was only a short step towards its final repeal in 1846, but the process of erosion had begun. Indicative of Wellington's unacknowledged conversion is the fact that there was no general defection on the part of would-be reformers within his government. For while Huskisson did resign in May 1828, Peel returned to the Home Office after having been omitted from Canning's and Goderich's cabinets, and many less prominent men followed his example.

The final events of the decade in the United Kingdom were in part shaped by political developments in Ireland. In order to understand how that island resumed a place at the centre of the British political arena, it is necessary to recall the situation created by Pitt's inability to achieve Catholic Emancipation following the Act of Union in 1800. What Pitt had failed to do was to make Catholics eligible either for *election* to Parliament or for appointment to any of a number of other offices. Catholics, including those in Ireland, could nevertheless *vote* for MPs. During the first quarter of a century following the Union, to be sure, this right to vote seemed relatively meaningless, inasmuch as it could not be used to send one of their own faith to Westminister. Furthermore, an election day generally found the uninformed, unorganized Irish tenant farmers, and even many small freeholders, being herded to the nearest county seat by agents of the local landlord, there to vote, without secrecy, in accordance with his stated wishes.

Then, in the mid-1820s, two previously unrelated currents came together to form a powerful stream of agitation for change. One stemmed from the adoption by England's own liberal Whigs and Radicals of religious emancipation as a necessary step towards a more popular form of government. In 1825 one of the leaders of the opposition in Parliament, Sir Francis Burdett, with the support of the most powerful 'new Whig' of all, Sir John Russell, introduced a bill calling for the abolition of religious tests as a limitation on eligibility to hold office. The bill survived its first reading, but not the final vote. For one thing, it faced the formidable opposition of Robert Peel, whose service as a youthful official in Dublin had left him uncharacteristically negative towards any reform affecting Ireland. Still more important, the Lords gave an unequivocal warning that their hostility was such as to make pointless any further discussion of the proposed measure. The problem, however, could not be indefinitely ignored.

Meanwhile – this was the second current – in Ireland there appeared a new political organization: the Catholic Association, founded in 1823 and soon possessed of a chapter in nearly every parish of the south and west. It had also begun to build an unprecedented resource, a campaign fund of its own. This was the Catholic Rent, created in 1824 for the purpose of collecting, and then disbursing, personal contributions solicited with help from the clergy. It proved so productive that by the end of its first year in existence its regular weekly yield was about £700.[12] Finally, the Association had found a leader, Daniel O'Connell, who was at once a shrewd lawyer (as witness his movement's success in skirting the perils of illegality) and an effective, if crude, public orator.

The Association, begun as an organ to express Catholic needs and grievances in the most limited, material sense, quickly broke loose from such modest aims and became a political force to be reckoned with. It instructed formerly bewildered peasants concerning their interests and their rights; and without recourse to the gentry, it turned out farm tenants to vote in hordes, under discipline which offered the police no excuse to complain of mob violence. In 1826, with O'Connell leading the campaign, the tenants of the marquess of Waterford defied his choice of his own brother for Parliament and instead elected another candidate, of necessity a Protestant, but one endorsed by the Association.

Similar upsets occurred in Louth, Armagh and several other counties. When angry landlords sought to retaliate by evicting their
disobedient tenants, the latter were given relief from the Catholic
Rent. Then, early in 1828, O'Connell took the last, long step. A
Catholic, and as such excluded from a seat in the House of
Commons, he nonetheless accepted nomination for a by-election
in County Clare. Again the farmers trooped in, voted quietly and
quietly went home. O'Connell's victory was so overwhelming
that his principal opponent actually withdrew before the final
day's voting.

The decision now moved back to Westminster. For the British
government, the issue was painfully clear. Would it defy the
Catholic voters of County Clare and refuse to seat O'Connell,
despite the orderly nature of his election? For a time Peel insisted
that such was the only course under the law and that any concession would be disastrous. Against his view stood not only the
Whig opposition but also a number of Tories, including some
Protestant Irish landowners, fearful of the burning and looting
that might ensue if the Association's thus far exemplary self-
control went unacknowledged. Although the final choice was
made by the duke of Wellington, with his great prestige and his
unquestioned conservatism, it was Peel, convinced at last, who
framed and presented the necessary legislation. In May 1828, after
155 years in force, the Test Act was repealed by both Houses.
Henceforth, no man could be excluded from office simply for
refusal to take the sacrament of the Church of England, though
he could still be so excluded for being a practising Roman
Catholic.

Some months later, in April 1829, the far more explicit and
positive Catholic Emancipation Bill became law. Under its terms,
communicants of the Roman Church were declared eligible to sit
in Parliament and to hold other public charges save for those
specified in a short list: lord chancellor, lord lieutenant of Ireland
and a few more. The government's surrender was far from total.
Catholic foundations were still denied either legal standing or
financial support from public taxes. Catholic office-holders were
required to swear a special oath to uphold the monarchy's Protestant succession. Almost 200,000 subjects in Ireland lost their
right to vote under a hurriedly established property qualification.
Nevertheless, in spite of the dogged survival of religious hostility,
the cutting line now was property, not creed. Another of the

ancient limits upon political action had begun to yield to calculations more typical of a frankly materialistic society.

In view of the initiatives of Canning and Huskisson and Peel,
the grudging flexibility of Wellington and the acquiescence,
however reluctant, of the king at each critical point, one may well
ask why the Tories fell from power in 1830. Part of the explanation must be sought in the death of George IV that June and
the threat which some men saw in the accession of his deeply
conservative brother, William IV. In the elections required by law
after a monarch's death, the Whigs made good use of this feeling,
increasing their strength in the Commons by some fifty seats.

Another factor, however, was the attitude of Wellington and
his cabinet colleagues. They had moved, or in some cases been
pushed, as far as they were prepared to go. Tariff reforms, legal
and judicial reforms, politico-religious reforms, all these the Tory
ministers had acceded to piecemeal. In so doing, no doubt, they
had helped to create the very expectations of further change that
drove them from office in November 1830. For what they could
not accept was the fundamental reform of Parliament itself, to
which Earl Grey and the Whigs were now committed. Huskisson
alone had believed in that, and Huskisson was gone – out of the
cabinet in 1828, killed in 1830 under the wheels of a steam loco-
motive at the opening of the Liverpool and Manchester Railway.
The steel gods of a new age, it seemed, took sacrifices even
among their own prophets.

THE RESTORATION CHALLENGED: FRANCE
AND THE LOW COUNTRIES

It would be idle to suggest that the British ferment of economic
expansion and political reform was at this early date fully matched
by any nation on the Continent. In western Europe, however,
other pressures, often characterized by variations upon the theme
of Catholic-liberal accommodation we have observed in the
United Kingdom, began to cast doubt on the permanence of the
Restoration's solemnly proclaimed alliance between throne and
altar. That alliance, be it said at once, could still deliver powerful
blows. In France, the Villèle ministry won passage in 1825 of an

Indemnity Law on behalf of aristocrats previously deprived of their lands by the Revolution. This was followed the next year by a Law of Sacrilege against defamers of the Catholic hierarchy. Finally, in 1827, the government struck at its critics in the middle class by ordering the dissolution of their most prized institution, the *Garde Nationale*, leaving the professional army unchecked by any form of citizens' militia. But progressive Catholics such as Lamennais and Montalembert were now joining their eloquent voices to those of secular liberals, among them Benjamin Constant, with his esteem for the British constitution, Victor Cousin, who recalled the anti-authoritarian side of Montesquieu's early teachings, and the sharp-tongued publicist and historian, Adolphe Thiers.

The first serious warning to the royalist-clerical party in France was the Liberal victory at the polls in November 1827, this despite a sharply limited franchise. It began to appear that a property qualification for voting would not protect a conservative régime if well-to-do businessmen decided they must oppose landed and Church interests. For the next two years Charles X temporized, seeking to lean on the compromise ministry of Martignac but in fact winning little praise from either the Right or the Left. By August 1829, the king had worked himself up to one of his characteristic displays of blind exasperation. He abruptly dropped Martignac and announced that the Prince de Polignac, nicknamed 'the Ultra of the Ultras', would head the government, without regard for any ministerial responsibility to the Chamber of Deputies.

Censured by the Liberals' parliamentary majority, Charles dissolved the Chamber in the spring of 1830, only to be rebuffed once more by a new Liberal victory in the May elections. His response – the July Ordinances dissolving the Chamber yet again, imposing further censorship and providing for revision of the electoral law – touched off the final crisis. Its full effects must be left to the succeeding volume in this series. Here, however, as a concluding tribute to the political sagacity of Charles X and Polignac, we should remark that within a matter of hours after the ordinances were promulgated on 26 July, the barricades were up in the streets of Paris. On the 27th, the capital was under rebel control; and just nine days later, a majority in the Chamber of Deputies proclaimed a new king of France, Louis Philippe of the house of Bourbon-Orléans. An entire conception of monarchy, that of the *ci-devant* Count d'Artois, had come crashing down, to be replaced by another more to the liking of his old bourgeois enemies.

The other notable instance of the Restoration's collapse in western Europe occurred in Belgium. There, in 1827, the king of the United Netherlands, groping for ways to control the Liberal and the Clerical opposition parties, attempted to strike at both almost simultaneously. By suddenly increasing the censorship, he proposed at least to muzzle 'Jacobins and separatists'. By negotiating a Concordat with the Vatican, which conferred on him the right of veto in all episcopal elections, he sought to bring Belgium's Catholic hierarchy to heel. The latter action turned out to be especially impolitic; for the Belgian prelates included many conservatives who had previously resisted demands from the younger and more impatient members of their flocks, such as the parliamentary deputy Baron de Gerlache, for collaboration with Liberals. Responding to the official publication of this Concordat, the bishops, enraged against the crowned Calvinist in the Hague, withdrew their previous objections to the alliance. Nothing more active on their part was required. In July 1828, the two parties' leaders announced agreement on joint demands for a responsible ministry, a free press, independence for all schools and the cessation of governmental interference in religious affairs.

Thus began the sundering of the United Netherlands, which nevertheless survived two more years of agitation, the rise of lower-class resentment over economic troubles, and a series of ineffectual attempts at suppression on the part of the royal government. Perhaps only the new French uprising of 1830 could have finally brought matters to a head at Brussels. In any event, within a month after the Parisians' July Revolution, the first unqualified demands for Belgian independence of the House of Orange appeared in print. On 4 October, amid threats of intervention by Russia and Prussia and counter-warnings from Great Britain to the eastern powers, the newly formed provisional government in Brussels declared its formal separation from the Dutch. A nine-year struggle was under way, destined to end as the rebels of 1830 insisted it must: with the creation of an independent Belgium.

AUTOCRACY REFURBISHED IN OTHER STATES

In northern and in most of central Europe, nothing comparable to the alarums and excursions of Britain, France and Belgium was to be found. The late 1820s witnessed no significant political developments either in the Scandinavian kingdoms or in Germany, though the accession of the philhellene Ludwig I as king of Bavaria in 1825 had raised shortlived hopes that the reform tradition of Montgelas might be revived there. With respect to Prussia, we should note the impressive growth of her tariff union: Hesse-Darmstadt joined the *Zollverein* in 1828, and in 1829 the two south German kingdoms, Bavaria and Württemberg, followed suit. For the time being, however, the commercial significance of these treaties gave no indication of being matched by political implications.

The only noteworthy political developments in all of *Mitteleuropa* during these years occurred in Switzerland and, in very different form, Hungary. For the Swiss, 1828 and 1829 saw the beginnings of constitutional advance, the 'Era of Regeneration'. Under the pressure of growing popular demands for broader suffrage and legal guarantees of individual rights, including freedom of expression, the ruling oligarchies in more than half of the twenty-two cantons began to make limited concessions. In its enunciation of democratic themes, this movement was at once nostalgic, looking back towards the French Revolution, and precocious, foreshadowing the more general agitation in other lands during the 1830s and 1840s. The actual changes in cantonal constitutions prior to 1830, however, were only modest hints of the future.

The same must be said of Hungary's major event of the decade, the revival of the Diet in 1825, following Francis I's unsuccessful twelve-year effort to rule without it. At first glance, the Hungarian Diet's structure and role seemed to mock liberal aspirations, for the upper house (called the Table of Magnates) was exclusively composed of the highest aristocrats, prelates and officials, while the Table of Deputies spoke only for the rural gentry and for a scattering of towns. Yet the Hungarian nobility of the 1820s, like the French of the 1780s, by insisting on its right to assemble, had restored the institutional setting for opposition to the Habsburg monarchy and Austrian dominance. From 1825 onward, the moderate liberal, Count Stephen Széchenyi, had a place in which to be heard; and close after him in time would come the much more radical nationalist and constitutionalist, Louis Kossuth, admired by many of the lower nobles.

In southern Europe, by contrast, the torpor which had followed the revolts of the early 1820s persisted through the remainder of the decade. Italian nationalism, which soon would lend strength to Giuseppe Mazzini's Young Italy movement, smouldered glumly beneath a blanket of authoritarian repression. Spain meanwhile offered no greater prospect of any serious liberal resurgence. Only Portugal, where Dom Miguel had deposed his niece in 1828, resounded to the catchwords of freedom. Even there, where civil war would end in 1834 with Miguel banished and Maria II again on the throne, the only meaningful victory was to be a dynastic one.

As for the Balkans, we have already watched Greece struggling towards independence through a welter of international complications and internecine disputes. Elsewhere, as earlier remarked of Bulgaria and the Danubian Principalities, there was no significant change. The gains in religious autonomy accruing to Serbia under the treaty of Adrianople in 1829 and the subsequent Turkish concessions to Milosh Obrenovich, including the title of Hereditary Prince in 1830, belong to the record of Ottoman decline, rather than to the uneven chronicle of growing liberty in Europe.

TURKEY AND RUSSIA

Oddly enough, considering the generally turbulent history of the 'Lesser Slavs' and the coming Polish Revolution of 1830, it was neither in the Balkan lands under Turkish rule nor in Warsaw under that of the tsars that the most explosive events occurred as our period drew to a close. Instead, the Ottoman and Romanov capital cities themselves witnessed a pair of crises, isolated no doubt but highly significant for the future. Let us look first at Istanbul.

We have seen how a combination of reactionary Bektashi dervishes and arrogant, as well as indolent, members of the Janissary corps had saddled Sultan Mahmud II with a bigoted religious policy and a corrupt, ineffectual military establishment. Humiliated by his impotence in the Greek crisis, whether in seeking to resist Russian and British diplomatic pressure or in dealing with his imperious Egyptian ally, Mahmud devoted the spring of 1826 to planning what can rightly be called a royal uprising. He began by convincing his religious entourage that only a complete military reform, involving the very structure of the army, would make possible their longed-for holy war against the infidel. Thereafter, he abruptly announced the formation of new military units and notified the Janissaries that they could· either enter the reorganized forces or leave his service.

On 15 June, as the sultan had expected, the corps revolted, defying the Sublime Porte with seeming impunity from behind the ramparts of the palatial Janissary barracks. In a bizarre scene, which coupled reminders of the Bastille with those of an army mutiny, Mahmud's own troops, surrounded and supported by a mob whipped up by dervishes, assaulted the fortified barracks. Once artillery had breached the walls, the horde of attackers swept into the luxurious compound, burning its contents and slaughtering its defenders. When the heavy pall of black smoke finally cleared after two days of fighting, several thousand Janissaries were dead (the precise number is unknown), and the power of the corps, indeed the corps itself, would never be revived. Ottoman despotism seemed more secure than ever; but an example had been set, an example of military opposition, with popular support, directed against a privileged caste. Many years later, the Young Turks would prove themselves, in an interesting way, the twentieth-century heirs of a sultan.

Only a few months before the Janissaries were massacred, a very different kind of example had been set in Russia. There the death of Alexander I in December 1825 triggered a peculiar succession crisis – and offered the Northern and Southern Societies, the United Slavs and other dissidents an unexpected opportunity to rebel. The presumptive heir was Alexander's brother, Constantine, the military commander in Warsaw. However, in view of the latter's stated disinclination to rule, his younger brother Nicholas had been designated to do so, under a pact concluded by the late tsar and both grand dukes. This seemed clear enough. However, when word came that their elder brother was dead of a fever in Taganrog, Nicholas and Constantine fell into a bewildering disagreement over procedure. The former insisted that he would not accept the crown until Constantine renounced it publicly, while the latter refused to undertake even the degree of imperial responsibility required to issue such a proclamation. Nicholas was in due course persuaded to announce his own accession, but not before the so-called Decembrist Revolt had taken place.

The initial rising occurred in St Petersburg, where members of the Northern Society spread rumours among the garrison troops to the effect that Nicholas was an illegal pretender and that Constantine, a sincere constitutional reformer (which he was not), was being wickedly prevented from assuming his rightful throne. On 14 December elements of the Moscow Regiment and several other Guard units, answering the call of Prince Troubetskoi and his fellow conspirators, announced their allegiance to Constantine and marched into the Senate Square. There the regiments stood numbly in the bitter cold for several hours, as if awaiting formal inspection, while the Northern Society's high command alternately made speeches and argued over what to do next. At dusk a cavalry brigade led by officers loyal to Nicholas charged the mutineers. When this effort failed, artillery was wheeled into the square and fired point blank at the half-frozen rebels, who finally broke into flight, leaving the pavement littered with their dead and wounded.

The rebellion was over in the capital, but in the far-off Ukraine the Southern Society, with help from United Slav leaders, persisted in trying to mount effective resistance. Late in December an insurgent army marched against Kiev, only to be routed it its first encounter with government forces. All the main figures in both Societies were captured, and five of them, including Colonel Pestel and the poet Ryleev, were hanged. Prince Troubetskoi, in view of his exalted birth, escaped with exile; but a special tribunal sent to Siberia more than 100 other accused conspirators. (This judicial body included the veteran reformer, Speransky, now seemingly intimidated by his autocratic new tsar, but also genuinely outraged by what seemed to him treason in the ranks.)

The Decembrist revolt, like the destruction of the Janissaries at Istanbul and the revival of the Hungarian National Diet, failed to change a basically autocratic pattern of government. Still, it shared with these other developments in the East a symbolic importance transcending its immediate effects. Far from reflecting any concessions to his critics, Nicholas I's thirty-year reign was in fact to be one of the most oppressive in all the long history of the Romanovs. In that sense, the Decembrists can be charged with having brought on their fellow subjects only grim reaction. Yet it is not too much to say that a particular Russian revolutionary tradition, at once romantic and libertarian, intellectual and melodramatic, first found expression in the chaotic events of 1825.

RESTORATION AND NEW DEPARTURES

If in the early 1820s a European could have been excused for thinking that he was living through a complete and permanent return to the Old Régime, by 1830 he might have decided that, on the contrary, the Revolution had been resumed and the Restoration relegated to the position of a mere interlude, a brief interruption in the process of change begun almost a half-century earlier. Indeed, if formulated with sufficient care, the latter proposition is even now all but impossible to refute. Our European of 1830, however, would have been wrong to conclude that some features of the contemporary situation – Parisians in revolt, Belgians rising against a foreign monarch, Britons deep in constitutional debate, Hungarians denouncing Austrian rule, Poles girding to resist Russians – represented literal *repetitions* of scenes from the 1780s. For the late eighteenth century's·revolutions were not being re-enacted in 1830, any more than the Old Régime had previously been reincarnated in all it details. Instead, the period between the Congress of Vienna and the July Revolution offers abundant proof that, while history plays many recurrent themes, it never repeats them without variations.

Let us recognize first that, whatever their intentions, the statesmen of Metternich's time, with their Congress System, their suspicion of change, their reliance on a conservative coupling of throne and altar, created something emphatically different in important respects from the Old Régime. For example, pre-1789 governments had in general displayed a notable lack of deference towards their respective church hierarchies. The legitimists of the Restoration were actual innovators, therefore, when they committed rulers, courtiers and bureaucrats alike to a solemn repudiation of Enlightenment scepticism.

To take another example, again admittedly one of degree, conservative monarchs after 1815 tended to count more heavily than had their predecessors before 1789 on organized military action against dissidents, undertaken both within and across national borders. It is true, as we saw in Chapter 5, that the 1780s had seen Prussian troops used in Holland, Austrian in Belgium and French in Geneva. Such scattered expeditions, however, could scarcely be compared with the almost ceaseless activity of regiments, from Peterloo to St Petersburg, from Spain's Trocadero to Italy's Novara, from Naples to Istanbul, in the period we have been examining. This change must no doubt be explained partly by the fact that great wars tend to bequeath increased armies, together with a penchant for using them, and partly too by the frequency, noted earlier in this chapter, with which regular military formations turned up on the insurgents', not the government's side.

Finally, with respect to official practices under the Restoration, it should be observed that police espionage and systematic censorship assumed a prominence they had never known in the eighteenth century. Here again, the altered nature of the opposition – organized parties, secret societies, press attacks, military cabals – must be kept in mind. If the Old Régime had deployed fewer *agents provocateurs* and left censorship largely to venal incompetents, the explanation must surely be that it had felt less threatened by the kinds of resistance to which it was accustomed. The fact remains that the French revolutionary experience had supplied rulers with increased motivation, as it also had suggested to them new possibilities, for coercive action against internal enemies.

Since the existing order in 1830 was basically different from that which succumbed in 1789, it should be no surprise to find that there were also major differences between the two revolutionary crises. The fact that many slogans, carried over from the earlier drama, were brought out and used again must not mislead us. The prominence of memories, legends and historical references inspired by the 'Great Revolution' was itself one of the elements which in 1830 distinguished the new crisis – not only in France, but in England and Belgium and Italy as well – from the earlier one. A revolutionary *tradition*, inspiring to some, terrifying to others, has been a factor in every revolution to occur in Europe during the nineteenth and twentieth centuries, as it could not have been in 1789.

What made the revolutions of 1830 non-repetitive in a much broader sense, however, was the set of ideas and groups involved.

Constitutional theories, nationalist sentiments, democratic credos, economic doctrines, some of them in existence but none of them as yet fully developed in the eighteenth century, had by now come vigorously into play. At the same time, political parties, classes and social groups, far removed from earlier conceptions of nobles, guildsmen or peasants, had emerged as units of action in this new world of national passions, of broad confrontations between conservatives and liberals, and of bewildering socio-economic change. By 1830, in others words, we are farther from 1780 than a span of fifty years might ordinarily suggest. Just how far can be better appreciated when we turn, as we now shall, to the realm of systematic thought.

NOTES AND REFERENCES

1   E. L. Eisenstein, *The First Professional Revolutionist: Filippo Michele Buonarroti, 1761–1837* (Cambridge, Mass., 1959).

2   E. Halévy, *England in 1815* (rev. edn, London, 1949), p. 381.

3   Population figures are from W. Köllmann, *Raum und Bevölkerung in der Weltgeschichte* (2nd edn, Würzburg, 1956), pt. III, pp. 143 ff.

4   W. L. Langer, 'Europe's initial population explosion', *American Historical Review*, vol. LXIX (1963).

5   David S. Landes, *The Unbound Prometheus* (Cambridge, 1969), pp. 41–123.

6   *Ibid*, p. 86.

7   *Ibid.*, p. 160.

8   J. H. Clapham, *The Economic Development of France and Germany, 1815–1914* (4th edn, Cambridge, 1955), p. 92.

9   H. Pirenne, *Histoire de Belgique*, vol. III (new edn, Brussels, 1950), p. 469.

10   G. Spini, *Risorgimento e protestanti* (Naples, 1956).

11   R. E. Pipes, 'The Russian military colonies, 1810–1831', *Journal of Modern History*, vol. XXII (1950).

12   The value of the 'Catholic Rent' is not easily translated into present-day monetary terms. However, some idea of the huge amount £700 a week represented at the time may be obtained by noting some sample wages in England in the mid-1820s: 14s *per week* for woolcombers and 10–12s for weavers (both in

Yorkshire), as little as 4s 6d for agricultural workers in the southern counties. Rates of income in Ireland, though not available in detail, were surely even lower. See J. L. and B. Hammond, *The Skilled Labourer, 1760–1832* (London, 1927), p. 201, and *The Village Labourer, 1760–1832* (London, 1932), p. 159.

13

PHILOSOPHERS, SCIENTISTS AND HISTORIANS

The half-century of Europe's intellectual history between 1780 and 1830 might at first glance appear to have been for the most part an interval of transition. On the one hand, the critical, rationalistic motifs of Enlightenment thought had been, if not obliterated, at least seriously challenged by the long revolutionary and military crisis. On the other hand, during the period of restoration and reassessment that began with Napoleon's overthrow a new world of ideas dominated by great systematizers – Comte, Marx, Darwin – could scarcely have been expected to emerge at once, fully formed.

Even under closer scrutiny there remains a good deal to be said for such a view, but in several important respects it calls for modification. It fails, for example, to take full account of the extent to which many of the Enlightenment's favourite themes retained their vitality while thrones toppled, old states disappeared and new social forces came to the fore. At another and more general level, to visualize any period, especially one so filled with debate, as nothing more than a hiatus or gap is to obscure the very meaning of *transition*. Just as the sovereign ideas of eighteenth-century *philosophes* went on claiming followers long after 1789, so the quest for more comprehensive systems of explication and prediction began well before 1830. Far from cutting our period loose from what went before and after, we need to recognize within its thought the intermingling of legacies from the past and anticipations of the future, as well as some contributions very much its own.

One major characteristic of the Revolutionary-Napoleonic era and its immediate sequel was, no doubt inevitably, the effort to comprehend a jumble of bewildering events. The interaction between ideas and occurrences, pondered during years of tumult and perhaps still more deeply thereafter, cast doubt on the ability of previous assumptions to explain what had happened. This confrontation inspired thinkers to search history, philosophy and observable human behaviour for theories that *would* give meaning to the past and if possible serve as guides to the future. As the present chapter's title seeks to make clear, we shall pay special attention to three broad intellectual disciplines. To do so is not to insist that only philosophical, scientific and historical endeavours were of interest to Europeans in our period. However, these three, particularly since the first of them included political, social and ethical speculation, offer a structure of sorts to what might otherwise become a formless survey.

POLITICAL SPECULATION: ENLIGHTENMENT AND REVOLUTION

Considering the narrative of the period, we should not be surprised at finding political issues, questions of man and the state, looming large among objects of intellectual concern. It is important in this regard not to misinterpret the legacy of the eighteenth century. The pre-1789 Enlightenment had not been rich or, for the most part, highly original in political theory. Montesquieu, to be sure, had espoused the separation of powers, not only among the executive, legislative and judicial branches of government, but also among different orders of men. Note, however, that his doctrine could survive only in the barest, most narrowly institutional terms in a society which saw the importance of 'orders' waning, as that of classes and parties increased. Rousseau had applied the theoretical (and quite old) notion of a social contract to the realization of popular sovereignty, had evoked the almost mystical concept of the General Will and had written movingly of the ethical grounds for reconciling external law with individual freedom; but he had said nothing about the actual bases and forms of modern government that could guide his admirers in action.

Voltaire, of course, had been interested in governmental power, especially for what it could do to further his chosen causes, such as the suppression of hereditary privilege and the overcoming of religious piety – or, as he saw it, superstition; but to the structure and functioning of government he remained largely indifferent. In pursuit of his aims, he would gladly have used the monarchy in France, Parliament in England, bourgeois voters in Geneva or the Hohenzollern autocracy in Prussia. As for such leading non-French figures as Hume, Lessing and Beccaria, not one had transmitted any political doctrine, strictly defined. The case of Immanuel Kant is more complex, and we shall have occasion to examine him a bit later in connection with one of the most important lines of political thought to develop within our period. Yet for Kant, as for Rousseau, questions of society and the state were generally subordinated to a central concern with personal morality.

Perhaps the best way to test the Enlightenment's contribution to political thought, once the Revolution came, is to consider the work of a man whose career formed a personal link of sorts between the two epochs: Marie Jean Antoine Nicholas de Caritat, marquis de Condorcet. In 1789, at the age of forty-six, Condorcet was already established as a famous philosopher and scientist. He welcomed the national uprising and became an active politician, serving in the National Convention after Louis XVI's deposition; yet he opposed the execution of the king, defended the cause of the Girondins (*see above*, pp. 130–1) and died in a Jacobin prison during the spring of 1794, thereby cheating Robespierre's guillotine of another victim. While hiding in Paris prior to his final arrest, he composed the *Sketch for a Historic Picture of the Progress of the Human Mind*, a document sometimes referred to as 'the testament of the eighteenth-century Enlightenment'.

The question before us here is how much of that testament was political, and the answer would appear to be: very little. There is no reason to belittle the poignant optimism with which this proscribed and hunted nobleman viewed his own times and what he confidently described as 'the future improvement of the human race'. For Condorcet, the history of mankind arranged itself into ten epochs, from the first ('Men United into Hordes') on through the eighth ('When the Sciences and Philosophy Threw off the Yoke of Authority') and the ninth ('Between Descartes and the Formation of the French Republic') to the glorious tenth, about to dawn. In this climactic epoch, the author foresaw 'the destruction of inequality between different nations; the progress of equality in one and the same nation; and lastly, the real improvement of man'.

It is a mistake to portray Condorcet, as is sometimes done, dreaming only of moral improvement and the miraculous perfection of human nature. A visionary he undoubtedly was, in the sweep and the irrepressible confidence of his views; but he did not ignore the need to advance *physical* wellbeing, in the hope that the resulting sense of security would breed benevolence and, at last, genuinely decent relations among mortals. The fact remains, however, that he was not a political theorist but a moralist and a scientist, cast in the prophetic mould.

If the Enlightenment had so little governmental theory to pass along, did the ideals, at once critical and reformist, of the eighteenth century have anything at all to offer a thoughtful man or woman of the ensuing period? They did, but their contribution lay primarily in posing practical aims and demonstrating practical methods for their pursuit. The Revolution in France, with its efforts to increase administrative efficiency, minimize unjust discrimination in legal and fiscal matters and make the welfare of a nation's entire population the measure of its government's success, was in those respects, *not* in its patriotic imperialism or its merciless attack on deviationists, an heir of the earlier reformers.

So obvious is this conclusion that we might easily overlook the more paternalistic and hence non-revolutionary side of the tradition, including the record of the more generous and sincere 'enlightened despots'. I am thinking not of cynical rulers such as Frederick II of Prussia or Catherine II of Russia, who exploited their much-publicized concern for Enlightenment in the interest of selfish autocracy, but rather of eighteenth-century princes genuinely, if not always prudently, swayed by the most humane currents of contemporary thought. These included Emperor Joseph II, his brother Leopold (grand duke of Tuscany for forty-five years and Holy Roman emperor from 1790 to 1792) and Charles III of Spain (died 1788). Without such monarchs to look back on, it seems doubtful whether monarchy itself could have survived the revolutionary crisis as well as it did.

Not only the enlightened despots, of course, but also a number of enlightened ministers represented to the new era an ideal of benign authoritarianism, which Napoleon and after him the crowned heads of the Restoration evoked as an actual theory of government. In Austria, where 'Josephinism' became a rallying cry within months of the reforming emperor's death in 1790, few individuals embodied that heritage so clearly as did Baron Joseph von Sonnenfels. Born in 1732, converted as a boy from Judaism to Catholicism at the behest of his recently ennobled father, Sonnenfels had a distinguished record as a public servant under the Habsburgs. Until the end of his long life in 1817, he represented the highest standards of honesty, efficiency and concern for the public good. As a Josephinist, he remained throughout a severe critic of his own adopted Church where issues of privilege and political influence were at stake; but his principal efforts in the intellectual sphere were directed towards rationalizing and humanizing the Austrian legal system. Appointed commissioner for the codification of laws in 1791, he laboured for two full decades on the project, which culminated in the Criminal Code of 1803 and the Civil Code of 1811, both of them in several important respects more liberal than the corresponding portions of the French Code Napoléon.

Other Enlightenment reformers included Prussia's Baron vom und zum Stein, whose efforts were sketched in an earlier chapter. For Stein, no less than for Sonnenfels, the value of responsible administration was beyond question, from the points of view of ruler and subjects alike. Not least among those state officials whose training and interests still identified them with the eighteenth century, even after 1789 appeared to have ended the Old Régime, were the Spaniards, Floridablanca and Aranda. Despite the attitude of Charles IV and their own dislike of the French Revolution, both men cherished the aspirations to improve Spain that had earlier inspired Campomanes and Jovellanos under Charles III. Finally, it is not difficult to find echoes of Enlightenment legalism and reformism, delivered from above, in political figures as widely separated as Maximilian von Montgelas (Bavaria's chief minister from 1799 to 1817), Count Stadion in Vienna and, in the England of the 1820s, Huskisson and Peel.

Yet when all has been acknowledged with regard to the Enlightenment's influence, it must be recognized that many conservatives were no more charmed by it after 1789 than they had been before. Equally important, and the more startling because of their recent appearance, were the assaults on the eighteenth century, both its evils and its proposed remedies, by men who insisted that nothing short of a clean and total break with old forms of government would suffice. The Revolution was an event, or better a flood of events; but it was also the expression of new and radical views concerning the state, the individual and the claims of both. These views characteristically went far beyond those of the Enlightened philosophers, demanding for the individual the right to participate in, not just benefit from, the formulation of public policy, but at the same time giving the state sweeping powers to reshape society, to pour the nation's manhood into war and to weed out dissident or 'useless' elements from the population, whence the Terror.

A good representative of the revolutionary position, in part because his career spanned the American and French revolts, is Thomas Paine, born an English Quaker in 1737. Having emigrated to the New World in 1774, Paine within two years made himself famous by publishing a pamphlet, *Common Sense*, which succinctly and energetically set forth the colonists' case for rebellion. To the extent that the American Revolution succeeded in breaking an old political tie and creating a new nation, it gratified Paine. To the extent that a war of independence fell short of immediately creating a powerful, centralized government, it disappointed him: Back in Europe on the eve of the French crisis, he found himself surveying revolutionary possibilities more to his liking.

By 1791, when he published the first section of another book, *The Rights of Man* (the second part appeared in 1792), his assault on authority and privilege was ready to be launched. His conclusion was uncompromising:

Whatever the form or constitution of Government may be, it ought to have no other object than the *general* happiness. When instead of this it operates to create an increased wretchedness, in any of the parts of society, it is a wrong system and reformation is necessary.

He denounced the 'gentlemen' who dismissed the rights of man as a faddish novelty, as though newness were itself a fault; and he offered in reply a metaphor in which the challenge of the future was expressed in the miracle of springtime:

. . . Though sleep will continue longer on some trees and plants than on others, and though some of them may not *blossom* for two or three years, all will be in leaf in the summer, except those which are *rotten*. What pace the political summer may keep with the natural, no human foresight can determine. It is, however, not difficult to perceive the spring has begun.

The buoyant revolutionary optimism of a Thomas Paine, like the careful language of the National Assembly's declaration, from which he took his book's title, seems a far cry from the harsh, suspicious preaching of Maximilien Robespierre before the National Convention, as it moved deeper and deeper into repression. Yet in fairness it must be conceded that the two revolutionaries' situations were scarcely comparable. Paine, the renegade Englishman, ran certain risks as a member of the Convention; but he bore no personal responsibility for converting precepts of political change – of the people's seizure of power in the state – into actual policies affecting public order, national finances and the prosecution of war.

Robespierre did bear such responsibility. The least engaging, in his pitiless self-righteousness, of all the Revolution's leaders, he was also the most consistent. The Terror he saw as a necessary work of purification, not as an end in itself, though he never had time to develop in any detail his vision of what France might become once the great purge was over. What saves him, for those who consider him saved, from the role of a bloodthirsty fanatic is the suggestion that beneath his heavy rhetoric lay an awareness of what a real revolution had to cost. That is, he drew chilling but, in his view, inescapable conclusions about the destruction of privilege and the creation of popular sovereignty, conclusions which involved an ever-widening effort to exterminate not only objectors but also laggards and compromisers, all in the name of human progress.

Any attempt to reduce the democratic wave of the Revolution to a coherent theory of the state encounters several obstacles. First is the variety of meanings different men, avowed 'revolutionaries' all, assigned to the Revolution as such. In this regard, it is instructive to contrast the incipient anarchism of Buonarroti with Babeuf's socialistic appeal to make the state a powerful agent for the material betterment of the population (*see above*, pp. 135 and 303). Second, vehement enemies of the Revolution, including William Cobbett in England (1775–1835), appropriated parts of its platform, the denunciation of corruption and favouritism, for example, thereby confusing still further the definition of popular revolt.

Third, and most important, modern democratic doctrine, when put to the test of application, had quickly revealed some serious internal contradictions and difficulties. It demanded participation by all citizens in the process of government; but in a large state, no such direct, continuing participation is in fact possible, and the practical effect of this demand is easily reduced to mass assent by plebiscite. The doctrine called for liberty to be guaranteed by equality; but the demand for equality, insofar as it went beyond equal opportunity and basic legal rights, turned out in many cases to threaten individuals' freedom to develop their differing abilities. It also soon became clear that an old régime is not toppled and replaced by a weaker one allowing increased personal freedom. Quite the contrary, a spiral of growing state power appeared implicit in successive shocks of revolution. The new nation, conceived as a 'people', made demands on all its citizens that could be enforced only by a strong, potentially oppressive government. Such observations do not suggest that we can or should discount the profound effect democratic aspirations have had upon the development of modern Europe; but they do caution against oversimplifying the practical effect of such aspirations.

THE PROLIFERATION OF POLITICAL THEORIES

Reactions against the Revolution, both as event and as theory, were of course intense – and no less varied than its claims. The earliest and one of the most telling counter-revolutionary statements was Edmund Burke's *Reflections* of 1790. As we saw in Chapter 7, Burke's chief insight, blurred but not negated by his imperfect knowledge of previous and existing conditions in France, lay in his definition of the state as an organism, the product of long, complex growth, not as a machine, which could from time to time be dismantled, cleaned, adjusted, even altered by a change of parts and reassembled like a watch or a power loom. The mechanical image, along with much accompanying brutality and injustice, he identified with the Revolution; and he considered it a tragic error.

Burke has retained his place as the founder of the modern conservative tradition in part because the positions adopted by many other critics of revolutionary aims and methods now appear too dated for present-day discussants. In 1811, to cite one example, the Russian historian, Karamzin, urged Alexander I by means of a famous memorandum drafted for the tsar's sister, Grand Duchess Catherine, to abandon Speransky's reform projects and return to the autocratic ways of Catherine the Great – not readily exportable as a conservative philosophy. At the other extreme, the poet Moritz Arndt lamenting Germany's spiritual humiliation or Samuel Taylor Coleridge apologizing to the recently conquered Swiss, in his 'France: An Ode' (1798), for ever having 'cherished one thought that . . . blessed your cruel foes'[1] were reacting to specific current events, not framing principles of government that offered the future a broad, continuing challenge.

Nevertheless, it cannot be said that Burke's answer to the Revolution was the only influential response at the time or that his temperate, relativistic form of conservatism was the period's sole legacy to anti-revolutionary thought. A quite different, flatly reactionary position was taken by Count Joseph de Maistre, the Savoyard nobleman driven from his homeland by the French invasion of 1792 and become in consequence the aristocratic *émigrés'* most impassioned spokesman. In some respects, Maistre appears as isolated from changing reality as was Karamzin. At the same time, there can be no denying his ability to link religious with political order in a manner more appealing to western Europeans of the generations that followed his own than the Russian's proposal to reintroduce enlightened despotism could ever have been.

In his *Considerations on France* (1796) and a large number of subsequent writings, Maistre equated impiety with rebellion, loyalty to the Roman Catholic Church with social stability, the Protestants of the past with the Jacobins of the present. At least once he suggested that the Inquisition, had it been maintained in full vigour, might have prevented the French Revolution. All this sounds slightly mad until one recognizes that on the Continent conservatives who lacked England's hard-earned political tradition were desperately groping for a´principle of order. In Maistre, they read that if governing aristocracies would only be devout, revolution stood condemned as sacrilege. The slogan 'Throne and Altar' neatly rephrased his message after 1815.

For the French Viscount Louis de Bonald, more restrained in expression but just as reactionary at heart, there could be no compromise with notions of civil equality and popular representation. In his eyes, even the modest constitutional concessions of Louis XVIII at the restoration of the Bourbon monarchy were both craven and foolhardy. The model, he insisted, should have been the glorious reign of Louis XIV, dead just 100 years when Napoleon fell from power. Using very similar arguments, the Swiss patrician, Ludwig von Haller, in his *Restoration of Political Science* (1816), hailed the return to power of kings, nobles and town oligarchs after the despicable interlude of anarchy. The corporatist repudiation of democracy has nowhere, I think, been more baldly stated.

Still another line of counter-revolutionary argument took a form which was also, to a degree, historical but more explicitly legalistic. When the earl of Eldon, England's lord chancellor (with one short interruption) from 1801 to 1827, boasted of the judicial campaign against individuals and newspapers charged with sedition, he did so in the stated belief that existing law was both a sacrosanct expression of established relationships and an instrument for the suppression of change. None of the provisions for orderly evolution defended by Locke in the seventeenth century and cautiously acknowledged by Burke in the eighteenth survived in Lord Eldon's theory. The law was there; let it be enforced. The legislation of the French revolutionary assemblies was not, in his view, law at all, being instead the destructive mouthings of unrestrained greed and envy. To the natural question just when, in the past, new legislation *had* been legal – as it must have been, to create the existing corpus of law – no clear answer was forthcoming from the lord chancellor. Eldon was himself willing to suspend parts of the constitution when necessary in the interests of repression, as witness the Six Acts of 1819; but to reformers he conceded no such right.

A more sophisticated expression of conservative legalism came from the Prussian scholar, F. K. von Savigny, one of the first professors appointed to the new University of Berlin in 1810. Savigny shared Lord Eldon's distaste for statutory change, but he devoted himself more seriously to finding the roots, and thus glorifying the mature wisdom, of existing law. With help from the famous student of folklore and Germanic customs, Jakob Grimm, he established himself as a legal historian of undeniable talent. His one frankly political treatise, *On the Vocation of Our Age for Legislation and Jurisprudence*, published in 1814, represented the most considerable effort by a student of law to refute the Revolution's central premise, namely, that civic institutions may be rightfully judged and, if found wanting, abolished on grounds of their irrationality or inequity, or both. In 1827, one of Savigny's disciples, Friedrich Stahl, published *The Philosophy of Law from an Historical Viewpoint*, inaugurating a career destined to carry his master's teachings forward into the nineteenth century.

It was perhaps inevitable that Germany, the land of Savigny and Stahl as of Fichte and Arndt and Gentz, should have been at the very centre of the reaction against the French Revolution. In this defeated and disorganized country, whose ancient foundations had crumbled in the great storm, the quest for order took on a special urgency, while the contagious fever of nationalism seemed, for many of the same reasons, particularly intense. Yet the picture is not that simple. For admiration of Burke, imitation of Maistre, concurrence with Eldon, loathing of Jacobins and French imperialists by no means exhausted the full range of the Germans' intellectual response. Still another line of argument, which was neither a literal extension of Enlightenment thought, an adaptation of revolutionary theses nor just another appeal to established authority, is encountered in Immanuel Kant, at the beginning of our period, and in Georg W. F. Hegel, near its end. In a summary discussion it is not possible to do justice to these founders of modern German philosophy. We should, nevertheless, seek to understand their efforts – differing but related, since Hegel owed much to Kant – to incorporate the experiences of their times into ambitious theoretical systems.

Kant, like many other intellectuals, was at the outset exhilarated by tidings of the French Revolution that reached him in the quiet East Prussian university town of Königsberg. It did not offend him to see human institutions subjected to the test of rational criticism. The issues involved belonged to the world of *phenomena*, amenable to understanding and ethical action, in short, to what he termed 'practical reason'. The limits of 'pure reason', which he had examined in his famous *Critique* of 1781, did not encompass political argument. Kant was without question a figure of the Enlightenment, one who admired Rousseau, believed in the pursuit of happiness (subject to his very special definition thereof) and demanded an end to the human mind's state of 'tutelage'.

Furthermore, in his *Eternal Peace* (1795), he favoured *republics*, though by that term he seems to have meant responsible governments combining freedom, power and law, a definition broad enough to cover 'responsible' monarchies, aristocracies and oligarchies, as well as democracies. Above all, Kant's moral philosophy imposed an absolute standard according to which an act's rightness depended not on its results but on the doer's motive or 'principle of action'. Hence, as a modern interpreter has observed, he 'supported [the French Revolution] not because of the immediate practical consequences, not because of its "deeds bad and good", but because of the state of mind manifested in its origins'.[2]

Why then did Kant, before his breakdown in 1798, come to oppose imitation of the Revolution in Germany and to repudiate the original in France? The answer must be sought in his view of human nature, which was more pessimistic than Rousseau's, and in his view of political change, which was distinctly evolutionary. The possibility that man's good will, his 'will to good', could ever be perfected to a point where he would be entirely happy obeying laws shaped by his own and others' wills, seemed to Kant slight, but also irrelevant. The *idea* of legality, the perfect meshing of personal morality and public order, was at the same time a vision of freedom, a goal that gave direction to history even though it might never be attained. While the slow striving went on within human nature, unrealistic attempts to leap forward, clutching for instant liberty, were hopeless, distracting and potentially retrogressive in their ultimate effect. Thus, Kant could both admire and deplore the Revolution as a well-motivated, doomed effort by imperfect mortals.

What had been in Kant a view of politics and history resting on ethical premises became in Hegel, the south German schoolteacher, a view of history according to which ethical judgments regarding politics became relative, their rightness or wrongness being dependent on the given stage of dialectical progress towards fulfilment of the Idea. The Idea is freedom, not in the sense of inalienable, natural rights but rather, as with Kant, in the sense of man's inner will and the state's outer compulsion reconciled. The emphasis, however, on freedom in Kant's definition of individual happiness, rooted in perfect morality and hence legality, has shifted in favour of discipline seen almost as a good in itself. Its ultimate expression now appears in the form of a highly authoritarian state, readily associated by many of Hegel's readers with a sort of idealized, much strengthened Prussian monarchy. In 1802, be it added, the philosopher published a book, *The Constitution of Germany*, in which he urged his fellow-countrymen to discard their false, anarchic illusions concerning freedom and study the great geniuses of state power, Machiavelli and Richelieu in particular.

Hegel, it must be said, would never have called himself a conservative, and indeed he was not one. His entire conception of the dialectic, as it emerges for instance from *The Philosophy of Right* and his *Natural Law and Political Science* (both published in 1821), is one of change, of progress towards the realization of freedom, achieved by challenges to and reversals of successive historical situations. Thus the dialectic explains progress in terms of collision. Hegel's mighty system of historical explanation presents its greatest difficulties to someone seeking the basis for judging a specific political régime, whether past or present. Since progress depends on opposition and the destruction of the *status quo*, the French Revolution as seen from the 1820s had been 'right'. Yet Napoleon's Empire too had been 'right' in reversing important aspects of the Revolution – that is, it had fulfilled its historical role – and the Restoration appeared just as 'right', in that it had emerged from the defeat of Napoleon as a valid next stage of the dialectic. The existing state thus both deserved men's allegiance at the time and faced certain overthrow in its turn, once the next level of development was ready to emerge. It is ironic but understandable that Hegel, for whom such terms as revolutionary and reactionary were literally without meaning as applied to himself, left behind him at his death in 1830 a body of thought to which monarchists and anti-monarchists in 1848, to say nothing of Communists and Fascists in our own day, could all turn for support of their several definitions of the state in relation to the individual. Karl Marx (born in 1818) owed him more than that: a theoretical framework for human history in its entirety.

SOCIAL THOUGHT

This era of spreading political debate, much of it launched from differing standpoints regarding history, also witnessed impressive growth in what we now call the social sciences, particularly in economics and sociology. Not that all theories of society propounded between 1780 and 1830 were, or sought to be, truly scientific. Much that was visionary flourished amid the appeals for objectivity, quantification and rigour in analysing evidence. In the minds of the scientific and the intuitive alike, however, decades of terrible warfare and the misery inherent in early industrialism posed – especially in the two great western powers, Great Britain and France – a challenge to explore the human relationships underlying law and government.

Even before the Revolution, the Enlightenment had produced, in Morelly and the Abbé Mably, for example, precursors of modern socialism's emphasis on poverty as the central problem of mankind and on collective action, even at the expense of liberalism's individualistic values, as the only answer. We have seen how unsuccessful Gracchus Babeuf had been in his attempt to push France towards a socialistic revolution after 1794. One of the opponents of 'big government' during the late eighteenth century had been the Count de Mirabeau, warning against the *fureur de gouverner* in his *Discourse on National Education* and in numerous speeches to the early revolutionary assemblies. Another was the Prussian aristocrat, philosopher and future reform minister, Wilhelm von Humboldt, author in 1792 of *Ideas for an Attempt to Fix the Limits of the State's Activity*. Nevertheless, as the spectacle of social dislocation, economic exploitation and mass suffering appeared to grow worse, there in time emerged a definite body of thought later identified by Marxists, more or less scornfully, as 'utopian socialism'.

Some of its opponents were in fact less theoretical than practical in the contributions they. sought to make. Robert Owen, the wealthy textile manufacturer, put his faith in demonstrating, at his mill town of New Lanark, Scotland, that out of unpromising materials a clean, orderly, well-fed, decently housed and adequately schooled industrial community could be assembled. Owen was in no sense a *state* socialist. He called instead for leadership from sensible businessmen and distrusted governmental intervention as strongly as had Mirabeau in France or Humboldt in Germany. Though he published several treatises, notably *A New View of Society* in 1813 and *The Book of the New Moral World* in 1820, he was seldom abstract and preferred to buttress his appeal by descriptions of New Lanark in operation. Certain English Radicals of the 1820s, Thomas Hodgkin, Charles Hall and others, would dwell on the labour theory of value and the social implications of unearned income, especially rent, in their indictment of capitalism. But it was Owen's prestige, his pragmatism and his evidence drawn from experience that really launched modern British socialism.

To understand the other great stream of socio-economic reformism, it is helpful to consider the succession of what an American scholar has called the 'prophets of Paris' – Turgot and Condorcet in the eighteenth century, followed by Henri de Saint-Simon, François Marie Charles Fourier and August Comte in the nineteenth.[3] Obviously, a great distance separates Turgot, the royal minister under Louis XVI, from Comte, the apostle of Positivism in the 1830s and 40s under King Louis Philippe. Yet beneath personal and doctrinal differences, can be discerned a persistent confidence in man's ability to find and correct the causes of social ills that was indeed prophetic no less in tone than in content.

For present purposes, the two most important of these French social theorists were the Count de Saint-Simon (1760–1825) and his slightly younger contemporary, Fourier (1772–1837). (Comte too wrote random pieces during our period and actually served for a time as Saint-Simon's secretary, but his own influence began to be strongly felt only after the revolution of 1830.) As for Saint-Simon himself, it would be hard to imagine a more bizarre figure. Born into a poor but respected family of the nobility, he began his career as an army officer, fighting in the American War of Independence and thereafter serving on special missions as a military engineer in Mexico and Spain, and as a diplomatic agent in Holland. During the French Revolution he made a fortune in land speculation, was imprisoned for almost a year at the height of the Terror and then, upon his release, launched a series of unsuccessful business enterprises made worse by his prolonged frustration as a writer. In 1812–13, literally maddened by failure to win influential support for his views, he spent several months in a Paris mental hospital. In due course, however, he recovered and began to attract the circle of younger men who, by the time of his death a dozen years later, would constitute nothing less than a cult.

Saint-Simon's ideas were diffuse, his knowledge uneven and his style sometimes turgid; but he clung doggedly, and in the long run persuasively, to a central insight, namely, that industrialism was forging a wholly new world. His treatise, *Of the Industrial*

System (1821), argued that the old order, grounded on feudalism
and Christianity, was in the process of being replaced by something altogether different. This prophesy's utopian element lay in
the vision of a well-ordered, increasingly productive society in
which the workers would grow affluent under the wise guidance
of scientists and business leaders. More to the point, however,
was Saint-Simon's recognition that the emerging industrial
economy was creating a new élite, a scientific-managerial
bureaucracy, in short a technocracy. He looked to a future in
which rational direction by this élite would ensure the betterment
of all mankind (note the echo of Condorcet).

Fourier, whose *New Industrial World* was written in 1827, might
have taken his title directly from Saint-Simon, but he was far less
willing than the now deceased seer to accept depersonalization
under a socialistic structure. Instead, many of the works of this
former commercial agent from Besançon are more concerned
with the psychological and sexual aspects of individual personality
than with society as a whole. If there was much of Condorcet in
Saint-Simon, in Fourier there lingered at least as much of Rousseau. Nevertheless, like Robert Owen, Fourier was attempting to
define a basis, at once progressive and practical, for improving
life in a changing Europe. His solution was not, as Saint-Simon's
and Owen's were not, the abolition of private property but rather,
in Fourier's case, an elaborate system of sharing the wealth. Small
industrial communities, which he named 'phalansteries', were to
be formed and their shared income disbursed in accordance with
the members' differing contributions: three-twelfths to manage-
ment, four-twelfths to the providers of capital and the remaining
five-twelfths to labour. With characteristic deference towards
psychology, Fourier sought to engage the worker's self-interest
in the task of production, as well as in the common life of the
industrial unit as a social organism.

These early socialists had to face several forms of resistance,
two of which deserve to be singled out for special attention. One
was romantic nostalgia for an older, explicitly medieval set of
values and relationships. In its political guise, we have already
encountered this motif in Maistre, Bonald and Haller (*see above*,
pp. 355–6). In its application to social forms, it appeared
particularly as the glorification of medieval times by a wide
variety of European writers. A good example of this tendency
was the French novelist and politician, Viscount F. R. de

Chateaubriand, who in 1802, long before the Restoration brought him to high office, published *The Genius of Christianity*, a wistful evocation of the ages of faith and order. Or consider the novels of Sir Walter Scott, with their brave and generous knights, sturdy yeomen and faithful servants. Scott's middle ages had their villains, evil individuals of all ranks, but its hierarchical social structure was portrayed as healthy and comforting. Whether it seemed so to medieval people may be debated; but there can be no question, judging from Scott's immense popularity, that he was giving a large segment of the early nineteenth-century reading public the kind of escape it wanted.

More solemn than Chateaubriand and more concerned with religion than Scott was the medievalism of the first generation of German Romantics, writing just before and after the turn of the century. In some cases their idealization of a golden past is ludicrous, as in the poet Wackenroder's title for a book submerged in bathos: *Heart-outpourings of an Art-loving Friar*. One of the several ardent converts to Catholicism who led this movement in Germany, and no doubt the ablest writer it produced, was the aristocratic Prussian, Friedrich von Hardenberg, who wrote under the pen name 'Novalis' and whose essay, *Christianity or Europe* (1799), was a sort of manifesto published just two years before its author's death. Here are some illustrative sentences:

> Those were bright glorious times, when Europe formed but one
> Christian land; when one Christianity dwelt throughout the civilized
> part of the world, and a great mutual interest bound together the most
> remote provinces of this wide spiritual empire. . . . A filial confidence
> closely united men to their instructions. . . . How contentedly could
> each one fulfil his daily work. . . .[4]

If Romantic corporatism accepted some organizing role for society, powerfully seconded by the Church, but rejected the egalitarian aspects of nascent socialism, the other antisocialistic attitude, that of the 'classical' economists, rested on the opposite pair of theses. These increasingly self-confident theorists had no use for corps or orders of men so dear to Romanticism, but neither did they share the socialists' commitment to extensive planning or control by the state. Born of generous efforts by eighteenth-century philosophers, notably Adam Smith and the French Physiocrats, to break down artificial, irrational barriers hampering commercial development and to discover the true springs of productivity, classical economics in our period was nevertheless moving rapidly towards becoming what its future critics would refer to as 'the dismal science'.

No single writer did more to buttress the forbidding side of this doctrine ruled by egoism and the free play of forces than did the Englishman Thomas Malthus. Denouncing what he considered the vaporizing of optimists such as William Godwin, the author of a utopian tract, *Social Justice*, Malthus in 1798 published an *Essay on Population*, a work that has continued ever since to influence not only economic thought but also the apologetics of imperialism and biological debates over environment and the development of species. For Malthus, the rationale of population growth, and hence of possible improvement in the masses' standard of living, was as clear as it was discouraging. Given mankind's apparent compulsion to produce offspring up to the absolute limit imposed by any given level of sustenance, the author saw no hope of lifting the race by increasing its food supply. Since by his calculations production of foodstuffs could at best increase, generation by generation, in no more than an arithmetic progression – 1, 2, 3, 4, 5 – while population, left to follow its natural tendency, would show a geometric progression – 1, 2, 4, 8, 16 and so on – the 'improvement of mankind' was an illusion beckoning its followers to disaster. The only reason the worst does not happen, he explained, is that natural checks, including famine, pestilence, war and 'vice' (i.e. venereal disease, abortion and infanticide) prevent the threatened rise in population from actually occurring.

Malthus did not seek to spell out any theory of wages or profits. Rather, he thought of himself as a scientific student of demography and, when urging self-restraint in regard to procreation, as a moralist. The implications of his theory for a ruthless young capitalism were none the less apparent. If anything more than subsistence only breeds misery for the mass of mankind, then bare subsistence should determine wages, all excess value created by technical progress and higher levels of industrial production being reserved to the entrepreneur and such stockholders as may have invested capital in his business. In actual practice, of course, the 'possessing classes' gradually revealed an increasing disposition, inspired by a mixture of pious altruism and enlightened self-interest, to deal back at least a fraction of the profits, in the form of largesse to support schools, hospitals, orphanages and other charitable institutions. Yet consider the distance separating Fourier's proposal to make the workers shareholders in his industrial communities from the spirit which informs Hannah More's 'Charge to the Women of the Shipham Club' (1801). The italics are Mrs More's:

Let me remind you that probably that very scarcity has been permitted by an all-wise and gracious Providence to *unite* all ranks of people *together*, to shew the *poor* how immediately they are dependent on the *rich*, and to shew the *rich* and *poor* that they are all dependent on *Himself*. . . . *You* are *not* the *only* sufferers . . . it has fallen in some degrees on all ranks. . . . We trust the poor in general, especially those that are well instructed, have received what has been done for them as a matter of *favour*, not of *right*.[5]

The subtlest and least harsh of the early classical economists was David Ricardo. A successful London businessman, descended from Sephardic Jewish immigrants from Spain by way of Holland, Ricardo saw himself as the disciple and continuator of Adam Smith. However, in his *Principles of Political Economy and Taxation* (1817) he went well beyond Smith's explanation of a healthy division of labour and exchange of products in a stable, though competitive, market. Ricardo, confronting a dynamic scene of accelerating and often ruthless expansion, pushed on to inquire 'into the laws which determine the division of the produce of industry amongst the classes who concur in its formation'. Gone is Smith's optimistic prospect of general enrichment of the whole society, to be replaced by the frank recognition that the classes – industrial capitalists, landed proprietors, labourers – are in direct conflict over their respective shares of the growing wealth.

By singling out the tension between landed and capitalist interests, including the former's desire for high grain prices and the latter's for inexpensive bread (as a factor directly influencing wages) Ricardo provided some of the earlier weapons for the long battle against the Corn Law (*see above*, p. 333). But still more important, by accepting labour as the essential variable determining a product's real cost, from which a classical economist would argue that wages, above all, must be limited if profits are to be high and capital is to accumulate for further investments, he riveted the attention of capitalist and socialist alike on a crucial issue. It was characteristic of Ricardo's balanced, dispassionate presentation of the issue that it suggested other responses than those of his own classical economics. Only two years after the *Principles of Political Economy and Taxation* appeared, the Swiss historian and social critic, Simonde de Sismondi, brusquely reversed the coin in his *New Principles of Political Economy* (1819): 'The earnings of the entrepreneur sometimes represent nothing but the spoliation of the workers.'[6]

Outside the range of socialistic, Romantic and classical economic writings, of course, many less sweeping but more concrete proposals for the betterment of society appeared during this same half-century. In Switzerland J. H. Pestalozzi began during the 1790s to demonstrate the importance of an open, challenging school environment for bringing out the best in any child; and his widely translated *How Gertrude Teaches Her Children* spread the Pestalozzian gospel of free, secular, humane education from East Prussia to Robert Owen's model school at New Lanark. Meanwhile, British Evangelical reformers, many of them Tories in politics, pressed for various moral reforms, including the abolition of slavery throughout the world and the advancement of religious education at home and abroad. Their most articulate spokesmen, the so-called Clapham Sect around William Wilberforce and Zachary Macaulay, failed to attack social and economic ills in England with sufficient zeal to win the respect of a Radical such as Francis Place; but they deserved better than the sneering criticism of the 'Saints' by William Cobbett.

Jeremy Bentham and his followers, the Philosophical Radicals, are not easy to place in the history of social thought *per se*, though Bentham's Utilitarian ethics and his confident use of the pleasure-pain standard of judgement had obvious legal and political implications. He was highly pragmatic in his view of society, as he had been conservative regarding government until convinced in the 1820s that only a broadened franchise and parliamentary reform could guarantee needed changes in the law. He rejected any notion of corporate interests, insisting that individuals alone provide the units for the pleasure-pain calculus; and his proposed judicial system was geared to the defence of personal rights, to rationally conceived punishments in criminal cases and, in civil, to both the protection of property and the minimizing of artificial inequalities in wealth. For the Utilitarian, a single good – the greatest happiness (most pleasure, least pain) for the greatest number of subjects – offered a clear and simple guide to the solution of any issue of social policy whatever. In this sense, Bentham's popular, because reassuring, theories of government, society and economics were inextricably bound up with his opinions concerning morality, of which more in a moment.

PHILANTHROPY, UTILITARIANISM AND THE CATEGORICAL IMPERATIVE

It can, I think, be said of the period we are considering that with respect to ethics, amid all the individual statements or restatements of personal views on right and wrong, there were three major themes that together have an especially strong claim to our attention. One of them, the ideal of philanthropy (literally, the 'love of mankind'), rested on a very old impulse to perform good works, an impulse sanctified by Hebrew scripture and the Christian doctrine of charity but not finally dependent on any formal religious teaching. A second theme, the Utilitarianism of Bentham's Philosophical Radicals, was firmly rooted in the rationalism and individualism of the eighteenth-century Enlightenment. The third, Immanuel Kant's 'categorical imperative', though its formulator was at once a *philosophe* and a devout Christian, rejected the Enlightenment's rational calculation of benefits to individuals as well as the ideal of simple charity as being, both the one and the other, incapable of supplying an independent standard of ethical judgement.

A word must be said about the role of organized religion in all this. There is no denying that in the late eighteenth and early nineteenth centuries, as in all ages, theological premises continued to shape the ideas of innumerable men and women with respect to the moral life. For the Evangelical 'Saints' and for the more radical Nonconformists in England, for Catholic converts among the German Romantics, for such strikingly different Catholics by birth as Bonald, Chateaubriand and Constant in France, for inward-looking Old Lutherans in Prussia and Old Believers in Russia, specific versions of the Christian message presumably dictated specific responses to the recurring choices that punctuate each personal life. The same was assuredly true of the increasingly divergent varieties of Judaic belief, whether orthodox, conservative or modernist.

Yet the contributions of theology as such to ethical debate during the half-century under discussion were remarkably thin. By that I mean only to point out the extent to which such discussion was pursued without heavy reliance on theological references or proofs. The Catholic revival brought with it, at least for the first couple of decades after 1815, little evidence of new energy at the upper reaches of formal thought and even less altering of doctrinal guidance in personal or social ethics. As for the Protestants, even a divine such as the University of Berlin's F. D. Schleiermacher (died 1834), who addressed himself to a rethinking of God's relationship to His creatures, quite explicitly denied that religion must give practical, ethical guidance to those creatures in their relations with one another. The reforming zeal of the Nonconformist fathers of the early Factory Acts in England, as well as the stirrings of what would become Social Catholicism on the Continent, revealed not so much the direct application of abstract theology to the problems of mankind as the generous, but also very general, impulse of Christian humanism. Church leaders could insist on the continuing relevance of the moral teachings of Christ – or Moses – but they could scarcely have been expected to satisfy the demand of an increasingly sceptical civilization for standards not dependent on any particular religious belief.

Of the three themes mentioned at the beginning of this section, philanthropy did, of course, offer a chance for the pious to demonstrate their 'applied religion'. Thus Pitt's old friend, Wilberforce, and other members of the Clapham Sect denounced human slavery as an affront to the equal love of God for all mankind and at the same time pressed to bring the Bible into the lives of the poor as the greatest bounty and consolation mortals could receive. Even Wilberforce, however, implied on occasion – as did Zachary Macaulay more frequently and more emphatically – that slavery was equally an affront to human reason and goodness of heart. In many other cases, including those of Owen and Fourier, the ideal of philanthropy required no divine sanction at all, a circumstance that won Owen in particular the enmity of the Evangelicals. About the most that can be said of the philanthropic impulse was that it rallied men and women, some of them religious, others not, who found in the commandment to do good to others sufficient inspiration to lead them out of the moral desert of naked self-interest.

Less sentimental, but seemingly more precise, was the Utilitarian assertion that a good act is one that serves to maximize the pleasure and minimize the pain of individual humans, including the doer as one, but no more than one. If we are anxious to choose the 'right' action among several open to us, we need only ask ourselves which, in the event, is likely to bring the greatest happiness to the greatest number. Critics of the Benthamite creed have pointed out the lack of any logical connection between, on the one hand, a hedonistic (that is, pleasure-oriented) definition of happiness combined with an egoistic (self-centred) notion of motivation and, on the other hand, a faith that social progress must result from the rational effort by individuals to promote a quantitative increase in the total supply of human happiness. The Utilitarian usually replies partly by denying that his idea of happiness is limited to animal pleasures and partly by asking: 'Have you a clearer, more measurable criterion to offer?'

Perhaps a more serious charge against the Utilitarian ethic is that it does not seek to evaluate the goodness of men but only of their actions, that it addresses itself not to *motives* but to the ascertainable *effects* of behaviour. If stated too harshly, this accusation is not altogether fair, at least not to Bentham; for in his *Principles of Morals and Legislation* (privately circulated in 1780, but first published in 1789) he was much interested in human 'dispositions' – good, bad or altogether depraved. He did, however, insist on separating the 'tendency' of the act, i.e. its influence on human happiness, from the 'motive which gave birth to it'. This distinction permitted him to call the sale of bread to a hungry man, at the regular price, a good deed which nevertheless offers no basis for judging the baker to be either better or worse than other men. If the price were extortionate, of course, the motive – and hence the baker – would be bad, as would the tendency or effect. The *theft* of bread for selfish reasons is bad as regards both tendency and motive; but a theft motivated by the desire only to feed starving children ceases to be mischievously motivated though it remains a lawless and antisocial, hence a bad, act.

Utilitarian teaching also provides for acts of good tendency *and* generous motivation (pure beneficence), not to mention others of good tendency and 'semisocial' motivation – the love of reputation, for instance – recognizing that the charitable distribution of bread to the poor might be of either type. Bentham and his followers, in their eagerness to define and to encourage socially useful reforms, including new legislation, did in fact often seem to examine 'tendencies', i.e. practical effects, of behaviour more intently than they sought to evaluate motives. As a practical matter, if a given member of Parliament were willing to support a revision of the penal code, for example, they found it difficult to keep worrying about the degree of altruism, as opposed to political calculation, that lay behind his vote.

At just this point the era's other great ethical system collided head-on with Utilitarianism. For Kant, the categorical imperative is binding on man without regard to the results of specific acts. It is an ethic of pure intention – moral evil being entered upon or avoided the moment an individual decides to do something, or not to do it. The will is 'good in itself' if it wills good, whence Kant's own approval of the French Revolution's initial impulse, notwithstanding his eventual condemnation of its results (*see above*, pp. 357–8).

In his *Fundamentals of the Metaphysics of Morals* (1785), the Koenigsberg philosophy professor framed the categorical imperative in these terms: 'In all cases I must act in such a way that I can at the same time will that my maxim should become a universal law.' At first glance this may seem only an unnecessarily complicated version of the Golden Rule; but it is in reality quite different from the invocation, at once benign and practical, to 'do unto others as thou would'st have them do unto you'. For what Kant is saying is that your every act, at whatever cost to yourself or to other people, must express a principle of action that can stand the test of *rational* (not necessarily charitable) appraisal. Specifically, can or cannot that principle be universalized? Can it be generalized indefinitely without becoming self-contradictory? By this test, theft is evil because its 'maxim', to use Kant's term, would if universalized put an end to all private ownership and thus rob theft itself of meaning. Similarly, murder is evil because if universalized the principle of man's right to kill another by his own decision would obliterate human life – and with it, the crime of murder. The same could be said of adultery in relation to marriage.

Certain of his critics have suggested that in practice Kant's rule tends merely to support social institutions and the general welfare, that it is in reality little more than Utilitarianism disguised as Idealism. Such a claim, however, ignores the distinguishing characteristic of the Kantian imperative, namely, its passing of moral judgement on the individual will *before* a given act has occurred and *irrespective of the results*. It is a judgement coloured neither by self-interest nor by considerations of social usefulness. Furthermore, the simple examples given above are not the only ones that could be imagined. In other possible scenarios the happiness of the greatest number *may not benefit even incidentally* from an individual's obedience to the categorical imperative.

Take the case of a man tempted to lie, in order to conceal information which a small but heavily armed gang of criminals will surely use to destroy him, his family and a whole village of his neighbours. Is he morally justified in lying? 'Of course,' Bentham would say, with a shake of the head at such a foolish question. 'No,' Kant would insist, 'for the principle of untruth, if universalized, would extinguish the very idea of truth and hence of lying as well.' There is no evidence that the philosopher actually expected anyone to be capable of such Stoic indifference to his own and others' immediate wellbeing. But for Kant this standard of moral purity is what the 'good will' must strive toward, a peculiarly chilly East Prussian image of the Grail.

THE NATURAL SCIENCES

Although both Kant and Condorcet were contributors to scientific inquiry, while major scientists such as Joseph Priestley in England and Antoine-Laurent Lavoisier in France became deeply involved in political action (the latter dying on the guillotine in 1794), the progress of science in our period must be treated as an essentially independent phenomenon. With two exceptions – the great public institutions for research and teaching created by revolutionary-imperial France and the crucially important University of Berlin, founded by a Prussia reacting to defeat at the hands of Napoleon – there are no important links between the achievements of pure science and the chronicle of public events from 1780 to 1830. Instead of being hampered by international conflict, many of those achievements showed a high degree of communication and cooperation which survived the divisive effects of warfare between peoples.

The closing decades of the eighteenth century, both before and after 1789, witnessed the growing institutionalization of learning in general and of science in particular. The establishment in 1780 of the American Academy of Arts and Sciences at Boston, in the western reaches of the European world, the appearance of new academies in Dublin and Turin during the ensuing three years, the creation of the Literary and Philosophical Society of Manchester in 1785, like that of the less formal Lunar Society of Birmingham a decade before, all testify to the era's organizing ability. Similarly, according to the tabulation of a modern specialist in this field, of the sixty-nine scientific journals founded in the second half of the century, twenty were launched in the 1780s and twenty-five in the 1790s.[7]

As for revolutionary France, not the delirious first five years but the less dramatic period of the Directory constituted a time of expansion for the 'scientific establishment'. When the *Institut National* was founded in 1795, as the supreme arbiter of higher learning, science was ensconced as the largest of the three divisions. Almost simultaneously, the *Ecole Polytechnique* began its work of bringing rigorously selected students together with the élite of French scientists and engineers. Another creation of the Directory, the *Ecole Normale Superieure*, was, as we know, less successful until its thorough restructuring by Napoleon in 1812 (*see above*, pp. 187–8); but it too was destined to have a major role in the systematic teaching of science. During the first years of the new century the establishment of technological and scientific institutes, or *Technische Hochschulen*, in a half-dozen of the larger German cities reflected the prestige of the French model. Perhaps the most tangible symbol of that prestige, the metric system, extended its sway over the Continent decade by decade, providing a conveniently standardized language of measurement to the still growing array of scientific, mathematical and medical journals.

Italian, Swedish and Dutch names appear prominently in the chronicle of this scientific crusade, but the overwhelming majority of its leaders were Frenchmen, Britons or Germans. From their Parisian institutes and schools, the French dominated many fields with lofty self-assurance, though never with indifference to developments taking place elsewhere. In England the twin traditions of individual, often amateur, endeavour and unofficial associations relying on private patronage continued, with many of the most important contributions being made by men of a distinctly practical bent, as opposed to strong theoretical, especially mathematical, concerns. (Scottish scientists, though equally practical, seem to have included in their ranks rather more of the theoretical and mathematically trained, perhaps because Scotland's universities as such were already heavily involved in scientific inquiry even before our period.) But it was the Germans who relied most consciously on the concentration of research in their numerous and widely scattered centres of learning. The latter had for the most part escaped the torpor into which their French and English counterparts had fallen in the seventeenth and eighteenth centuries and now entered the nineteenth with Berlin in particular prepared to supply the organizing and radiating point for a proud system of academic science. These national differences were not absolute – new, French-style technical institutes appeared alongside Germany's historic universities, and the British Isles had their formal Royal Academy as well as their Lunar Society – but the general lines of differentiation are worth identifying for the help they offer in understanding several distinctive styles of attack on the problems of science.[8]

In the space available, it is impossible to more than suggest the range and briefly illustrate the significance of the late eighteenth and early nineteenth centuries' scientific contributions. In mathematics, the application of differential equations to physics and astronomy by J. L. Lagrange in his *Analytical Mechanics* of 1788 and the precision of Gaspard Monge's *Treatise of Descriptive Geometry* (1799) gave scientists the algebraic and geometric tools they needed to penetrate relationships previously difficult to fathom and often still more difficult to record. The work of these two Frenchmen created powerful echoes in Germany, both in the isolated brilliance of Karl Friedrich Gauss (1777–1855), measuring celestial orbits at the University of Göttingen, and in the mathematical seminar begun in 1825 by Karl Jacobi at the University of Berlin.

The modern scientist's other essential instrument, along with mathematical conceptualization and notation, has of course been observation pursued with ever-increasing ingenuity and exactitude, as well as sophistication in the designing of controlled experiments. Nowhere was this last quality more impressively displayed than in chemistry, suddenly emergent from centuries of descriptive vagueness and bizarre deductions. As early as the 1770s the English Nonconformist minister, Joseph Priestley, had isolated oxygen and shown its general relationship to both combustion and respiration. Within only a few years Priestley's friend and correspondent, Lavoisier, had demonstrated in his laboratory at Paris that air is not an element, as it had long been assumed, but a compound of which only about one-fifth is respirable and combustible. These discoveries, supported by Daniel Rutherford's concurrent achievement in isolating nitrogen or 'noxious air', began a chain of important investigations that by the turn of the century had not only revolutionized the learned world's understanding of gases, liquids and fire (overthrowing the old belief in 'phlogiston' as a 'combustible principle', an actual substance supposedly released by all substances when burning) but also opened a challenging field of inquiry into the nature of compounds in general.

Thus in 1808 John Dalton in England announced a system for classifying atoms by weight, as opposed to shape. The next year, in France, J. L. Gay-Lussac published the ratios by which *numbers* of particles combine in various gases. By 1815 an Italian, Amedeo Avogadro, was ready to argue that the combining unit of compounds, the molecule, might itself be a particular cluster of discrete atoms. Even without reference to Avogadro, the way was now clear for the great Swedish chemist, J. J. Berzelius, to issue in 1818 his pioneering work, a table of elements and compounds, with the former's combining weights and the symbols by which they are still identified. Just as Jacobi had carried French mathematic analysis back to the University of Berlin, so another gifted German, Baron Justus von Liebig, upon his return to the University of Giessen from Paris in 1826, set up an important chemical laboratory on the basis of his own studies under Gay-Lussac. It was decades before all the implications of theories such as Avogadro's would be recognized; but by 1830 the 'chemical revolution' was already well past its first stage.

Advances in a much older science, astronomy, can best be epitomized by the career of Pierre-Simon Laplace – made Count de Laplace by Napoleon and a marquis by Louis XVIII. His *System of the World* (1796) and its sequel, the multi-volume *Celestial Mechanics* (1799–1825), lent powerful support to the Newtonian explanation of gravitational force. It also spelled out in detail the nebular theory of the solar system's derivation from the cooling of an original mass of incandescent gases. His *Analytical Theory of Probabilities* (1812) meshed with the efforts of Gauss at Göttingen to reconcile perfection in celestial movement with the practical difficulties of human observation. The success of Sir William Herschel as far back as 1781 in identifying a previously unknown planet, Uranus, from his Slough observatory had done much to encourage observers; but profound mathematicians on the Continent still pondered the irreducible degree of error.

Like chemistry – which it was beginning to influence profoundly – physics was moving rapidly ahead. With respect to electricity, it is perhaps enough to point out that many of the basic terms we use for various processes and units of measurement are themselves tributes to scientists of the period under review. 'Galvanizing' (stimulating particles by the use of current) recalls Luigi Galvani of Bologna (1737–98), demonstrator in 1786 of the effect of electrical impulses on a frog's nerves and muscles; the 'volt' (energy), Alessandro Volta of Como (1745–1827), inventor of the condenser, the electrometer and, in 1800, the 'electric pile' or wet-cell storage battery; the 'ampere' (current), A. M. Ampère of Paris (1775–1836), mathematical student of electromagnetism and rival of Avogadro as a precursor of atomic research; finally, the 'ohm' (resistance), Georg Simon Ohm of Cologne (1787–1854), analyst of the relationship among energy, resistance and current. A crowning achievement, quite literally dynamic, was Michael Faraday's work in London during the 1820s on the production of electrical current from a magnetic field.

Another area of the highest importance to physics was the study of heat. In 1799 an American-born researcher, Sir Benjamin Thompson, who had also been named Count von Rumford by the elector of Bavaria, released the results of experiments proving that heat in itself is weightless and hence immaterial, a necessary basis for investigating its properties as a form of energy. Just twenty-five years later this particular cycle of discoveries reached its culmination in the treatise of a French *polytechnicien*, N. L. Sadi Carnot, constituting nothing less than the manifesto of thermo-dynamics as a pure science: *Reflections on the Motive Power of Heat*. Here, as in several other areas already noted, the contribution of mathematical abstraction and prediction, specifically Joseph Fourier's *Analytical Theory of Heat* (1822), was very great. A comparable summary of investigations into optics by a succession of English and French scientists would provide the background for Thomas Young's and Augustin Fresnel's quite separate, but mutually reinforcing, demands in the first quarter of the nine-teenth century for the abandonment of the corpuscular in favour of a wave theory of light. The Englishman's and Frenchman's findings were further buttressed by the electroscopic experiments of a Bavarian optician, Joseph von Fraunhofer (1787–1826).

In two other scientific disciplines, those of geology and biology, great debates raged over the formation of the planet Earth and the origin of its creatures. Dominating the geological argument was the disagreement between the Neptunists, who credited the action of water with the formation of rocks and the shaping of terrain, and the Vulcanists, who emphasized the role of igneous matter, that is, its initial emergence from the cooling of burning gases and its subsequent eruptions from the earth's still molten interior. By 1785, however, when James Hutton published his *Theory of the Earth* in Edinburgh, something like the eventual synthesis of aqueous and igneous explanations was emerging, in that Hutton evoked both water *and* heat as agents in the fashioning of the surface of the globe.

As a matter of fact, Hutton's efforts to resolve one geological debate were to be overshadowed by his contribution to the initiation of another, involving the relationship between prehistoric and historic events. For his 'uniformitarian' doctrine insisted that all past changes, however remote in time, must somehow be explainable by the operation of slow cooling, sedimentation, erosion, eruption and other phenomena still observable in his own day. To the shocked rejoinder from biblical literalists, but also from many scientists, that such a scheme posited absolutely preposterous stretches of elapsed time, Baron Christian Leopold von Buch, a Prussian nobleman, replied in 1810 that his analysis of Scandinavian rocks proved previous estimates, whether theological or scientific, with respect to the earth's age to be wholly inadequate. Others joined Buch in seeking to stretch geology's available time frame; and in 1830 a Scottish compatriot of Hutton, Charles Lyell, began to publish his magisterial *Principles of Geology*, a fully developed statement of the uniformitarian position.

Biology was a subject that owed undeniable debts to Lavoisier and Laplace for early experiments with respiration in the former's Parisian laboratory, to the Germans Karl von Baer and Friedrich Wöhler for their pioneering discoveries during the late 1820s in embryology and organic chemistry, respectively, to the histologist, Xavier Bichat, and the physiologist, Francois Magendie, French giants of the intervening period. However, the most visible and exciting struggle, as seen by contemporaries, was waged over the familiar issue of animal species, their origin and differentiation. It was no accident that this conflict paralleled those of the geologists, for the two sciences shared a common interest in palaeontology and especially in the use of fossils as evidence.[9]

The three main protagonists were all Frenchmen working in the great research centres of the Empire and the Restoration monarchy. The Chevalier de Lamarck, author of *Zoological Philosophy* (1809) and a *Natural History of Invertebrates* (1815–22), in the latter work revealed the skills of an able anatomist, classifying organisms by rigorously examining their structures and functions. Already in the earlier book, however, he had shown a more impressionistic, even poetic, side in his insistence on the organism's ability to adapt directly to its environment and then, in reproducing itself, to transmit the characteristics produced by that adaptation. Whatever Lamarck's view may have contributed to a general interest in some process of evolution, there remained a great distance yet to be travelled between his image of a single giraffe, passing on by immediate inheritance the long neck it had developed by constant stretching for leaves on high branches, and the yet unborn Darwinian doctrine of natural selection.

Lamarck's more conservative colleague, G. L. C. Cuvier, came nearer to adumbrating that aspect of Darwin's eventual system, as published in 1859. For while he insisted on the fixity of species, each designed by its Maker to function successfully in its particular environment, in his *Animal Kingdom* (1817) Cuvier was very close to asking how environmental *changes* might affect a species by favouring some and not others of the individual variants which even his notion of fixity had to recognize. Here, as his direct opponent, Etienne Geoffroy Saint-Hilaire (1772–1842), was to charge, a presupposition not unlike that of some geologists concerning the earth's age blinded Cuvier to the fact that in rejecting Lamarck's notion of inheritance of acquired characteristics, he need not have clung to eternal, because divinely created, species. In 1830, just as our period ended, Geoffroy Saint-Hilaire's assault on behalf of biological metamorphosis against Cuvier's belief in fixity erupted in the august surroundings of the French Academy of Sciences.

Before leaving the history of science, in one of its most exciting times, we should note the interaction between scientific advances and several other important aspects of European life. The 'scien-

tific method' was increasingly admired and emulated by practitioners in other fields of knowledge. Saint-Simon thought himself
a thorough-going scientist, whatever the Marxists would say later
– in support of their own claim to being truly scientific. Auguste
Comte in the 1820s was already writing of the need for careful
observation, exact quantification and dispassionate analysis of
society, while coining such phrases as 'social physics' to describe
his concerns. History composed in accordance with scientific standards was becoming for some an explicit ideal at about the same
time, as we shall shortly observe; and economics appeared even
more susceptible to the quantifying, if not yet the abstractly mathematical, aspects of scientific methodology.

In the light of this obvious carry-over into other disciplines, it
seems ironic that the period we are discussing should have seen
the first clear signs of a split in the world of learning, between
scientists on the one hand and, on the other, those scholars who
clung to the verbal and individualizing preoccupations of what
they saw as the 'humane' thinker. This confusion over the boundaries of the humanities, born of a forgetfulness concerning the
central place of science in the tradition of man-centred knowledge,
continues to plague us today. It can be blamed in part on
historians, belletristic authors, classicists and others who have
shown themselves too lazy or too self-satisfied to recognize in
scientific rigour one of the highest qualities of human thought, and
in scientific progress towards our doubtless never-to-be-complete
understanding of the world a cultural achievement having implications for history, literature and the other arts as well.

In part also, however, the schism which was appearing in the
early nineteenth century was the fault of the scientists themselves.
Even though many did not, as some did, heap scorn on literature's fascination with the idiosyncratic and on history as uncomprehending narration, scientists nevertheless tended increasingly
to draw apart in a sort of international fraternity – or to be more
accurate, a number of distinct fraternities, as special fields prolif-
erated within science itself. The French *Ecole Polytechnique*, the
German universities and *Technische Hochschulen* made the scientist
a professor, but he was becoming a special kind of professor who
concentrated on his seminars for advanced students and often
seemed to care more for his correspondence with fellow specialists
in other cities and other nations than for conversation with his
non-scientific colleagues at home. A broader, more generous

conception of humane learning remained available, as it still does, to help pull together a culture increasingly splintered by the centrifugal force of expanding knowledge, but no one looking back on the age of Monge and Lagrange and Joseph Fourier, of Berzelius and Gauss and Lyell can fail to appreciate the intensity of the force as such.

One area of European culture that felt the shock of science with special acuteness was traditional religion. The dispute between Cuvier and Geoffroy Saint-Hilaire over fixity versus metamorphosis of species became, for a conservative theologian, an agonizingly important confrontation in which Cuvier *had* to be right if adoration of God's role as a perfect Creator was to survive. The success of a chemist such as Wöhler in synthesizing an organic substance (urea) carried an implicit challenge to the most sacrosanct assumptions about the nature of life itself. But not even biological research had such startling implications for religion as did geological inquiry. The geologist was probing the very history of the planet, not as a sudden construction by the God of Genesis but as the work of heat and cold, of water and air that could only be envisaged as having consumed prodigious amounts of time. If Hutton and Lyell and their fellow uniformitarians were right, if man could understand how the globe on which he lived had assumed its present form simply by observing processes still going on, what was left of the drama of Creation? Modern theology had as yet barely begun to grope towards a conception of God and the world sophisticated enough to co-exist with this merciless destroyer of 'old truths', the scientist.

If the spiritual side of existence was rocked by the advance of the sciences, the other, material, side showed curiously little effect, at least for the time being. That the political history of this period should have been quite separate from the scientific is easy to accept; but most students are surprised to find a comparable lack of connection between science and that other powerful complex of changes, the Industrial Revolution. Yet it is true that technology seemed to have a distinct chronology and a practical, inventive, largely non-theoretical life of its own. Like most generalizations, the above is subject to qualification. In the 1780s, for example, the great French chemist, Count Berthollet, applied the experimentally established bleaching properties of chlorine to a textile industry previously burdened with the need to bleach cloth on sunning frames in open fields; and in 1816 Sir Humphrey

Davy, relying partly on his theoretical knowledge of combustion, invented a miners' safety lamp which would not ignite subterranean gases because of metal gauze screening the oil flame.

Nevertheless, it would be easy to exaggerate the number and significance of such exceptions. Thus, while James Watt knew of Joseph Black's discovery of 'latent heat' in the 1760s, there is no evidence that Watt required any such concept in order to develop the separate condenser for his improved steam engine – experience with the old Newcomen engine was all he needed. Even such important discoveries as the method for extracting soda from seawater (patented by Nicolas Leblanc at Paris in 1791), or the usefulness of large leaden vessels for the economical production of sulphuric acid, came not from the laboratories of pure science but from direct, empirically based efforts to meet felt needs of the chemical industry itself. The findings of scientists with respect to electricity, magnetism, thermodynamics, molecular structure, botany, geology and many other subjects would in time revolutionize industry, agriculture and mining, to say nothing of communications; but that revolution still lay well ahead, beyond 1830 and the purview of the present volume.

HISTORIOGRAPHY

The period we have been studying, important to the historian for its social, ethical and scientific thought, witnessed one further development at once original and portentous: the birth of history as both a separate discipline and a profession. Several different influences and impulses combined to produce this phenomenon. Once achieved, the emergence of history as an object for systematic inquiry and, still more, of 'historicism' as an intellectual stance had sweeping implications for modern thought in general.

Throughout most of the nineteenth century, and well into the twentieth, the *eighteenth* was so regularly, and wrongly, dismissed as 'anti-historical' that more recent writing may actually have gone too far in the opposite direction, underestimating the changes in this field which did come only in the late 1700s and especially in the early 1800s. We are regularly reminded today that learned Benedictine monks and other early archivists had been assembling documentary collections for decades before Voltaire's *Age of Louis XIV* offered, in 1752, a novel conception of cultural history, that Montesquieu had written some ancient, and Hume some British, history, that Gibbon's *Decline and Fall of the Roman Empire* (1776–88) still stands as a towering, if idiosyncratic, classic. All this is true; it is important not to underestimate either the Enlightenment's historical reach or its grasp. Nevertheless, it is equally necessary to recognize that when dealing with the past most eighteenth-century writers showed less genuine empathy than antiquarian curiosity, the latter often guided by didactic purpose. For some of them, including Rousseau and Condorcet, history was not strictly speaking a field of inquiry at all, but instead a canvas on which to present the vast theoretical designs they hoped would shape mankind's response to contemporary conditions.

No doubt the easiest to identify among several stimuli to the reconstruction of history for its own sake was the challenge of the Revolutionary-Napoleonic epoch itself, the call to interpret the present at least partly in the light of the past. Burke tried his hand at some French history in his *Reflections* of 1790, though this was far from being the essay's strongest feature. Maistre, the counter-revolutionary émigré, was by no means unskillful in his use of historical arguments designed to link the Revolution with the Reformation and other past challenges to authority; and he used history to lecture aristocrats on their impiety, sloth and ignorance. On the other side, in defence of the Revolution, French writers such as the journalists, Adolphe Thiers and François Mignet, both of whom began publishing histories in 1823, offered detailed arguments based on the record of their own times. Thus, well before 1830 the great debate over the Revolution, destined to engage Michelet, Tocqueville and many after them, was in full swing.

Certain other influences fed the growth of historical interest, without relating directly to the events of the age. One of these was the upsurge in archaeology and in fascination with systematic exploration – as opposed to literary admiration – of classical and pre-classical antiquity. This effort received its greatest lift from Napoleon's doomed expedition to Egypt in 1798. The future emperor had with him several French archaeologists, who stayed on in the Nile valley and delta for several years after General

Bonaparte had slipped home to become first consul. It was a squad of soldiers working for them who in 1799 uncovered at Rosetta, near Alexandria, a stone bearing inscriptions in Greek, ancient Egyptian hieroglyphic and 'demotic' (or shorthand) hieroglyphic characters. Not until 1822 was it made clear by Champollion that the two Egyptian texts were identical in meaning with the Greek (a section of dynastic chronicle from the Ptolemaic period); but once that guess proved correct, the deciphering of Egyptian records suddenly unlocked a whole world of history. The thrill of excitement that ran through educated society in Europe at the finding of this magic key was comparable to that inspired in our own day by photographs and geological samples brought back from the surface of the moon.

It was the classical world of the Greeks and Romans, however, that continued to grip most firmly the modern imagination. The two-volume *History of Rome* published in 1811–12 by a lecturer at the University of Berlin, Barthold Georg Niebuhr, was a major attempt to get beyond both Gibbon's polemics and the long-revered Livy's inaccuracies to a 'scientific' recovery of the Roman drama, from pre-Republican origins to the end of the Empire. Niebuhr was no stylist; but especially in his much expanded second edition of 1827–32, after further research during a seven-year sojourn as Prussia's emissary to the Vatican, he added greatly to his era's understanding of Roman legal, political and social institutions.

By the time Niebuhr published his first edition, the other branch of classical history, that dealing with Greece, could boast some striking advances of its own. The eighteenth century, like the middle ages and the Renaissance, had of course nourished strong views concerning ancient Hellas. Rousseau had surprised his fellow-Encyclopedists by praising disciplined, unphilosophical Sparta over Athens; and Goethe's entire life, from his youthful sense of 'Germanness' in the 1770s through his discovery of Italy (both old and new) to the form and values of the second, 'classical' part of *Faust*, was in one sense a long pilgrimage back to the civilization of Greek antiquity. In 1805 the poet published *Winckelmann and His Century*, a tribute to the scholar whose *History of Ancient Art* (1764) had done so much to inspire interest in Egyptian, Etruscan, Roman and, above all, Greek aesthetics. In the 1820s, with the Greek War of Independence, that interest soared higher still, as Lord Byron hailed:

The isles of Greece, the isles of Greece!
Where burning Sappho loved and sung . . .
Eternal summer gilds them yet.

(Don Juan, Canto III, Stanza 86)

This continued, and indeed intensifed, reverence for classical antiquity needs to be stressed, not least because our period might otherwise appear to have been wholly in the thrall of another, more novel historical awakening: the rediscovery of the middle ages. The romantics' fascination with what they took to be a world at once orderly and colourful, that of the medieval church and feudal-manorial society, has already been mentioned in connection with their political and social ideas. But there was more to it than a mere rejection of the Revolution's levelling tendencies, or a revulsion against the ugliness they saw in modern cities, factories and parliaments. Here again the eighteenth century had bequeathed several important themes. Giambattista Vico's regard for the *spirit* of once-scorned ages past, Herder's love of the old 'folk language' enshrined in Alsatian idiom, Justus Möser's exaltation of the annals and the customs of his home town in Lower Saxony (*Osnabrückische Geschichte,* 1768 ff.) all had emphasized the value to be found in Europe's history between the age of Rome and that of the Renaissance.

By the early nineteenth century, older collections of medieval charters, edicts and other 'diplomas' were being supplemented by ambitious new projects in the field of documentary recovery, editing and publication, best typified by the *Monumenta Germaniae Historica* launched in 1823 by the Hanoverian archivist, G. H. Pertz, with the active support of the old Prussian reform minister, Baron vom und zum Stein. Here, of course, we perceive the force of patriotism as a motive for antiquarian delving. The same motive, combined with a passion for order and symmetry, would soon, under the July Monarchy, inspire French scholars to catalogue documents of the middle ages and the Old Régime resting in scores of departmental and municipal archives.

The marked increase in the volume of archaeological and documentary sources available in the first years of the new century has moved certain observers to relate this phenomenon to the Industrial Revolution. It may be true that, for better or for worse, some modern historians have been satisfied to take the supply of raw material at hand and to convert it into a finished, marketable product by sifting and smelting, moulding parts and ultimately assembling them in accordance with a preconceived pattern or blueprint. That, however, is scarcely an adequate description of how most history is written. Much more influential – leaving aside the impulse to nurture history as an accepted form of literature – have been two other preoccupations, one scientific, the other philosophical, which are still as influential, despite countless mutations, as they became in the first decades of the nineteenth century with the mature Hegel and the youthful Ranke.

The philosophical attempt to define the structure of human history and to characterize the process it embodies is older than the scientific effort to recreate the past according to the canons of a new discipline. For present purposes, I must relegate to the sphere of theology such medieval visions of Providence working through history as St Augustine's *City of God*, in which mortal strivings and errors are only dim reflections of the true drama of redemption from sin, the divine offer of salvation and the final triumph of Christ's second coming. I must also set aside certain other figures, notably Vico at the beginning of the eighteenth century, who, however suggestive of later concerns, were not representative of any major intellectual movements in their own times. Instead, let me suggest that the search for a philosophy of history, as process, began only in the late 1700s and was to a remarkable degree concentrated in Germany.

The German thinkers of this period included some whose chief contributions lay in their insistence on 'understanding' (*Verstehen*) at the highest, or at least most general, level of abstraction. Some of these men, including Wilhelm von Humboldt (1767–1835), proceeded from many of the rational, individualistic assumptions of the Enlightenment. Others, above all Humboldt's colleague in the University of Berlin, Schleiermacher, clung to a more explicitly theological outlook – not Augustinian, but dedicated to explaining God to man by every available means, including the penetration of history's workings. A rather different contribution, less abstract but more substantial in its multifaceted richness, was that of Herder, in his *Ideas for the Philosophy of Human History* (1784–91).

Once again, however, it was the mind of Immanuel Kant that produced the questions and suggested the answers ensuing generations were to find especially stimulating, if at times exasperating. In his essay, *An Idea for a Universal History from the Cosmopolitan Point of View* (1784), Kant examines the natural laws governing human acts, which were in his terms 'phenomenal' – not the 'noumena' that lie beyond the reach of practical evaluation. Almost inevitably, having adopted such language, he slipped into the highly debatable identification of historical with scientific laws. Equally important, however, he strove to give meaning to history by falling back on two of his favourite general concepts: (1) the idea of freedom as man's ability to shape laws for himself on the basis of reason applied to historical experience, and (2) the possibility of progress through the conflict or collision of egoism, lust and ignorance with the reasoned responses of a humanity gradually becoming surer of its way. Here, as in so many other connections, Kant's piquancy lay in the coupling of his generally gloomy view of human nature with his positive assertions about the power of reason to educate men and women in self-discipline. This message he formulated abstractly, but its relevance to the chaotic world of Europe after 1789 is not hard to recognize.

The younger generation of German historical thinkers influenced by Kant included Friedrich Schiller, whose inaugural discourse as a professor at Jena in 1789 took the form of a lecture on universal history – what it is and why we study it. The great poet's answers include a genuine historicist's appeal to recapture, through research and vicarious understanding, all we can learn of past societies, their religious beliefs, artistic values and social structure, as well as their wars and politics. Less future-oriented than Kant, he saw the present, however imperfect, as the final stage of human progress about which a student of history could justifiably offer opinions. That is to say, the future might well hold further promise, but it was not of a kind even the most 'philosophical' historian could pretend to delineate.

In another of these contemplative Germans, F. W. J. Schelling, especially in his *System of Transcendental Idealism* (1800), we encounter in its purest form the idealistic view of history, namely, that it is, along with nature, one of the two expressions of the Absolute – perhaps most aptly described as pure Reason at work in the world – and that it is compounded of the intelligible thoughts and actions of intelligent beings. This conception (which, like the rest of its author's systematic Idealism, was to have a particularly strong influence upon the nineteenth-century

Russian intelligentsia) dignified both mankind and its history. However, the limitations of such a credo when applied to the reconstruction of real thoughts and actions, often irrational and even unintelligible, account for Schelling's failure to shape western historical thought, despite all his insistence that the Absolute could, in one or another of its manifestations, be found everywhere in action.

The culminating figure in this German idealistic school of historical philosophy, of course, was Hegel; and his published lectures on the *Philosophy of History* (1822–23) may be taken as that school's most sweeping pronouncement. The Swabian sage, some of whose political views, themselves strongly shaped by historical tenets, we have already noted in passing, was indebted to Kant for the importance of 'antinomies', that is, of conflicts and collisions of ideas in history. However, unlike both Kant and Schelling, he denied that history and nature are related as to their laws and structures. Nature, he insisted, knows only the repetition of phenomena in cycles or in recurrences that may be complex but are nonetheless predictable if we know all we need to about the conditions and the variables involved. This was helpful to some of the experimental chemists of the day, notably to Liebig (*see above*, p. 374), but not to the pre-Darwinian biologists searching for a dynamic principle of evolution.

History, on the other hand, was for Hegel neither aimless nor even cyclical. Instead it was the record of human *thought*, progressing across the centuries towards greater and greater rationality, which in turn constitutes true freedom of the will. The process he perceived was not a direct, linear advance, but instead a dialectical one of theses or motivating ideas generating their own antitheses and of the syntheses resulting from such conflicts becoming new theses, each capable in its turn or eliciting a new antithesis.

Whereas Hegel owed much to Kant, and presumably to Schelling, with respect to his historical idealism, he shared with Schiller the belief that the dialectical process he was describing must be seen as eventuating in the present. That process, as was to be pointed out in attacks on Marx's later adaptation of it, *need* not be seen as ending at any particular stage or point in time; and both theorists have been criticized for setting their own, by no means self-evident, terms for arbitrarily ending the game, so to speak. To Marx the end would be the classless society, the proletarian thesis become final synthesis. To Hegel, quite unnecessarily from a philosophical point of view, the emerging pattern of national state power, especially as embodied in the Prussian monarchy, promised the realization of full freedom of the rational will under recognized and accepted discipline. Perhaps if he had shared Schiller's vision of history as concerned with much besides law or politics, Hegel might have seen his own times as part of an ongoing experience, more complex than his dialectic perhaps, but no less interesting.

Less as a reaction against philosophical idealism applied to history than as an effort to satisfy history's own demands for knowledge and objectivity, another strand of Germany's great contribution in this period began to appear in the 1820s. We have already seen how archaeology and the spreading interest in documentary collections had been providing more and more source material for students of the past. On the other hand, the works of Thiers, Mignet and other chroniclers of the Revolution seemed to challenge the very possibility of history's being written without partisan bias.

It would be difficult to imagine a complete and candid interesting work of history which avoided all acknowledgement of the author's point of view; but in Leopold von Ranke we encounter a man neither committed to methaphysical theorizing nor abjectly imitative of scientific canons, yet determined to reconstruct as fully and fairly as possible the narrative to be found in the great archival centres of Berlin, Vienna, Venice, Rome, Paris and elsewhere. His often quoted (and frequently misconstrued) promise that he would seek to write history 'as it really was' appeared in the preface to his first major work, *The History of the Latin and Germanic Peoples from 1494 to 1535*, which appeared in 1824 and the next year won the young Saxon-born teacher in Frankfurt-on-the-Oder an adjunct professorship at the University of Berlin.★ The study, as its title indicates, was a fresh appraisal of the Reformation, seen in the context of the European state system and set against the background of differing 'Romance', i.e. Latin, and Teutonic civilizations. The goal of recreating objective reality in carefully documented detail (*not* of achieving total recall, which

---

★ A thoughtful and informed discussion on the famous phrase *wie es eigentlich gewesen* appears in F. Gilbert, 'What Ranke Meant', *The American Scholar*, volume 56 (1987), pp. 393–7.

he recognized as impossible) would sustain Ranke through a long lifetime of research and writing and made him, among other things, the first man to earn a substantial income as a professional historian.

As has already been suggested, Ranke was not detached from the times in which he lived. His next major publication after the *Latin and Germanic Peoples* was a timely book on *The Serbian Revolution* (1828); and in the 1830s he became what amounted to a political journalist, albeit an exceedingly scholarly one, as he attacked the revival of French revolutionary influences. The latter he detested above all because history was for him a story about states, powers – despite the rather misleading reference to 'peoples' in the title of his maiden work. Years later, in 1871, when Germany's Second Empire was founded under Bismarck's leadership, Ranke would hail the end of the 'revolutionary episode' as though history itself had in some sense been interrupted for eighty-two years. Yet this deeply conservative observer of his age, who is reliably reported to have been called to a chair in Berlin in 1825 by the hated censor of German academic life, Kamptz, to counteract liberal agitiation,[10] never abandoned his quest to objective erudition. In fact, even he expressed worry over the Prussian censorship in the 1820s and chose to have his own works published in Saxony. It must be added that his judgement of *individuals* in history, regardless of their nationality or religion, was remarkable for its balance and fairness.

Ranke's colleague at Berlin in 1825 (and for five years thereafter, before moving to Halle) was Heinrich Leo, a former *Burschenschaftler*, an admirer of Hegel, a devoted historian of medieval Italy, an advocate of ecumenical peace among Christian denominations and a vehement opponent of Ranke. Scorning 'source criticism' as a method, Leo sought instead a total grasp of cultural history. Before the middle of the nineteenth century, he was to become, in strictly political terms, more conservative than Ranke; but in the 1820s he opposed his famous rival on grounds both of vaguely defined 'progressivism' and of distaste for what he considered the mechanistic approach of archival specialists.

It is tempting today to applaud Leo for having criticized scientific history, since we are apt to judge the latter by the arrogance of some of Ranke's disciples. But Ranke himself was distinctly cautious about scientism; and his methodological rigour, his energy, his patience, his search for basic themes in political history all combine to justify the attention he continues to receive from students of the nineteenth-century European mind. If we find his ideas dated, this is because they presupposed a political and diplomatic structure we no longer accept as an ideal; but the same would be true of a modern scientist judging, while still respecting, the ideas of a Laplace, a Cuvier or for that matter, reaching still further back in time, a Newton.

NOTES AND REFERENCES

1 A. Cobban, ed., *The Debate on the French Revolution*, 2nd edn (London, 1963), p. 379.

2 K. Jaspers, *The Great Philosophers*, tr. R. Manheim (New York, 1962), p. 355.

3 F. Manuel, *The Prophets of Paris* (Cambridge, Mass., 1962).

4 Translated by Klaus Epstein in J. Hexter, ed., *The Traditions of the Western World* (Chicago, 1967), pp. 542–3.

5 A. Cobban, ed., *The Debate on the French Revolution*, 2nd edn (London, 1960), p. 415.

6 Quoted in F. Artz, *Reaction and Revolution* (New York–London, 1934), p. 209.

7 D. McKie in *The New Cambridge Modern History*, vol. VIII, p. 136.

8 C. Gillispie in *The New Cambridge Modern History*, vol. IX, *passim*.

9 The most important recent survey of scientific debates in this period, with emphasis on biology, is E. Mayr, *The Growth of Biological Thought; Diversity, Evolution and Inheritance* (Cambridge, Mass., 1982).

10 M. Lenz, *Geschichte der Königlichen Friedrich-Wilhelms Universität zu Berlin* (Halle, 1910), vol. II, pp. 255–7.

14

SOCIETY AND CULTURE IN 1830

This chapter is shorter than those that have preceded it, for two reasons. First, we are now looking backward; and while the present volume may serve to introduce its readers to mid-nineteenth-century conditions, it cannot pretend to give a comprehensive overview of things to come. Second, our journey from 1780 to 1830 had best end with attention paid to a quite specific question, namely, to what extent and in what ways had European society and culture *changed* between those two dates? Was our particular half-century just an arbitrary slice of time cut from an ongoing chronicle? Or can it also claim to have witnessed a transformation in forms and values so crucial as to make the revolutionary-Napoleonic era a true turning point in the history of the peoples of Europe? Several different kinds of analysis may help to answer that question.

THE GROWTH AND DISTRIBUTION OF POPULATION

We have already observed that the rise in population continued apace from the eighteenth on into the nineteenth century (*see above*, pp. 305–7). A Europe of some 230 million inhabitants in 1830 was bound to differ in many important respects from one of perhaps 165–170 million in 1780. This was especially true because by the second quarter of the nineteenth century these added millions had made their presence felt especially in the cities.

At the end of our period, to be sure, even the largest of Europe's urban centres had not wholly lost the character of congeries of small towns only partially absorbed by the 'metropolitan sprawl' of London and Paris, Vienna and Berlin. Yet such cities were on the way to acquiring their modern form as vast organisms destined, as Oswald Spengler would remark in the twentieth century, to have more traits in common one with another than any shared with the provincial towns of its own country. Numerous men and women who were children in 1830 lived out their entire lives within the confines of these huge municipalities, often without ever having seen the countryside save on rare and fleeting occasions.

Wealth there was in the city, for those who controlled the factories and for the suppliers of goods needed by the swelling ranks of urban dwellers. But for many more there was only the misery of smoke and filth and disease – and the constant, nerve-racking dread of unemployment. As Robert Southey wrote in his *Colloquies* of 1829:

The new cottages [stand] naked, in a row. How is it, said I, that every thing which is connected with manufactures presents such features of deformity? . . . Time cannot mellow them; Nature will neither clothe nor conceal them; and they remain always as offensive to the eye as to the mind.[1]

Southey shared this distaste with other nature-lovers such as Chateaubriand in France and Novalis in Germany, but it touched as well certain non-aesthetic social critics and journalists. Robert Owen's real, and Charles Fourier's imaginary, workers' colonies were conceived partly out of a desire to escape the worst features of urban concentration. For William Cobbett, in his *Political Register* of 12 July 1817, it was the contrast between potential natural wealth and actual poverty that was most shocking:

Here are the resources! Here is the wealth! Here are all the means of national power, and of individual plenty and happiness! And yet, at the end of these ten beautiful miles, covered with all the means of affording luxury in diet and in dress, we entered that city of Coventry, which, out of *twenty thousand inhabitants*, contained at that very moment upward of *eight thousand miserable paupers*.[2]

This quotation from Cobbett suggests a condition which by 1830 was one of two especially striking features of urban life in relation to that of fifty years before. The poor had known hunger, disease and idleness in eighteenth-century cities, as the drawings of Hogarth alone suffice to prove. But previous fluctuations in lower-class income – as between low wages and actual destitution – had been less abrupt than those resulting from the factory system. The extremes of affluence and misery generated with ‑bewildering speed by that system seemed more cruel even than the endemic inequities of an earlier day.

The second contrast between 1780 and 1830 arose from the fact that whatever its failings, and they were many, the Old Régime's complex of guilds and parishes had provided, with the family, a set of crude cushions against absolute hopelessness for most inhabitants. It was the apparent loss of even the most rudimentary sense of social responsibility that aroused critics of the new economic order and would lead Marx and Engels, at least part of the time, to wax as nostalgic as the most romantic admirer of the middle ages. A classical economist, on the other hand, could argue from Malthus (*see above*, pp. 364–5) not only that wages *should* be low and employment precarious but also that alms represented nothing more than social folly. This presumably applied to the agrarian poor, driven by enclosure from common lands, no less than to city workers.

Considering the background of rising population, rural want and urban problems, one might expect to encounter massive emigration to other lands throughout the early nineteenth century. Here, however, we must take care; the picture is not that simple. For one thing, poverty will not by itself make emigrants of people lacking the means required to pay travel costs. Furthermore, the American economic crisis of 1819 and settlers' reports home concerning the harsh, uncertain conditions of life in the young United States, the parallel findings of emigrants sent to Canada under official British auspices and the suffering of Germans in Brazil, or along the lower Danube, en route to the Russian Caucasus, all served to discourage many who might otherwise have left their homes in Europe. Specific disasters, such as the 'famine summer' of 1822 in Ireland and the winter floods of 1825 in the Rhineland, produced periodic surges of emigration; but compared to what lay ahead, they were brief in duration and limited in scale.

In 1830, following a dreadful winter for virtually all of Europe and amid equally bitter political and social upheavals in many lands, the great 'Atlantic migration', as one economic historian has called it, was about to enter an unprecedented phase.[3] Through the early 1820s, Tsar Alexander's Polish dominions had seemed more attractive to emigrants, especially Germans, than had the United States. So, for shorter periods, had Brazil and Canada and the Caucasus, though no reliable statistics are available. As the decade ended, however, a dramatic change was taking place. American industry was beginning to organize itself, demanding in the process a greatly increased labour force and at the same time guaranteeing a somewhat more hospitable welcome than it had previously shown recruits from Europe. The movement beginning about 1830 is best illustrated by the fact that the number of westbound transatlantic passengers during the next ten years was *five times* the corresponding figure for the 1820s. By 1900 some 35 million people would have made the crossing to the United States alone. After a complicated history of false starts and disillusionments, the westward rush was on, contrasting sharply with the relatively cautious attitude towards emigration still typical of the early nineteenth century.

SOME ASPECTS OF DAILY LIFE

Although details of food and dress and manners can sometimes amuse without revealing much that is fundamental to history, the latter would be cold and inhuman if it ignored the most mundane, but also the most tangible, features of life in the past. A brief excursion into day-to-day social reconstruction is therefore necessary before we touch upon higher realms of culture as commonly defined. Changes in what people wear, what they eat and what they say or do in ordinary social intercourse reveal other, often more elusive, features of human existence: hopes, tastes, estimates of others, conceptions of comfort, security and personal success.

The dress of aristocrats and of upper income groups in general is of course the easiest to study, not only because such clothing was shown in fashion magazines at the time but also because the garments' intrinsic value led to their survival in museums and private collections. The changes between 1780 and 1830 in the case of well-to-do women's apparel can best be summarized by contrasting the high, elaborate wigs and sweeping satin or brocaded gowns of Marie Antoinette and her entourage with the very different silhouette of ladies in 1830. During the intervening period, the 1790s had witnessed, at least in France and French-dominated Europe, some extreme affectations, including near nudity of bosoms and thin, streaming gowns, while the succeeding Empire style, though more chaste in its use of opaque materials and simple sheath skirts, had retained high waists and very low necklines. By the end of our period, however, this classical model had yielded to something quite different: a lateral emphasis on bare shoulders (for evening) above high, straight necklines, pleated and ruffled leg-of-mutton sleeves, wasp waists and wide, flaring skirts, built out over pantaloons and crinoline underskirts of horsehair or stiff cotton. Women's hair styles in the 1820s had replaced the curls or natural coiffures of the Empire with topknots, often elaborated to form bizarre rolls, wings and horns. These were still to be seen in 1830, but the topknots had become simpler and were in some cases being wholly replaced by curls or rolls over the ears. Millinery, on the other hand, had reached one of its extremes of variety and fancy, ribbon-bedecked straws and wide-brimmed hats of flowers vying with all manner of lacy caps and bonnets.

The 'high style' for men had also changed markedly. If the excesses of French dandies (*Incroyables*) under the Directory and of Beau Brummel's English imitators under the Regency were no more to be seen, neither were the tricorns, bicorns and various forms of cocked hat, the colourful satin suits with knee breeches (as in Gainsborough's 'Blue Boy') or the expansive, embroidered waistcoats of the 1780s. Instead, the favoured costume for the affluent male now tended to combine a double-breasted tail coat or cutaway of sombre hue, lighter-coloured long trousers, a high collar with cravat or scarf and a top hat, usually with a rolled brim and flaring crown. Powdered wigs had largely disappeared, save for ceremonial use and for regular wear by certain stubborn old-sters. More popular now was free falling-hair, long but not queued, for those who fancied themselves romantics, and for most other men, short-cut hair with a curled forelock piled up in front. Relatively few moustaches and still fewer beards were to be seen at this time; but sideburns lacking that name as yet, and usually more slender than bushy, were in vogue.

No glimpse of *haute couture*, of course, would in itself suffice to distinguish the earliest from the latest years included in our survey. Throughout history, the dress of farmers and workmen has changed less drastically than that of people having sufficient money and leisure to follow the fashions. Nevertheless, we know from sketches and written accounts that shorter hair and either breeches or trousers were supplanting the manes or queues and the smocks or aprons of eighteenth-century labourers. Lower-class women wore simple bonnets or caps little influenced by the millinery explosions in Mayfair, the Tuileries or Charlottenburg; but these same women, as compared with their grandmothers, had adopted simpler – and in summer cooler – clothes, with cloaks or short capes when needed. Their plain skirts and aprons lacked the bulk rather puzzlingly apparent in even the humblest of eighteenth-century costumes.

What of the middle classes? At this point there emerges a significant fact, noted by virtually all historians of dress, namely, that the difference in clothing between aristocratic and comfortable, but non-noble, groups in society was becoming less and less apparent. To be sure, almost anyone could still have told, simply by looking at those present, whether he or she was at a dinner in Vienna's Esterházy palace or in the town house of an Austrian banker, at a garden party given by the duke of Saxe-Weimar or one arranged by the newly enriched Krupps of Essen. Yet the contrast was not so striking as it would have been, in 1780, between princely and bourgeois gatherings. In part, no doubt this reflected a decline in acceptance of the high nobility's theoretical *separateness* from the rest of society, as opposed to the *superiority* in degree that was still generally conceded. But it also revealed the effects of mass production in the field of textiles. Whatever the cause or causes, by 1830 European clothing characteristically drew less of a distinction between the titled and the non-titled than between the well-to-do and the poor. Even in the case of cotton cloth, unquestionably a boon to all but the most deprived levels of society, there remained a great difference between fine muslin or poplin on the one hand and coarse denim on the other.

Changes in the European diet – or better, diets – are more difficult to define in general terms than are those in dress. However, at least three features of our period deserve notice. One was the increase in availability and consumption of starchy and/or sweet foods. The production of cereal grains was rising steeply:

rye in the Junker estates of eastern Germany, wheat in Bavaria, northern Italy, southern France and England, maize (Indian corn) in the Danube valley, oats in Scotland. Even before the great influx of Russian and American grain in the second half of the nineteenth century, the flour used in bread, cakes, noodles and porridge was being milled at a rate which, save for the very worst years, appears to have been gaining on even a rising population.

Meanwhile, as earlier noted, the potato was at or near its high point of relative importance. This very popularity and intensive cultivation, however, brought certain dangers, as revealed by the Irish famine of 1822. For the potato, like any other inbred organism, could and did develop diseases of its own; and even this hardy ground dweller was not immune to periodic freezes, floods or droughts. The suffering in Ireland, if truth be told, seemed at first to have provided only a brief and all too easily forgotten warning. Not until the more protracted, as well as more wide-spread, potato famines of the 1840s would the possible tragedy implicit in excessive reliance on a single food source lead Euro-peans to diversify somewhat their pattern of edible crops. Still, when one considers the dependence on potatoes and bread in most of Europe even today, one arrives at some idea of the importance attached to carbohydrates a century and a half ago.

Increased availability of starches, combined with the rise of sugar imports from the American canefields and in beet sugar production at home, suggests that that non-existent figure, the average European, may have been hungry less often in 1830 than his grandparents had been in 1780, but that he was not necessarily any healthier. From a nutritional standpoint, the really significant changes – a substantial rise in the consumption of proteins and a purposeful increase in the serving of fresh fruits and garden vegetables when available – awaited greater knowledge about diet, which came to northern and western Europe around the middle of the nineteenth century, and to the south and east considerably later than that. In 1830 an egg or a 'bit of meat' was still a rarity for a large proportion of the European population; and while the tomato's slow rise towards popularity continued, many potential users clung to an old belief in its poisonous nature.

A second feature of dietary history, the importance of regional variations, can be noted only briefly here. The *average* Englishman or Englishwoman probably had more pudding and a little more meat than did his or her counterpart in northern France. The latter in turn could depend on more, and better cooked, fresh vegetables. Most Italians had to make up in cereal *pasta* what they lacked in virtually all meats save poultry or veal and sausages padded with flour and garlic. Gruel or porridge was common almost everywhere for the poor; but while the Russian or Bulgarian might add onions or leeks, and the Pole a scrap of pork rind, a Dane was more likely to have on the side some cheese with a hen's or duck's egg, while the Alsatian or south-west German would turn to cabbage, especially in the form of sauerkraut. Salt fish was consumed in varying quantities almost everywhere in Europe; but the beverages used to wash it down differed considerably, depending on the region. Larger quantities of beer than of wine were consumed in most of north and central Europe, more wine than beer in the south and south-west; for, aside from the special case of Great Britain's reliance on imported port, sack, hock and claret, the beer and wine 'trade' was still in its infancy. The recently increased system of canals might have served; but in fact neither brewing, distilling nor wine-making would emerge as an important industry, pitched to national and foreign markets, until the coming of the railway and the steamship. In 1830, a well-stocked cellar remained one of the surest signs of uncommon taste *and* affluence.

The third characteristic of food as a feature of our period's social history is particularly significant, in that it demonstrates a parallel with the record of clothing. This is the distinction between wealth and poverty, as opposed to that between social ranks traditionally defined in legal or honorific terms. In Russia, for example, great aristocrats, merchants and government officials seem to have adopted tea-drinking as a regular practice by the end of Alexander I's reign; yet the Russian masses would scarcely know this exotic beverage for another half-century. Berlin's courtiers, army officers, bankers, merchants and bureaucrats might enjoy Rhenish wines and Dutch cheeses, as well as dinner *à la française*, and then consume jelly-cakes and cream buns with coffee or chocolate later in the evening, while their humbler fellow subjects ate, usually at midday, a collation of gruel or rye bread, potatoes and perhaps some lard or salt pork, helped along by thin beer. In France, where eighteenth-century cookbooks had carefully distinguished the *cuisine bourgeoise* from the *cuisine des grands* (aristocrats), the well-to-do in cities and chateaux now enjoyed, without regard to rank or calling, a diet whose refinement bore little or no relation to the bread and cider of a Norman farm hand or the fish stew and sour wine of a longshoreman on the Mediterranean coast.

A society divided into a reduced number of crudely defined categories was bound to show, in manners as in food and dress, fewer distinctions and less exact indicators of status than had that of the Old Régime. Yet in the sphere of decorum, of public social behaviour, some fairly obvious gradations did survive the onslaught of class differentiation in terms of wealth or poverty. In most countries there were many representatives of old families who clung to a notion of gentility, of *politesse*, regardless of their economic situation. At the other extreme, even among the rich, noble and non-noble alike, there were numerous self-styled Bohemians (in this sense, 'gypsies') who defied social conventions and showed their self-conscious alienation from tradition by turning for company to thieves, vagabonds and prostitutes, while jeering at the sharp business practices and furtive adulteries of the 'respectable'. Finally, almost everywhere there were subtle barriers of inflection in speech and ease in manner that made it more difficult for the new rich to ignore their background than they had perhaps expected.

These variants in behaviour, if exaggerated, might lead us to underrate the self-confidence of rich men, or to ignore the burden of deference that bore down on poor men and women. It is nevertheless true that while wealth, or a lack of it, set some Europeans apart from others without regard to traditional nuances, a residue of the old society remained. Still to be seen were the supple, witty, often dissolute creatures of princely courts and aristocratic salons. There were equally comfortable but more heavily self-righteous merchants, bankers and government officials, who worshipped the solid bourgeois values, preached honesty (even when they did not always practise it) as preferable to polish, and sternly denounced the lewdness in speech which certain aristocrats sought to share with 'the lower orders'. Lastly, defying assignment in economic terms (which would have placed many of them below skilled labourers), there were hordes of impecunious but orderly clerks, small shopkeepers and minor bureaucrats, the Uriah Heeps of a persistently status-conscious society.

CHANGING THEMES IN ARTS AND LETTERS

For a long time historians almost routinely described the period after 1815 as one dominated by the clash of neoclassical and romantic motifs in the plastic and visual arts, in music and in literature. Just how an allegiance to the discipline, symmetry and monumentalism of the Greco-Roman inheritance could co-exist in a single culture with the more emotional, personal and often, by association, medieval preoccupations of the romantics was not always made very clear. Their reciprocal hostility, however, tended to be taken for granted. An increased familiarity with the shadings and varieties of both neoclassicism and romanticism has helped to illuminate the less tidy but more authentic relationship we can now discern between these powerful schools of taste.

To overdraw the contrast between neoclassical order on the one hand and, on the other, romantic sentimentalism, obscures the ways in which both styles expressed the fascination of Europeans with the faraway, be it antique Greece and Rome or the Gothic middle ages or the 'mysterious East'. True, the classical ideal had since the Renaissance been the more familiar of these standards of reference, and seemingly the more nearly timeless. It was also easier than the romantic to combine with representational realism in art. Take, for example, the Grecian scenes and Napoleonic portraits of the painter J. A. D. Ingres (1780–1867), a student of Jacques-Louis David in Paris but also of Italian masters in Florence and Rome. Yet the exotic and the exaggerated also appear in Ingres's work, notably in the languorous nudes of his Moorish harem scenes. If the long lifetime of Goethe, ending with his death in 1832, was in some of its aspects a journey from pre-romantic enthusiasm to neoclassical restraint, the still longer life of Ingres was an odyssey, at once brilliant and baffling, in the opposite direction. Similar warnings against hasty judgement speak to us from the passionate yet carefully constructed symphonies of Beethoven (1770–1827) – admired by the ageing Goethe even as they were claimed by the romantics, and from the intermingling of stylistic canons in the paintings of Théodore Géricault (1791–1824) and Eugène Delacroix (1798–1863). Note especially Delacroix's 'Liberty', an only partially draped Grecian goddess, rallying top-hatted male insurgents of Paris at the barricades in 1830.

The neoclassical and the romantic, however intertwined, can

still be usefully distinguished by anyone who seeks to visualize the European cultural scene in the early nineteenth century. On every side, it seemed, there loomed Greco-Roman edifices some of them undertaken before the Revolution but many more produced during the generation after Napoleon I made himself a new Caesar. Even a short list of examples serves to remind us of what neoclassicism meant for the architecture of the period: in Paris, Chalgrin's Arch of Triumph (1806–1837), the *Bourse* or stock exchange (1808–26), the Church of Saint Madeleine (started under the old monarchy, but redesigned and recommenced in 1807); in Milan, Cagnola's Arch of Peace (1806 ff.); in London, John Nash's great curving Regent Street (1813 ff.); in Berlin, Schinkel's State Theatre (1818–21) and his Old Museum (1822–28); in Bavaria, Leo von Klenze's Glyptothek or museum of sculpture (1816–30) at Munich and his Parthenon-like 'Valhalla' near Regensburg (begun in 1830).

Spurred by archaeological discoveries, by philhellene rapture during the Greek War of Independence and by the impulse to commemorate military heroics and dynastic triumphs, architects not unnaturally looked for inspiration to the grandeur of ancient Greece and Rome. So too did sculptors such as Antonio Canova (1757–1822) in Italy, Gottfried Schadow (1764–1822) and Christian Rauch (1777–1857) in Prussia, Ludwig Schwanthaler (1802–48) in Bavaria and Bertel Thorwaldsen (1770–1844) in Denmark. Finally, among the painters, after J.-L. David and J.-B. Regnault (1754–1829) came the generation of François Gérard (1770–1837) and P. N. Guérin (1774–1833), Frenchmen who glorified their powerful nation by using allegories from classical antiquity.

Even the less ambitious style called 'Biedermeier' in Germany – a domesticated, bourgeois adaptation of 'Empire' – can best be understood in terms of its relation to more imposing models of neoclassical dignity and balance. The term *Biedermeier* (or *Biedermaier*) did not actually appear until 1850, in the title of a book by Ludwig Eichrodt called *Poems of the Swabian Schoolteacher, Gottlieb Biedermaier*; and by then it was already an evocation, at once wistful and gently derisive, of the prudence, docility and limited horizons of German middle-class existence from 1815 until 1848 or even later. In house construction, it connoted simple, boxlike rooms with large windows – no rococo swirls or domes. In home furnishings, it stood for curved, but not ornate, chairs and settees, commonly of cherry wood or mahogany veneer instead of gilt or ivory-painted surfaces. In dress, it dictated sombre colours and modest concealment of ladies' bosoms and men's calves. In manners, it stressed the pleasures of evening coffee or chocolate around the family's round parlour table, of Sunday walks in the local park, of a leisurely clay pipe smoked over the books and magazines in the town's public reading room.

In the case of romanticism too, we can use a set of stylistic assertions and applications to recapture other parts of Europe's varied cultural life, as long as we recognize the immense range of individual traits displayed by the romantics themselves. Just as writers such as Shelley, Keats and, later, Heine, would be impossible to equate with Wordsworth, Novalis or Chateaubriand, in terms of political and religious attitudes, so in visual art, the mystical genius of William Blake (1757–1827), painter, engraver and poet, had little save mystery itself in common with the eerie seascapes and dark woods of his fellow-countryman J. M. W. Turner (1775–1851) or the terrifying 'Black Studies' of Goya in the years of madness preceding his death in 1828. Yet Blake, Turner and Goya all expressed the rejection of measured, classical rationalism. So did several Germans, including the romantic landscape painter, Caspar David Friedrich (1774–1840), and the rebellious student of Schadow, Adolf Schroedter (1805–75), in his jumbled medieval vision of Don Quixote poring over manuscript volumes with a lance tilted against the table next to him.

Nevertheless, in 1830 the full efflorescence of romanticism in painting – the pre-Raphaelites in England, for example, or the medieval scenes of Moritz von Schwind (1804–71) in Germany – still lay in the future, as did the bulk of the Frenchman Honoré Daumier's (1810–79) very unromantic but equally anticlassical caricatures of ancient myths and heroes. Since the Gothic revival in architecture too was only impending at the close of our period, it seems fair to say that neoclassicism, challenged on several sides as it had often been before, continued to hold the high ground on the battlefield of plastic and graphic taste.

A considerably different conclusion emerges when one turns to music. Even allowing for the mixture, earlier noted, of neoclassical and romantic elements in Ludwig van Beethoven's works, musical composition during our fifty-year time span showed an undeniable movement away from abstract rules governing form, towards more personal and often more passionate self-expression by composers and performers alike. It was also an era of larger and larger, though not necessarily more sophisticated, audiences, a time marked by the proliferation of musical societies and construction of spacious, permanent concert halls and opera houses. Like newspapers, journals of opinion and the flood of new novels, to which we shall turn in a moment, the musical performances of the early nineteenth century appealed increasingly to large urban gatherings.

At the beginning of that century, F. J. Haydn (1732–1809), *Kapellmeister* to successive princes Esterházy in Vienna, was Europe's reigning orchestral composer. Since the 1790s, despite his apparent immersion in an aristocratic court culture, Haydn had been producing symphonies, such as the 'Surprise' and the 'Clock', for large London audiences and choral masterpieces for performance primarily in Austria. Both sets of works delighted new masses of admirers. Many of the symphonies were mischievously.amusing; and the oratorios were popular in their appeal – 'The Seasons', for instance, being based on a romantic poem by James Thomson presenting idyllic scenes of peasant life.

It would be a mistake to assume that in becoming broader and more accessible, Haydn's work became a less important influence on other German composers who followed him. His identification with Austria, for example, was in itself enough to make Beethoven emigrate from the Rhineland to Vienna. In 1830 Beethoven had been dead for three years; but his music continued to excite intense controversy. His Ninth (and last) Symphony, first performed in 1824, struck many of the cognoscenti as too elaborate, even wild, to qualify as a great achievement. Yet both the music and the messsage of the 'Ninth', its final movement incorporating a chorale drawn from Schiller's 'Ode to Joy', stirred powerful emotions in countless listeners. Just as his overture to Goethe's *Egmont* in 1811 had caught the spirit of political freedom from that drama of Flemish resistance to Spanish rule, so now the use of Schiller's words permitted Beethoven to salute the ideal of brotherhood among all free men. Though in the 1820s his string quartets were generally, albeit mistakenly, taken to be mere reversions to the formal chamber music of the preceding era, his symphonies and overtures already exercised a growing influence on public taste.

While Haydn and, somewhat less obviously, Mozart had given Beethoven a basis for form on which to build his original structure of genius, another German composer owed the late eighteenth-century masters a debt of a different kind: the ability to elaborate simple melodies into complex vocal arrangements with instrumental accompaniment. This was Franz Schubert (1797–1828), the first and greatest writer of *Lieder*. The hold of these dramatic, and often exceedingly difficult, songs on presentday audiences springs both from admiration for the performers' virtuosity and from fascination with the stories being told. Drawing on poems by Goethe and others, Schubert composed hundreds of *Lieder*, including the haunting *Erlkönig* of 1815; but neither these works nor his 'Unfinished Symphony' (1822) had won full recognition at the time of his death. It was rather as the harbinger of new extensions of romanticism that he figured in the history of our period. The same could be said of Louis Hector Berlioz (1803–69), whose *Symphonie fantastique*, the first major work of the French romantic school, was completed in 1830.

A word more deserves to be said about music, specifically about the continuing success of opera. This was the age of G. Rossini's (1792–1868) greatest successes: *Tancred* (1813), *The Barber of Seville* (1816) and *William Tell* (1829). It was also the age of Karl Maria von Weber (1786–1826), whose *Der Freischütz* in 1821 and *Oberon* in 1826 really started the development of nineteenth-century German opera – as Beethoven's popular, but dramatically less successful, *Fidelio* in 1805 did not. Considering the fact that earlier works, especially those of Mozart and Gluck, continued to be performed on dozens of stages to ever growing audiences, it is easy to appreciate the importance of opera, viewed as a social institution.

When discussing literature, no less than when considering music, one has to see aesthetic achievements partly in relation to a changing society. This is true of romantic poetry in the 1820s, when the lyrics of Keats (1795–1821) and Shelley (1792–1822) in England, like the translations of Ludwig Tieck (1773–1853) and August Wilhelm von Schlegel (1767–1845) in Germany, were opening new vistas of imagination, while the name of Lord Byron (1788–1824) became a household word even in remote corners of Europe. It is perhaps still more emphatically true of a genre which in 1830 was approaching its zenith of popularity and power: the novel.

The rise of this prose form to pre-eminence as the mid-nineteenth century's most significant contribution to world literature has been explained in a number of ways. Its audience, for example, can be shown to have comprised an expanding literate public, one produced by the democratization of at least elementary education in many countries and fed by circulating libraries and journals that featured serialized fiction. To some devotees of eighteenth-century novelists, Defoe, Fielding and Richardson in England, Prévost and Diderot in France, the young Goethe in Germany, the emergence of mass readership and the growing responsiveness of authors and publishers to the demands of popular taste seem in retrospect to have been destructive of literary quality. As from 1830, however, and indeed for some decades thereafter, it would be unfair not to credit the best in novel-writing with a significant enrichment of European letters.

Among all the causes that might be cited for the novel's popularity, two seem particularly relevant to our concerns. The first has to do with the rise of historical awareness, under the dual influence of romanticism and nationalism. Sir Walter Scott (1771–1832), whose *Waverley* appeared in 1814, produced a literally epoch-making series of historical romances, including *Kenilworth* (1821), *Quentin Durward* (1823) and *Ivanhoe* (1825). Across the Channel in France, Prosper Mérimée (1803–70), who was destined to write *Carmen* at mid-century, had in 1828 already published a novel of rebellion, *La Jacquerie*. Not all historico-nationalist enthusiasm was expressed in prose, as witness Alexander Pushkin's epic poem in Russian, *Ruslan and Liudmila* (1820) and his tragedy, *Boris Godunov* (1825), frankly modelled on Shakespeare's history plays. Probably the very best product of this entire movement, however, *was* a novel, Italy's finest drawn from history: *I Promessi sposi* (*The Betrothed*) by Alessandro Manzoni (1785–1873), published in 1825–27. It is in essence a tender love story, but the rich background of seventeenth-century Lombardy under Spanish domination makes it a classic of its kind.

Other countries, lacking a Manzoni, were less fortunate than Italy, perhaps because mere imitation of Scott could not take the place of verve and originality. Thus several emulators of *Waverley* failed in Spain; Tieck's historical novels fell short of real success in Germany; and even certain intrinsically better works, such as the Polish romance, *Jan z Tęczyna* (1825) by J. U. Niemcewicz (1757–1841), and a Hungarian drama laid in the thirteenth century, *Bánk Bán* by József Katona (1798–1830), are less interesting as literature than as evidence of their authors' intense patriotism. The same was true of the Belgian Hendrik Conscience's Flemish romances, the first of which were published in the 1830s. Yet the sheer volume of such efforts is in itself significant.

A different type of novel, concerned with introspection, manners and often tense personal relationships, was also coming into its own in our period – not, be it said at once, without having had precursors in the eighteenth century and even earlier. This brings us to a second explanation for the novel's popularity. The nineteenth century was a time when society was changing in several obvious respects, but when numerous other features, including notions of decorum, still hung on from the past. Thus the evolution of personality, both within itself and in its social setting, held a fascination not difficult for us to appreciate. The novel of personality and of manners employed, usually at any rate, a style that was detached, sometimes almost clinical, rather than empathetic or sentimental. Author joined reader as a cool and often amused, albeit keenly interested, observer of the human condition.

This method Jane Austen (1774–1832) carried to an unrivalled state of polish in her portrayals of middle-class English provincial life: *Pride and Prejudice* (written in 1796–97, but published only in 1813), *Sense and Sensibility* (1797–98, published in 1811), and several later novels, including her most subtle, *Emma* (1816). There is no exciting action in her works, as there is in Scott's, and none of the richness of Manzoni's historical tapestry, but instead the patient dissection of moods and motives achieved by chronicling the details of daily life. The reader is held by a lucid style and the ripple of a quiet wit. On the Continent, Goethe had explored an individual's education in *Wilhelm Meisters Lehrjahre* (1795–96). In *Wilhelm Meisters Wanderjahre* (1821–29), he concentrated on the same hero's later travels and development. Between these novels, in 1809, he produced a truly psychological drama of love and renunciation, *Elective Affinities* (*Die Wahlverwandtschaften*). And in 1830, almost unnoticed for the moment but in due course to be hailed as one of Europe's most brilliant novels, appeared *The Red and the Black* (*Le Rouge et le noir*) by a Frenchman from Dauphiné, Marie-Henri Beyle (1783–1842), who wrote under the name Stendhal and whose theme was the mixture of religion, ambition, passion and violence in the downfall of young Julien Sorel.

The role of nationalism, of pride in a 'fatherland' politically defined, has been emphasized in discussing historical novels and plays. Another aspect of patriotism in the record of European letters has still to be noted. This was the early nineteenth century's enthusiasm for folklore, for dialects, for vernacular literature. Scott's *Lay of the Last Minstrel* (1805) breathed fervent Lowland Scottish sentiments, couched in picturesque local idiom. In 1806–8, Achim von Arnim (1781–1831), his wife, Bettina (1785–1859), and her brother, Clemens Brentano (1778–1842), published the first of many versions of romantic German songs of magic, *Des Knaben Wunderhorn*. Even more important for the future, Jakob Grimm (1785–1863) and his brother Wilhelm (1786–1859), both of them destined for international renown as philologists, in 1812–15 issued the first edition of their collected German fairy tales, *Kinder- and Hausmärchen*.

Interest in folklore and vernacular dialects was not exclusively self-centred. The Grimms recaptured Irish, Scandinavian and Slavic legends, as well as those of their native Germany; and in 1824 Jacob Grimm translated into German the first Serbian grammar to receive such recognition. Nevertheless, the patriotic impulse to glorify one's *own* people's tongue and traditions was as powerful as it was widespread. This was especially true of spokesmen for nationalities living under what seemed to them alien rule. Consider for instance the *Historical Songs of the Poles* (1816) by Niemcewicz, (*see above*, p. 404) and the inspirational *Poems* (1822–23) of Adam Mickiewicz (1798–1855), or Henrik Anker Bjerregaard's (1792–1842) anthem, 'Sons of Norway' (*Sönner ab Norge*), written in defiance of the Swedes in 1820. The first published story in Flemish prose, *Jellen en Mietje* by Karel Brockaert (1767–1826), first appeared in 1811, when Belgium was under French rule; but it retained its popularity during the years of Dutch domination after 1815. Nowhere was the mounting interest in vernacular literature and in local chronicles stronger than in the Balkans, where Vuk Karadžić (1787–1864), Ranke's old friend and source of information concerning the Serbian rebellion, had by 1830 published several of his collections of South Slavic folk poetry. In 1829 a Bulgarian scholar living in the Ukraine, Yurii Venelin, completed the first comprehensive history of his people and their customs to be printed in the native language, *The Bulgarians Ancient and Modern*.[4]

This general tendency suggests a footnote of some importance to the history of the years between 1780 and 1830. It will be recalled that earlier in this volume (*see above*, pp. 44–50) we had to distinguish between the aristocratic and characteristically cosmopolitan 'high' culture of Europe on the eve of the French Revolution and the far less widely appreciated, but more deeply rooted, 'low' culture of popular traditions and language. That distinction still existed in 1830, but it had become less sharp. On the one hand, we have observed the growing popularity, in the most literal sense, of serious music, poetry and, above all, fiction. On the other hand, eminent historians, philologists and literary figures had turned to folk themes for inspiration, as well as for subject matter. Not the least significant effect of the Revolution's dual legacy of democratic ideals and nationalistic fervour was the narrowing of the gap between 'high' and 'low' cultures in the age that followed.

NOTES AND REFERENCES

1 Quoted by R. Williams, *Culture and Society, 1780–1850* (New York, 1960), pp. 23–4.

2 *Ibid.*, p. 14.

3 M. L. Hansen, *The Atlantic Migration, 1606–1860* (Cambridge, Mass., 1941).

4 R. J. Crampton, *A Short History of Modern Bulgaria* (Cambridge, 1987), p. 10, observes that many years prior to the publication of Venelin's work, the monk Paiisi Hilendarski had composed a narrative of the Bulgarian empires, 'in a lively mixture of Old Church Slavonic and contemporary Bulgarian'. However, as Crampton also points out, while this late eighteenth-century manuscript circulated in numerous handwritten copies, it did not appear in print until 1845, at Budapest.

15

CONCLUSION

In his provocative treatment of Europe before 1914, Arno J. Mayer has endowed the *ancien régime* with a stubborn resiliency that deserves much of the blame for some of our own century's worst troubles. 'Though losing ground to the forces of industrial capitalism,' he writes, 'the forces of the old order were still sufficiently willful and powerful to resist and slow the course of history, if necessary by recourse to violence.'[1] The present volume seeks to arrive at no such sweeping judgement of the European scene before 1789 or on the virtues of the Great Revolution's uneven efforts to change it. My approach nevertheless has in common with Mayer's a strong conviction that while the half-century from 1780 to 1830 erased or at least dramatically altered much that was familiar, it did not mark a clean or total break with the past.

Our search for that period's place in modern history began with chapters devoted to major features – social, cultural, diplomatic, military and political – of Europe in the decade of the 1780s. We then turned to the French crisis, including both its domestic and its exported aspects, proceeding thereafter from the fall of the monarchy through the sequence of republican experiments to the authoritarian outcome under Napoleon Bonaparte. The last segment of this survey took up political, intellectual and social as well as other cultural aspects of the post-1815 situation. All along the way, certain issues kept reminding us of questions posed at the outset. Only now, however, is there an opportunity to raise for a final time the central query: how different *was* the Europe of 1830 from that of 1780?[2] That in turn leads straight to one of history's universal problems. For as the late Carl Becker liked to remind students in his seminar, two truths about human affairs must always be borne in mind, because both are true. One is that the world may change, but it changes slowly; the other, that while the world may change slowly, it does change.

Consider for a moment some of the arguments *against* the idea of a sharp break between the Old Régime and post-Napoleonic Europe. They are substantial, and they rightly take issue with any simplified notion of discontinuity. In the realm of ideas, to cite only one example, it has been very plausibly maintained that both the end of the seventeenth century, with Locke, Newton, Bayle and Leibniz, and the turn of the nineteenth, with Einstein, Freud, Weber, Pareto and Lenin, represented far deeper shifts in conceptions of mankind and its world than did the period we have been examining. Intervening figures who reached maturity around 1830 – Auguste Comte, Karl Marx, John Stuart Mill – have with growing frequency been referred to as still eighteenth-century *philosophes*, in the light of their rationalistic and utilitarian assumptions. From that point of view, even Hegel appears more the product of certain idealistic and progressive traditions than the inventor of a wholly new philosophical system. Turning to literature and art, one is reminded that well before 1780 first Rousseau and then the young Germans of the *Sturm und Drang* movement had espoused values which would later be called 'romantic' while an older 'classicism' remained powerful, especially in architectural taste, long after 1830.

Other pronounced strands of historical continuity were unbroken by the Revolution or, despite having been interrupted for an interval, were quickly reconnected in 1815. Dynastic diplomacy, like the cosmopolitan aristocrats to whom it was largely entrusted, continued to dominate international relations in the age of Metternich. Strategic and tactical theories of warfare, whether on land or at sea, had not been overturned by the struggles from Valmy to Waterloo, at least so far as most holders of actual commands were concerned, however earnestly such writers as Clausewitz and Jomini might strive to convince their contemporaries of the need for 'new' approaches. As for the political map of Europe in the 1820s, though the Holy Roman Empire had vanished, its successor, the German Confederation, possessed a number of undeniably familiar features; Italy remained splintered into many fragments while Poland was still divided under

Russian–Prussian–Austrian control; Norway had exchanged Danish for Swedish rule, and Belgium had passed from Austrian to Dutch; one Bourbon had recovered the crown of France and another that of Spain. Even with regard to economic development, the Industrial Revolution was by 1830 only beginning to make its full impact felt on the Continent.

Together, reflections such as these suggest that there really was no significant watershed cutting across the landscape of Europe at the turn of the eighteenth century – that instead, as can happen in nature, clouds of dust whipped up by a violent wind were only briefly mistaken for mountain ranges. A conclusion of this sort seems consistent, does it not, with the biological fact that 'life goes on' and new human generations do not in fact abruptly replace older ones but instead, like the countless individual lifetimes of which they are composed, overlap each other endlessly? And yet, so bland a flattening-out of history offers an inadequate approximation of what this period represented as a segment of Europe's past. To achieve fuller understanding we need to bear in mind some other features of our story and of the era with which it has dealt.

Among those features was not just the modification but in many instances the fundamental reorganization of major governments. Administrative recasting designed to meet revolutionary France on something like its own terms led to changes in state structure from Russia and Alexander I's new central ministries, through Prussia with the reforms Stein launched in 1807, to the England of Addington's income tax and the far-reaching implications of his efforts to introduce collection at the source. In warfare, while drill manuals might remain conservative, the realities of battle would never again, after the *levée en masse*, return to those of the eighteenth century. In politics, the introduction of democratic demands, buttressed by popular patriotism and focused on the making of written constitutions, brought alterations in the tone and content of public life which the Restoration proved able to withstand only briefly and never to thrust wholly out of sight. In the realm of aesthetics, while one would be foolish to envision altogether clear stylistic breaks, there can be no denying the change of atmosphere, a rise in emotional temperature that came with the full onset of romanticism, especially when joined to liberal and patriotic impulses.

All these aspects of change during our period deserve to be treated at least as seriously as the lines of continuity we also traced. Nevertheless, it might still be maintained, the balance between continuity and change seems no more than that, a roughly equal offsetting of the old and the new, likely to be matched by many other half-centuries in history. That is why at just this point a further and perhaps decisive element of difference between 1780 and 1830, having to do with social structure, action and attitdues, assumes crucial importance. For in the course of our *particular* half-century, as was emphasized in Chapter 3, *orders* (nobility, clergy, bourgeoisie) were to a remarkable degree replaced by *parties* and *classes*, as the key to how people were grouped, or grouped themselves, within the general population.

This change, like many others, did not occur without warning at the outbreak of the Revolution, nor was it total when it came. In the decade before 1789 political parties became increasingly visible – Patriots and Orangists in the Dutch United Provinces, Republicans, Moderates and Patriots in Poland, and so on. We saw class conflict break into the open with the *affaire Reveillon* at Paris almost on the eve of the Estates General's being called to order (*see above*, pp. 108–9). Conversely, nobility, clergy and, to a much more limited degree, bourgeoisie survived well beyond 1830 as orders legally defined; and in some countries, of course, they still do. Nevertheless, the change that took place was of deep and lasting importance.

One way of gauging the shift is in terms of the revived Roman title 'citizen', elevated by the French Revolution to a level of prestige it has enjoyed in a growing number of nations ever since. To become a citizen is to acquire a rank that makes noble birth or religious ordination, if not irrelevant, certainly not decisive. Another index is the shift in the basis for honorific status, and more particularly for what some modern sociologists call generalized, as distinct from specialized, status. Under the Old Régime a noble, *any* noble, had enjoyed to some degree this 'generalized status'. Today we accord it to, among others, war heroes, astronauts, film and sports stars, scientists – and the rich. People in the mid-nineteenth century, dazzled by new wealth and by industrial and commercial ingenuity, honoured *especially* the rich, regardless of birth, far more willingly than had Europeans in the eighteenth.

It is interesting to recall that Napoleon himself, in a portentous linking of attributes, had signalled the new day with his decree of 1808 establishing the Imperial Nobility. Remember that titles could be conferred by the emperor on anyone he chose; but in order to be passed along by inheritance, every such title had to be accompanied by a legally specified financial legacy as well. Nobility thus was revived, even in France; but in its new form it was in the first instance justified by service, not birth, and could be sustained only by family wealth.

Does the rise in importance of economic gradations signify the complete triumph of classes as the only authentic units of social conflict and political action? By no means. It is now widely agreed among historians, and other observers who disagree about much else, that men and women seldom act exclusively in pursuit of economic interests, rationally perceived, or only in groups defined by shared economic motives. Increased knowledge concerning the mixed and shifting composition of revolutionary crowds, for example, served to cast doubt on some of the premises of 'primitive' Marxian analysis. This new scepticism may serve a useful purpose in warning us not to see class struggle behind all the other kinds of conflict known to history. Equally dangerous, of course, albeit less likely to occur, would be the opposite form of oversimplification: shrugging aside class conflict as insignificant. Since time immemorial poor and rich *have* struggled against one another for advantage, with economic self-interest, often mixed with other issues of status and freedom, very much at stake.

The break between 1780 and 1830 – the true basis for speaking of a Revolutionary-Napoleonic watershed – was, in any case, more complex than any mechanical displacement of orders by classes or parties. It can be seen in two developments. One, which we have been discussing, was the *relative* increase in the attention paid to wealth, at the expense of birth, calling or religious affiliation, as a factor in determining personal or group influence. The other, clearly discernible by the 1820s and still more so in the revolutions of 1830, was the expanding role of political parties, sometimes class-based to be sure, but just as often linking prosperous with needy citizens, aristocrats with commons, for the defence of religious or regional interests, and on occasion still broader goals.

As members of a society thus conceived and a political order so constructed, preoccupied with such issues as national unification, constitutional democracy, the division of industrial production and its profits, Europeans in 1830 already stood a long way from the world of their eighteenth-century forebears. It was in fact a longer way than the passage of just any half-century of time might have been expected to carry them. In a very real sense, they looked back to the Old Régime across a historic watershed, and so do we today.

NOTES AND REFERENCES

1 *The Persistence of the Old Régime: Europe to the Great War* (New York, 1981), p. 4.

2 For the author's own introduction to this theme, see F. L. Ford, 'The Revolutionary-Napoleonic Era: How Much of a Watershed?', *American Historical Review*, vol. LXIX (1963), pp. 18–29.

BIBLIOGRAPHY

The following bibliographical essay, like those appended to companion volumes in this series, relies heavily on works available in English but extends to titles in other languages wherever and whenever their intrinsic importance appears to justify such inclusion. In keeping with series policy, the bibliography has been divided by headings which correspond to chapter titles employed in the text. Some of the books or articles mentioned here have already been cited in endnotes. A number of the more specialized footnote references, however, are not repeated, for what I hope the reader will recognize as sensible reasons.

One other comment, this one having to do with the age of various works, should perhaps be offered in advance. The summary to follow contains more than eighty new titles, some merely added to those in the original 1970 edition, others inserted in place of earlier entries. Nevertheless, despite this process of accretion and substitution, a considerable number of works dating from the first part of the twentieth century and a smaller, but not insignificant, number produced in the nineteenth have retained their positions in this new reckoning. The period under consideration began, after all, over 200 – and ended more than 150 – years ago, years filled with searching, often passionate debate marked by contributions from some of the true shapers of modern historical understanding. Many of the books produced by such historians have never, or at least not yet, been surpassed. Others have been superseded by further research and analysis. The resulting mixture of insights both old and new is what a present-day synthesis must strive to incorporate, and that mixture is of necessity reflected in its bibliography.

GENERAL WORKS

A good place to begin is with the *New Cambridge Modern History*, volume 8, *The American and French Revolutions, 1763–93*, ed. A. Goodwin, and volume 9, *War and Peace in an Age of Upheaval, 1793–1830*, ed. C. W. Crawley (both Cambridge, 1965). Less recent but still very useful, especially for their bibliographies, are the corresponding volumes in W. L. Langer's series, *The Rise of Modern Europe*: L. Gershoy, *From Despotism to Revolution, 1763–89* (New York–London, 1944); C. Brinton, *A Decade of Revolution, 1789–99* (New York–London, 1934); B. Bruun, *Europe and the French Imperium, 1799–1814* (New York–London, 1938); F. B. Artz, *Reaction and Revolution, 1814–1832*, (New York–London, 1934). There are three competing French series, the most highly compressed of which is *Clio: Introduction aux études historiques*, including E. Préclin, *Le XVIIIᵉ siècle*, 2 volumes (Paris, 1952); L. Villat, *La Révolution et l'Empire*, 2 volumes (2nd edn, Paris, 1940–42); and J. Droz, L. Genet and J. Vidalenc, *Le XIXᵉ siècle*, part I: *Restauration et révolutions, 1815–71* (2nd edn, Paris, 1963). More expansive, but offering less detailed bibliographical guidance, are two volumes of the *Histoire générale des civilisations*: R. Mousnier, E. Labrousse and M. Bouloiseau, *Le XVIIIᵉ siècle: Révolution intellectuelle, technique et politique, 1715–1815* (Paris, 1953), and R. Schnerb, *Le XIXᵉ siècle, 1815–1914* (Paris, 1955). The third of these collaborative enterprises, *Peuples et civilisations*, while more readable than *Clio*, is rather narrower in scope than the *Histoire générale*. The four volumes devoted to our period, however, have benefited from particularly frequent and diligent revision: P. Sagnac, *La Fin de l'Ancien régime et la Révolution américaine, 1763–1789* (3rd edn, Paris, 1952); G. Lefebvre, *La Révolution française* (3rd edn, Paris, 1963); the same author's *Napoléon* (5th edn, Paris, 1965); and F. Ponteil, *L'Eveil des nationalités et le mouvement libéral, 1815–1848* (Paris, 1960, replacing the previous volume by G. Weill).

Two major collections deal with special aspects of general history. The *Histoire des relations internationales*, ed. P. Renouvin, offers as volumes 3, 4 and 5 (part one): G. Zeller, *De Louis XIV à 1789* (Paris, 1955); A. Fugier, *La Révolution française et l'Empire napoléonien* (Paris, 1954); and P. Renouvin, *Le XIXᵉ siècle: De 1815 à 1871* (Paris, 1954). In another field, the *Cambridge Economic History of Europe*, volume 6, *The Industrial Revolutions and After*, ed. H. J. Habakkuk and M. Postan (Cambridge, 1965), contains the excellent 328-page chapter on 'Technological change and industrial development in west Europe, 1750–1914' by D. Landes, whose later work, *The Unbound Prometheus* (Cambridge, 1969), incorporates those same pages, somewhat revised. Also available is perhaps the best overview of the rural economy of the Old Régime, W. Abel, *Agricultural Fluctuations in Europe from the Thirteenth to the Twentieth Centuries*, written in German but trans. O. Ordish (London, 1980).

Turning to major national histories, we have two volumes of the *Oxford History of England*: J. S. Watson, *The Reign of George III, 1760–1820* (Oxford, 1960), and E. L. Woodward, *The Age of Reform, 1815–1870* (Oxford, 1938). The participants in the general French series mentioned above naturally give detailed attention to their own country's history. In addition, volume 9, part one, of the magisterial *Histoire de France des origines jusqu'à la Révolution* under the general editorship of E. Lavisse is entitled *Le Règne de Louis XVI, 1774–1789*, ed. H. Carré, P. Sagnac and E. Lavisse (Paris, 1911). The best introductions to Germany are the 8th revised edition of B. Gebhardt's *Handbuch der deutschen Geschichte*, ed. H. Grundmann, volumes 2–3 (Stuttgart, 1955–60), and the briefer but nevertheless substantial *Deutsche Geschichte im Überblick* ed. P. Rassow (2nd edn, Stuttgart, 1962). A survey in English by a distinguished German émigré to America is H. Holborn, *History of Modern Germany*, volume 2, *1648–1840* (New York, 1964); but at once the most profound and the most original treatment of the pre- and post-Napoleonic scene is F. Schnabel, *Deutsche Geschichte im neunzehnten Jahrhundert*, 4 volumes (rev. edn, Freiburg, 1948–51). Austria's past is reviewed by R. A. Kann, *A History of the Habsburg Empire, 1526–1918* (Berkeley, 1974), to which may be added R. Bauer's well-balanced *Oesterreich: Ein Jahrtausend Geschichte im Herzen Europas* (Berlin, 1977). Among several full histories of Spain, one of the most judicious and surely the most handsomely illustrated is A. Ballesteros y Beretta, *Historia de España y su influencia en la historia universal*, volumes 9–10 (rev. edn, Barcelona–Buenos Aires, 1956–58). F. Soldevila, *Historia de España*, volumes 6–7 (Barcelona, 1958–59), also should be mentioned, especially for its fine bibliographies. Of special value because of its broad Luso-Hispanic view is S. G. Payne, *A History of Spain and Portugal*, volume 2: *1700–Present* (Madison, 1973). Quite different in scope and purpose is the penetrating interpretive essay by J. Vicens Vives, *Aproximación a la historia de España* (3rd edn, Barcelona, 1962). Spain's neighbour to the west receives more concentrated treatment in A. H. De Oliveira Marques, *History of Portugal* (New York, 1972), volume 2 of which is relevant for present purposes.

In rather puzzling contrast to the Iberian countries and Germany, not to mention France or England, Italy offers relatively few general treatments of its eighteenth- and nineteenth-century past. However, appropriate chapters from L. Salvatorelli, *A Concise History of Italy*, trans. B. Miall (New York, 1940) may be usefully supplemented by A. J. Whyte, *The Evolution of Modern Italy, 1715–1922* (Oxford, 1944). Europe's smaller nations have also been subject to recently increasing coverage. B. J. Hovde, *The Scandinavian Countries* (Ithaca, 1948), has been joined by T. K. Derry, *A History of Scandinavia: Norway, Sweden, Denmark, Finland and Iceland* (Minneapolis, 1979), as well as by F. D. Scott, *Sweden: The Nation's History* (Minneapolis, 1977), and O. Feldbaek, *Danmarks historie*, volume 4: *Tiden 1730–1814* (Copenhagen, 1982). Turning to the Netherlands, one will find guidance in E. H. Kossmann, *The Low Countries, 1780–1840* (Oxford, 1978), and in J. A. Van Houtten, *An Economic History of the Low Countries, 800–1800* (New York, 1977). Two national studies, B. H. M. Vlekke, *The Evolution of the Dutch Nation* (New York, 1945), and H. Pirenne, *Histoire de Belgique*, are now both quite out of date; but the latter has been republished with well-chosen illustrations (Brussels, 1950), and Vlekke retains its usefulness if used in conjunction with such a book as S. Schama, *Patriots and Liberators*, discussed below under the heading for Chapter 5.

Looking towards eastern Europe, one finds Polish historical studies well synthesized in W. H. Reddaway *et al.*, *The Cambridge History of Poland*, volume 2 (Cambridge, 1941) For later interpretations, however, it would be wise also to consult J. K. Fedorowicz *et al.*, eds., *A Republic of Nobles: Studies in Polish History to 1864* (Cambridge, 1982). In the sprawling Russian field, we should note that G. Vernadsky, *A History of Russia* (New Haven, 1929), as well as N. V. Riasanovsky's later and much more detailed work under the same title (New York, 1963), serve to introduce the reader to other surveys by continental scholars, including P. Milyukov, C. Seignobos and L. Eisenmann, *Histoire de Russie*, volumes 2–3 (Paris, 1932–33), and V. Gitermann, *Geschichte Russlands*, volumes 2–3 (Zurich, 1945–49), the latter made attractive by its excellent maps and illustrations. For the Ottoman Empire, we must still rely heavily on J. W. Zinkeisen, *Geschichte des osmanischen Reiches in Europa*, volumes 6–7 (Hamburg-Gotha, 1859–63); but important facets of that area's history are dealt with both by L. S. Stavrianos, *The Balkans since 1453* (New York, 1958), and R. Ristelhueber, *A History of the Balkan Peoples*, trans. S. D. Spector (rev. edn, New York, 1971).

CHAPTER 2: THE SOURCES

Given the nature and subject of this chapter, numerous references to published sources have been incorporated into the text itself, pp. 5–13. Certain other titles, however, deserve to be identified here. An essential guide to older catalogues and collections of documentary sources is P. Caron and M. Jaryc, editors, *World List of Historical Periodicals and Bibliographies* (rev. edn, Oxford, 1939). A more specialized listing of memoirs, correspondence and other materials will be found in F. M Kircheisen, *Bibliography of Napoleon* (London, 1902). For national selections of central importance see Caron's and his successive collaborators' several *Bibliographies des travaux publiés . . . sur l'histoire de la France depuis 1789*, beginning with a volume devoted to works published 1866–97 (Paris, 1912); J. B. Williams, *A Guide to the Printed Materials for English Social and Economic History, 1750–1850* (New York, 1926); and Germany's magisterial 'Dahlmann-Waitz', *Quellenkunde der deutschen Geschichte*, launched by F. C. Dahlmann in 1830 but revised by various continuators down to the 10th edition, ed. H. Heimpel, H. Geuss *et al.* (Stuttgart, 1965). Papers having to do with international relations are catalogued by D. H. Thomas and L. M. Case, *Guide to the Diplomatic Archives of Western Europe* (Philadelphia, 1959), while H. Temperley and L. M. Penson, *A Century of Diplomatic Blue Books, 1814–1914* (Cambridge, 1938), combines a listing of the Foreign Office's Parliamentary papers with evaluations of such key figures as Castlereagh and Canning. A recently completed statistical reference of great importance for the early modern period is E. A.

Wrigley and R. S. Schofield, *The Population History of England, 1541–1871: A Reconstruction* (Cambridge, Mass., 1981). Among important studies of newspapers and periodicals as historical sources should definitely be included Arthur Aspinall, *Politics and the Press. c. 1780–1850* (London, 1949); the first volume of the official *History of 'The Times': The Thunderer in the Making, 1785–1841* (London, 1935); Rene de Livois, *Histoire de la presse française* (Lausanne, 1965); and K. Schottenlohr, *Flugblatt und Zeitung* (Berlin, 1922). Finally, although the work is itself of considerable substantive value, R. Williams, *Culture and Society, 1780–1830* (New York, 1960), should be mentioned here because of its author's discussion of literary sources and their value to social history.

CHAPTER 3: THE OLD RÉGIME: SOCIETY AND CULTURE

Much valuable material concerning social and cultural subjects can be found in political narratives of the period, some of which are cited below with reference to later chapters. A political analysis which nonetheless relies heavily on economic and social explanations, including demographic factors, is P. Goubert, *L'Ancien Régime*, 2 volumes (Paris, 1969–73). This mention of population questions calls into view, in addition to the volume edited by Wrigley and Schofield already cited, several related studies, including M. R. Reinhard, *Histoire de la population mondiale* (Paris, 1949); W. Köllmann's more detailed treatment in part 3 of *Raum und Bevölkerung in der Weltgeschichte* (2nd edn, Würzburg, 1956); C. Cipolla, *The Economic History of World Population* (7th edn, Baltimore, 1978); and the most recent, M. W. Flinn, *The European Demographic System, 1506–1820* (Baltimore, 1981). Comparative studies of parallel groups in different countries include *The European Nobility in the Eighteenth Century*, edited by A. Goodwin (London, 1953), and E. Dolléans, M. Crozier *et al.*, *Mouvements ouvriers et socialistes* (Paris, 1950). The latter collection supplies chronology and bibliography, ranging far beyond the history of labour movements narrowly defined.

Analyses of French society are understandably abundant. P. Sagnac, *La formation de la société française moderne*, volume 2: *1715–1788* (Paris, 1946), remains significant, as does F. Olivier-Martin, *L'organisation corporative de la France d'ancien régime* (Paris, 1938). For thoughtful treatment of a previously neglected subject, the administration of feudal estates during early modern times, see R. Forster, *The Nobility of Toulouse in the Eighteenth Century* (Baltimore, 1960), together with G. V. Taylor, 'Non-capitalist wealth and the origins of the French Revolution', *American Historical Review*, volume 72 (1967). Works on Great Britain include the revised editions of G. D. H. Cole and R. Postgate, *The British People, 1746–1946* (London, 1961), and P. Mantoux, *The Industrial Revolution in the Eighteenth Century* (rev. edn, London, 1961). Two studies of the Irish scene worth noting are C. Maxwell, *Country and Town in Ireland under the Georges* (rev. edn, Dundalk, 1949), and L. M. Cullen, *An Economic History of Ireland since 1660* (New York, 1972). To these Cullen has added a more general volume on the same country, *The Emergence of Modern Ireland, 1600–1900* (London, 1981). In a very different vein, Q. D. Lewis treats an important aspect of British popular culture in her *Fiction and the Reading Public* (London, 1932).

The Spanish situation is well analysed both by R. Herr, *The Eighteenth-century Revolution in Spain* (Princeton, 1958), and by William J. Callahan, *Church, Politics and Society in Spain, 1750–1874* (Cambridge, Mass., 1984). W. H. Bruford, *Germany in the Eighteenth Century* (Cambridge, 1935), and F. K. Luetge, *Deutsche sozial- und wirtschafts-Geschichte* (Berlin, 1952) are useful introductions. E. M. Link, *The Emancipation of the Austrian Peasant, 1740–1798* (New York, 1949), while perhaps too favourable to Maria Theresa, offers an admirable summary of agrarian conditions and Habsburg projects to improve them. On the empire of the Romanovs, see D. S. Mirsky, *Russia: A Social History* (London, 1931), and J. Blum, *Lord and Peasant in Russia* (Princeton, 1961). More specialized contributions include R. Portal, *L'Oural au XVIIIe siècle* (Paris, 1950), and G. Sacke, 'Adel und Bürgertum in der Regierungszeit Katharinas II. von Russland', in *Revue belge de philologie et d'histoire*, volume XVII (1938).

CHAPTER 4: THE EUROPEAN STATE SYSTEM

There exist a number of manuals summarizing the diplomatic history of Europe under the Old Régime. The most recent, and from the French point of view the best, is G. Zeller, *De Louis XIV à 1789* (Paris, 1955); volume 3, part 2 of *Histoire des relations internationales*, ed. P. Renouvin; but M. Immich, *Geschichte des europäischen Staatensystems von 1660 bis 1789* (Berlin-Munich, 1905), has yet to be surpassed for its balance and brevity. The first volume of A. Sorel's *L'Europe et la Révolution française* (Paris, 1885), despite its title, is in large part a critical analysis of eighteenth-century diplomatic mores. For a penetrating discussion of the industrial revolution's effects on armed conflict – and vice versa – see J. U. Nef, *War and Human Progress* (Cambridge, Mass., 1950). A. Vagts, in his *History of Militarism* (rev. edn, New York, 1959), though particularly concerned with technical problems, does not overlook civil–military relations. A classic work on naval questions is A. T. Mahan, *The Influence of Sea Power upon History, 1660–1783* (Boston, 1890), carried further in some respects by P. M. Kennedy, *The Rise and Fall of British Naval Mastery* (New York, 1976). A good analysis of how foreign offices conducted their business is D. B. Horn, *The British Diplomatic Service, 1689–1789* (Oxford, 1961), while a thoughtful treatment of legal and philosophical aspects, may be found in F. H. Hinsley, *Power and the Pursuit of Peace* (Cambridge, 1963).

CHAPTER 5: POLITICAL ISSUES

In many ways the best general introduction to this period in European politics would be a combination of two works, R. R. Palmer, *The Age of the Democratic Revolution*, volume 1: *The Challenge* (Princeton, 1959), dealing with the years 1760–91, and C. B. A. Behrens, *The Ancien Régime* (New York, 1967), a work which can be usefully compared with W. Doyle, *The Old European Order, 1660–1800* (New York, 1978), and the still more recent volume by O. Hufton, *Europe: Privilege and Protest, 1730–1789* (Ithaca, 1980). In part because of the interest aroused by Sir Lewis Namier's theories, the past several decades have produced a number of important studies of British political life, including H. Butterfield, *George III, Lord North and the People, 1779–1780* (London, 1949); R. Pares, *King George III and the Politicians* (Oxford, 1953); I. R. Christie, *Myth and Reality in Late Eighteenth-century British Politics* (London, 1970), as well as his *Wars and Revolutions: Britain 1760–1815* (Cambridge, Mass., 1982); J. Brooke, *King George III* (London, 1972); and B. W. Hill, *British Parliamentary Parties, 1742–1832* (Boston, 1985). Ireland's history is partially illuminated by these and related studies, but special mention should be made of R. B. McDowell, *Irish Public Opinion, 1750–1800* (London, 1943).

Although numerous books devoted to the French crisis will be treated separately below, three works of widely differing emphasis need to be included in any pre-1789 survey: C. E. Labrousse, *La crise de l'économie française à la fin de l'ancien régime* (Paris, 1944), a revealing study of prices and profits; R. Darnton, *The Literary Underground of the Old Régime* (Cambridge, Mass., 1982); and a much more sweeping overview by Jean Egret, *The French Prerevolution, 1787–1788*, trans. W. D. Camp (Chicago, 1977). For the Low Countries, P. Geyl, *De Patriottenbeweging, 1780–1787* (Amsterdam, 1947), and S. Tassier, *Les démocrates belges de 1789* (Brussels, 1930), are basic analyses of the Dutch and Belgian crises, though Geyl's book has been largely superseded by S. Schama, *Patriots and Liberators: Revolution in the Netherlands, 1780–1813* (New York, 1977).

Turning to central Europe, Prussia under Frederick William II is the focus for H. Brunschwig, *La crise de l'état prussien à la fin du XVIIIᵉ siècle* (Paris, 1947), while an interesting comparison between the French and Prussian situations will be found in C. B. A. Behrens, *Society, Government, and the Enlightenment: The Experience of Eighteenth-century France and Prussia* (New York, 1985). The most general treatment of German reactions to revolutionary ideas is F. Valjavec, *Die Entstehung der politischen Strömungen in Deutschland, 1770–1815* (Munich, 1951), which can now be supplemented by consulting H. Dippelt, *Germany and the American Revolution*, trans. B. A. Uhlendorf (Chapel Hill, 1977). Although the Habsburgs' version of enlightened despotism has aroused considerable interest in the past couple of decades, as evidenced, for example, by E. Wangermann, *The Austrian Achievement, 1700–1800* (London, 1973), it is still impossible to dispense entirely with two treatments both of which are more than three-quarters of a century old: P. von Mitrofanov, *Joseph*

II: *Seine politische und kulturelle Tätigkeit* (Vienna–Leipzig, 1910), and H. Marczali, *Hungary in the 18th Century* (Cambridge, 1910).

With respect to most other European countries, there is little need to mention here titles not cited elsewhere in the present essay. A new work of signal importance for Russian history, however, is I. De Madariaga, *Russia in the Age of Catherine the Great* (New Haven, 1981). In view of Poland's dramatic role during this period, note should also be taken of D. Stone, *Polish Politics and National Reform, 1775–1788* (Boulder, 1976), as well as J. Fabre, *Stanislas-Auguste Poniatowski et l'Europe des lumiéres* (Paris, 1952). Rather surprisingly, Fedorowicz's *A Republic of Nobles*, cited above under GENERAL WORKS, does not include an essay on the fateful 1780s as such. It does, however, contain one by Barbara Grochulska entitled 'The Place of the Enlightenment in Polish History', pp 239–58. The geographically restricted but historically very revealing Genevan crisis occupies several chapters in the *Histoire de Genève des origines à 1798*, published by the Société d'Histoire et d'Archéologie de Genève (Geneva, 1951).

CHAPTER 6: UPHEAVAL IN FRANCE

For an introduction to this vast subject, the reader may turn to the excellent new paperback series, *The French Revolution*, published in English by the Cambridge University Press through arrangement with Editions de La Maison des Sciences de l'Homme. Its three volumes dealing with the crucial decade, each the work of an established French scholar, are by M. Vovelle, *The Fall of the French Monarchy, 1787–1792*, trans. S. Burke (Cambridge, 1983); M. Bouloiseau, *The Jacobin Republic, 1792–1794*, trans. J. Mandelbaum (Cambridge, 1983); and D. Woronoff, *The Thermidorean Régime and the Directory, 1794–1799*, trans. J. Jackson (Cambridge, 1983). Concerning the mid and late 1790s, one can also consult M. Lyons, *France under the Directory* (Cambridge, 1975)

Certain older treatments survive as monuments of historical literature, though long since overtaken by later research, not to mention changes of approach. Two such are T. Carlyle, *The French Revolution*, ed. C. Fletcher (New York, 1902), first published in 1837; and J. Michelet, *Histoire de la Révolution française*, written between 1848 and 1851 (rev. edn, Paris, 1952). Others among the now classic studies retain their interest primarily because of their authors' strongly expressed views. Thus, A. Aulard, *The French Revolution: A Political History, 1789–1804* (London, 1910), employed what might be called the 'official' terms of the Third Republic. J. Jaurès, *Histoire socialiste de la Révolution française* (Paris, 1922–24), as the title indicates, adopted an entirely different set of assumptions. More extreme even than Jaurès in his attack on Aulard from a Marxist angle was the work first published in 1921 by the formidable A. Mathiez, *The French Revolution* (New York, 1962). This view of a 'capitalists' revolution', overcoming (indeed betraying) more radical aspirations, has been restated with somewhat greater sophistication by A. Soboul, *The French Revolution, 1787–99*, trans. A. Forrest and C. James (New York, 1975). Among efforts to bring changed perspectives to the drama as a whole, that advanced by A. Cobban, *The Social Interpretation of the French Revolution* (Cambridge, 1964), suggesting that not a modern capitalist class but an older-style bourgeoisie 'won' the struggle, continues to fuel energetic arguments, some of the most recent to be found in L. Hunt, *Politics, Culture and Class in the French Revolution* (Berkeley, 1984). A special place among contemporary additions to such literature, however, must be reserved for F. Furet's elegant quartet of reflective essays, published in French as *Penser la Révolution française* (Paris, 1978), and in English, trans. E. Forster, as *Interpreting the French Revolution* (Paris–Cambridge, 1981), earlier mentioned in the introduction to the present volume.

In addition to these general surveys and reflections, a number of works devoted to special topics can be cited here, though the profusion of such studies imposes an obvious need for careful selection. C. Brinton, *The Jacobins* (New York, 1930), was recognized from its first appearance as a pioneering application of historical sociology, while R. R. Palmer has written on the powerful Committee of Public Safety, *Twelve Who Ruled* (rev. edn, Princeton, 1958). What constitutes in many respects a sequel to both of these works is supplied by I. Woloch, *Jacobin Legacy: The Democratic Movement under the Directory*, (Princeton, 1970). Especially since the appearance of J. Godechot's masterful study, *La contre-révolution* (Paris, 1961), translated into English by S. Attanasio as *The Counter-Revolution, Doctrine and Action, 1789–1804* (New York, 1971), a good deal of scholarly attention has been paid to the nature and structure of internal opposition, often with an emphasis on regional movements. L. A. Hunt, *Revolution and Urban Politics in Provincial France, 1786–1790* (Stanford, 1978), which centres on a pair of selected municipalities, Troyes and Reims, applies modern forms of social analysis. R. Cobb, *Paris and Its Provinces, 1790–1802* (Oxford, 1975), employs a wider canvas for the following decade, as does the well-chosen set of articles on topics other than revolutionary activity, G. Lewis and C. Lucas, eds., *Beyond the Terror: Essays in French Regional and Social History* (New York, 1983). The end of the *ancien régime* and the ensuing decade of revolution are examined with special reference to French journalists by J. R. Censer, *Prelude to Power: The Parisian Radical Press, 1786–1790* (Baltimore, 1976), and by J. D. Popkin, *The Right Wing Press in France, 1792–1800* (Chapel Hill, 1980). Still another aspect of political conflict has attracted the attention of S. Scott, *The Response of the Royal Army to the French Revolution* (Oxford, 1978), with obvious emphasis on the interests and attitudes of the French nobility; but a more extended inquiry into the latter subject is P. Higonnet, *Class, Ideology and the Rights of Nobles in the French Revolution* (New York, 1981). Underlying a great deal of this regional, class and occupational analysis are careful statistical studies including D. Greer's invaluable monographs, *The Incidence of the Terror during the French Revolution* (Cambridge, Mass., 1935) and *The Incidence of the Emigration during the French Revolution* (Cambridge, Mass., 1951), as well as P. Dawson, *Provincial Magistrates and Revolutionary Politics in France, 1789–1795* (Cambridge, Mass., 1972). Biographical works too, although only a few can be cited here, obviously provide an important point of entry into the revolutionary chronicle. Robespierre, of course, has continued to attract close attention from A. Mathiez's early, but still influential, *Etudes sur Robespierre, 1758–1794* (new edn, Paris, 1973) to the same author's translated collection, *The Fall of Robespierre and Other Essays* (New York, 1968); G. Rudé, *Robespierre: Portrait of a Revolutionary Democrat* (New York, 1976); and D. Jordan, *The Revolutionary Career of Maximilien Robespierre* (New York, 1985). Another recent biography of a major figure is by N. Hampson, *Danton* (New York, 1985).

CHAPTER 7: THE REVOLUTION BEYOND FRENCH BORDERS

An indispensable two-volume synthesis of the Revolution's European-wide ramifications is J. Godechot, *La Grande Nation* (Paris, 1956), 2 volumes, while R. R. Palmer continued *The Age of the Democratic Revolution* into the period after 1791 with a second volume, *The Struggle* (Princeton, 1964). National studies of course make up a major portion of the available bibliography on Europe as a whole. Concerning England, see S. Maccoby, *English Radicalism, 1786–1832: From Paine to Cobbett* (London, 1955); A. Cobban, *The Debate on the French Revolution, 1789–1800* (London, 1950); relevant sections of I. R. Christie, *Stress and Stability in Late Eighteenth-century Britain: Reflections on the British Avoidance of Revolution* (Oxford, 1984); the same author's *Wars and Revolutions: Britain 1760–1815* (Cambridge, Mass., 1982); and F. P. Lock, *Burke's 'Reflections on the French Revolution'* (Boston, 1985). For other parts of the British Isles, H. W. Meikle, *Scotland and the French Revolution* (Glasgow, 1912), and R. Hayes, *Ireland and Irishmen in the French Revolution* (London, 1932), though old, still deserve notice. A clear analysis of the founding of the Batavian Republic will be found in R. R. Palmer, 'Much in little: The Dutch Revolution of 1795', *The Journal of Modern History*, volume 26 (1954); but S. Schama's work, *Patriots and Liberators*, previously noted under Chapter 5, goes well beyond most earlier work on the Netherlands in this period. With respect to Germany, Valjavec's book, *Die Entstehung der politischen Strömungen in Deutschland* (see above, p. 420), and J. Droz, *L'Allemagne et la Révolution française* (Paris, 1949), can be usefully supplemented by M. Botzenhart's *Reform, Restauration, Krise: Deutschland 1789–1847* (Frankfurt-on-Main, 1985). G. P. Gooch, *Germany and the French Revolution* (London, 1920), has in some important respects now been surperseded by T. C. W. Blanning, *The French Revolution in Germany: Occupation and Resistance in·the Rhineland, 1792–1802* (Oxford, 1983). Switzerland's experience is examined in detail by H. Buechi, *Vorgeschichte der helvetischen Revolution*, volume 1: *Die Schweiz in den*

Jahren 1789–1798 (Solothurn, 1925). More than just literary reactions in Italy are dealt with in P. Hazard, *La Révolution française et les lettres italiennes, 1789–1815* (Paris, 1910), a work that can be used in tandem with C. Lombroso *et al.*, *La vita italiana durante la rivoluzione francese e l'impero* (Milan, 1900). By far the most valuable study of the Habsburg dominions is the volume by E. Wangermann, *From Joseph II to the Jacobin Trials* (London, 1959). As for Russia, C. de Larivière, *Catherine II et la Révolution française* (Paris, 1895), despite its age, deserves attention, as does a biography by D. M. Lang, *The First Russian Radical: Alexander Radishchev, 1749–1802* (London, 1959).

CHAPTER 8: BONAPARTE FROM CONSUL TO EMPEROR

A remarkably sustained essay devoted to past historians' treatments of Bonaparte's career and its significance is P. Geyl, *Napoleon: For and Against* (London, 1949). Another important treatment of the same general problem, A. Guérard's *Reflections on the Napoleonic Legend* (New York, 1923), was followed more than a quarter of a century later by his *Napoleon I* (New York, 1956). The best recent 'total history' of the reign, including its social and economic aspects, is L. Bergeron, *France under Napoleon*, trans. R. R. Palmer (Princeton, 1981); but a student wishing to learn more about the emperor's personality and intellect will find an absorbing array of source readings in J. C. Herold, ed. and trans., *The Mind of Napoleon: A Selection from His Written and Spoken Words* (New York, 1955).

On the structure of French government and society, a comprehensive manual is J. Godechot, *Les institutions de la France sous la Révolution et l'Empire* (Paris, 1951). Valuable treatments of specific institutional features include J. Regnier, *Les préfets du Consulat et de l'Empire* (Paris, 1907); C. Durand, *Etudes sur le Conseil d'état napoléonien* (Paris, 1949); I. Collins, *Napoleon and His Parliaments, 1800–1815* (New York, 1979); and E. d'Hauterive *et al.*, *La police secrète du premier Empire*, 4 volumes (Paris, 1908–63). J. Valynseele's two genealogical studies, *Les maréchaux du premier Empire* and *Les princes et ducs du premier Empire, non maréchaux* (Paris, 1957 and 1959) are rather narrowly antiquarian in purpose but contain much of interest concerning the highest levels of Napoleon's new aristocracy. Among scores of works dealing with religious affairs, four should, for varying reasons, be singled out here: A. Latreille, *L'Eglise catholique et la Révolution française*, volume 2: *L'Ere napoléonienne et la crise européenne, 1800–1815* (Paris, 1950); H. Walsh, *The Concordat of 1801* (New York, 1933); R. Anchel, *Napoleon et les juifs* (Paris, 1928); and finally, though it deals with Calvinist Huguenots over a long period, to the exclusion of the French Lutheran minority, B. C. Poland, *French Protestantism and the French Revolution* (Princeton, 1957).

CHAPTER 9: NAPOLEON AND THE NATIONS OF EUROPE

Among surveys of diplomatic history, still the most thorough is A. Fugier, *La Révolution française et l'Empire napoléonien* (Paris, 1954), volume 4 of *Histoire des relations internationales*, ed. P. Renouvin. Also worth consulting as a sequel to M. Immich's work in the same series (see above, p. 419) is A. Wahl, *Geschichte des europäischen Staatensystems, 1789–1815* (Munich–Berlin, 1912). Two still older treatments, which retain their interest in part because of their strongly argued theses, are A. Sorel, *L'Europe et la Révolution française* (see above, p. 419), committed to the view that Napoleon fought a hopeless struggle for France's 'natural frontiers' against the relentless opposition of rival powers, and E. Bourgeois, *Manuel historique de politique étrangère*, volume 2: *Les révolutions, 1789–1830* (Paris, 1898), emphasizing Bonaparte's obsession with the Middle East. More specialized studies worth noting are H. Deutsch, *The Genesis of Napoleonic Imperialism* (Cambridge, Mass., 1938); E. Kraehe, *Metternich's German Policy*, volume 1: *The Contest with Napoleon, 1799–1814* (Princeton, 1963); E. A. Whitcomb, *Napoleon's Diplomatic Service* (Durham, N. C., 1979); E. Gulick, *Europe's Classical Balance of Power* (Ithaca, 1955); and O. Connelly, *Napoleon's Satellite Kingdoms* (New York-London, 1965).

The authoritative treatment of England's diplomatic role is volume 1 in the *Cambridge History of British Foreign Policy, 1783–1919*, ed. A. W. Ward and G. P. Gooch (Cambridge, 1922), modified in important respects by C. K. Webster, *The Foreign Policy of Castlereagh, 1812–1815* (London, 1931), and subsequently by R. Glover, *Britain at Bay: Defence against Bonaparte, 1803–14* (New York, 1973). Numerous biographies, notably J. H. Rose, *Life of William Pitt* (New York, 1924), and P. Guedalla, *Wellington* (New York, 1930), give valuable accounts of the great conflict. Significant monographs dealing with Germany, among them R. C. Raack, *The Fall of Stein* (Cambridge, Mass., 1965), and H. Berding, *Napoleonische Herrschaft und Gesellschaftspolitik im Königreich Westfalen, 1807–1813* (Göttingen, 1973), may be used with such broader works as F. Meinecke, *Das Zeitalter der deutschen Erhebung, 1795–1815* (6th edn, Göttingen, 1957), trans. and ed. P. Paret as *The Age of German Liberation* (Berkeley, 1977): G. Ritter, *Stein: Eine politische Biographie* (rev. edn, Stuttgart, 1958); and C. Prignitz, *Vaterlandsliebe und Freiheit: Deutscher Patriotismus von 1750 bis 1850* (Wiesbaden, 1981). For eastern Europe, two earlier works may be consulted, M. Handelsmann, *Napoléon et la Pologne, 1806–1807* (Paris, 1909); S. Tatishchev, *Alexandre Ier et Napoléon, d'après leur correspondance inédite, 1801–1812* (Paris, 1891); and F. Tarlé, *Napoleon's Invasion of Russia, 1812* (London, 1942). A more recent work is H. Ragsdale, *Détente in the Napoleonic Era: Bonaparte and the Russians* (Lawrence, 1980), while M. Raeff, *Michael Speransky: Statesman of Imperial Russia, 1772–1839* (The Hague, 1957) remains an important biography. Concerning the western Mediterranean countries, see M. Artola, *Los origenes de la España contemporanea* (Madrid, 1959);

G. H. Lovett, *Napoléon and the Birth of Modern Spain* (New York, 1965), 2 volumes; A. Fugier, *Napoléon et l'Espagne, 1799–1808* (Paris, 1930), as well as his *Napoléon et l'Italie* (Paris, 1947); and C. Zaghi, *Napoleone e l'Italia* (Naples, 1969). Finally, two studies of the central figure in Sweden's crucial relations with Bonaparte are F. D. Scott, *Bernadotte and the Fall of Napoleon* (Cambridge, Mass., 1935), and T. T. Hojer's monumental *Carl XIV Johan*, volume 2: *Kronprinstiden* (Stockholm, 1943), while another important aspect of Scandinavian involvement receives attention in O. Feldbaek, *Denmark and the Armed Neutrality, 1800–1801* (Copenhagen, 1980).

CHAPTER 10: THE DIMENSIONS OF VIOLENCE

Major surveys devoted to military history include Nef, *War and Human Progress*, and Vagts, *A History of Militarism*, both mentioned earlier in this essay; but special attention should be paid to a pair of more recent studies, W. McNeill, *The Pursuit of Power: Technology, Armed Force and Society since A. D. 1000* (Chicago, 1982); and M. Van Crefeld, *Command in War* (Cambridge, Mass., 1985). The standard work on the revolutionary forces remains R. W. Phipps' five volumes, *The Armies of the First French Republic* (London, 1926–39), supplemented by specialized monographs such as M. Lauerma, *L'artillerie de campagne française pendant les guerres de la Révolution* (Helsinki, 1956). G. E. Rothenberg has written specifically on the struggles of the First Empire: *The Art of Warfare in the Age of Napoleon* (Bloomington, 1978). For Great Britain, consult C. Oman, *Wellington and His Army* (Oxford, 1954); A. H. Burne, *The Noble Duke of York* (London, 1949); and *The Letters of Private Wheeler, 1809–28*, ed. B. F. Liddell Hart (London, 1951). The important case of Prussia's army has been studied by W. O. Shanahan, *Prussian Army Reforms, 1786–1813* (New York, 1945), and by G. Ritter, *Sword and Sceptre*, volume 1 (Coral Gables, 1969), originally published as *Staatskunst und Kriegshandwerk* (rev. edn, Munich, 1959). An interesting sidelight is supplied by J. A. Lukacs, 'Russian armies in western Europe: 1799, 1814, 1917', *American Slavic and East European Review*, volume 13 (1954). J. Naylor, *Waterloo* (London, 1960), and C. Duffy, *Austerlitz 1805* (London, 1977) offer lucid accounts of major individual battles, something M. Glover does for an entire theatre of operations in *The Peninsular War* (Hamden, Conn., 1974), and in *Wellington's Army in the Pensinsula, 1808–1814* (New York, 1977). Theoretical aspects are examined in three chapters of *Makers of Modern Strategy*, originally edited by E. M. Earle with G. Craig and F. Gilbert, but now available in an editon revised under the direction of P. Paret (Princeton, 1986). Probably the most provocative, because negative, among recent treatments of Bonaparte as a field commander is O. Connelly, *Blundering to Glory: Napoleon's Military Campaigns* (Wilmington, Del., 1987).

Naval history can be approached through two classics of A. T. Mahan, *The Influence of Sea Power upon the French Revolution and Empire*, 2 volumes (14th edn, Boston, 1918), and *The Life of Nelson* (rev. edn, Boston, 1943), though these have since been updated by G. Marcus, *The Age of Nelson: The Royal Navy, 1793–1815* (New York, 1971), and by D. Pope, *England Expects* (London, 1959). Two interesting works on amphibious warfare are A. Vagts, *Landing Operations* (Washington, 1946), and E. H. S. Jonas, *An Invasion That Failed: The French Expedition to Ireland, 1796* (Oxford, 1950). For the United Kingdom's pivotal role in the economic struggle, see W. F. Galpin, *The Grain Supply of England during the Napoleonic Period* (Philadelphia, 1925), and F. Crouzet, *L'économie britannique et le blocus continental, 1806–1813* (Paris, 1958). Finally, 'fiscal warfare' is discussed by J. M. Sherwig, *Guineas & Gunpowder: British Foreign Aid in Wars with France, 1793–1815* (Cambridge, Mass., 1969).

Inasmuch as two new sections, on non-military violence, have been added to Chapter 10 of this revised edition, several works bearing on the subject deserve mention here, among them G. Rudé, *The Crowd in the French Revolution* (Oxford, 1959), and P. Caron, *Les massacres de septembre* (Paris, 1935). An especially interesting monograph dealing with the interplay of political and judicial motives is David P. Jordan *The King's Trial: Louis XVI vs. the French Revolution* (Berkeley, 1979). There are, of course, other studies having less to do with the French Terror than with general aspects of crime, prosecution and punishment, one such being J. H. Langbein's *Torture and the Law of Proof* (Chicago, 1977), earlier alluded to on page 256, above. Regarding assassination in particular, the present author's volume, *Political Murder: From Tyrannicide to Terrorism* (Cambridge, Mass., 1985), contains at least brief treatment of the deaths of Gustav III, Marat, Tsar Paul I, Perceval in England and Kotzebue in Germany, as well as suggestions for further reading.

CHAPTER 11: THE EUROPEAN STATE SYSTEM AFTER 1815

In addition to numerous national histories, there are several works dealing with international affairs during the post-Napoleonic period that invite attention here. The best short study of the subject remains H. Nicolson, *The Congress of Vienna* (London, 1946), from which one may go on to such sharply focused studies as E. Kraehe, *Metternich's German Policy*, volume 2: *The Congress of Vienna* (Princeton, 1983). Four scholars have directed close attention to major diplomats of the 'congress era': H. von Srbik, *Metternich: Der Staatsmann und der Mensch*, (Munich, 1925), 2 volumes; G. Lacour-Gayet, *Talleyrand* (Paris, 1928–34), especially volume 2; C. J. Bartlett, *Castlereagh* (London, 1966); and H. Temperley, *The Foreign Policy of Canning, 1822–1827* (London, 1925). Srbik also deals at length with the German problem in his *Deutsche Einheit*, volume 1 (Munich, 1935). Two excellent monographs concerning Alexander I are those by W. Naef, *Zur Geschichte der Heiligen Allianz* (Bern, 1928), and F. Ley, *Alexandre Ier et sa Sainte-Alliance (1811–1825)* (Paris, 1975). Books of a more essayistic nature include H. G. Schenk, *The Aftermath of the Napoleonic Wars* (London, 1947); L. C. B. Seaman, *From Vienna to Versailles* (London, 1955); and H. A. Kissinger, *A World Restored: Metternich, Castlereagh and the Problems of Peace, 1812–22* (Boston, 1957). The crucial events in Greece are dealt with by C. M. Woodhouse, *The Greek War of Independence* (London, 1952), and D. Dakin, *The Greek Struggle for Independence, 1821–1833* (Berkeley, 1973). For further discussion of this topic one may consult *The Movement for Greek Independence, 1770–1821: A Collection of Documents* (London, 1976), ed. R. Clogg, who has also edited a volume of essays, *The Struggle for Greek Independence* (Hamden, Conn., 1973).

CHAPTER 12: RESTORATION POLITICS

Historians have long been aware that politics cannot be well studied in exclusively political terms. For the post-1815 era, therefore, it is essential to make use of, among other aids, D. S. Landes, *The Unbound Prometheus* (Cambridge, 1969). Additional contributions by economic historians comprise two works by W. O. Henderson, *The Industrialization of Europe, 1780–1914* (New York, 1969) and *The Zollverein* (2nd edn, London, 1959); J. H. Clapham, *The Economic Development of France and Germany, 1815–1914* (4th edn, Cambridge, 1955); H. Kellenberg, *Deutsche Wirtschaftsgeschichte*, volume 2: *Vom Ausgange des 18. Jahrhundert bis zum Ende des Zweiten Weltkriegs* (Munich, 1981); and H. R. C. Wright, *Free Trade and Protection in the Netherlands, 1816–1830* (Cambridge, 1955). For the religious background, one can consult J. N. Moody *et al.*, *Church and Society: Catholic Social and Political Thought and Movement, 1789–1950* (New York, 1953); and K. S. Latourette, *Christianity in a Revolutionary Age* (New York, 1958–9), volumes 1–2. Of the principal countries, Great Britain has been the subject of an especially large number of works dealing with political developments. Even the most select enumeration must take note of E. Halévy, *England in 1815*, and its sequel, *The Liberal Awakening 1815–30* (both rev. edns, London, 1949); K. G. Feiling, *The Second Tory Party, 1714–1832* (London, 1938); A. S. Turberville, *The House of Lords in the Age of Reform* (London, 1958); and D. Read, *Peterloo: The Massacre and Its Background* (Manchester, 1958). An important adjunct to that list is J. A. Reynolds, *The Catholic Emancipation Crisis in Ireland, 1823–1829* (New Haven, 1954).

With respect to France after 1815, the best single work is G. de Bertier de Sauvigny, *La Restauration* (Paris, 1955), though F. B. Artz, *France under the Bourbon Restoration* (Cambridge, Mass., 1931) retains its value, while S. Kent, *The Election of 1827 in France* (Cambridge, Mass., 1975), provides an illuminating case study. The Belgian situation is perhaps best approached by turning first to H. Pirenne, *Histoire de Belgique*, volume 3 (new edn, Brussels, 1950), then to C. Bronne, *L'Amalgame: La Belgique de 1814 à 1830* (Brussels, 1948), and H. Haag, *Les origines du catholicisme libéral en Belgique, 1789–1839* (Louvain, 1950). An excellent synthesis dealing with Germany is F. Schnabel, *Deutsche Geschichte im neunzehnten Jahrhundert*, volume 2: *Monarchie und Volksouveränität* (Freiburg, 1949), to which may be added K.-G. Faber, *Deutsche Geschichte im 19. Jahrhundert: Restauration und Revolution*, volume 3/I, part 2 of the multi-volume Athenaion *Handbuch der Deutschen Geschichte* (Wiesbaden, 1979). Prussia's emerging role is emphasized in T. Nipperdey, *Deutsche Geschichte, 1800–1866: Bürgerwelt und starker Staat* (Munich, 1983). On Austria, see A. J. P. Taylor, *The Habsburg Monarchy, 1809–1918* (London, 1948). A judiciously assembled collection of readings, *Metternich's Europe, 1813–1848*, ed. Mack Walker (New York-London, 1968), contains a number of selections bearing not only on Austria but on the other major powers as well.

Southern Europe may be studied with the help of R. Gambra Ciudad, *La primera guerra civil de España, 1821–23* (Madrid, 1950); G. T. Romani, *The Neapolitan Revolution of 1820–21* (Evanston, 1950); and M. Petrocchi, *La restaurazione romana, 1815–1823* (Florence, 1943). Several portions of C. and B. Jelavich, eds., *The Balkans in Transition* (Berkeley, 1963), can be profitably combined with chapters 3 and 4 of D. Djordjevic and S. Fischer-Galati, *The Balkan Revolutionary Tradition* (New York, 1981). Another welcome addition to this literature is R. J. Crampton, *A Short History of Modern Bulgaria* (Cambridge, 1987). Much more than just Poland's eventual uprising is examined in R. F. Leslie, *Polish Politics and the Revolution of November 1830* (London, 1956). Of the many studies devoted to Russian affairs, M. Zetlin, *The Decembrists*, trans. G. Panin (New York, 1958), serves as a worthy successor to A. G. Mazour, *The First Russian Revolution, 1825* (Berkeley, 1937), while a welcome biography is M. Raeff's *Michael Speransky* (see above, p. 425) continues to its subject's death in 1839. A significant study of financial policies and sluggish industrialization in Russia is K. Heller, *Die Geld- und Kreditpolitik des russischen Reiches in der Zeit des Assignaten, 1768–1839/43* (Wiesbaden, 1983).

CHAPTER 13: PHILOSOPHERS, SCIENTISTS AND HISTORIANS

Among the literally countless works devoted to intellectual history, it is impossible to cite all of those the author has found helpful in one connection of another. For political, social and ethical thought, often inextricably intertwined, the following should be noted: G. Sabine, *A*

History of Political Theory (3rd edn, New York, 1961); J. Lough, *The Philosophes and Post Revolutionary France* (New York, 1982); F. Manuel, *The Prophets of Paris* (Cambridge, Mass., 1962); and by the same author, *The New World of Henri Saint-Simon* (Cambridge, Mass., 1956); E. Halévy, *The Growth of Philosophical Radicalism* (rev. edn, London, 1949); C. Brinton, *Political Ideas of the English Romanticists* (London, 1926); R. Aris, *History of Political Thought in Germany from 1789 to 1815* (London, 1936); L. Krieger, *The German Idea of Freedom* (Boston, 1957); K. W. Epstein, *The Genesis of German Conservatism* (Princeton, 1966); and C. Schmitt, *Politische Romantik* (2nd edn, Munich, 1925).

A deservedly influential study of the portentous shift from eighteenth-century cosmopolitan values to nineteenth-century nationalistic ones in Germany is F. Meinecke, *Weltbürgertum und Nationalstaat* (7th edn, Munich–Berlin, 1928), trans. R. Kimber as *Cosmopolitanism and the National State* (Princeton, 1970). A collection of long essays by the famous German scholar, K. Jaspers, *The Great Philosophers*, trans. R. Manheim (New York, 1962), contains one of the best available summaries of Immanuel Kant's thought, though the work as a whole has in many respects been superseded by F. Copleston, *A History of Philosophy*, volume 7: *Fichte to Nietszche* (Westminster, Md., 1985). For the other major German philospher dealt with in this chapter, see J. H. Shklar, *Freedom and Independence: A Study of the Political Ideas of Hegel's Phenomenology of Mind* (New York, 1976). In the growing array of studies dealing with the history of science and its offspring, technology, I would single out two works by C. Gillispie, *Genesis and Geology* (Cambridge, Mass., 1951), and *The Edge of Objectivity* (Princeton, 1960); together with A. and N. Clow, *The Chemical Revolution* (London 1952); E. Mayr, *The Growth of Biological Thought; Diversity, Evolution and Inheritance* (Cambridge, Mass., 1982); H. E. Sigerist's collected essays, *On the History of Medicine* (New York, 1960); and F. Klemm, *A History of Western Technology* (New York, 1959).

There are, of course, many manuals of historiography; but doubtless the most important single interpretation of the period here dealt with is F. Meinecke, *Die Entstehung des Historismus* (Munich–Berlin, 1936), also available as *Historicism: The Rise of a New Historical Outlook*, trans. J. E. Anderson, rev. H. D. Schmidt (London, 1972). Still well worth consulting is R. G. Collingwood's highly personal *The Idea of History* (Oxford, 1946), on which certain remarks concerning the German school to be found in my Chapter 13 have been based. An anthology edited by F. Stern, *The Varieties of History* (New York, 1956), contains good selections perceptively introduced, while B. Mazlish, *The Riddle of History: The Great Speculators from Vico to Freud* (New York, 1966), offers an interesting guided tour through 'metahistorical' writings. Concerning the special, but important, case of Russia one may consult J. L. Black, *Nicholas Karamzin and Russian Society in the Nineteenth Century: A Study in Russian Political and Historical Thought* (Toronto, 1975).

CHAPTER 14: SOCIETY AND CULTURE IN 1830

Valuable contributions to the social history of Great Britain in the later years of our period include A. Briggs, *The Age of Improvement* (London, 1959); D. Thomson, *England in the Nineteenth Century* (London, 1964); and R. M. Hartwell, ed., *The Industrial Revolution* (New York, 1970). On daily life in France and Germany, see R. Burnand, *La Vie quotidienne en 1830* (Paris, 1957), and G. Bianquis, *La Vie quotidienne en Allemagne à l'époque romantique* (Paris, 1958). Two basic works for the study of population movements are M. L. Hansen, *The Atlantic Migration, 1607–1860* (Cambridge, Mass., 1941), and M. Walker, *Germany and the Emigration, 1816–1885* (Cambridge, Mass., 1964).

Varieties of food and dress may be approached through E. P. Prentice, *Hunger and History* (New York, 1939); B. Payne, *History of Costume* (New York, 1965); and F. Boucher, *20,000 Years of Fashion* (New York, 1967). The best introduction to the pictorial and plastic arts is still G. Pauli, *Die Kunst des Klassizismus und der Romantik* (Berlin, 1925), volume 14 of the *Propylaen-Kunstgeschichte*. Available in English, but actually more heavily Germanic than Pauli in its emphasis, is F. Novotny, *Painting and Sculpture in Europe 1780–1880* (London, 1960). Also important, in the light of French painting's crucial place in nineteenth-century European art, is W. Friedlaender, *David to Delacroix*, trans. R. Goldwater (Cambridge, Mass., 1952). The soundest general manual of musical development is probably still A. Einstein, *A Short History of Music*, trans. E. Blom (5th edn, London, 1948); but see also Einstein's more specialized *Music in the Romantic Era* (New York, 1947) and J. Barzun, *Berlioz and the Romantic Century* (Boston, 1950). An interesting study of popular taste in literature, suitable for use in conjunction with Q. D. Leavis, *Fiction and the Reading Public* (see above, p. 419), is R. D. Altick, *The English Common Reader* (Chicago, 1957). Unfortunately, comparable analyses are lacking for the Continent, but some idea of literary currents in Europe as a whole may be derived from a perusal of the selections assembled by H. E. Hugo, ed., *The Romantic Reader* (New York, 1957). Among national studies, a handful of especially helpful entries merit inclusion here: R. Jasinski and later collaborators, *Histoire de la littérature française*, volume 2 (rev. edn, Paris, 1966); P. Moreau, *Le Romantisme* (Paris, 1932); F. Flora, ed., *Storia della letterature italiana*, volume 4 (rev. edn, Milan, 1956); R. Pascal, *The German Novel* (Manchester, 1956); and D. S. Mirsky, *A History of Russian Literature* (New York, 1927).

MAPS

Map 1 Europe in 1780

Map 2 The French Republic by Departments (1790)

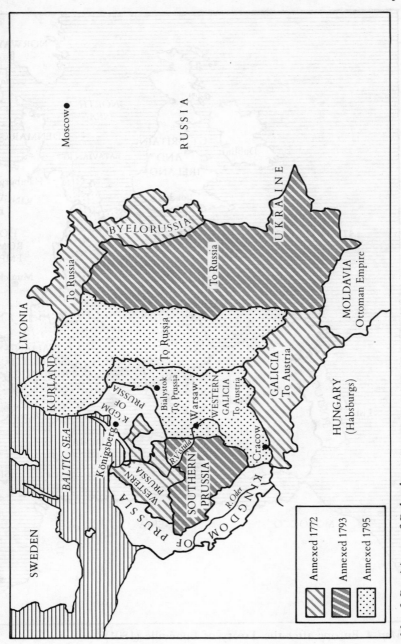

Map 3 Partitions of Poland

Annexed 1772
Annexed 1793
Annexed 1795

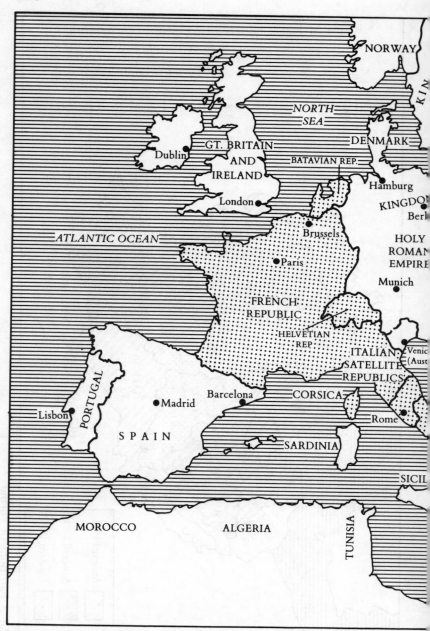

Map 4 Europe after the Treaty of Lunéville (1801)

OM OF SWEDEN

St. Petersburg

Stockholm

BALTIC SEA

French Republic with subsidiary
republics and occupied territories

OF PRUSSIA

RUSSIA

(PORTION
OUTSIDE
EMPIRE)

Warsaw

Prague

Cracow

Vienna

HABSBURG
DOMAINS

Budapest

MOLDAVIA

(PORTION
OUTSIDE
EMPIRE)

WALLACHIA

BLACK SEA

SERBIA

BULGARIA

O T T O M A N   E M P I R E

RUMELIA

ALBANIA

Ionian Islands

GREECE

MEDITERRANEAN SEA

EGYPT

439

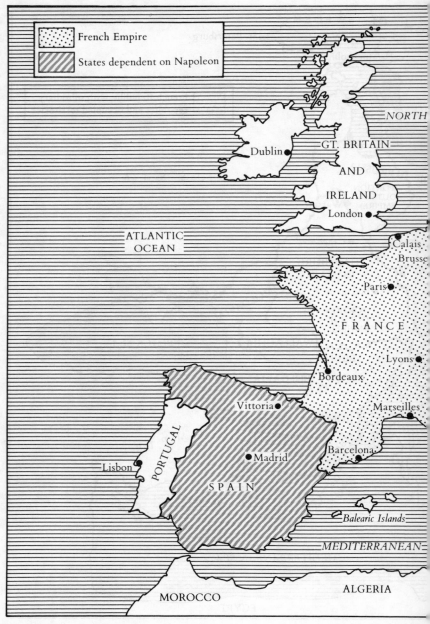

French Empire

States dependent on Napoleon

NORTH

GT. BRITAIN

AND

IRELAND

Dublin

London

ATLANTIC
OCEAN

Calais

Brusse

Paris

F R A N C E

Lyons

Bordeaux

Vittoria

Marseilles

PORTUGAL

Barcelona

Lisbon

Madrid

S P A I N

Balearic Islands

MEDITERRANEAN

MOROCCO

ALGERIA

Map 5 **Europe in 1812**

NORWAY

FINLAND

Stockholm

SWEDEN

BALTIC SEA

RUSSIA

SEA

Copenhagen

Tauroggen

Hamburg

KINGDOM OF PRUSSIA

terdam

Berlin

Warsaw

RHENISH
FEDERATION

AUSTRIAN
EMPIRE

Strasbourg

Vienna

Munich

Budapest

ILLYRIAN PROVINCES

Milan

Venice

rin

Genoa

OTTOMAN

CORSICA

EMPIRE

Rome

ITALY

Naples

Ionian Islands

SARDINIA

SEA

SICILY

UNISIA

Map of Europe in 1810 after the Congress of Vienna.

Map 6 Europe in 1815 (after the Congress of Vienna)

St. Petersburg

Moscow

Königsberg

Warsaw

DM OF
OLAND
uss)

RUSSIAN EMPIRE

Kiev

USTRO-
Budapest
ONARCHY

MOLDAVIA

WALLACHIA

SERBIA

BULGARIA

BLACK SEA

O T T O M A N

Constantinople

E M P I R E

EGYPT

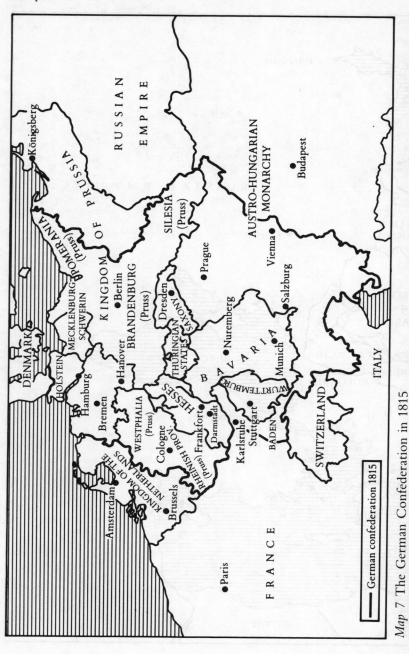

Map 7 The German Confederation in 1815

Map 8 Italy in 1815

Index

(Dates shown for rulers are those of their reigns, preceded in some cases by birth and death dates as well. For certain other individuals birth and death dates are shown.)